# CD START INSTRUCTIONS

D0807527

**1** Place the CD-ROM in your CD-ROM drive.

**2** Launch your Web browser.*

**3** From your Web browser, select Open File from the File menu. Select the CD-ROM drive (usually drive D for PCs and the Desktop for Macs), then select the file called Welcome.htm.

\* We have included the Microsoft Web browser Internet Explorer on this CD in case you do not have a browser or would like to upgrade or change your browser.

## Minimum System Requirements

This software is designed to work on both Macintosh and Windows operating systems.

**1** Macintosh System

Computer: 68020

Memory: 8MB of RAM

Software: System 7.0 or higher

Hardware: 2X CD-ROM Drive

**2** Windows System

Computer: 386 IBM PC-compatible

Memory: 8MB of RAM

Software: Windows 3.1, NT, or 95

Hardware: 2X CD-ROM Drive

**Note:** System requirements vary depending on what software you download from this CD. Please view all available readme files before installation or prior to startup of installed software included on this CD.

# *HOW* <u>to</u> Program

# CGI

## with Perl 5.0

# HOW _to_ Program

# CGI

## with Perl 5.0

# S T E P H E N · L I N E S

Ziff-Davis Press
An imprint of Macmillan Computer Publishing USA
**Emeryville, California**

| Publisher | Stacy Hiquet |
| Acquisitions Editor | Simon Hayes |
| Development Editor | Simon Hayes |
| Copy Editor | Katherine Krause |
| Technical Reviewer | Bryan Taylor |
| Production Editor | Ami Knox |
| Proofreader | Jeff Barrash |
| Cover Illustration and Design | Megan Gandt |
| Book Design and Layout | Bruce Lundquist |
| Indexer | Anne Leach |

Ziff-Davis Press, ZD Press, and the Ziff-Davis Press logo are trademarks or registered trademarks of, and are licensed to Macmillan Computer Publishing USA by Ziff-Davis Publishing Company, New York, New York.

Ziff-Davis Press imprint books are produced on a Macintosh computer system with the following applications: FrameMaker®, Microsoft® Word, QuarkXPress®, Adobe Illustrator®, Adobe Photoshop®, Adobe Streamline™, MacLink®Plus, Aldus® FreeHand™, Collage Plus™.

Ziff-Davis Press, an imprint of
Macmillan Computer Publishing USA
5903 Christie Avenue
Emeryville, CA 94608

ISBN 1-56276-460-8

Manufactured in the United States of America

10 9 8 7 6 5 4 3 2 1

# Table of Contents

# Acknowledgments

My undying gratitude goes to Pagan Kennedy for the many takeout meals she brought me as I worked on this book, and for the solicited and unsolicited advice she lavished upon me. I also wish to thank many other friends for their support during the last few months. Tommy Poggio, my advisor at MIT, was tremendously understanding when I announced that I was embarking on this project, and proved to be understanding throughout. I'm also very grateful to my editor, Simon Hayes, for his patience and encouragement.

# Introduction

CGI programs are the engines behind dynamically changing Web pages, fill-in forms, chat-rooms and bulletin boards, online catalogs and shopping systems, search pages, games, and much more. Perl is the programming language of choice for creating such applications, and without it, the Web today would be far less interactive and useful than it is.

This book is an extended tutorial both on how to create programs for the Common Gateway Interface and on how to program with Perl 5.0. I have written it for people who already know some of the ins and outs of HTML authoring, and who want to add CGI programming, or computer programming in general, to their skill sets. Perhaps you have been assigned to add some interactive presentation or data collecting functions to your company's Web pages, or perhaps you would like to make CGI programming a part of your next job. If you are like many of my friends, you might also want to add impressive gadgets and automation to your own personal or artistic pages. Using this book, you can learn how to do any of these things and more. In fact, as you learn Perl, you will be able to start writing your own CGI programs almost immediately.

I do not assume any prior acquaintance with Perl or with software engineering in general, but will lead you all the way from Perl's basic data types and logical constructs to advanced programming techniques and strategies. Along the way, I thoroughly explain how the Common Gateway Interface works, and illustrate new topics with complete working examples. Other books on CGI present example programs as if their workings were self-evident, or refer the reader elsewhere for explanations of actual programming techniques. In this book, I discuss all the example programs in considerable detail, and explain what each Perl function or operator does in both the particular instance and in general. In addition, the usages of the most important functions and logical constructs are also illustrated by many small coding fragments. If you work through this book, you will learn enough about CGI and programming in Perl that you will be able to design and implement your own interactive applications for the World Wide Web.

# How This Book Is Organized

The ideas behind CGI are not difficult, but there are some things you need to understand well before you can write CGI programs that really do what you want them to do. Therefore, each chapter begins with a general introduction to the concepts it will cover. Throughout this book, I have tried not only to tell you what works, but to explain *how* it works, and in many cases, even *why* it works the way it does.

Chapter 1, "The Common Gateway Interface on the World Wide Web," explains how CGI works with the client/server architecture of the Web, and presents several simple examples of CGI programs written as Perl scripts.

Chapter 2, "Tools for CGI Programming with Perl," discusses some of the history and different versions of Perl, and tells you how to get and install Perl 5 on Unix, DOS/Windows, Macintosh, and other platforms. It also reviews and provides pointers to some useful libraries and other online resources for Perl and CGI programming.

Chapter 3, "Getting Started with Forms," explains how HTML forms work with CGI programs. Its examples show you how to create forms and then process their input data using CGI programs.

Chapter 4, "Input through the Common Gateway Interface," describes all the different kinds of CGI input there are, and explains how to get, parse, and decode this input using a general purpose function.

Chapter 5, "Output through the Common Gateway Interface," describes all the different kinds of CGI output there are, and demonstrates how to serve files other than HTML text from a Perl script. Its examples include image and sound animation using the server push mechanism.

Chapter 6, "Creating Dynamic Documents and Interfaces," explains safe and efficient ways for CGI programs to read, write, create, share, and destroy files on a Web server. Its examples show you how to create textual and graphical access counters, a dynamically generated pie chart, and a self-modifying form.

Chapter 7, "Maintaining State in Multiple-Page Applications," explains how CGI programs can keep track of and maintain a persistent context with client browsers. Its examples cover the use of hidden fields, short-term cookies, and Netscape persistent cookies, as well as sending form input by e-mail and interfacing a CGI program with a database.

Chapter 8, "Searching, Indexing, and Reorganizing Information," describes how search engines work in general, and shows you how to get started in implementing a search page for your own site.

Chapter 9, "Designing and Implementing Interactive CGI Applications," discusses the creation of CGI applications in broader terms, as a task of software engineering. It also explains some techniques for parsing files and filtering textual information in general, which is one of CGI's most frequent roles. It ends with a presentation of general  CGI programming tips and techniques.

Chapter 10, "The Future of CGI," discusses the place of CGI with regard to the rest of the World Wide Web, past, present, and future. It reviews some of the advantages and disadvantages of using CGI today, and points out some of the directions in which changes are likely to occur in the not too far distant future.

Finally, the Appendix, "Regular Expressions in Perl," can be used both as a tutorial and as a reference on the use of regular expressions in Perl. It contains complete specifications of the elements of regular expressions, the rules governing what and how they match, and Perl's pattern matching and search/replace operators.

# Conventions Used in This Book

▶ **Boldface** is used for all Perl code and user commands that appear in the main body of text. In text set apart from the main body, boldface indicates user input.

▶ *Italics* are used to introduce new terms, and occasionally for emphasis.

▶ ALL CAPS are used for HTML tags and attributes, environment variables, and several programming abstractions that are not peculiar to Perl, such as the filehandles STDIN and STDOUT.

▶ Programming code appears in Courier font.

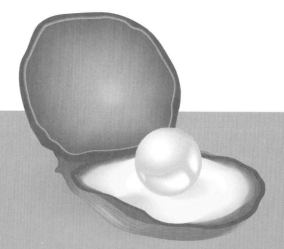

# Examples of Some Simple CGI Scripts

# Back to What It Is: CGI as a Standard Interface

# Chapter 1
# The Common Gateway Interface on the World Wide Web

From a user's point of view, CGI lets you do things such as buy, sell, vote, play games, chat with other users, search for news or how-to tips, and customize remote Web pages for your own use. Without CGI programs, a Web server can offer only static documents and links to pages on other servers. With CGI programs, the Web becomes truly interactive, informative, and, above all, useful.

From a developer's point of view, CGI provides a way for Web servers to run external onsite programs and incorporate their output into the pages they serve. These external programs can interact with users and dynamically create new Web pages, complete with audio and graphics generated on-the-fly.

The Common Gateway Interface is actually a standardized set of conventions specifying how these external programs are to interface with the Web server. CGI is not a programming language, although it is often spoken of as if it were. CGI programs can be written in C, Perl, Visual Basic, AppleScript, or any other programming language, as long as they adhere to CGI's conventions. CGI programs are often called *scripts* because the first ones were written in Unix shell scripting languages (such as sh, csh, and bash). To a Web server, however, one CGI program is just about the same as another; the server invokes a script written in a scripting language such as Perl or VBS in exactly the same way as one written in C or Visual Basic and then compiled into a binary executable. Every CGI program must accept data from the server and send back a document according to a standard set of conventions—in other words, through one common interface. The programmer's task is to create a program that complies with this standard interface; only compliant programs will have their output relayed by the server to the user.

All the CGI programs installed at a given Web site share that site's Web server as their common gateway to the Internet and their sole means of interfacing with browsers. Unlike the contents of an ordinary HTML file, the output of a CGI program cannot be viewed by a browser without going through a server first. When you request a CGI program by its URL, the server at that URL's Web site actually

**1**

runs the CGI program on your behalf, supplying it with any additional input your browser sends along with the URL, and directing its output back to your browser. The CGI program is thus entirely dependent on its server, and yet all of this happens according to a standard, prescribed protocol. Running the same CGI program under a different vendor's server software or installing it at a different site should not require any major modifications. In this sense, then, to a CGI program one Web server is just about the same as another. Such portability is possible because both the program and the server comply with CGI as a standard set of interface conventions.

This overview of CGI gives you, I hope, an intuitive feeling for the concepts behind its full name: the Common Gateway Interface. As a formal standard, CGI is all about how external programs interface with Web servers; browsers are not even a part of this loop. The really interesting interactions, however, do take place between CGI programs and Web browsers, with the server acting only as an all-but-invisible intermediary. To explain how this seemingly direct interaction is possible, I'll first describe what Web servers and Web clients do and how they interface with each other in the absence of CGI.

## What Web Servers and Web Browsers Do

Web servers are programs that run continuously, always waiting for requests from Web clients (browsers). The computers they run on are usually remote from their clients, and they receive their clients' requests via the Internet, by "listening" for them at virtual devices called *ports*. When a server receives a client's request for a transaction or a document, it can either attempt to satisfy that request by itself (for instance, by sending back a document) or pass the request on to some other program (in particular, to a CGI program—but we'll get to that in a moment).

Browsers, such as Netscape Navigator and Internet Explorer, are by far the most common Web clients. A browser is a full-blown application that displays a Web page inside a window surrounded by buttons, menus, and all the other gadgets that constitute the browser's graphical user interface. But whether the user is mousing around with these gadgets or with the links on the Web page itself, the browser is always doing the same thing: translating the user's mouse clicks and keystrokes into requests to be sent to the appropriate Web servers. In the absence of CGI, such a request must remain very simple; it can hardly amount to anything more than a set of instructions for retrieving a document by its URL. This only provides the user with an interface to fixed documents. The next section describes what servers and browsers do with these simple requests.

## How Browsers Get Servers to Send Documents

Consider what happens when a user clicks on a link to an ordinary HTML document: Essentially, the browser requests the document by its URL, and the server on which the document lives sends it to the browser, right? But how does the request get from the browser to the server? What does the server know about the browser? And how does the browser know whether to display a returned document as text or HTML, play it as a Wave sound, or show it as a Quicktime movie?

The basic answer to these questions is that all of this information must be sent back and forth by the browser and the server, and in certain cases negotiated and agreed upon, before the browser will even begin to download and display a document. Figure 1.1 shows the connections that are made and the messages that are sent when a browser retrieves a document from a server.

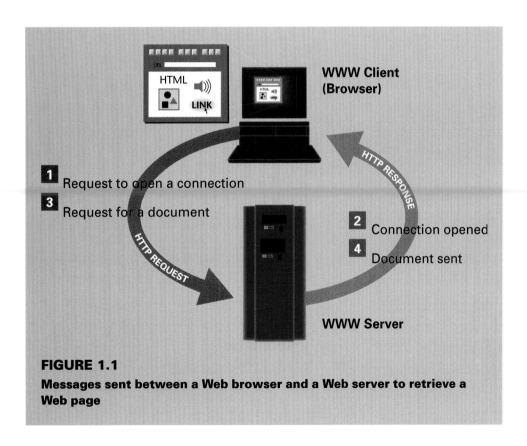

**FIGURE 1.1**
**Messages sent between a Web browser and a Web server to retrieve a Web page**

## The Sequence for Requesting, Downloading, and Displaying an Ordinary Web Page

The following steps explain what happens behind the scenes at both ends of the browser/server connection when a browser requests an ordinary Web page:

1  The user clicks on a link to a document. For the purposes of this discussion, the URL will be http://www.site.domain/directory/homepage.html.

2  The browser translates the server name, www.site.domain, into an Internet address such as 18.23.0.22., and contacts the Web server there with a request to open a connection for communicating via the Hypertext Transport Protocol (HTTP). (HTTP is a communications protocol that governs all data flow on the Web.) If the server accepts, a two-way connection is opened.

3  The browser sends the remainder of the URL, namely /directory/homepage.html, to the server as part of a second request.

4  The server translates this partial URL into a filename and a local (absolute) directory path. Using the example URL, the filename would be homepage.html and the directory path would be something like /etc/httpd/Web/directory, although the exact path would depend on that particular Web server's configuration.

5  The server sends an appropriate HTTP message header back to the browser, telling it what kind of document the server is about to send. This header is followed immediately by the contents of the file, sent as a binary stream of bytes, or 8-bit characters. In this example, the file's contents happen to be HTML text, but a digital audio or image file would be treated just the same. When the server is finished sending, it closes the connection.

6  The browser parses any HTML tags in the stream of bytes as they come in, and it begins to display the resulting page in a window. If there are any embedded tags, such as <IMG SRC="http://www.site.domain/images/home.gif">, that require the browser to download more documents for inline display, the browser might begin fetching the other documents before it continues to draw the page. In this case, the browser would go back to step 2 with each new URL until all the documents that make up the Web page were retrieved.

7  The browser finishes loading the page. Most browsers do not wait for the server to close the connection before they begin drawing the document, but they do indicate when the page has been completely loaded.

For instance, Netscape Navigator displays the word "Done" in its status line when the loading has been completed (see Figure 1.2).

Notice in Figure 1.2 that the Web server itself is invisible to the user. At most only its name shows up, as part of the URL in the Location field above the page. All communication with the server is handled by the browser, and the user can surf from one page to another as if the links in the pages themselves are the only control interface. This server transparency is part of the beauty of the Web, giving users the impression that there is a direct interaction between browsers and CGI programs.

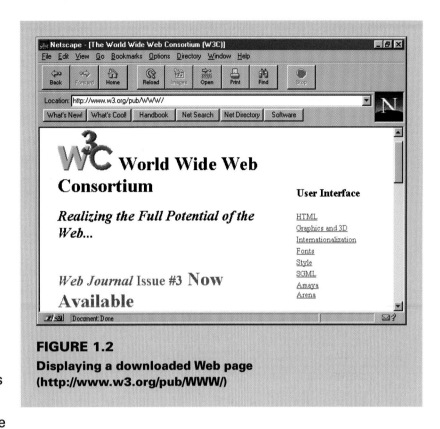

**FIGURE 1.2**
**Displaying a downloaded Web page
(http://www.w3.org/pub/WWW/)**

### Try It: Getting a Web Page without Using a Browser

If you have access to a Unix shell account on a machine connected to the Internet, or if your communications software provides a Unix-like **telnet** command, you can retrieve Web pages directly without using a browser. Simply **telnet** to port 80 (the port that Web servers listen to by default) of any Web server and type in requests as if you were using a browser. For example, at a Unix shell prompt, you would enter the following (user input is in boldface):

```
unix% telnet www.w3.org 80
Trying 18.23.0.22 ...
Connected to www.w3.org.
Escape character is '^]'.
GET /pub/WWW/ HTTP/1.0
```

The port number, **80**, after the Internet name is necessary; if you do not include it, the computer on which the server is running (if it's a Unix machine) will most likely prompt you to log on as a user; with a non-Unix server you might not even get so much as an error message. If your **telnet** program cannot find www.w3.org

by name, substitute the server's Internet Protocol public socket (IP) address, **18.23.0.22**, instead. Type the **GET** in all capital letters, and after you have typed in the protocol and version number, **HTTP/1.0**, press Enter twice. You should be rewarded with something like the following reply:

```
HTTP/1.0 200 Document follows
Server: CERN/3.0A
Date: Fri, 02 Aug 1996 17:23:11 GMT
Content-Type: text/html
Content-Length: 6071
Last-Modified: Thu, 18 Jul 1996 17:59:56 GMT

<HTML>
<HEAD>
                    . . . LONG DOCUMENT HERE . . .

</BODY></HTML>
Connection closed by foreign host.
```

The first six lines of this reply are HTTP headers. There is always a blank line between these and the contents of the document proper. Now if you really were a browser, and not a person faking a request using **telnet**, you might display the page as in Figure 1.2.

You can use the same kind of GET request to induce a Web server to run a CGI program and send you its output; this can be useful for debugging your own scripts. Note that if you leave off the HTTP/1.0 from the GET request you'll still get the document, but without any headers; this isn't as useful for seeing what's going on. (When a browser receives a document without headers, it won't display it but will usually ask whether you want to save the document to disk.) To really impersonate Netscape Navigator 3.0 or some other browser, you'd have to tell the server a little more about yourself, but you get the basic idea.

## How Browsers Get Servers to Run CGI Programs

A client request for a CGI program has the same form and contains the same type of URL as a request for an ordinary HTML page. Only the path or filename in the URL itself might provide a clue that what it references is a program instead of a static document. For example, the URL http://www.site.domain/cgi-bin/query references a CGI program. Most Web servers assume that any file in the /cgi-bin directory is a CGI script. Some also assume that any filename with a certain extension, such as .cgi or .doit, is a CGI script.

The first four steps of the CGI calling process are the same as those for retrieving a static document. But when the URL is resolved into a full path and filename, the server determines that this URL points to an executable program rather than an ordinary document. Instead of sending the contents of the file that contains this program back to the browser, the server executes the program and sends its output. This might not yield any advantage over sending a static file, except that the server also tells the CGI program everything it knows about the client, and the program can use this information to tailor its output for just that particular client and request. This is what makes it possible for a CGI program to create custom pages or otherwise respond to user input as if it has a direct connection to the user's browser. Figure 1.3 shows the connections that are made and the messages that are sent when a browser invokes a CGI program.

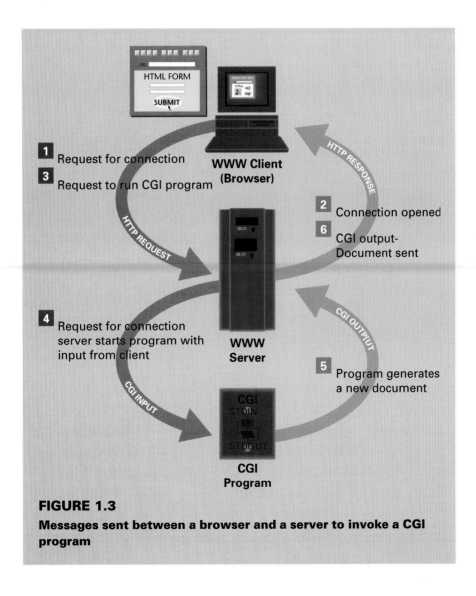

**FIGURE 1.3**

**Messages sent between a browser and a server to invoke a CGI program**

## The Sequence for Requesting, Downloading, and Displaying the Output of a CGI Program

Here is an overview of what happens behind the scenes at both ends of the browser/server connection when a browser requests a CGI program:

1 The user clicks on a link to a CGI program. For the purposes of this discussion, the URL will be http://www.site.domain/cgi-bin/welcome-script.

2–4 These steps are the same as for retrieving a static document.

5 Instead of sending the contents of the file containing the requested CGI program, the server creates a special environment in which to run this program. This environment includes *environment variables*, which contain generic information about the Web server and the client browser as

# Runtime Environments and Standard Input/Output

No computer program runs in isolation, at least not on a computer that's also running a Web server. Computer operating systems execute each program in its own runtime environment, which generally includes some ready mechanisms that enable the program to communicate with whoever invoked it and to interface with the rest of the computer. The details vary with the operating system, naturally, but if your system can run Perl, it's capable of furnishing its runtime environments with everything they need to run scripts as Unix-like CGI programs.

Under the Unix operating system, a program's runtime environment is quite explicit and readily accessible. Unix runs all programs as *processes* and treats practically everything that isn't a process as a file, including hardware devices and anything that resembles a stream of data going into or coming out of a process. Every process starts off with its own set of environment variables as well as three standard *I/O streams*, or virtual devices that are already open for input and output. In keeping with Unix's penchant for treating everything as a file, these streams are also known as *virtual filehandles*. (The word "virtual" refers to the fact that these filehandles are always defined, even when they are not associated with any actual file. In general, a *filehandle* is just a variable used in a programming language such as Perl to represent a file that's open for reading or writing.) These three filehandles well as data specific to the request. It also includes three virtual filehandles—STDIN, STDOUT, and STDERR—for standard input and output; the program can use these to communicate with the server. (If you are not familiar with these terms, see the sidebar, "Runtime Environments and Standard Input/Output.")

**6** The program executes, referring to the environment variables and reading from STDIN at will.

**7** The program outputs the proper MIME headers by writing them to its STDOUT filehandle. MIME stands for Multipurpose Internet Mail Extensions; some common types of MIME headers are text/html, text/plain, and image/gif. (The text/plain type often shows up in e-mail

are named STDIN, STDOUT, and STDERR, which are mnemonics for *standard in*, *standard out*, and *standard error*. Both as general-purpose symbols and as the names of special, predefined variables, these three mnemonics permeate Perl, C, csh, and most other Unix-originated programming languages, as well as the often terse argot of Unix's online manuals (known as *man pages*). You'll be seeing them throughout this book.

When you start a Unix program from a command line, STDIN is by default mapped to the keyboard for input, and both STDOUT and STDERR send their output to your terminal screen by default. It may seem strange to identify hardware devices with filehandles, but, after all, the devices do input or output streams of characters, and DOS uses STDIN, STDOUT, and STDERR in the same way Unix does. As programs in their own right, many Unix and DOS commands redirect these defaults for STDIN and STDOUT internally, and both Unix and DOS allow you to redirect input and output externally by using the symbols <, I, and > on the command line. When you redirect a program's output, you're really redirecting its STDOUT; when you redirect its input, you're really redirecting its STDIN. This is the mechanism underlying command-line pipes: a pipe is formed whenever one program's STDOUT is connected directly to another program's STDIN. For example, the DOS command

```
c:\dos> type oldfile.txt | sort > newfile.txt
```

redirects **type**'s STDOUT to **sort**'s STDIN using the pipe symbol I, and it redirects **sort**'s STDOUT into a text file instead of to the screen using the redirection symbol **>**.

A similar sort of redirection is often set up when one program runs another one—for example, when a Web server runs a CGI program. The first program, or *parent process*, starts up the second one as a child process and directs its own STDOUT to feed into the STDIN of the child. Conversely, the child's STDOUT starts off as directed back into the STDIN of the parent, closing the loop. In other words, the parent is connected to the child via two one-way pipes. This is exactly how Web servers run CGI programs as child processes, and this is why CGI programs are often spoken of as interacting directly with Web servers and only indirectly with Web clients (browsers). From a CGI program's point of view, anything it reads from STDIN comes from the server, and anything it writes to STDOUT goes back to the server.

The other major part of a CGI program's runtime environment is its set of environment variables. In Unix, there are three basic methods by which a parent process can pass information to a child process:

▶ If the parent creates the child with a pipe from its own STDOUT to the child's STDIN, as described above, the parent can write information into this pipe. The child must read from the pipe to get the information.

▶ The parent can start the child with a parameter list, which is just an ordered set of words or character strings. This is equivalent to starting the child with a set of command-line arguments.

▶ The parent can start the child with an arbitrary set of environment variables, which are names paired with values. Every process has its own set of environment variables, often spoken of as simply its *environment*. The parent can simply pass the child a copy of its own environment or make up a new one. (A Web server generally gives a CGI program part of its own environment and supplements this with other environment variables specific to the Web client's request.)

In CGI, pipes to STDIN are used quite often for processing forms, whereas command-line arguments (the second method described above) are rarely used except for a few special purposes, such as handling server-side image maps. Environment variables, however, are pervasive. As you'll see in the course of the next few chapters, they are used to tell a CGI program practically everything it can know about the remote browser and the particulars of the request that caused its Web server to execute it in the first place. ∎

headers.) These headers tell the server, and in turn the client, what type of document will follow. This discussion will assume that the document is an HTML document.

8   The program writes the rest of its output to its STDOUT filehandle. The server reads the data stream from this filehandle and passes it directly to the client.

9   The program exits, and the server, which has been waiting for the program to terminate, closes the connection to the client.

10   The browser parses the data stream and displays the resulting page the same way it would display the stream of bytes from an HTML file sent directly by the server. (See steps 6 and 7 in the earlier discussion about retrieving a static document.)

That's basically all there is to it! All the essentials of CGI program invocation take place in steps 4 through 8. But if this still seems complicated, don't worry. A few simple examples will make everything much clearer.

# Examples of Some Simple CGI Scripts

Many CGI programs can be written in only a few lines of Perl, as in the examples offered here. It is well worth your while to learn how the code in these examples works because you will use some of it over and over in the programs you create yourself. More importantly, you can learn some of the basic principles of CGI programming from them and easily generalize and apply these principles to even the most complex CGI programming tasks.

All of the examples in this section were written for a Web server running on a generic Unix platform. They can also be made to run on a Windows platform if DOS versions of the Unix commands that they reference are installed; ports of these and many other simple Unix programs are readily available on the Internet (see Chapter 2). I'll provide some instructions on how to install these scripts as CGI programs on a Unix Web server after I show you how the first of them works as a simple Perl script.

For a few pointers on how to install CGI programs on Windows and Macintosh platforms, see Chapter 2.

## Example 1A: Using MIME-Type Headers to Implement a Town Crier Program

In this first example, you will create a script that generates a Web page containing dynamically updated information. The page displays a "Howdy, World" message, followed by the local date and time (see Figure 1.4).

If your browser downloaded and displayed this page from an ordinary HTML file stored on a Web server, the HTML text in that file might look like Listing 1.1.

This ordinary HTML code is, in fact, what the hello.cgi script outputs, with two exceptions:

▶ Because the Web server has no way of knowing in advance what kind of document the script will output, the script itself must be responsible for outputting a MIME header describing the kind of document that will follow. In this case, the document is an HTML text document. The wrong header can result in such folly as a GIF image displayed in a browser window as text.

▶ The script must substitute the local date and time each time it generates the page.

Listing 1.2 shows the Perl script hello.cgi, which generates the Web page in Figure 1.4.

Let's go through this script line by line. The first line is essential to making the script run as a Perl program. It tells the Web server to execute the script using the Perl interpreter located in the /usr/local/bin directory. Because of this line's first two characters, Unix programmers call it a *pound-bang command line.* (See the sidebar, "The Pound-Bang Command Line," for details.)

The second line in the script is just a comment, giving the name of the file and a brief description of what the script does. In Perl, comments always begin with a pound sign. (The converse, that every line beginning with a # is a comment, is almost true. The

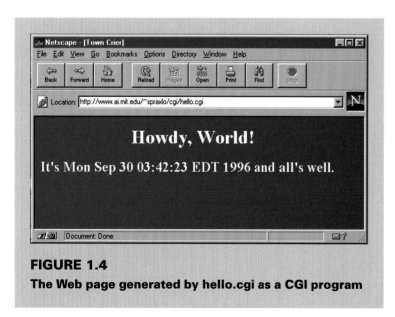

**FIGURE 1.4**
**The Web page generated by hello.cgi as a CGI program**

**LISTING 1.1    An ordinary HTML text file that might generate the Web page in Figure 1.4**

```
<HTML><HEAD><TITLE> Town Crier </TITLE></HEAD>
<BODY BGCOLOR=NAVY TEXT=WHITE>
<H1><CENTER> Howdy, World! </CENTER></H1>
<H2> It's
Mon Sep 30 03:42:23 EDT 1996
and all's well.
</H2></BODY></HTML>
```

**LISTING 1.2    The hello.cgi Perl script, which generates the Web page in Figure 1.4**

```
#!/usr/local/bin/perl
# hello.cgi — say hello and tell the date and time

# Output the MIME-type header, followed by two newlines:
print "Content-type: text/html\n\n";

print "<HTML><HEAD><TITLE> Town Crier </TITLE></HEAD>\n";
print "<BODY BGCOLOR=NAVY TEXT=WHITE>\n";
print "<H1><CENTER> Howdy, World! </CENTER></H1>\n";
print "<H2> It's \n";
print `date`; # date is a Unix command that tells the date and time
print "and all's well.\n";
print "</H2></BODY></HTML>\n";
```

first line, beginning with **#!**, is one of the very few exceptions.) Comments won't slow your programs down and might actually speed up their readability.

The entire body of this script is composed of **print** statements. In Perl, the **print** operator generally sends everything in its argument list to the standard output filehandle, STDOUT. If the script was called as a CGI program, sending output to STDOUT means sending it to the Web server, which will send it on to the browser that requested it.

The first **print** statement outputs the MIME content-type header for HTML. (This is step 7 in the CGI program invocation sequence detailed earlier.) In other words,

```
print "Content-type: text/html\n\n";
```

# The Pound-Bang Command Line

When the Web server invokes the script shown in Listing 1.2, the Unix pre-processor reads the first line

```
#!/usr/local/bin/perl
```

which tells it to execute the script using the Perl interpreter located in the directory /usr/local/bin. The same thing happens if you invoke this script by entering its name as a command line. Suppose you've saved this script as a Unix-executable file named hello.cgi; in a Unix shell (whose command prompt might just happen to be unix%), the command

```
unix%  hello.cgi
```

will be exactly equivalent to

```
unix%  /usr/local/bin/perl  hello.cgi
```

which tells the preprocessor to fire up a copy of Perl and feed the program file hello.cgi to it. If you have access to a Unix shell account, try it!

In order for the pound-bang command line to work, it must be the very first line in the file—simply because that's where the Unix preprocessor looks for it. There should be no space before the pound sign (#), but most systems do permit a space after the exclamation point (**!**), or *bang.* If you install the script on a Web server platform running Windows NT or OS/2, you might need to change this first line to indicate where Perl lives on that machine. For example, if Perl is installed as C:\perl5\perl.exe, change the first line to **#!/perl5/perl.exe**. On a Windows 95 or Macintosh system, the pound-bang command line shouldn't make any difference, unless you include in it a command-line option such as **-w**. If the Windows or Macintosh port of Perl checks this line at all, this option would cause it to output compiler warnings intermixed with the script's normal output. This might help with debugging, but it is probably not what you want from an installed CGI program.

You'll be seeing this pound-bang command syntax at the beginning of scripts throughout this book.

prints the string

```
Content-type: text/html
```

followed by two newlines, which are represented inside the quotation marks as **\n\n**. The two newlines are absolutely necessary because HTTP requires a blank line between the header and the body. If the blank line is missing, the Web server will ignore the rest of the script's output and send the browser an error message. Why? Because it's expecting every line up to the blank one to be an HTTP header. (PC users should refer to the sidebar, "A Note on Carriage-Return Characters for PC Users," for more information.)

The blank-line convention allows headers to be sent in any order, as long as they're all sent ahead of the main document. But if the Web server encounters something other than an HTTP header before the terminating blank line, the header is probably incomplete; as a result, the server may not know how to send the document correctly, and if it were to send it anyway, the browser might lack the necessary information to display it properly. An HTTP-compliant server will not send the requested document following a broken header but will send an error status header followed by an error message instead.

Following the MIME content-type header and the blank line, the script must output the HTML document itself. The **print** statements output the document one line at a time. Only the third line from the bottom is different from the HTML code shown in Listing 1.1:

```
print `date`; # date is a Unix command that tells the date and time
```

As the comment in the code indicates, **date** is a Unix command, but you can obtain a port of the **date** command for MS-DOS, as I'll explain later in this chapter.

Inside a Perl script, a command enclosed in backquotes (`), also known as *back-ticks,* is executed by the system, and the result is then substituted into the expression as a literal value. If you typed **date** at a Unix or DOS command-line prompt, you'd see something like this:

```
prompt> date
Thu Aug  1 09:23:45 EDT 1996
prompt>
```

The string returned between the prompts is exactly what Perl substitutes for `**date**` in the print statement. It includes the newline at the end, as you can see by

# A Note on Carriage-Return Characters for PC Users

If your script is running on a DOS or Windows platform, you might need to print two CRLFs (carriage-return/new-line combinations) to output the blank line, as in

```
print "\r\n\r\n"
```

However, most implementations of Perl for PCs will translate **\n** to **\r\n** for you.

Web browsers must be able to display pages served from any platform, regardless of its carriage-return/new-line convention for plain text files. Unix ends lines with a newline, also known as ASCII 10 or the line feed character (LF), represented in Perl and other Unix programming languages as **\n**. Macintosh ends lines with a carriage-return (also known as CR, ASCII 13, or **\r**). Only PCs running DOS or Windows use both; the combination is usually written symbolically as CRLF.

Since HTTP transfers data as "raw" binary streams, rather than as ASCII or "cooked" text, any reasonable browser will properly display plain or HTML text files with or without the carriage-return/newline characters, and if the browser can do this with the text that makes up the body of a displayed page, it can also do it with the text that makes up the HTTP headers.

Nevertheless, some Windows Web servers may need the carriage-return/newline characters in order to parse the headers output by CGI programs. If you have access to CGI scripts already installed on your Web server, you might want to follow their example. Most Web server software distributions provide examples as part of their installation kits.

If your script will run only on a Unix or Macintosh system, you'll rarely need to worry about this issue. Even though the current draft of the HTTP 1.1 specification calls for every HTTP protocol element, including headers, to end with a CRLF, and not a bare CR or LF character, no Unix or Macintosh Web servers or browsers that I know of actually balk at bare LFs that terminate HTTP header lines or any other element of the protocol. Indeed, in the Unix and Macintosh programming worlds, it's extremely rare to see a Perl script that pays any attention to these considerations. Server-side animations, as explained in Chapter 5, may be one of the few exceptions (and even then other problems are much more common).

comparing the script with the listing of its output (see Listing 1.1). There is no explicit newline in the statement

```
print `date`;
```

but one is printed nonetheless, as part of the value substituted for **`date`**. A useful description of what backquotes do in Perl is that they "literally place the results back into" the backquoted expression.

I'd like to add one more comment about the content-type header: If this script specified the MIME type text/plain instead of text/html, the rest of its output would be exactly the same, but a browser receiving this output would display it differently. Instead of parsing the tags, making "Town Crier" the document's title and "Howdy, World" its headline, the browser would display the tags along with everything else as literal text (see Figure 1.5).

## How to Install a CGI Script on a Web Server Running under Unix

Installing a Perl script as a CGI program on a Unix Web server is quite straightforward, assuming you have sufficient privileges. Not all Internet service providers (ISPs) allow users to install their own CGI scripts, so if you're in doubt, ask your site administrator. Many commercial ISPs charge extra for allowing users to serve CGI programs from their own directories, and some insist on installing all CGI programs themselves, after charging the user a fee to check for security holes. At least a few will waive such fees and checking requirements once you convince them that you know what you're doing.

Depending on the Web server's configuration, scripts may need to reside in a certain directory for the server to be able to run them as CGI programs (as opposed to simply serving up their contents as documents or sending only error messages). Most Web servers can be configured to treat any file with a designated extension (such as .cgi) as a CGI program, which allows scripts to coexist with static documents in the same user directories. However, this feature is not the default setting in any popular Unix server software, nor is it commonly used by commercial ISPs. Most do follow the convention of making a directory named /cgi-bin a home

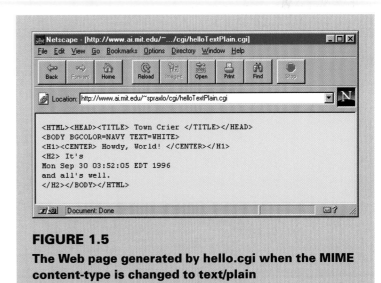

**FIGURE 1.5**

**The Web page generated by hello.cgi when the MIME content-type is changed to text/plain**

only for CGI programs, but the absolute path of this directory varies, as do the ISPs' policies regarding its use. Some Web sites and Internet service providers will let you maintain the equivalent of your own /cgi-bin directory, especially if you are paying them to host your pages as a virtual site—that is, if your site appears to be running its own dedicated Web server. (If you actually are setting up your own Unix Web server, follow its installation instructions and pay particular attention to what they say about ScriptAlias directories and adding MIME types.)

Once you have the sufficient access privileges and know the proper directory in which to install your CGI scripts, you can install your script on the server. The next several pages describe how to install the Example 1A script on a Unix Web server, starting with these four steps:

**1** From an editor or word processor, save the script as an ordinary text file. (From a word processor, you might have to choose Text Only in the Save As dialog box.) It's customary to give Perl scripts the extension .pl, as in hello.pl, but when scripts are installed as CGI programs, this suffix is usually either dropped or changed to an extension recognized by the server. For this example, save the script as hello.cgi. If this file isn't already on the Unix system, upload it there now.

**2** Mark this file as world-executable and world-readable using the Unix change-mode command: **chmod 755 hello.cgi**. Some server installations also require the file to be group-writable (but not world-writable); in this case you would use **chmod 775 hello.cgi**. If you have a Unix shell account, you can enter either of these commands on the command line (and enter the command **man chmod** to read **chmod**'s manual page). If you are restricted to FTP access only, you can still issue the same command on hello.cgi as a remote file once you've uploaded it; any FTP-compatible or Unix-enabled file transfer utility should give you this option. (For more on viewing and changing access permissions, see the sidebar, "Using **ls** and **chmod** to View and Change a File's Access Permissions in Unix.")

**3** If the file is not already in the /cgi-bin directory (or its equivalent) on your Web server, move or copy it there now. (The Unix commands are **mv** and **cp**, respectively.) This should make its URL something like http://yoursite .yourdomain/cgi-bin/hello.cgi. Again, if you are not sure where the /cgi-bin directory is on your server machine, or if you need permission to put your files there, ask your systems administrator. Alternatively, if your server recognizes the .cgi suffix, you can install the file in any directory from which the server serves ordinary HTML documents; its URL will vary accordingly.

**4** Enter the URL from step 3 into your browser's Go To or Open URL field, or create a link to it in an HTML page and click on that. Your browser should receive the script's output and display it as a new page.

## Troubleshooting the Installation of a CGI Perl Script under Unix

If the four steps above fail to produce the correct results, try following these simple rules for troubleshooting:

▶ If you get an error message that says something such as "404 File Not Found," first check to make sure that the URL is correct and then check the file's access permissions.

▶ If you get an error message that says something such as "403 Forbidden" or "Permission Denied," check the permissions first of the file itself and then of its parent directory (which should, in general, be 755).

▶ An error message that says something such as "500 Server Error" or "Internal Misconfiguration" usually indicates one of two things: Either the server isn't configured to run any CGI program out of that directory or, if other scripts do run there, this particular script is at fault. To find out whether it's the latter problem, and to locate such a problem within the file, you might try running the same program from the command line. Perl provides several command-line options for diagnosing errors; two of the most useful option flags are **-c** and **-w**. The **-c** option only checks the script's syntax without actually running it; the **-w** option runs the script and intermixes compiler warnings, if any, with the script's normal output. If the script passes the first test, as in

```
unix% perl -c hello.cgi
hello.cgi syntax OK
```

try the **-w** option; the output should then match Listing 1.2 (except for the current date and time, of course).

## Where Is Perl Living on Your Unix System, and Which Perl Will Run?

There is one more fairly common question that might pop up when you are installing your first CGI script at a given site: Where in the world is Perl? If the path given for Perl in the pound-bang command line is incorrect, you'll most likely get a "Server Error" message in your browser window; if you try to run the script from the command line, you may get an even more cryptic error message, such as "file not found" (meaning that /usr/local/bin/perl or whatever your script has in its pound-bang command line was not found). To find Perl on a Unix (or Linux) system, use the **which** or **whereis** command. Here's an example that uses **which**:

```
unix% which perl
/usr/bin /perl
```

The Unix **which** command returns the *first* directory in your path that contains the Perl interpreter. This tells you which program would actually be executed if you entered **perl** at the beginning of a command line without specifying any preceding directory.

The Unix **whereis** command will return *all* the occurrences in your path, plus the location of the Unix manual page, as in

```
unix% whereis perl
perl:  /usr/bin/perl  /usr/sbin/perl  /usr/man/perl
```

# Using ls and chmod to View and Change a File's Access Permissions in Unix

To view a file's current access permissions, use the Unix command **ls -l** (the directory listing command **ls** with the long format option **-l**). The **ls** command is available both in Unix shells and in interactive FTP sessions. Some FTP server configurations always run **ls** with the **-l** option, and some provide a **dir** command as an alias for **ls -l** (as do some Unix shells). Be forewarned: Most Unix FTP programs interpret a command such as **ls -l hello.cgi** to mean "get a listing of a remote file named -l and save it as a local file named hello.cgi, overwriting the local file if it already exists." To avoid this headache, either use **dir** (if it's available) or use **ls -l** without a filename. (This will list all the files in the current directory in long format.) Below is an example showing the output of **ls -l** in a Unix shell:

```
unix:/usr/spraxlo/public_html/cgi> ls -l hello.cgi
-rw-rwxr—   1 spraxlo  webuser       409 Sep 27 21:23 hello.cgi
```

A file's access permissions appear as the first field in a long-format directory listing. The very first character in this ten-character field will be a **d** if what's listed is the name of a directory; the first character will be a different letter if the listed item is some other kind of special file. A dash (**-**) in this position means that the

A path in Unix is very similar to a path in DOS: It is the ordered list of directories that contain the executable files you can use as commands. When you issue a DOS or Unix shell command at a prompt or from within a program, the system looks in these directories and runs the first program that matches the name of your command. In either case, the system determines your process's current path by examining an environment variable ($PATH in Unix, **%path** in DOS). Incidentally, many small Unix utility programs such as **which** and **whereis** have also been ported to DOS.

If you don't have access to a Unix shell account, you might try looking for **perl** or **perl5** (actually, try **perl\***) in the following likely directories: /bin (for RedHat Linux), /usr/sbin (for SGI IRIX), /usr/bin or /usr/local/bin (for general Unix systems), or /usr/local/gnu/bin (for other, nonstandard Unix systems). Otherwise, ask your systems administrator for help.

listed item is an ordinary file. The next nine characters are interpreted as three sets of 3 bits each. The first set indicates the file access permissions that the system will grant to the file's individual owner, the second set indicates the permissions granted to other members of the file's user group (or "group ownership"), and the last set indicates the permissions granted to all other users. Within each set, the three letters **r**, **w**, and **x** indicate permission to read, write, and execute the file as a program, respectively. (If the item is a directory, "permission to execute" means permission to search the directory for a specified file and "permission to read" means permission to search it for any files.) The presence of one of these letters indicates that the permission is granted; a dash in the place of a letter means that the corresponding permission is denied.

In the example above, the permissions field **-rw-rwxr—** indicates that to its owner, **spraxlo**, hello.cgi is readable and writable; to any member of the group named **webuser**, other than **spraxlo**, the file is readable, writable, and executable; and to all other users, the file is readable only. The category of all other users is also referred to as "the rest of the world," or just plain "world," as in "hello.cgi is world-readable." Relative to a given user or file, "the world" does not include random users on the Internet, but it does include any user who can log into or run a process on the same computer. (By running a process I mean just running a program—for example, an FTP server or a Web server.)

These particular permissions should prevent hello.cgi from being executed as a CGI program. Here's why: In Unix, all processes are effectively owned and run by users, and when one process spawns another (for instance, when a Web server starts up a CGI program), the child process generally inherits the same owner, or effective user ID, as its parent process. A Web server is at the beck and call of users outside the system, so to minimize the damage that might be caused by an errant CGI program or by a hacker who is able to gain some control over the Web server and spawn off other processes, the server itself should have as few privileges inside the system as possible. In particular, the Web server should not be able to read, write, delete, or execute any file it doesn't own, unless that file is so marked with the least restrictive permissions possible; that is, unless it is world-readable, world-writable (which also means world-deletable), or world-executable. Thus the effective user ID of any Web server process should be excluded from membership in any user group designated for ordinary, human users (**webuser**, in this example). In other words, a Web server should always run as part of the "rest of the world," and not enjoy group ownership privileges over any human users' files.

To change a file's access permissions, use the Unix command **chmod** (pronounced "ch'mod"). Like **ls**, the **chmod** command is also available both in Unix shells and in interactive FTP sessions, but the FTP version is less flexible than the shell version. With the shell version of **chmod**, you can specify the permissions symbolically, as in

```
unix:/usr/spraxlo/public_html/cgi> chmod u+x,g-w,o+rx hello.cgi
unix:/usr/spraxlo/public_html/cgi> ls -l hello.cgi
-rwxr-xr-x    1 spraxlo   webuser        409 Sep 27 21:23 hello.cgi
```

which, as you can see from the changed directory listing, adds execute permission to the owner's (user's) permission set, subtracts write permission from the group's set, and adds execute permission to the world's (other's) set. A useful shortcut is **ch +x**, which adds execute permission to all three user categories—owner, group, and world. (The abbreviations **u**, **g**, and **o**, which stand for user, group, and other, were chosen to avoid the confusion that might result if **w** were used for both "world" and "write.")

At an FTP prompt, you must specify **chmod**'s permissions fields as octal (base-8) numbers. The symbolic permissions **r**, **w**, and **x** correspond to the numbers **4**, **2**, and **1**, respectively, and to get the octal number representing the permissions granted in each user category, you simply add up the corresponding numbers. The result is a number from **0** to **7**, inclusive. For example, read and write permissions correspond to **4 + 2**, or **6**, whereas **7** indicates read, write, and execute permissions. To get the whole access permissions field, simply string the numbers from each category together; thus **-rw-rwxr—** translates to **674** and **-rwxr-xr-x** translates to **755**. For a complete example showing how to use **ls -l** and **chmod** in a command-line-oriented FTP session, see Listing 1.3.    ∎

**LISTING 1.3    A complete command-line-oriented FTP session, illustrating the use of the commands** dir **(an alias for** ls -l**) and** chmod

```
UnixOne% ftp manarola.ai.mit.edu
Connected to manarola.ai.mit.edu.
220 manarola FTP server ready.
Name (manarola.ai.mit.edu:spraxlo): spraxlo
331 Password required for spraxlo.
Password:  [the password is not echoed]
230 User spraxlo logged in.
Remote system type is UNIX.
Using binary mode to transfer files.
ftp> cd public_html/cgi
250 CWD command successful.
ftp> dir hello.cgi
200 PORT command successful.
150 Opening ASCII mode data connection for '/bin/ls'.
-rw-r—r—   1 spraxlo   user        409 Sep 27 21:23 hello.cgi
226 Transfer complete.
ftp> chmod 755 hello.cgi
200 CHMOD command successful.
ftp> dir hello.cgi
200 PORT command successful.
150 Opening ASCII mode data connection for '/bin/ls'.
-rwxr-xr-x    1 spraxlo   user        409 Sep 27 21:23 hello.cgi
226 Transfer complete.
ftp> bye
221 Goodbye.
UnixOne%
```

## How to Make This Same Script Work in MS-DOS or Windows

Ports of many Unix commands are available for MS-DOS (and thus for the DOS command prompt in Windows). A full-featured port of the Unix **date** command by Frank Whaley can be found as part of the Unix95 archive at S. Zurgot's Virtually Unix Web site (http://www.itribe.net/virtunix/). If you already have Perl installed on an MS-DOS/Windows system, here is one prescription for making the Example 1A script work there:

1 Determine what your installed version of Perl is by using the command **perl -v**. The response should indicate a port of Perl version 5.001 or greater for Windows 95 or Windows NT; ports for Win32s may give you problems.

2 Install the MS-DOS port of **date**, and any other command-line programs that you will use similarly, in a directory on the same drive as perl.exe and your Perl scripts. For instance, you might have a full pathname of c:\unix\date.exe.

3 To ensure that the script calls this date program rather than MS-DOS's built-in **date** command (which would cause the script to hang until you typed Ctrl-C), change the line in the script to the reflect the program's full pathname:

```
print `/unix/date`;
```

or, if don't care to make your scripts portable to other systems,

```
print `c:\\unix\\date`;
```

For compatibility's sake, I strongly recommend using the version with forward slashes (/)and generally eschewing both drive names and backslashes as directory separators in path specifications. Perl will translate the forward slashes to (single) backslashes as needed. As shown in the second version above, the backslashes must be doubled because Perl uses \ as a special quotation or "escape character"; its most common usage is to force other special characters, such as $, to be taken literally instead of interpreted. It *escapes* otherwise special characters from their special meanings. When \ is applied to itself, as in \\, the result is, quite literally, \ Including the drive specification (C:) can also be tricky, because in some versions of DOS, the C: command always means "change to drive C," and anything after the colon is ignored. However, the most recent ports of Perl for PCs seem to fix this problem.

4  Alternatively, you can avoid conflicts with DOS's built-in **date** command by changing the Unix executable's name from date.exe to unixdate.exe and then adding the directory c:\unix to your command path. For example, you could issue the command

```
path = %path%c:\unix;
```

from a DOS prompt or insert it into (the equivalent of) your autoexec.bat file. Then change the line in the script to

```
print `unixdate`;
```

(If you are using some early port of Perl, such as Perl 5 for Win32s, forward slashes may not be properly translated into backslashes, and so putting the date program in the default path of the system as unixdate might be the only reliable way to call it as an external executable program, using backquotes.)

Now you should be able to run the script from a DOS prompt, like this:

```
c:\doswin\examples> perl hello.cgi
```

The results should be the same as in Listing 1.1.

5  From this point, installing this script as a DOS/Windows CGI program is similar to installing it as a Unix program. Save the script as a text-only file (in your computer's native CRLF-line-terminated text format) and move or copy it into your Web server's script directory. In O'Reilly's WebSite, for example, the default installation configuration uses the directory C:\WebSite\cgi-shl (in addition to several others). To mark the script as an executable program under Windows, you'll probably need to make an *association* between its file extension (such as .cgi) and your installed Perl program. (See Windows Help if you are not sure how to do this.) I recommend using the extension .cgi if it isn't already associated with another program, or something new such as .plc if .cgi is already in use. Don't use .pl, because that will also mark all your Perl library files as executables; associate them with your favorite text editor instead. This should be enough to get your hello.cgi script up and running.

## A Native Perl Alternative to the Unix date Command: time and ctime

Perl provides an alternative to the backquoted Unix **date** command in hello.cgi: a pair of functions named **time** and **ctime**. A *function* in Perl is just a subroutine that always returns a value, so you can always use it as if it were just the value that it returns. For example, in the **print** statement

```
print "According to my computer's system clock, it's ", &ctime(time);
```

the value returned by the **time** function becomes the argument to **ctime**, whose return value is in turn the second argument to the **print** operator. In the case of hello.cgi, you can simply substitute **&ctime(time)** for `date` as the argument to the **print** function; that is, change the line

```
print `date`; # date is a Unix command that tells the date and time
```

to

```
print &ctime(time); # ctime is a function that returns a Unix-like¬
date and time
```

Like **print**, the **time** function is built right into Perl; the only difference is that, since **time** accepts no arguments, you can't do anything with it *except* use it as if it were just a literal value. As a function, however, **time** always returns the current time as the number of seconds elapsed since midnight, December 31, 1969, Greenwich mean time (GMT). The **ctime** function takes a time represented in this way and converts it to a human-readable format. On a Unix system, this format is usually identical to that returned by the **date** command; on PCs, Macintoshes, and other platforms, the format will be very similar.

In Perl, a library or user-defined function is identified by an ampersand prefixed to its name, as in **&ctime**; however, an ampersand prefixed to the name of a built-in function will cause Perl to spit out an error message and abort execution. The **ctime** function is actually defined in a file named ctime.pl, and in order for Perl to execute a call to the **ctime** function, this file must be included as part of your script. The standard way of including a library file in a Perl script is to use the **require** operator, as in

```
require "ctime.pl";
```

You can place such a **require** statement anywhere in your script after the pound-bang command line and before your first call of the **ctime** function, but it's customary to place it at the very beginning, following any header-type comments. If you know where the file ctime.pl resides on your system, you could put its full path as the argument to the **require** operator, but since it is part of Perl's standard library, Perl should be preconfigured to know where to find it. (On Unix systems, the most likely place for it is in /usr/local/lib/perl/lib; for NTPerl and MacPerl, it is usually in a subdirectory named lib in whatever directory the perl.exe program or MacPerl application is installed.) Listing 1.4 shows the revised script, hi-ctime.cgi, which uses Perl's **time** and **ctime** functions in place of the Unix **date** command.

Since the output of **ctime** is quite similar to that of the Unix **date** command, the Web page that this modified script outputs should be practically the same as the one shown in Figure 1.4.

## Example 1B: Counting Down with a Non-Parsed Header

The previous example showed the importance of the HTTP content-type header and the MIME type it specifies. A full-fledged HTTP header contains lines specifying other characteristics of the document as well, such as its length. The Web server usually supplies these other header lines for you. The server sends these header lines ahead of the output of your script, making the content-type line the last line in the full header. Here's an example:

```
HTTP/1.0 200 OK
Date: Fri, 02 Aug 1996 09:23:45 GMT
```

**LISTING 1.4    The hi-ctime.cgi script, which uses Perl's time and ctime functions in place of the Unix date command**

```perl
#!/usr/local/bin/perl
# hi-ctime.cgi — say hello and tell the date and time
require "ctime.pl";

print "Content-type: text/html\n\n";

print "<HTML><HEAD><TITLE> Town Crier </TITLE></HEAD>\n";
print "<BODY BGCOLOR=NAVY TEXT=WHITE>\n";
print "<H1><CENTER> Howdy, World! </CENTER></H1>\n";
print "<H2> It's \n";
print &ctime(time); # ctime is a function that returns a Unix-like date and time
print "and all's well.\n";
print "</H2></BODY></HTML>\n";
```

```
Server: NCSA/1.3
MIME-version: 1.0
Content-type: text/html
```

The first line is mandatory—most browsers require it so that they can handle the document correctly. It identifies the protocol and its version number (HTTP version 1.0), gives the transaction status code (200 always means success in HTTP), and ends with a short, optional comment. The next three header lines shown in the code above are optional, but without this first line, some browsers will print the rest of the header and the script's output as a page of plain text.

Web servers send the same header lines ahead of the content, regardless of whether the content is a static HTML document or the output of an ordinary CGI script. In the case of a CGI script, you can bypass this server intervention simply by prefixing the script's filename with the **nph-** prefix. (The *nph* stands for *non-parsed header*.) Most servers send the output of any CGI script with a name such as nph-countdown directly to a client browser, without adding to or in any way checking the output. This can be useful for sending out lengthy documents—such as a long list of search results or an audio stream encoded on-the-fly—as they are generated. Non-parsed-header scripts can also be used to introduce simple time sequences into a document, which is useful for playing games or tricks.

## How to Make a Non-Parsed Header Script Work

To make a non-parsed-header script work correctly, you must do three things:

1 Prefix the name of your script with **nph-**, as in nph-countdown.cgi.

2 Unbuffer your script's output. By default, all output from a Perl script to STDOUT is buffered; that is, it is actually sent only when a certain block size (such as 512 or 1,024 bytes) is reached or when the script exits with a less-than-full buffer. To see smaller chunks of output, you either have to wait or change the buffering scheme. You can turn buffering off by setting Perl's special variable **$|** to a nonzero value, as in

```
$| = 1;
```

It is usually best to put this statement close to the beginning of your script, before any output operators such as **print**.

3 Because the Web server won't supply any HTTP headers, your script itself must output at least the mandatory headers. Here's an example:

```
print "HTTP/1.0 200 OK\n";
print "Content-type: text/html\n\n";
```

The first step alone will make the server send the output of your script as is, but without a valid HTTP header as described in step 3, the client browser won't do the right thing with the document. The second step guarantees that the output will be sent to the server at least at every newline so that short lines will print individually instead of in large blocks. As a mechanism for bypassing the server and connecting directly to a client browser, however, non-parsed-header scripts are far from perfect. All of your script's output to STDOUT is still going to the server, and even though the server is supposed to send this output on to the browser without changing it, it may still hold this output up for a moment or two within its own internal buffering or caching system, especially if it's busy. If your browser doesn't start displaying this countdown right away, try reloading the script's URL. If that doesn't work, try editing the script to change the MIME content from text/html to text/plain.

It's also a good idea to send the Server: *software* header, where *software* refers to the kind of Web server software that you are running. This lets the browser know what kind of a server it is receiving data from. I'll show you how to do this a little later, in Example 1D.

## Counting Down with a For Loop

The CGI script in this example outputs some initial lines of text and then counts down for 10 seconds before outputting its final lines. In Figure 1.6, the user apparently chose not to wait and see what would happen when the countdown got to 0; he or she hit the browser's Stop button instead. Listing 1.5 shows the script that generates the countdown page.

As advertised, this script unbuffers its output before reaching its first print statement (by setting **$l = 1**), and then it outputs a minimal but valid HTTP header. Two other things are new

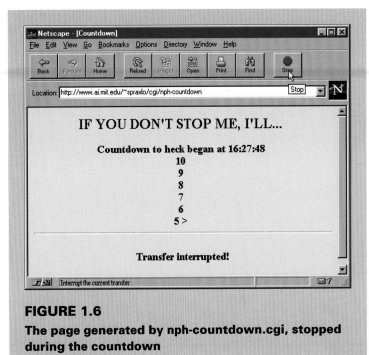

**FIGURE 1.6**

**The page generated by nph-countdown.cgi, stopped during the countdown**

**LISTING 1.5   The nph-countdown.cgi script, which generates the Web page shown in Figures 1.6 and 1.7**

```perl
#!/usr/local/bin/perl
# nph-countdown.cgi — count down and say Aw Heck! in HTML

$| = 1;    # unbuffer all subsequent output

print "HTTP/1.0 200 OK\n";
print "Content-type: text/html\n\n";

print "<HTML><HEAD><TITLE> Countdown </TITLE></HEAD>\n";
print "<BODY BGCOLOR=#FFFFFF><DIV ALIGN=CENTER>\n";
print "<H2> IF YOU DON'T STOP ME, I'LL... </H2>\n";

print "<H3>Countdown to heck began at ", `date +%T`;
for ($count = 10; $count > 0; $count—) {
  print "<BR>", $count, "\n";
  sleep 1;
}
print "</H3><H2>...AW HECK, I'LL JUST STOP MYSELF!</H2>\n";
print "<H3>Countdown to heck ended at ", `date +%T`, "</H3>\n";
print "</DIV></BODY></HTML>\n";
```

here: the format argument **+%T** in the backquoted **date** command and the **for** loop that prints and decrements the **$count** variable ten times.  I'll explain the format argument in the **date** command first.

In most flavors of Unix, the **date** command accepts any argument beginning with a plus sign as a format string, as in

```
date +%T
```

or

```
date +"Today's date is %D"
```

The **date** command goes through the format string and replaces the symbols that begin with percent signs with bits and pieces of the current date and time. In the code lines just shown, it would replace **%T** with the time, formatted as *HH:MM:SS* (*hours:minutes:seconds*) and **%D** with the date, formatted as *MM/DD/YY*. Some flavors of Unix define many more format symbols; a few (such as Mach on a NeXT machine) don't accept format strings at all. For details about your Unix system, refer to the manual page on this command. You can view this page by typing **man date** at a Unix shell prompt. If you are using a DOS port of the Unix **date** command, as described above, try the command **date -h** (or **unixdate -h**) to see a list of options.

When the line

```
print "<H3>Countdown to heck began at ", `date +%T`;
```

is executed in the script, it should print something like

```
<H3>Countdown to heck began at 16:23:45
```

(if indeed it is 4:23 p.m.). Remember that **print** outputs all the arguments in its comma-separated list, one right after another.

The actual countdown is performed by this **for** loop:

```
for ($count = 10; $count > 0; $count-) {
    print "<BR>", $count, "\n";
    sleep 1;
}
```

Here the name **$count** represents a scalar variable. Scalars are Perl's fundamental data type. A scalar value is either a number or a string of characters—or both. Perl converts between the two as needed, so you can use numbers as strings and strings as numbers. A scalar variable is just a variable whose value is always a scalar—that is, a number or a string. You can assign it a numerical value like this

```
$count = 10;
```

or like this

```
$count = 5 + 5;
```

and still print it as part of a string like this

```
print "You've got $count seconds... ";
```

You don't have to do anything special to tell print to output the numeral 1 followed by the numeral 0 rather than, say, the tenth character in the ASCII character set.

Conversely, you can set **$count** equal to the string **"10"**, as in

```
$count = "10";
```

print it as above, and then perform arithmetic operations on it and print it again, as in

```
$count = $count - 1;
print "The count is now $count\n";
```

In Perl, the name of a scalar variable always begins with a dollar sign (**$**), and any word or expression beginning with a **$** identifies a scalar variable. Arrays and other complex data types in Perl are always made up of scalars as their basic elements.

As stated previously, the actual countdown is accomplished using the **for** loop, and the only place the **$count** variable appears is as the index or "dummy" variable in this for loop, in which it is always evaluated as a number.

The syntax of a **for** loop in Perl can be the same as in C and in some other programming languages, except that the curly braces around the statements in the **for** loop's body are mandatory, not optional. In the countdown script, the first expression inside the parentheses initializes the **$count** variable to the value **10**. The middle expression, separated from the other expressions by semicolons, tests the conditional statement **$count > 0** each time before the statements in the for loop's body are executed. If **$count** is greater than **0**, Perl will print the line

```
<BR> $count
```

where *$count* is the current value of **$count**. The value is followed by a newline. Then the loop will sleep for 1 second. After the body of the **for** loop has executed, the last expression inside the parentheses, which decreases the value of **$count** by **1**, is executed. In Perl, as in C, the auto-decrement operator (the two minus signs after the variable in **$count—**) makes the expression

```
$count—
```

equivalent to

```
$count = $count - 1
```

When **$count** reaches **0**, the conditional in the middle of the parentheses fails, and the loop terminates immediately, without printing or decrementing **$count** again.

The overall effect of the **for** loop is to print the numbers in the countdown one by one in a column down the center of the page in the browser. Figure 1.7 shows the generated page run to completion.

The date/time command is placed before and after the loop to report how long the countdown really took. Remember, once the script begins, it doesn't wait for server parsing or feedback of any kind. A reported ending time of more than 10 seconds later than the reported beginning time indicates that the Web server machine on which the program ran was very busy, perhaps due to the activities of the server software itself. If the difference between reported times is exactly 10 seconds but it took your browser much longer to display the countdown, it's probably your connection that was (temporarily) slow.

## Example 1C: Using Environment Variables (%ENV) to Tell Fortunes

When a Web server invokes a CGI script to satisfy some client browser's request, it can pass information about that client

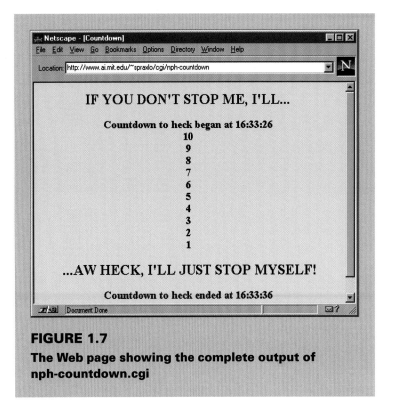

**FIGURE 1.7**

**The Web page showing the complete output of nph-countdown.cgi**

and its request to the script in several different ways. The simplest way is through environment variables. As discussed earlier, these are variables that the script inherits from its surroundings at runtime. The Web server actually creates a special environment every time it runs a CGI script, and it sets variables in this environment that represent such things as the kind of browser making the request and its host machine's Internet name and address. Inside the script, this information is free for the taking. The script has only to refer to the environment variables by their names. More precisely, the environment variables are accessible inside any Perl script as the elements of a predefined associative array named **%ENV**. (See the sidebar "Ordinary and Associative Arrays in Perl" for more information.)

The script in this example uses several environment variables that contain information about the client and the request in an attempt to lend a wee bit of credibility to the fortunes it tells. Figure 1.8 shows the resulting Web page.

The variables used to create this page were

▶ REMOTE_HOST, the Internet name of the browser's host machine, if it has one and if the server enables Domain Name Server (DNS) look-ups.

▶ REMOTE_ADDR, the IP address of the browser's host machine. This variable is always set.

# Ordinary and Associative Arrays in Perl

### An Ordinary Array Is Like a Single-Column Table

An ordinary array in Perl is an ordered list of values that are referred to, or *indexed*, by their position numbers. An ordinary array is like a single-column table, in which you can look up the value in a particular cell by its row number. To refer to an ordinary array value in Perl, you can subscript the array's name with a numerical index in square brackets. For example,

```
$entry = $normalArray[2];
```

sets the scalar variable **$entry** to the value in position 2 of the array, which is marked as being a normal array by the **$** prefix and **[]** suffix attached to the *identifier* **normalArray**. An identifier in Perl is any string of letters and digits that begins with a letter. (Perl also treats the underscore character as a letter.) Array position numbering usually begins at 0, so this would actually be the array's third cell entry, or *element*.

All the entries in an array must be scalar values, and any expression that refers to a particular element of an array must begin with **$**, as in **$suits[3]**. When referring to an ordinary array as a whole, however, you must prefix its name with an at sign (**@**). Technically speaking, the identifiers **normalArray** and **suits** are *names*, but they are not the names of arrays. Without a prefix such as **$** or **@**, a bare identifier such as **suits** is ambiguous; it could be either a name of a filehandle or a literal scalar value. Here is an example that shows how to refer to an array as a whole:

```
@suits = { 'Spades', 'Hearts', 'Clubs', 'Diamonds'};
```

This statement initializes the **@suits** array to contain four literal strings as its entries numbered 0 through 3. The expression **$suits[1]** would then evaluate to the scalar value **Hearts**. For example,

```
print $suits[1], " are wild.\n";
```

would output the line

```
Hearts are wild.
```

### An Associative Array Is Like a Set of Named Variables

An associative array in Perl is different from an ordinary array: Instead of referring to the entries in an associative array by number, you can look them up by name. The named entries in an associative array are called simply its *values*, whereas the *names* of the entries are called its *keys*. A key can be any arbitrary string, long or short. You can think of keys as keywords for looking up the associative array's entries; each key is associated with a unique value.

To refer to a value in an associative array, you subscript the array's name with that value's key string inside curly braces. For example,

```
$oneValue = $assocArray{'someKey'};
```

sets the variable **$oneValue** to whatever value is associated with the key '**someKey**'. To place a new value into an associative array, just switch the two sides of the equation. For instance, the expression

```
$reverseSuits{'Hearts'} = 1;
```

assigns a value of 1 to the '**Hearts**' key. The string '**Hearts**' need not be already defined as a key in the associative array. If it does already exist, its old value will be replaced. Otherwise, a new entry will be created for the key and its associated value.

You can also think of an associative array as a list of paired entries. Whereas an ordinary array is an ordered list of values, indexed by position number, an associative array is a set of pairs of elements, indexed by the first element of each pair (the key). In fact, you initialize an associative array as a set of comma-separated pairs. Here's an example:

```
%suitNames = { 'Arm',    'Armani',
               'BB',     'Brooks Brothers',
               'SNR',    'Sears & Roebuck',
             }; # the last comma in a list is ignored
```

(The name of an associative array as a whole always begins with a percent sign.)

So you can view the keys either as the names of the array's entries or as non-numerical array indices. Either way, the upshot is that you can associate arbitrary values with arbitrary strings—that's why these arrays are called associative arrays.

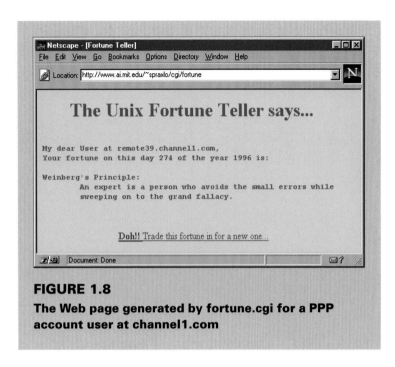

**FIGURE 1.8**
**The Web page generated by fortune.cgi for a PPP account user at channel1.com**

▶ REMOTE_IDENT, the user name associated with the browser, if one is given.

▶ HTTP_REFERER, the URL of the page from which the browser followed a link to this script, if any.

▶ SCRIPT_NAME, the relative URL of the script itself.

▶ SERVER_NAME, the Web server's Internet host name, alias, or IP address, as the server would refer to itself in a URL.

## The Unix Fortune Teller, CGI-Style

Listing 1.6 shows the fortune.cgi script, which generates the Unix Fortune Teller page.

Some of the environment variables that appear in this script might not always be defined. For instance, if the user typed the URL into the browser instead of clicking on a link, there would be no HTTP_REFERER variable in the script's run-time environment, and the line

```
$http_referer = $ENV{'HTTP_REFERER'};
```

would set **$http_referer** to the null value, which in Perl evaluates to **0** in a numerical context or to the empty string (**''**) in a string context. The script uses this fact to set some default values for its output. If the **$remote_ident** variable acquires no value from the associative array **%ENV**, it is set to the string **"User"**. Similarly, if **$ENV{'REMOTE_HOST'}** is not defined, **$remote_host** is assigned a default value of **$ENV{REMOTE_ADDR}**.

These default settings allow the script to address the user at least by his or her Internet address, if not by name. If the script has a URL for a referring page, it will reveal this information, too, in order to convince the user of the fortune teller's clairvoyance. When the user simply hits the Reload button or clicks on the link at the end of the page, however, it would seem less than prescient if the seer

**LISTING 1.6    The fortune.cgi script, which generates the Web page shown in Figures 1.8 and 1.9**

```perl
#!/usr/local/bin/perl
# fortune.cgi — tell the user's fortune and let 'em try again

$remote_ident = $ENV{'REMOTE_IDENT'};
$remote_host  = $ENV{'REMOTE_HOST'};
$http_referer = $ENV{'HTTP_REFERER'};
$script_name  = $ENV{'SCRIPT_NAME'};
$server_name  = $ENV{'SERVER_NAME'};

if (! $remote_ident) { $remote_ident = "User"; }
if (! $remote_host ) { $remote_host  = $ENV{'REMOTE_ADDR'}; }/-

print "Content-type: text/html\n\n";
print "<HTML><HEAD><TITLE>  Fortune Teller  </TITLE></HEAD><BODY>\n";
print "<H1><CENTER> The Unix Fortune Teller says... </CENTER></H1>\n";
print "<BR><B><PRE>\n";
print "My dear $remote_ident at $remote_host,\n";

$this_scripts_url = "http://$server_name$script_name";
if ($http_referer) {
  if ($http_referer eq $this_scripts_url) {
    print "Didn't I just tell you your fortune?\n";
  }
  else {
    print "You were sent here by $http_referer\n—nothing is by chance.\n";
  }
}

print "Your fortune on this ";
print `date +"day %j of the year 19%y is:"`; # date +format, %j for julian
print "\n";
print `/usr/games/fortune`;
print "</PRE></B><BR><BR><CENTER>\n";

print "<A HREF=$script_name>\n";
print "<B>Doh!! </B> Trade this fortune in for a new one...</A>\n";

print "</CENTER></BODY></HTML>\n";
```

announced that the user had just come (again) from the very same page. Therefore, the referring URL must be compared with the script's own URL to see whether it is the same. The script's own URL is constructed out of the two environment variables $SERVER_NAME and $SCRIPT_NAME. These environment variables must be extracted from the **%ENV** associative array and placed into the scalar variables (which in this script just happen to have the same names in lowercase) before their values can be interpolated into the string on the right-hand side of the assignment statement:

```
$this_scripts_url = "http://$server_name$script_name";
```

(Here the slash between the server name and the document pathname is included as the first character in the string contained in **$script_name**.) Then in the compound conditional statement

```
if ($http_referer eq $this_scripts_url) {
    print "Didn't I just tell you your fortune?\n";
  }
  else {
    print "You were sent here by $http_referer\n—nothing is by¬
chance.\n";
  }
```

the **eq** operator tests for equality between the two strings. If the referring URL matches the URL of the script itself, letter for letter, the script's output points this out; otherwise, the URL of referring page is shown.

The Unix **date** command is then called with a somewhat elaborate format string enclosed in quotation marks. The **date** command returns this format string with the Julian date and the two-digit year in place of **%j** and **%y**, and the returned string is immediately printed. Likewise, the lines returned by the Unix program /usr/games/fortune are printed as is, all inside the PRE tags. (This path for the Unix fortune program is fairly standard, but you may need to locate it on your system using the **which** command, as explained above.)

Finally, the script uses the $SCRIPT_NAME environment variable to present a link back to itself, offering the user a chance to trade his or her fortune in for a new one. Notice that the full URL is not needed here as it was when comparing this script's URL with that of the referring page. The situation here is the same as it is in any static HTML page: A link to any page on the same site requires only the relative URL. (That's all a browser would include in a get request anyway.)

## Example 1D: Fortunes and Status Codes

This example puts it all together: calling an external program such as date or fortune, using environment variables, using non-parsed headers and if-then flow control, and looping. In addition, it introduces two new concepts: CGI query strings and HTTP status codes.

Passing a CGI query string is probably the most prevalent means of sending user input from browsers to CGI programs. CGI query strings often show up in URLs as strings appended to the document URL following a question mark. For instance, the string **user@other.com** is the CGI query string in the following URL:

```
http://www.site.domain/cgi-bin/finger?user@other.com
```

Decoding and processing query strings will be major topics in Chapters 3 and 4. The example in this section simply tests for the presence of a query string, ignoring the string's actual contents.

### How to Use HTTP Status Codes

The HTTP status code is always a part of the first header a Web server or non-parsed-header CGI program sends back to the browser. The countdown script in Example 1B returned status code 200, indicating success. Other codes denote failures, such as "Document Not Found" or more ambiguous responses such as "Document Moved" (which might precede a forwarding address). A complete listing of the HTTP status codes and their intended meanings is available at http://www.w3.org/hypertext/WWW/Protocols/HTTP/HTRESP/.html. Most servers and browsers do not support all of them. Table 1.1 lists the most commonly used codes.

Some of the codes shown in Table 1.1 are codes that your browser might never let you see. For instance, if your browser supports automatic redirection, instead of displaying status code 302 with an error message from the server, it will accept the new URL from the server and take you directly to the found document. Of course, you can still see the 302 message by using the **telnet** method, as shown here:

```
unix% telnet www.w3.org 80
Trying 18.23.0.22 ...
Connected to www.w3.org.
Escape character is '^]'.
GET / HTTP/1.0
HTTP/1.0 302 Found
Server: CERN/3.0A
Date: Thu, 08 Aug 1996 22:55:58 GMT
Location: http://www.w3.org/pub/WWW/
```

```
Content-Type: text/html
Content-Length: 342

<HTML>
<HEAD>
<TITLE>Redirection</TITLE>
</HEAD>
<BODY>
<H1>Redirection</H1>
This document can be found
<A HREF="http://www.w3.org/pub/WWW/">elsewhere.</A><P>
You see this message because your browser doesn't support automatic
redirection handling. <P>
<HR>
<ADDRESS><A HREF="http://www.w3.org">CERN-HTTPD 3.0A</A></ADDRESS>
</BODY>
</HTML>
Connection closed by foreign host.
```

Status codes are illegal in the output of ordinary, parsed-header CGI scripts; inserting one there might cause the server to send a 500 ("Internal Error") code.

**TABLE 1.1    COMMON HTTP STATUS CODES**

| Code | Meaning | Description |
| --- | --- | --- |
| 200 | Success | The request has been carried out. A document usually follows. |
| 202 | Accepted | The request has been accepted but is still being processed. |
| 204 | No Response | The browser shouldn't change anything. |
| 301 | Document Moved | This usually means that the document has been moved to another server. |
| 302 | Document Found | The document is on this server but at a different location than originally indicated. |
| 400 | Bad Request | The request's syntax was bad (for example, if get instead of GET was used). |
| 401 | Unauthorized | The server restricts the document to authorized clients (those with passwords). |
| 403 | Forbidden | The request is denied due to file access permissions requirements or other reasons. |
| 404 | Not Found | The request found no matching document. |
| 500 | Internal Error | The server unexpectedly failed to fulfill the request. |
| 501 | Not Implemented | The request is for a feature that the server doesn't handle. |
| 502 | Service Overloaded | The server temporarily refuses to process any more requests. |

If your non-parsed-header script outputs any of these codes, it's responsible for following the code with an appropriate message. The script in Example 1D sends the 200 or 204 status header, depending on the input it receives. The 204 code means that the browser shouldn't do anything; in particular, it shouldn't load a new page or even reload the current one.

## A Fortune Teller that Keeps On Going and Going

The script in this example contains a stripped-down version of the code from the previous example. A significant difference is that, by default, this fortune teller will keep on sending fortunes to the client browser forever. The Web page produced by this script is shown, in part, in Figure 1.9.

There are two ways to stop this script's verbal outpouring. One way is the same as the method used in the countdown example: Hit the browser's Stop button. The other way is to click on the link that this script repeatedly places in its own output. As in the previous example, this script uses the $SCRIPT_NAME environment variable to present a link back to itself, but this time the extra string **?STOP** is appended to the URL specified in the link. When the script is called using this slightly modified URL, its output is completely different: It sends only the 204 ("No Response") status header, a content-type header, and a message that your browser should completely ignore. What actually stops the script from sending

more output is the click on the link (clicking on any link should stop further downloading and display of the current page), but what keeps the browser from reloading or switching to another page is the 204 status header. Of course, some browsers have been known to flunk this test (see Figure 1.10). Listing 1.7 shows the code.

Here the environment variables are accessed in the usual way, through the associative array **%ENV**. **$ENV{'$SERVER_SOFTWARE'}** specifies the server program that the server machine is running; some examples are Apache, CERN, Netscape,

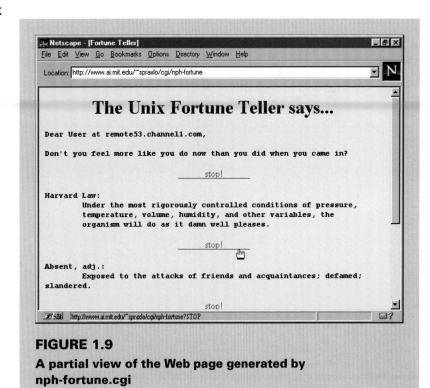

**FIGURE 1.9**
**A partial view of the Web page generated by nph-fortune.cgi**

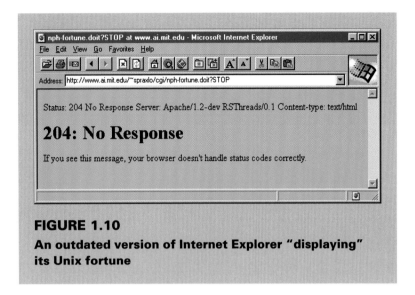

**FIGURE 1.10**
**An outdated version of Internet Explorer "displaying"**
**its Unix fortune**

and NCSA. This information is saved to the scalar variable **$server_software** and then sent to the client as part of the script's non-parsed header.

As in the previous example, the variable **$remote** is set to the Internet name of the browser's machine (using REMOTE_HOST) if this is available; otherwise, it's set to the remote machine's Internet address (which is always available from the environment variable REMOTE_ADDR). As a conditional, **unless** means *if not*; that is,

```
unless (EXPRESSION)
```

is equivalent to

```
if (! EXPRESSION)
```

where **!** is the negation operator. The whole statement,

```
$remote = $ENV{REMOTE_ADDR} unless $remote = $ENV{REMOTE_HOST};
```

takes advantage of the fact that in Perl, as in C, the value of an assignment statement in a conditional is the same as it is in any other context: the value on the right-hand side of the equal sign. Thus the entire statement could be rewritten verbosely as

```
$remote = $ENV{REMOTE_HOST};
if (! $remote) {  # if $remote is 0 or the null string, then
  $remote = $ENV{REMOTE_ADDR};
}
```

Most experienced Perl programmers, however, prefer the conciseness of the version shown previously.

The use of the environment variable QUERY_STRING is one way for a CGI program to receive variable input, such as the information a user types into an HTML form, from a client. In a GET request, this information is appended to the URL as

**LISTING 1.7    The nph-fortune.cgi script, which prints the user's fortune until it is told to stop**

```perl
#!/usr/local/bin/perl
# nph-fortune.cgi — tell the user's fortune over and over...

$script_name     = $ENV{'SCRIPT_NAME'};
$server_software = $ENV{'SERVER_SOFTWARE'};
$remote          = $ENV{'REMOTE_ADDR'}
  unless $remote = $ENV{'REMOTE_HOST'};
$query_string    = $ENV{'QUERY_STRING'};

$| = 1;

if ($query_string) {
  print "Status: 204 No Response\n";
  print "Server: $server_software\n";
  print "Content-type: text/html\n\n";
  print "<H1>204: No Response</H1>\n";
  print "If you see this message, your browser\n";
  print "doesn't handle status codes correctly.<P>\n";
  exit;
}

print "HTTP/1.0 200 OK\n";
print "Server: $server_software\n";
print "Content-type: text/html\n\n";

print "<HTML><HEAD><TITLE>   Fortune Teller  </TITLE></HEAD><BODY>\n";
print "<H1><CENTER> The Unix Fortune Teller says... </CENTER></H1>\n";
print "<B><PRE>Dear User at $remote,</PRE></B>\n";
while (1) {
  print "<B><PRE>", `/usr/games/fortune -w`, "</PRE></B>\n";
  print "<CENTER> <A HREF=$script_name?STOP>_____stop!_____</A> \n";
  print "</CENTER>\n";
}
print "</BODY></HTML>\n";
```

an encoded string following a question mark. In this example, the URL plus the query string is likely to be

```
http://www.site.domain/cgi-bin/nph-fortune?STOP
```

The **STOP** comes from the link in the default, never-ending Web page generated by the nph-fortune script itself. The first page the user sees is the default page—this script is actually capable of outputting two entirely distinct Web pages. If the script is requested without a query string, it will bypass the first conditional and enter this infinite loop

```
while (1) {
    output a fortune and wait a moment
    output the STOP link
}
```

where **1** is always true. The result is the script's default output; actually, the script will never even reach the statement

```
print "</BODY></HTML>\n";
```

If the script is called with a query string, however, as from the link

```
<A HREF=$script_name?STOP>_____stop!_____</A>
```

where the script's partial URL is substituted as the value of **$script_name** when it is printed, the output is quite different, as shown in Listing 1.8.

The script outputs these lines and then exits. The rest of the statements in the file are never executed.

A browser that receives this output should not display it as a Web page; in fact, it shouldn't do anything at all. This code makes it possible to stop the default page's verbiage without loading a new page. In effect, clicking on the **stop!** link causes the script to do the same thing the server would have had to do if the user

**LISTING 1.8    The output from nps-fortune.cgi when the script's partial URL is passed to it**

```
Status: 204 No Response
Content-type: text/html

<H1>204: No Response</H1>
If you see this message, your browser
doesn't handle status codes correctly.<P>
```

had hit the browser's Stop button. This is one more way in which CGI scripts usurp or enhance the functions of Web servers.

# Back to What It Is: CGI as a Standard Interface

If you have followed the examples in this chapter, you should now have a better and more practical understanding of what CGI is and how it works. Formally, the CGI specification covers three aspects of the interaction—or cooperation, if you will—between Web servers and CGI programs:

▶ How a Web server starts up a CGI program within its own special environment

▶ How the server passes on to this program any data sent by a Web client that requested the program's execution

▶ How the CGI program sends its output to the Web server, which may or may not process this output further (for instance, by parsing and adding to the header) before sending it on to the requesting client

This book will cover all three of these aspects of CGI in considerable detail. The first two items in this list form the main topics of Chapter 3; the third is the central focus of Chapter 5. After that, the book will concentrate mainly on the processing that takes place *between* CGI input and output. The topics covered in these later chapters will include processing the actual data collected from forms, searching your Web site and maintaining a database, and generating graphics on-the-fly. And along the way, I will be explaining Perl features and programming techniques as they are introduced.

Chapter 2 tells you how to get and install Perl on your system if you don't have it already and then discusses other tools and libraries that you might find useful for CGI programming with Perl. Chapter 3 presents an introduction to creating and processing some easy forms, and then Chapter 4 moves right on to the topic of CGI input.

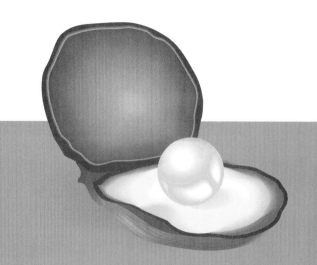

# Chapter 2
# Tools for CGI Programming with Perl

Perl has been available as a programming language on Unix systems since the late 1980s, when it gained a reputation as an excellent tool for searching and rearranging large amounts of text, manipulating files, and managing processes. These capabilities made it a favorite of Unix systems administrators and programmers. As Perl's capabilities have grown, so has its popularity. Perl's migration to PCs and Macintoshes began in the early 1990s, and now it's easy to obtain stable adaptations of Perl versions 4 and 5 for MS-DOS, Windows 95 and Windows NT, Amiga, MacOS, OS/2, and several other platforms. It has also become by far the most widely used language for writing CGI scripts.

## Why Use Perl?

From the beginning, Perl has been very handy for generating reports—or, to put it more generally, for extracting large amounts of data and reducing the data to nicely formatted text. Perl's creator, Larry Wall, originally named it as an acronym: PERL stands for Practical Extraction and Report Language. Over time, Perl also developed into an easy-to-use networking language, providing facilities that allow programs to communicate, via sockets, with processes running on other machines. Advanced security features and interfaces to many popular database facilities have also found their way into Perl. These capabilities make Perl a nearly ideal language for accomplishing the fundamental tasks of CGI: creating the HTML texts of dynamic Web pages, manipulating the data returned from interactive forms, and saving this information in plain text files and in databases.

Moreover, Perl is easy to learn and use. Beginning programmers have no trouble recognizing Perl's simple data types and clearly marked variables. They like Perl because of its straightforward style, its forgiving syntax, and its quick development cycle, both in terms of the learning curve and in terms of writing the actual code. You can begin writing useful programs right away, without having to be an expert programmer, and concern yourself with all the fine points and special features later. With Perl, you don't have to worry much about the right way to do things. One of Perl's slogans is, "There's more than one way to do it."

Experienced software professionals like Perl for its flexibility, its sensible default variables, and its predictable behavior. If you already know Unix shell or C programming, Perl may seem more like a different dialect than a foreign language to you. You won't need to learn a completely new way of thinking, because a great deal of what Perl is and does was devised in the same spirit as Unix and C. Conversely, if you are new to Unix or need to perform some tasks on Unix platforms but do most of your work in Windows, MacOS, or on some other platform, Perl is a good starting point and can provide you with many shortcuts.

## Perl vs. Unix:
## A Common Toolbox vs. a Scattered Bag of Tricks

The difference between Perl and Unix or DOS shell scripting is that with Perl you've got one well-designed toolbox full of functions that work together, whereas the deficiencies of shell scripting languages constantly force you to rely on external programs that have no common calling interface. Perl offers many powerful built-in functions, so instead of having to master a dozen other file and text processing utilities, you need to learn only the equivalent functions within Perl, all of which share a common interface. If you already know how to use Unix commands or their DOS equivalents, you can easily call them from within a Perl script and retrieve the results (just as the Unix **date** command was called in the examples in Chapter 1). However, as you learn Perl, such habits may soon vanish.

## Perl vs. C and Visual Basic:
## Interpreted vs. Compiled Languages

The difference between Perl and a language such as C or Visual Basic is that Perl is interpreted, not compiled. This means that you can execute a Perl program as soon as you've saved the code as an ordinary text file, just as you can with a shell script or a batch file. You don't have to compile the file into object code or link it with any other files before you run it, as you must with a program written in C or Visual Basic.

## Conclusion

All of this allows you to develop Perl scripts very quickly and modify them easily. It also allows you to be creative and learn about Perl's capabilities by trying them out. It is much easier to try out a new feature when all you have to do is type in a line of code and hit Save before running your modified program. (Or, if you're editing a script that is already installed as a CGI program, all you have to do is save it and hit Reload in your browser.)

One more reason to use Perl for CGI programming is that so many other programmers already have. The vast majority of CGI programs currently running on the Web are Perl scripts. Many generous souls have made their favorite Perl scripts freely available on the Web, and there are several Usenet newsgroups devoted to Perl, Perl scripting specifically for CGI, and CGI programming in general, wherein Perl is now the lingua franca.

In short, Perl is a great language for CGI programming and is well worth learning even if you will be programming primarily on platforms other than Unix.

# Differences between Perl Versions 4 and 5

The biggest difference between Perl versions 4 and 5 is that Perl 4 favors a procedure-oriented approach to programming, while Perl 5 provides much greater support for object-oriented programming techniques. In procedure-oriented programming, functions and subroutines tend to be centered around performing many general tasks and a few application-specific procedures. Data structures, small or large, are usually subordinate to these procedures. Object-oriented programming reverses this, making functions revolve around data structures (*objects*) and certain kinds of objects called *classes*. Objects and classes are also spoken of as *encapsulating* both data and class functions, also known as *methods*, which operate only on a given object's or class's data.

For example, inside a word processor implemented as a procedure-oriented application, there might be only one search function for searching the text of any document; either the application represents different kinds of documents the same way internally or the function itself must behave differently on different documents. Inside a word processor implemented with object-oriented techniques, however, different kinds of documents are likely to be given different internal presentations, each with its own text-searching function.

There are advantages and disadvantages to either orientation. Procedure-oriented programming styles feel more natural and straightforward to most beginning programmers and generally make it easier to get small programs up and running. However, there is a tendency in procedure-oriented programming to represent even large, application-specific objects very generically, so that their components can be manipulated by many small, general-purpose functions. In large applications, such representations are often error-prone.

Object-oriented programming (OOP) suffers from the opposite problem. In OOP there is a tendency to reinvent many small functions as methods that work only with specific object classes. OOP applications also tend to demand greater effort in the initial design stages. However, once you get the hang of OOP as a general approach, its techniques can make it easier to isolate the various parts of a large application from each other, thereby shielding data and making it easier to catch and handle errors.

One of the best things about the incorporation of object-oriented programming into Perl 5 is that it is nearly invisible, unless you write your script to use specific object-oriented classes. Perl represents classes as modules, and using one of them is very much like calling the functions from an included library. It usually requires little or no effort to adapt scripts written for Perl 4 to run under Perl 5, and there is every reason to use Perl 5 for all new development work. All of the scripts in this book were written for use with Perl 5, although most will also run under Perl 4.

# How to Get Perl for Your Computer

Perl is free and very widely available on the Internet. Perl is already installed on probably the majority of all Unix systems, since it started on the Unix platform, but Perl versions 4 and 5 have also been adapted to run on almost any computer that can run a Web server, including Amiga, Macintosh, MS-DOS, OS/2, VMS, Win32s, Windows 95, and Windows NT. These adaptations, or *ports*, are freely distributed by FTP sites all over the world, and you can download any of them using your Web browser or any FTP-enabled file-transfer utility program.

All of the different ports of Perl are very similar to the original Unix implementation, so I would urge you to install Perl 5 on your own computer, even if the Web server on which you will install your scripts runs on a different platform. Although you need a Web server to actually run your scripts as CGI programs, you can do a lot of development and testing on your local machine first. This will save you a lot of time, especially in debugging, and will save the Web server from running completely untested code.

Perl has always been written in C, and installation kits generally come in two forms: as precompiled binary executables ready to install along with all their library and other support files, or as compressed archives containing all the source code for rebuilding the binary executables and installing Perl from the ground up. Unless you have a fair amount of experience programming in C, go with the first option. Perl's original Unix creators and many of its porters to other platforms have put a lot of effort into making the installation procedure as automatic and fail-safe as possible, but with computers there's always one more way for something to go wrong, and if a problem arises when you are rebuilding Perl from the source code, you may suddenly need a lot of programming know-how to fix it.

## CPAN: A Primary Perl Resource

Many Perl distribution sites are members of an umbrella organization known as CPAN, which stands for Comprehensive Perl Archive Network (see Figure 2.1). CPAN member sites tend to be up-to-date and to include nearly all of the Perl version 4 and 5 ports to other operating systems. An HTML interface for the entire contents of standard CPAN mirror archives is currently under construction.

The main CPAN site is in Finland (ftp.funet.fi), but a very popular U.S. site is maintained at the University of Florida: ftp://ftp.cis.ufl.edu/pub/perl/ CPAN/. This particular site also maintains lists of frequently asked questions and answers about Perl (the Perl FAQ and Meta-FAQ), as well as archives of the Perl Usenet newsgroups (in /pub/perl/comp.lang.perl and similar directories). As I'll describe in the sections that follow, there are other, non-CPAN sites that specialize in Perl for particular platforms, but when you are in doubt about where to get anything having to do with Perl, look first to CPAN.

## Perl for Unix

Perl was created for Unix and can run on almost any Unix platform. In fact, if you are a user at any large or commercial Unix site, chances are Perl is already installed on your Unix machine, especially if it shares file systems with a Web server.

### Where to Get Perl for Unix Platforms

Perl for Unix is usually distributed only as a compressed archive source kit. Within a CPAN FTP site, the directory containing the latest released version of Perl 5 is usually

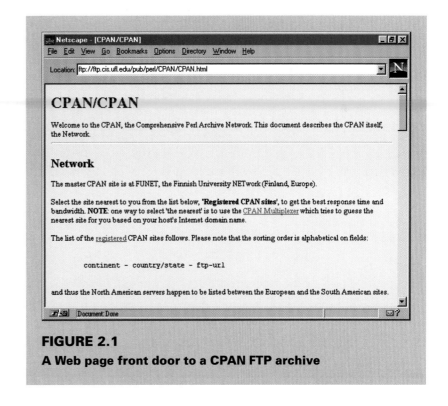

**FIGURE 2.1**

**A Web page front door to a CPAN FTP archive**

CPAN/src/5.0 or perl/src/5.0. For example, some complete URLs for downloading the latest version of Perl are

▶ ftp://ftp.cis.ufl.edu/pub/perl/CPAN/src/5.0/latest.tar.gz

▶ ftp://ftp.metronet.com/pub/perl/src/5.0/latest.tar.gz

▶ ftp://genetics.upenn.edu/perl5/src/5.0/latest.tar.gz

(At all of these sites, latest.tar.gz should currently be linked to perl5.003.tar.gz in the same directory.) The latest beta versions are kept in /src/5.0/unsupported (relative to the top-level directory).

The Unix source kits contain scripts that automate as much of the installation procedure as possible, but again, unless you are an experienced C programmer (or are blessed with beginner's luck), you might face a steep learning curve in rebuilding Perl from the source kit.

## Where to Install (or Find) Perl on a Unix Machine

It's customary for the current version of the Perl interpreter to be installed as the executable file /usr/local/bin/perl and for the code libraries it uses to live under the directory /usr/local/lib/perl. Larry Wall, Perl's creator, recommends that you install the interpreter as /usr/bin/perl, but at that location it is liable to be deleted during system upgrades, and therefore many sites reserve the directory /usr/bin for software bundled with the operating system. It is therefore common to create a symbolic link from wherever the Perl executable is actually installed to /usr/bin/perl so that the executable can be invoked using this pathname, too.

Many Unix sites are now switching over from Perl versions 5.001 and 4.036 to Perl 5.003. Their systems administrators might keep one of the version 4 releases available as /usr/local/bin/perl4 and create a *symbolic link* from /usr/local/bin/perl to usr/local/bin/perl5.003. (A symbolic link in Unix is like a shortcut to a file in Windows or an alias on Macintosh systems.)

On other sites, Perl still refers to Perl version 4, and it is version 5 that your scripts might have to call explicitly, as with this pound-bang command line:

```
#!/usr/local/bin/perl5
```

Most of the Perl CGI scripts you'll see in this book, or find on the Web, begin with

```
#!/usr/local/bin/perl
```

and assume that this pathname points to the latest version. To get the actual version number of any installed Perl program, invoke it with the command-line option **-v**, as in **/usr/bin/perl -v**. If Perl is installed elsewhere on the Unix system you use, you'll need to change this pathname. (For information on how to find Perl on your system, see the sections in Chapter 1 on installing hello.cgi.)

## Perl 5 for Windows 95, Windows NT, and Win32

Ports of Perl 4 to MS-DOS and Windows 3.1 were made by several different parties, and these are still in use on 16-bit Windows platforms (see the next section). As of Perl 5, however, all ports are 32-bit only and have come from one source. At Microsoft's behest, HIP Communications ported Perl 5.01 to Win32s and later to Windows NT. Both of these ports will work under Windows 95, but the Windows NT version seems to work much better than the Win32's version. The current build corresponds to Perl version 5.001, unofficial patchlevel 1l for Windows NT and patchlevel m for Win32s. As in Unix, you can get the version and patchlevel of an installed version of Perl by invoking it with only the **-v** option at a DOS command prompt, as shown here:

```
C:\perl5> perl -v

This is perl, version 5.001

        Unofficial patchlevel 1.1

Copyright 1987-1994, Larry Wall
Windows NT port Copyright (c) 1995 Microsoft Corporation.  All rights
reserved.
        Developed by hip communications inc., http://info.hip.com/info
        Windows NT Perl 5.001.a Built Jul 28 1995@16:46:31
Perl may be copied only under the terms of either the Artistic License
or the
GNU General Public License, which may be found in the Perl 5.0 source
kit.

C:\perl5>
```

The version here can be identified more briefly as 5.001l. Conversely, the long form of identification for Perl 4.036 is usually Perl version 4.1.8, patchlevel 36.

## Where to Get Perl 5 for Windows NT and Windows 95 (NTPerl)

Perl 5.0 source kits and precompiled binaries for various 32-bit Windows platforms can also be obtained from any CPAN-member FTP archive. For example, one URL for the latest source distribution is

▶ ftp://ftp.metronet.com/pub/perl/ports/winNT/perl5/perl5.001m/CurrentBuild /110-src.zip

and one URL for the latest version precompiled for "wintel" machines (Windows on Intel Pentium and x86 machines) is

▶ ftp://ftp.cis.ufl.edu/pub/perl/CPAN/ports/winNT/perl5/perl5.001m/ CurrentBuild/110-i86.zip

The original distribution site is http://www.perl.hip.com/, which also provides an HTML interface (see Figure 2.2).

## Where to Install Perl 5 for Windows NT and Windows 95

On a Windows system, the binary executable perl.exe should live in the same directory with all of Perl's library and other support files. A common path for the main directory is c:\perl5, but it doesn't really matter what it's called or where it is on your system as long as it contains the subdirectory called lib, which contains the code for a library of functions that Perl can call. There should also be a subdirectory called doc, which contains Perl's documentation in the form of .htm files. If you are installing the main directory yourself—for instance, from a .zip archive—it's a good idea to put it on the same drive with your CGI scripts, and your scripts should definitely be on the same drive with any external programs that they may call (as date.exe is in the hello.cgi example in Chapter 1).

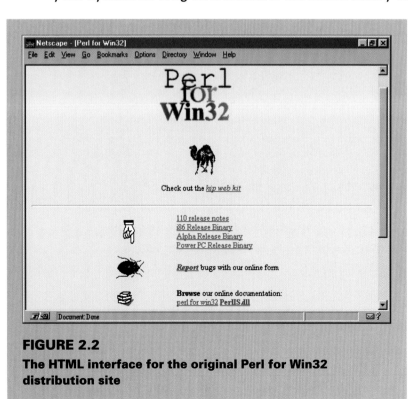

**FIGURE 2.2**

**The HTML interface for the original Perl for Win32 distribution site**

The C source code for these ports of Perl 5 is available from the same places (hip.com and most CPAN archives). If you want to rebuild Perl from the source code, you'll need  Microsoft Visual C++, which was used for the original port.

## Perl 4 for Windows 95, Windows 3.1, and MS-DOS

Most CGI Perl scripts will run just fine under Perl 4 unless they include object-oriented coding or linking schemes. Perl 5's dynamic linking model, along with the many libraries available for linking, constitute one of the main advantages of using Perl 5. On the other hand, Perl 4 has a large installed base, and some scripts written for Perl 4 do break under version 5. If you need to write portable code, it's a good idea to keep a copy of Perl 4.036 around, too. If you have both, keep them in their own directories (\perl4 and \perl5, for instance); you'll probably also want to re-name the version 4 perl.exe to perl4.exe.

### Where to Get Perl 4 for Windows and MS-DOS

Several ports of Perl 4 for Windows and MS-DOS platforms are available from ftp://ftp.ee.umanitoba.ca/pub/msdos/perl/perl4. The most popular is probably BigPERL4, which corresponds to the official Unix version 4.036 and also works under Windows 3.1. It's called "big" because it uses virtual memory and is able to address up to 32MB of RAM. (With Perl 5 on a 32-bit Windows machine, this is not an issue.) Be warned that some distributions of Perl 4 contain only the source code, with no precompiled binary executables.

**Denny's Perl 4 for Windows NT and Windows 95**   Another popular port of Perl 4.036 for Windows is Robert Denny's Perl for Windows NT and Windows 95, available from http://www.ora.com/software/. Denny developed this version specifi-cally "in order to provide a Perl environment for the O'Reilly WebSite Web server," of which he is the author.

This port of Perl is actually an enhancement of the original NTPerl kit from ftp://ftp.intergraph.com/pub/win32/perl/, which you will need in order to install this port. Both the Denny version and the NTPerl kit come with installation instructions, but if you are installing onto a Windows 95 platform, Robert Denny's instructions supersede those of Intergraph. Basically, you install the original Intergraph version manually and then replace some of its executables with those from the Denny distribution. Denny's upgraded features include support for standard input/output (STDIO) sockets (which enables Perl to run the libwww-perl packages) and mutex support (which enables CGI scripts to synchronize access to shared objects).

## Perl for the Macintosh: MacPerl 4 and 5

MacPerl is the only port of Perl in common use on the Macintosh. Matthias Neeracher ported both versions 4.036 and 5.001 as different versions of MacPerl. MacPerl 5 is now stable and preferred over MacPerl 4; the current release is MacPerl 5.07r1m, which dates back to March 12, 1996. MacPerl 5 also runs as a native application on PowerPC Macintoshes.

### Using MacPerl as a Standalone Application and MPW Tool

MacPerl 4 and 5 both come in three different distribution kits: as a standalone application; as a tool application for use with Macintosh Programming Works (MPW) 3.2 or later, which is now a part of Metrowerks's CodeWarrior; and as a C source code kit for rebuilding either the application or the tool. Both the standalone application and the MPW tool provide a console window for testing and debugging scripts and are scriptable with AppleScript. If you plan to use MacPerl only to serve or test CGI scripts, you are probably better off with the application version. If you will also be programming in Java or C on the Macintosh, get the tool version as well.

MacPerl is able to compete with AppleScript as a CGI programming language with advanced features for the Macintosh and yet is still highly compatible with Unix Perl. Despite the many differences between Unix and the Macintosh operating system (MacOS), it is very easy to write MacPerl scripts in such a way that they can run unchanged under Unix, which also makes them easy to port to other platforms.

### How to Install a Perl Script as a CGI Program on a Macintosh

To run a Perl script as a CGI program on a Macintosh Web server such as MacHTTP or its commercial successor, Starnine/Quarterdeck WebStar, you will also need AppleScript and a special MacPerl extension, MacHTTP CGI Script.

AppleScript is a MacOS system extension that comes with MacPerl. It is also a standard part of MacOS 7.5 and is widely used by other applications. (To use MacPerl, you need System 7.1 or later.)

The MacHTTP CGI Script extension is an application extension specific to MacPerl; unfortunately, it is not presently included in the distributions of MacPerl itself or the MacHTTP family of Web servers. (The next section explains where to get it.) Its purpose is to insert AppleScript code into your script file's resource fork, enabling it to handle AppleEvents. Such code is commonly called "glue," and the resulting semi-autonomous application is called an *applet* (meaning "little application," not "little AppleScript program").

All this may sound complicated, and in fact it would be if you had to use ResEdit to edit the script's resource fork yourself, but now it can be done automatically. Once the MacHTTP CGI Script extension is placed in MacPerl's extensions folder (which is either a subfolder in the MacPerl application directory or a subfolder named MacPerl in your system's preferences folder), all you have to do is save your script as a MacHTTP CGI Script in MacPerl's Save dialog box. Then just put the resulting applet in the same folder with the Web server's application folder (or a subfolder of that folder). Macintosh Web servers are close to being plug-n-play. You needn't worry about any special filename extension or path variables; just request the CGI applet by its URL, and the server will do the rest.

## Where to Get MacPerl and Its "CGI Glue" Extension

The current releases of MacPerl 4 and 5 are freely available from any CPAN mirror site. Here are two possibilities:

▶ ftp://uiarchive.cso.uiuc.edu/pub/lang/perl/CPAN/ports/mac/ (in Illinois)

▶ ftp://ftp.demon.co.uk/pub/mirrors/perl/CPAN/ports/mac/ (in Great Britain)

Another popular distribution site for MacPerl and CGI-related Macintosh software is ftp://nic.switch.ch/software/mac/perl (in Switzerland), but the FTP server may disallow downloads if you are not connecting from an educational site (with .edu as part of your domain name). You can also get MacPerl, including the latest beta test version and extended source code distributions, from ftp://mors.gsfc.nasa.gov/pub/MacPerl/Applications or from Matthias Neeracher's own FTP distribution site, ftp://err.ethz.ch/pub/neeri/ (also in Switzerland; this site tends to be very busy).

The MacPerl "CGI glue" extension for use with MacHTTP is available from Neeracher's own site, ftp://err.ethz.ch/pub/neeri/MacPerl/PCGI.sit.hqx.

# Editors and Development Environments for Perl

Perl scripts are plain text files, which means that they can be written and edited with just about any text editor or word processor. Many simple text editors give you an advantage in speed and clarity: They load and save files quickly and display all text files in a fixed-width font that's optimized for screen viewing rather than for printing.

A full-featured word processor might give you the ability to edit, search, and even keep track of many files at once, but you might need to disable some of its "automatic" features (such as auto-save, automatic spell-checking, word wrap, and "smart" quotes) and avoid any commands that would add formatting or non-ASCII-printable characters (such as boldfaced or indented text and "curly" quotation marks). You'll also want to make sure that you're saving your scripts as text-only files. If you will be editing a lot of these scripts, you might also want to change your default font to a fixed-width screen font such as Courier, Ohlfs, or Monaco (for the Macintosh).

Editors that are designed for programmers usually provide features such as automatic indentation and some way of keeping track of the level of nested parentheses. Some can even parse the code as you write it and display various pieces of the syntax in different colors or warn you about apparent errors. In general, these advanced features are meant to help you check your code's syntax or even its logic as you go. They are usually reconfigurable, and your choice of features is a matter of taste.

Emacs is one such text editor that is extremely popular with programmers. It was originally developed for Lisp and C programmers in a Unix environment, but it has long since been ported to just about every other operating system under the sun. (The name *Emacs* derives from *Editing MACroS*, although other acronyms abound.) Richard Stallman originally created Emacs at the MIT Artificial Intelligence Lab, and it is freely distributed by GNU under the terms of its General Public License from ftp://prep.ai.mit.edu/pub/gnu. The latest GNU Windows version, along with instructions for installation, can be found at www.cs.washington.edu/homes/voelker/ntemacs.html. The GNU versions and most recent ports come with a built-in Perl mode. Several other Perl-mode extensions are freely available on the Internet (for example, Perl Plus by Hirose Yuuji at www.comp.ae.keio.ac.jp/lab/okoma/yuuji/perlplus.el). If you use a Perl mode, Emacs can do some of your code formatting and syntax checking for you as you write, and it can automatically display various types of code elements in different colors.

Because Perl is an interpreted language, it has no need for its own compiler or linkers, and thus a special development environment just for Perl might be considered overkill. At any rate, with the partial exception of MacPerl, no Perl development environments exist. Nevertheless, if you are already accustomed to a particular programming environment designed for a language such as C or Visual Basic, you might be able to tweak it to create projects in Perl code as well. At the very least, you can probably use some of its advanced editing capabilities with your scripts.

# Some Useful Libraries for Perl and CGI

There are many common tasks in CGI programming that must be performed every time you generate a new page or process the input from a form. Tasks such as outputting HTTP headers or decoding a query string hardly vary from one Web page to another, so you will often find yourself using the same pieces of code over and over again. A good thing to do in this situation would be to rewrite those repeated pieces of code as generalized subroutines and gather them into a library that you can reference in all of your CGI projects.

An even better idea would be to have an expert do it for you. Once you understand how to use a well-designed set of subroutines to accomplish the basic, common tasks of CGI, you can focus your attention on the things that make your site distinctive and your programs an effective part of that. There's no need to reinvent the wheel when what you want to do is build a rocket.

Best of all would be to use a library created by experts and already in widespread use, so you can be sure that all the subroutines have been thoroughly debugged and will efficiently perform their appointed tasks. Also, when there is a large base of fellow users, there are likely to be several people you can refer to for help if something goes wrong or when you are just learning.

Well, the software engineering in this world is rarely so perfect that you can trust somebody else's code in every detail, but there are in fact many public domain Perl libraries. The routines in these libraries allow you to accomplish such common tasks as creating forms and parsing their input, and there are even a few public forums and archives of frequently asked questions and answers pertaining to the libraries' use. Three of these widely used Perl libraries are cgi-lib.pl, CGI.pm, and libwww-perl.

## A Simple Starter Library: cgi-lib.pl

The small but effective cgi-lib.pl library is concerned mainly with parsing and manipulating the data that users enter into forms. The entire library is contained in one Perl source file written by Steven Brenner and named cgi-lib.pl. It is available from http://www.bio.cam.ac.uk/cgi-lib/ (see Figure 2.3). To call its subroutines in your own scripts, you have only to install this file in Perl's default library directory and include the following line in your script:

```
require "cgi-lib.pl";
```

This tells the Perl interpreter to process your script as if the contents of the file cgi-lib.pl were literally there in your own script in place of the **require** directive.

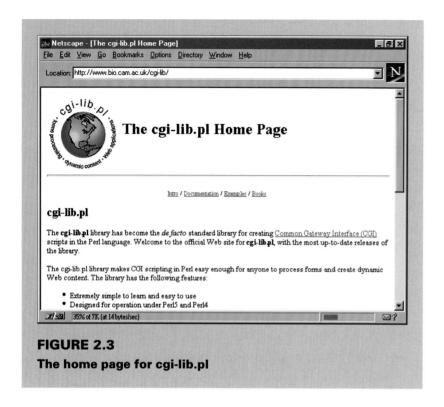

**FIGURE 2.3**
**The home page for cgi-lib.pl**

Perl will first look for the cgi-lib.pl file in the directory in which your script is located, and then it will search in its own default library directory. On a Unix system, Perl's library directory is usually in /usr/local/lib/perl; on a Windows or Macintosh platform, it's usually the subdirectory named lib in the same directory with perl.exe or the MacPerl application program.

The cgi-lib.pl file contains half a dozen subroutines that perform the basic tasks of parsing form input, printing all the keys and values of an associative array such as **%ENV**, and outputting an error message as a complete HTML document. Two of its one-liners could have been used in the examples in Chapter 1: one that outputs the ubiquitous HTTP header

```
Content-type: text/html\n\n
```

and another that returns the complete URL of the script itself (as you did in the fortune.pl example).

## CGI.pm: A Full-Featured CGI Forms Module for Perl 5

CGI.pm contains subroutines that do everything cgi-lib.pl can do and much more. It is geared toward not only parsing the input from forms but also creating forms as output from the same scripts that process the user-entered data sent to the server. You use CGI.pm to create forms by calling its functions to generate HTML form elements for you, rather than explicitly printing out all the tags yourself. Using its methods may not be as intuitive as outputting all the necessary HTML code yourself, but it can make your scripts more consistent and succinct.

Loosely speaking, CGI.pm is a Perl 5 library; you install it in Perl's lib directory and use its subroutines in just about the same way you use those of cgi-lib.pl. Technically, though, CGI.pm is a Perl *module.* (That's what the .pm stands for.) Instead of including the entire contents of the CGI.pm file in your own script using a **require** directive, you put the line

```
use CGI;
```

near the top of your script. Perl will then include only those parts of CGI.pm that your script actually uses.

CGI.pm was developed by Lincoln Stein and is available as freeware from http://www-genome.wi.mit.edu/ftp/pub/software/WWW/. It comes with its own installation instructions and documentation that explains its use in detail.

Stein has also written cgi-utils.pl, which is an extension of Steven Brenner's cgi-lib.pl and is available from the same site: http://www-genome.wi.mit.edu/WWW/tools/scripting/cgi-utils.html. Stein's offerings are well-documented and tend to be very portable; CGI.pm has been used successfully with the WebSite server under Windows NT and Windows 95, the MacHTTP server with MacPerl 5 under MacOS, and even the port of Perl 5 for the VMS operating system.

## The libwww-perl Utilities Collection

Developed in a collaborative effort, libwww-perl is not one library but a collection of utility libraries and test scripts. It's based on Perl version 4.036, and its intention is to support as much of HTTP version 1.0 as possible in order to facilitate the creation of Web tools and client programs. Although its focus is not on CGI programming per se, it contains a great many bits and pieces that are worth looking at for their ideas and techniques. The libwww-perl distribution is a public giveaway from the University of California at

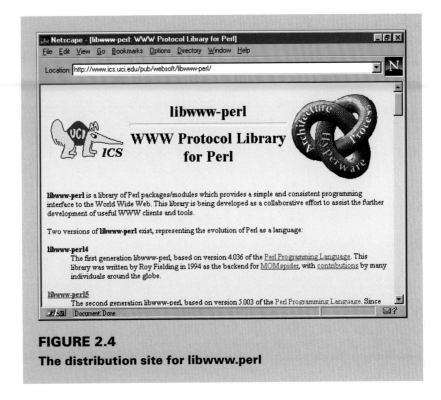

**FIGURE 2.4**
**The distribution site for libwww.perl**

Irvine (see Figure 2.4). The latest versions are available from http://www.ics.uci.edu/WebSoft/libwww.perl/.

This Web site is also the home of the MOMspider (Multi-Owner Maintenance Spider), which was created in Perl by Roy Fielding. Its function is to crawl entire Web sites and report any problems it finds, such as missing links or inaccessible documents. Spiders and other site maintenance tools will be discussed in some of the later chapters in this book.

## Graphics On-the-Fly with libgd.a and GD.pm

The most frequently used tool for dynamically generating GIF images on the Web is probably libgd.a, which is actually a C library. GD.pm is a Perl module that serves as a "wrapper" for libgd.a—that is, an external calling interface that allows you to call libgd.a's C routines for creating and drawing GIF images from within a Perl script. (*GD* stands for *GIF Draw.*) Thomas Boutell originally wrote libgd.a in C for Unix, and then Lincoln Stein created GD.pm as something of a port to Perl. You still need to have libgd.a installed on your system before GD.pm will work, but both can be used on platforms other than Unix. You can find both libgd.a and GD.pm, along with a great deal of information about CGI programming, on Thomas Boutell's own site, http://www.boutell.com/ (see Figure 2.5). Or you can go directly to the original distribution sites for each: libgd.a is available from http://siva.cshl.org/gd/gd.html, and GD.pm is distributed from http://www-genome.wi.mit.edu/ftp/pub/software/WWW/ GD.html. In this book we will use both libgd.a and GD.pm to generate dynamic documents in Chapter 6.

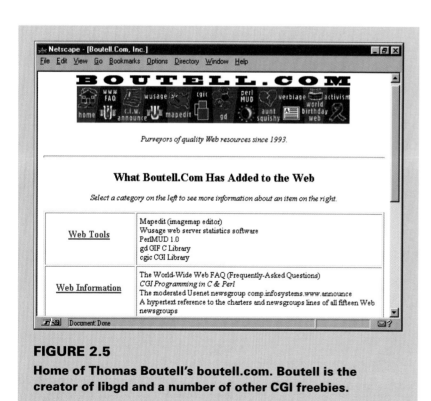

**FIGURE 2.5**
**Home of Thomas Boutell's boutell.com. Boutell is the creator of libgd and a number of other CGI freebies.**

# Other Online Resources for Perl and CGI

There are many other distribution sites for Perl and CGI-related libraries in addition to the ones described in this chapter, and sites that serve up free Perl scripts and information about their use are too abundant even to list. The most complete lists are maintained online rather than in any printed form, yet often the best way to find a utility or example script for a certain task is still to search with one of the Web's global search engines such as AltaVista or Yahoo! This section lists just a few more online resources for CGI programming with Perl.

## Informative Perl/CGI Web Sites

Here are a few Web sites that provide many sample scripts and informative links for CGI programming with Perl:

▶ **http://www.worldwidemart.com/scripts/**    Matt Wright's Script Archive contains many well-written scripts that have been tested by a large number of users. If you are looking for a ready-made Perl CGI script, this is a good place to start (see Figure 2.6).

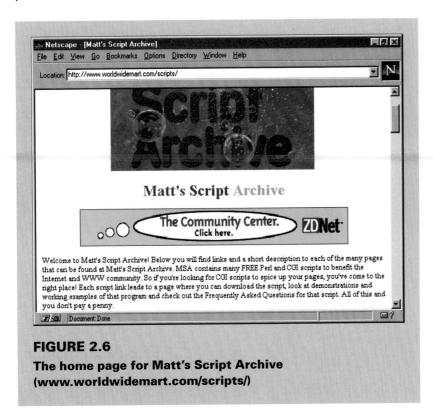

**FIGURE 2.6**

**The home page for Matt's Script Archive (www.worldwidemart.com/scripts/)**

▶ **http://www.seds.org/~smiley/cgiperl/csh.htm** The Web page formerly known as Mooncrow's CGI/PERL Source Page is now maintained by Mr. Guy Smiley. This page provides dozens of links to sample Perl scripts, tutorials, and reference sources.

▶ **http://www2.primenet.com/~buyensj/ntwebsrv.html** Jim Buyens maintains a very comprehensive, well-organized, annotated list of links to resources for running a Web server under Windows NT (see Figure 2.7). The list includes CGI and Perl among a great many other categories.

▶ **http://www.greyware.com/greyware/software/** Greyware Automation Products maintains a large list of freeware and shareware scripts and programs for Windows NT, many of which will also work with Windows 95. These include CGIShell, a CGI wrapper program that allows you to use Delphi, Visual Basic, and other GUI programming environments with Windows-based Web servers such as EMWAC.

▶ **http://enterprise.ic.gc.ca/~jfriedl/perl/** Jeffrey Friedlander's Perl Stuff includes a number of useful CGI and networking libraries, as well as scripts whose functionality goes way beyond the basics of CGI programming.

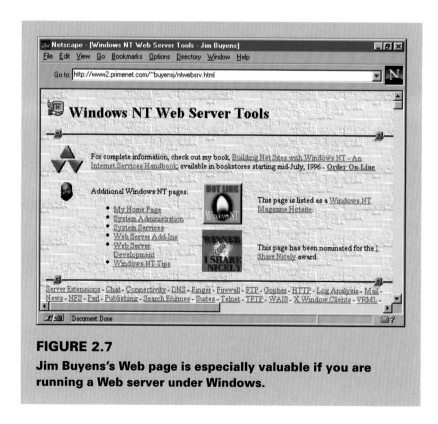

**FIGURE 2.7**
**Jim Buyens's Web page is especially valuable if you are running a Web server under Windows.**

Some of these scripts may not be easy for a beginner to understand, but they come with user manuals that make them, by most programmers' standards, extremely well-documented.

▶ **http://www.iserver.com/cgi/library.html**   This site contains many sample scripts for using image maps, building a guestbook or Web index, and creating server-push animations.

▶ **http://www.ora.com/software/**   This site contains Perl for Windows NT, libraries of Visual Basic routines, and many other tools for use with Robert Denny's WebSite Web server for Windows NT and Windows 95.

## Web Sites for Learning Perl in General

Several other sites focus on learning Perl in general, not necessarily for CGI programming. Three Web sites that showcase a great deal of reference information and provide links to other resources for learning Perl are

▶ Tom Christiansen's Perl Page: http://www.perl.com

▶ Metronet's Perl 5 WWW Page: http://www.metronet.com/perlinfo/perl5.html

▶ Learning Perl: http://www.teleport.com/~rootbeer/perl.html

## Newsgroups Devoted to Perl and CGI

The main Usenet newsgroup for discussions about programming techniques and problem-solving with Perl as a language is comp.lang.perl.misc. For news about Perl, check comp.lang.perl.announce.

For CGI in general, the main newsgroup is now comp.infosystems.www.authoring.cgi, although others are likely to spring up. For discussions about CGI and particular browsers and servers, there are also groups such as comp.infosystems.www.servers.ms-windows and comp.infosystems.www.browsers.mac.

A good way to keep tabs on the proliferation of newsgroups pertinent to CGI programming is to check Yahoo!'s categories under http://www.yahoo.com/yahoo/Computers/World_Wide_Web/ and http://www.yahoo.com/yahoo/Computers_and_Internet/Internet/World_Wide_Web/ CGI__Common_Gateway_Interface/.

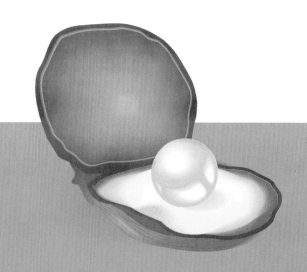

# Chapter 3
# Getting Started with Forms

This chapter introduces HTML forms and the CGI programs that handle them. It begins with an overview of how forms work with CGI, and then it focuses on how forms take in user input and send this data to CGI programs. You'll come to a better understanding of some of the technical issues that are involved in designing forms, and then you'll move right on to creating and processing a form that illustrates how to use all of the basic HTML input elements.

In the exercise, you first design the form based on the information you'll need, and then you write the CGI program based on the implementation of this form. You will thus create two separate files: an HTML file that displays the form and a Perl script file that processes its input.

## How HTML Forms Work with CGI

When you fill out a form on a Web page, you are often presented with an array of virtual input devices. You interact with each input device in its specialized way, and both the particular mechanics of these devices and the overall design of the form tend to shape your actions as you fill out the form or make your selections.

Behind the scenes, each input field is specified by its own HTML element, as defined by an INPUT tag or a SELECT tag. These elements are laid out between the form's opening and closing FORM tags the same way other HTML elements are laid out between a page's opening and closing BODY tags. A simple example is the HTML file shown in Listing 3.1, which puts one input field in each of its five paragraphs.

Browsers parse these HTML input elements and display them as the form's menus, selectable buttons, and text boxes (see Figure 3.1). No CGI programming is necessary to simply make the form accept and display user input; this is all handled by the browser that displays the form. Indeed, once a server has sent a Web page that contains a form to a browser, it generally closes the connection just as it would after sending any other HTML document.

**LISTING 3.1    The HTML text of a Web page that contains a form**

```
<HTML><HEAD><TITLE> Simple Form </TITLE></HEAD>
<BODY BGCOLOR="beige">
<FORM ACTION="http://www.site.dom/cgi-bin/simplex" METHOD=GET>


<H2> This simple form gives you... </H2><B>


<P> One checkbox to click on/off:
<INPUT TYPE="checkbox" NAME="Chekov">


<P> One pair of radio buttons to choose between:
<INPUT TYPE="radio" NAME="radioBand" VALUE="AM"> AM
<INPUT TYPE="radio" NAME="radioBand" VALUE="FM" CHECKED> FM


<P> One pull-down menu with three choices:
<SELECT NAME="menuChoice">
<OPTION> One
<OPTION> Two
<OPTION> Infinity
</SELECT>


<P> And a single-line text field:
<INPUT TYPE="text" SIZE=24 NAME="oneLine"
        VALUE="Edit this text">


<P> To submit this form,
<INPUT TYPE=SUBMIT VALUE="Press Here">


</FORM>
</B></BODY></HTML>
```

When the user *submits* a filled-out form, however, something new happens. The browser gathers up all the data the user has entered and sends it to a Web server as part of a request to execute a CGI program. How does your browser know where to send the data? Every form begins with a FORM tag, inside of which is the ACTION attribute. This attribute specifies the URL to which your browser should submit the form's data. For example, suppose that a form begins with the tag

```
<FORM ACTION="http://www.site.dom/cgi-bin/simplex">
```

The attribute ACTION="http://www.site.dom/cgi-bin/ simplex" tells the browser that the input to this form should be sent to, and processed by, the CGI program /cgi-bin/simplex on the HTTP server www.site.dom.

Exactly *how* the browser submits the form's input data to the designated CGI program will be the major focus of this chapter and the next.

In general, your browser sends the form's data to the specified Web server, and this server passes the data on to the named CGI program. The CGI program processes the data in whatever way pleases its programmer, and then, like any other CGI program, it outputs a new document. This document goes back to the

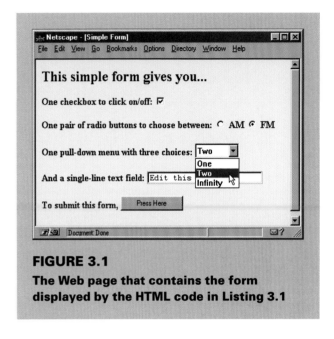

**FIGURE 3.1**

**The Web page that contains the form displayed by the HTML code in Listing 3.1**

server, and the server in turn sends it back to the browser. When the browser displays the new document returned by the CGI program, the sequence is complete. You never actually see the server or the CGI program, of course; you see only the documents they output. (See the sidebar entitled "CGI Back Ends and HTML Front Ends.")

But what does the form itself do? Isn't it just a bunch of HTML code that tells the browser what to display? Yes, it is just HTML code, but those HTML tags contain pieces of vital information in their attributes, and this undisplayed information is sent along with the form's user-entered data as input to the CGI program. Basically, each input field in the displayed form has its own name and value. The field's value changes to reflect user input, but its name is fixed by the form's author. When the form is submitted, the data from each input field is sent as a *name=value* pair. That's how the CGI program can tell which data values come from which input fields.

For example, the INPUT element in

```
Tell me, what color are your eyes?
<INPUT TYPE="text" NAME="eyecolor" VALUE="brown">
```

generates the text field shown here:

Tell me, what color are your eyes? brown

Its default value, **brown**, is displayed only when the form first appears; the user can change this displayed value to any other string. The name **eyecolor**, however, is not displayed and cannot be changed by the user.

The default input data from this text field would be

```
eyecolor=brown
```

but if the user changes **brown** to **emerald**, the browser will send

```
eyecolor=emerald
```

CGI programs rely on the names in variable *name=value* pairs such as this one to distinguish among the values submitted from a form's various input elements. Without the name **eyecolor**, the CGI program that is to process this data would have no way of determining what the value brown or emerald referred to.

# CGI Back Ends and HTML Front Ends

Because CGI programs run behind the scenes, or "in back of" the pages, they are often called *back ends,* and the pages they run behind are called *front ends.*

A single CGI program might generate a page, process any user input entered into the page, and generate a different page in response. In this case, the CGI program is said to be *backending* the page or pages. Conversely, a form that *frontends* a CGI program can serve as its complete graphical user interface, acting in concert with the back end as if the two together were one seamless application.

The browser, server, CGI program, and even the HTML in the form itself must all play their parts to achieve this smooth operation. The browser displays the form and gathers user input. The server receives the request with the data from the form and runs the CGI program. And when the program has processed the data, it returns a new document to the browser through the server.

## Forms with More Than One Input Field

This pairing of name and value is especially important when a form contains more than one input field. For example, if the form in Listing 3.1 were submitted with the values shown in Figure 3.1, the browser would establish a connection and send the following GET request to the server at www.site.dom:

```
GET /cgi-bin/simplex?Chekov=on&radioBand=FM&menuChoice=Two&oneLine=
Edit+this+text  HTTP/1.0
```

Here all of the form's input data is strung together into what is known as a *query string*, which is appended to the CGI program's relative URL following a question mark. (You might be familiar with such strings, which sometimes appear in a browser's location field.) The browser treats the resulting extended URL the same way it would an ordinary URL, sending it to the server as part of an HTTP GET request. Because the whole thing is sent in the same way as any other URL, it must be encoded as a URL. In particular, any spaces in the original input data are replaced by plus signs. A question mark separates the query string from the program's name, and within the query string ampersands separate the *name=value* pairs from each other. Decoding the query string back into pairs is then straightforward, and every CGI program accomplishes this decoding in pretty much the same way. Later in this chapter, I'll explain how to do so using Perl.

This scheme of representing all the input data as *name=value* pairs and encoding the pairs into a single query string is the basic mechanism for passing user-entered data from forms to CGI programs. Each INPUT and OPTION element in an HTML form is responsible for submitting one *name=value* pair, which you might think of loosely as the name of a variable and its assigned value. There are many more details you'll need to know about how the various kinds of input elements generate their submitted *name=value* pairs, but you can already see how the NAME attributes inside a form's INPUT and SELECT tags are used to give order to the data, dividing it up into easily manageable bits and pieces.

Other schemes for distinguishing the input entered in one field from that entered in another are of course possible, but if the form is to communicate its data to the CGI program, some kind of standard convention is needed. That's just what CGI is all about. The scheme of sending the data as *name=value* pairs is fairly powerful and quite general, but, more to the point, it's part of the CGI standard. It works because that's how CGI programs, by definition, expect to receive their input.

There is thus an intimate relationship between a form and the CGI program that processes it. In the big-picture view, the role of the HTML form is to take in user input and feed it in an organized way to the CGI program. The form's HTML elements not only specify the appearance of the displayed Web page, they also specify the appearance of the data sent to the CGI program. The CGI program must be designed to expect the particular *name=value* pairs whose names come from the NAME attributes in the form's HTML tags, and, conversely, the form must be designed to give the CGI program the named values it expects. It is therefore quite natural for a form and the CGI program that handles the form's input to be designed by one person. And as you shall see by the end of this chapter, there are also many advantages to using one CGI program both to generate the form and to handle its input, especially if that program is an easily modifiable Perl script.

# How to Create a Form

The best way to create a form for CGI processing is usually to design the form as an HTML document. Begin by asking yourself, "What information do I want from the user, and what is the clearest way to ask for it?" Think of the form's various input devices as ways to constrain the user's answers to exactly the information you seek, no more and no less:

▶ Use checkboxes to ask simple yes-or-no questions.

▶ Use radio buttons to force a choice of exactly one of several short alternatives. (Actually, if you initially display the form with no buttons checked, the user doesn't have to pick one. In that case, no *name=value* pair will be submitted for that group. But once a user has picked one radio button in a group, he or she can't revert to selecting none.)

▶ Use pull-down menus to let the user choose one option from a list. The name of each option should be short enough to fit onto one line.  You must provide at least one choice, but you can provide up to as many choices as will fit vertically on the user's screen.

▶ Use scrollboxes to allow the user to choose an option from a longer list or to make multiple selections from a single list.

▶ Use range elements to allow the user to input numbers that won't fit easily into a menu or a group of radio button values—for instance, when all fractional numbers between a given minimum and maximum are valid.

▶ Use text fields only when the information doesn't lend itself to one of the above devices or when you don't want to provide predefined choices.

Whether the user is to enter text as single words, lines, or whole paragraphs depends on how this text will be used as information, but most users prefer the guidance afforded by small text boxes rather than large, multiple-line text areas (which force them to make decisions about item order, line breaks, and so on).

As far as the CGI program is concerned, these input devices are all pretty much the same: There's no discernible difference between the data that originates as menu selections and the data that comes from named checkboxes or radio buttons. What's important is that the form collects the right information.

A form is a kind of graphical user interface. It's usually the only means your CGI program has for communicating with the user, and to get clear input, the form must present clear choices. When designing a form, then, you should first concentrate on its options and capabilities from the user's point of view, and then design its particular HTML input elements and the CGI program to handle this input accordingly.

## Creating the HTML for a Design-Your-Own-Sandwich Form

In this section, you'll begin Example 3A by creating and implementing a form for designing your own deli sandwich (see Figure 3.2). When you are creating any form, it helps to know the basics of how the various HTML input elements work, but you certainly don't need to know all the details to get started. For now, I'll explain only as much as you need to know to understand the decisions behind the design and implementation of this example form. The HTML code for the form in its entirety is shown in Listing 3.2. I'll go through it step by step.

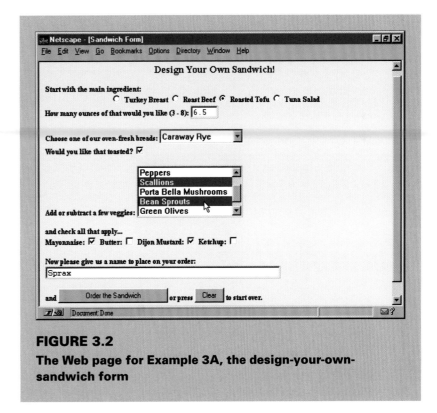

**FIGURE 3.2**

**The Web page for Example 3A, the design-your-own-sandwich form**

---

**LISTING 3.2    sandwich.html, the HTML text for a design-your-own-sandwich form**

```
<HTML><HEAD><TITLE> Sandwich Form </TITLE></HEAD>
<BODY BGCOLOR="beige">
<!- sandwich.html ->
<FORM ACTION="http://www.site.dom/cgi-bin/sandwich" METHOD=GET>

<H2><CENTER> Design Your Own Sandwich! </CENTER></H2><B>

<P> Start with the main ingredient: <P><CENTER>
<INPUT TYPE="radio" NAME="protein" VALUE="Turkey Breast" CHECKED> Turkey Breast
<INPUT TYPE="radio" NAME="protein" VALUE="Roast Beef"> Roast Beef
<INPUT TYPE="radio" NAME="protein" VALUE="Roasted Tofu"> Roasted Tofu
<INPUT TYPE="radio" NAME="protein" VALUE="Tuna Salad"> Tuna Salad
</CENTER></P>

How many ounces of that would you like (3 - 8)?
<INPUT TYPE="range" SIZE="6" MIN="3.0" MAX="8.0" NAME="oz" VALUE="5.0">
<BR>

<P> Choose one of our oven-fresh breads:
<SELECT NAME="bread">
<OPTION> Baguette
<OPTION> Buckwheat
<OPTION> Caraway Rye
<OPTION SELECTED> Pumpernickel
<OPTION> Tomato-Pecan
<OPTION> Twelve-Grain
<OPTION> Whole-Grain Rice
</SELECT>

<BR> Would you like that toasted?
<INPUT TYPE="checkbox" NAME="toasted" VALUE="toasted">


<P> Add or subtract a few veggies:
<SELECT NAME="veggies" MULTIPLE SIZE="5">
<OPTION SELECTED> Lettuce
```

**LISTING 3.2    sandwich.html, the HTML text for a design-your-own-sandwich form
(Continued)**

```
<OPTION SELECTED> Tomatoes
<OPTION> Peppers
<OPTION> Scallions
<OPTION> Porta Bella Mushrooms
<OPTION> Bean Sprouts
<OPTION> Green Olives
<OPTION> Garlic Pickles
</SELECT>

<P> and check all that apply...<BR>
Mayonnaise:     <INPUT TYPE="checkbox" NAME="mayo" CHECKED>
Butter:         <INPUT TYPE="checkbox" NAME="butter">
Dijon Mustard: <INPUT TYPE="checkbox" NAME="mustard">
Ketchup:        <INPUT TYPE="checkbox" NAME="ketchup">


<P> Now please give us a name to place on your order: <BR>
<INPUT TYPE="text" SIZE=50 NAME="name">

<P>  and <INPUT TYPE=SUBMIT VALUE="Order the Sandwich">
or press <INPUT TYPE=RESET  VALUE="Clear">
to start over.


</FORM>
</B></BODY></HTML>
```

## The FORM Tag and Its Attributes

All forms live inside HTML documents, and every form begins and ends with a
FORM tag. The form in sandwich.html begins with

```
<FORM ACTION="http://www.site.dom/cgi-bin/sandwich" METHOD=GET>
```

The ACTION attribute tells the browser *where* to send the form's data; the METHOD
attribute tells the browser *how* to send it. The data from this form will go to
/cgi-bin/sandwich on the HTTP server www.site.dom, but since you are designing

the cart before the horse, the specified CGI program doesn't yet exist. During a form's initial development phase, you might want to direct its data submission to a CGI test script that simply echoes back the *name=value* pairs or environment variables that are sent to it. This can also be useful for debugging a form or its CGI back end independently. I'll show how to do this in the next chapter.

GET is the default method for submitting a form, so this METHOD attribute actually isn't required. The other possibility here would be METHOD=POST, which I'll also explain in the next chapter. Recall that when a form is submitted to a CGI program using METHOD=GET, all of the form's input is URL-encoded as a single query string and appended to the CGI program's pathname, as in

```
GET /cgi-bin/somescript?query_string HTTP/1.0
```

(Incidentally, you can use this fact to test a CGI script by itself, without going through any form. Just type in the query string yourself after the script's URL in your browser's Go To field.)

## Placing the Input Fields into the Form

Now you can begin placing the form's actual input fields. Ideally, your considerations at this stage should be more about taking an order for a custom-made sandwich than about programming a computer.

Let's start with the main ingredient, the sandwich's source of protein. You'll let the user choose one of four sources. You could present this choice as a pull-down menu, but then only the default choice would be visible when the page first appeared. You could use a scrollbox to show all four choices at once, but that wouldn't make it clear to the user that he or she is allowed only one choice. A series of checkboxes would be even worse; the user could definitely click on more than one of them. You could give the user explicit instructions, but it would be better not to let the user make mistakes and to make the form so clear that no instructions are necessary.

**Using Radio Buttons**   A group of radio buttons is the best solution. All four choices will be visible at all times, each is selectable with a single mouse click, and it's clear that the user gets only one choice:

```
<P> Start with the main ingredient: <P><CENTER>
<INPUT TYPE="radio" NAME="protein" VALUE="Turkey Breast" CHECKED¬
Turkey Breast
<INPUT TYPE="radio" NAME="protein" VALUE="Roast Beef"> Roast Beef
<INPUT TYPE="radio" NAME="protein" VALUE="Roasted Tofu"> Roasted Tofu
```

```
<INPUT TYPE="radio" NAME="protein" VALUE="Tuna Salad"> Tuna Salad
</CENTER></P>
```

These four INPUT elements of TYPE="radio" form a group because they all have the same NAME attribute; only the values vary. The shared attribute NAME="protein" tells the browser that only one of the values can be picked; as with the buttons on some radios, when one is pressed in the rest pop out. With radio buttons, both the NAME and VALUE attributes are required, because these supply the selected *name=value* pair sent when the form is submitted.

**Input Fields for Entering a Number within a Specified Range**    To specify how much turkey or tofu goes into the sandwich, it's probably best to use an explicit number. Choices such as small, medium, and large tend to get translated into numbers anyway, and in this case there's no counterperson standing behind the form to answer questions, so it's best to be as explicit as possible:

```
How many ounces of that would you like (3 - 8)?
<INPUT TYPE="range" SIZE="6" MIN="3.0" MAX="8.0" NAME="oz"¬
VALUE="5.0">
```

The TYPE="range" input device lets the user enter a number within the range specified by MIN=*minimum* and MAX=*maximum* and starts by showing the default value given by VALUE=*number*. Unfortunately, most current browsers do not actually enforce these range restrictions, so the CGI program should do this itself to make sure that the number falls within the acceptable range. The SIZE="6" attribute specifies that the text box for entering the number should be 6 characters wide.

**Using Pull-Down Menus**    To let the user choose one of seven kinds of bread, a pull-down menu seems appropriate:

```
<P> Choose one of our oven-fresh breads:
<SELECT NAME="bread">
<OPTION> Baguette
<OPTION> Buckwheat
<OPTION> Caraway Rye
<OPTION SELECTED> Pumpernickel
<OPTION> Tomato-Pecan
<OPTION> Twelve-Grain
<OPTION> Whole-Grain Rice
</SELECT>
```

OPTION tags always appear between opening and closing SELECT tags. The name in the submitted *name=value* pair comes from the NAME="bread" attribute in the opening SELECT tag, whereas the value is given by the string after the OPTION tag. Alternatively, an OPTION tag can be written like this

```
<OPTION VALUE="cr"> Caraway Rye</OPTION>
```

so that the *name=value* pair sent if this option were selected would be **bread=cr** rather than **bread=Caraway+Rye**, but most programmers prefer the simpler format used in this form. The SELECTED attribute means that the option is the menu's default value. The selected value should be displayed in the entry window when the form first appears; this is the option that will be submitted unless the user chooses a different selection.

**Using Checkboxes**    A checkbox is perfect for this simple yes-or-no question:

```
<BR> Would you like that toasted?
<INPUT TYPE="checkbox" NAME="toasted" VALUE="toasted">
```

For checkboxes, the browser includes a *name=value* pair in the form's submitted query string only if the checkbox was checked. The VALUE attribute is optional. If it isn't there, the browser will supply the default value on, as in toasted=on. If the checkbox's INPUT tag does include a VALUE attribute, that value is used instead of on.

**Using Scrollable Menus (Scrollboxes) to Allow Multiple Selections**
Now for the veggies. There are too many of them to be displayed all at once, and the user should be able to pick more than one. Let's try using a scrollbox:

```
<P> Add or subtract a few veggies:
<SELECT NAME="veggies" MULTIPLE SIZE="5">
<OPTION SELECTED> Lettuce
<OPTION SELECTED> Tomatoes
<OPTION> Peppers
<OPTION> Scallions
<OPTION> Porta Bella Mushrooms
<OPTION> Bean Sprouts
<OPTION> Green Olives
<OPTION> Garlic Pickles
</SELECT>
```

Here the MULTIPLE attribute lets the user select more than one option, and SIZE="5" means that the displayed scrollbox should be big enough to show five options at a time. This scrollbox starts off with two default items selected. If multiple options are selected, the submitted query string will contain a *name=value* pair for each one, as in:

```
veggies=Lettuce&veggies=Tomatoes
```

The advantages of using a scrollbox are that it can display an arbitrarily long list, SIZE=*n* items at a time, and that it allows multiple selections. (Pull-down menus in HTML forms can do neither.) One disadvantage is that not every user will know how to choose multiple items that are not contiguous. In fact, the mouse button method and the key combination for doing so vary among different platforms and browsers. (Usually it's Ctrl-click on a PC, Command-click on a Macintosh, and single or multiple mouse button clicks on Unix workstations.)

A different way to let the user choose multiple items from a list is to present a list of checkboxes. For a short list, this is probably the clearest way:

```
<P> and check all that apply...<BR>
Mayonnaise:     <INPUT TYPE="checkbox" NAME="mayo" CHECKED>
Butter:         <INPUT TYPE="checkbox" NAME="butter">
Dijon Mustard: <INPUT TYPE="checkbox" NAME="mustard">
Ketchup:        <INPUT TYPE="checkbox" NAME="ketchup">
```

The resulting layout of these checkboxes in the page will be the same as for any other HTML elements: The multiple spaces following Butter: and so on are collapsed into one, so all the boxes appear on one line. Each INPUT element always has its own name; checkboxes are no exception. Each of these that is selected at the time the form is submitted will send its own *name=value* pair, as in **mayo=on**.

**Using a Single-Line Text Field**   Now that the user has designed the sandwich, let's at least get his or her name, if not a credit card number:

```
<P> Now please give us a name to place on your order: <BR>
<INPUT TYPE="text" SIZE=50 NAME="name">
```

The TYPE="text" attribute specifies a single-line text-entry field; SIZE=50 means that this text window should show 50 characters at a time. (Longer lines can be entered here, but to provide for multiple-line text fields, use TYPE="textarea", which is explained in the next chapter.) The *name=value* pair will be

```
name=whatever_the_user_enters
```

or just

```
name=
```

if the user doesn't enter anything. Including a default VALUE attribute in the INPUT tag would be one way to prevent nameless orders, but some users might assume that this default name was assigned to them specifically, which wouldn't be true. Later in this book, you'll learn how to specifically assign such default values, but for now you're leaving it up to the user to name his or her order (presumably for pickup).

**Completing the Form with Submit and Reset Buttons**    Finally, let's get the order sent to the deli server:

```
<P> and <INPUT TYPE=SUBMIT VALUE="Order the Sandwich">
or press <INPUT TYPE=RESET  VALUE="Clear">
to start over.
```

Input fields of TYPE=SUBMIT and TYPE=RESET are displayed as buttons with their values printed right on them. Browsers will supply default values such as **"Submit Query"** or **"Reset"**, but neither of these values is sent as part of the query string. Hitting a SUBMIT button causes the browser to send all of the form's input data in *name=value* pairs. Hitting a RESET button sends nothing. Instead, it causes the browser to reset all of the form's input fields to their default values.

# How to Process the Data Submitted from a Form

To handle the submission of a form, a CGI program must generally do three things:

1 Get the submitted data and parse it into information that the program can use.

2 Process this information to accomplish the form's purpose.

3 Output a new document, which the server will send back to the requesting browser.

To handle your designer-sandwich form, you'll write a Perl script that accomplishes each of these tasks in turn. When you're finished, you'll review the entire script. If you want to look over the whole script in advance, refer to Listing 3.6 later in this chapter.

## Getting and Parsing the Input from the Form

For a relatively straightforward form application such as the one in this example, just decoding the query string and parsing it into usable pairs of names and values is by far the most complicated part of the whole CGI process. Listing 3.3, which is the first part of sandwich-reply.cgi, shows the code for doing this. I'll explain this code in detail.

As you learned in the previous sections, all the information that a user enters into a form is represented by *name=value* pairs, and upon submission, these are all strung together and encoded as a single query string. If the sandwich form were submitted with the input values shown in Figure 3.2, the contents of the query string would be

```
protein=Roasted+Tofu&oz=6.5&bread=Caraway+Rye&toasted=toasted&¬
veggies=Scallions&veggies=Bean+Sprouts&mayo=on&mustard=on&name=Sprax
```

To get the form's input, then, your CGI program has only to get ahold of this query string. The simplest way to do this is through an environment variable. Recall that when a CGI program is called from the form using the GET method, the query string is appended to the program's URL and sent as part of the GET request. The server receives this string and passes it to the CGI program by way of an environment variable called QUERY_STRING. As explained in Chapter 1 (Example 1D), a Perl script can copy the value of this environment variable into an arbitrary scalar variable using an assignment statement such as

```
$sandwich_input = $ENV{'QUERY_STRING'};
```

That's the only line your script needs in order to get all the user input from the form.

## Decoding the URL-Encoded Query String

The variable **$sandwich_input** now contains the query string, but it's still encoded as if it were part of a URL. To translate this string into usable information, you need to parse it back into separate *name=value* pairs, convert these pairs into variables and values, and then undo the URL encoding process. The decoding steps are performed in reverse order compared to the encoding order; you must reverse the order to avoid problems that would arise if you tried to decode input values that contained the query string's special separation characters (**&**, **=**, and **+**).

**Parsing the Query String into *name=value* Pairs**   To separate the *name=value* pairs from each other, you have only to split the query string on each ampersand. In Perl, the **split** function does this and returns the separated

**LISTING 3.3** **The code for getting, decoding, and parsing the sandwich form's input (the first part of sandwich-reply.cgi)**

```perl
#!/usr/local/bin/perl
# sandwich-reply.cgi


############### STEP 1: GET AND DECODE THE INPUT FROM THE FORM: ###############


$sandwich_input = $ENV{'QUERY_STRING'};          # Get the query string


@name_value_pairs = split('&', $sandwich_input); # Split it into pairs


foreach $pair (@name_value_pairs) {              # Convert each pair...

  # Split the pair into a name and a value:
  ($name, $value) = split('=', $pair);

  # Translate any plus signs in the value string into spaces:
  $value =~ tr/+/ /;

  # Translate escaped hex numbers back into characters:
  $value =~ s/%(..)/pack("C", hex($1))/eg;

  # Convert the names and values into named, assigned variables;
  # that is, use each name as a key in an associative array and associate
  # it with all the values originally paired with that name, separating
  # multiple values for the same name with the null character...

  if (defined($order{$name})) { # If $order{$name} already exists,
    $order{$name} .= "\0";      # append \0 as a separator
  }                             # before appending the new value


  # Now append the value to the named entry in the associative array:
  $order{$name} .= $value;      # If $order didn't already have a value
}                               # for the key $name, it does now
```

substrings as the elements of an ordinary array. Here's an example of the **split** function:

```
@name_value_pairs = split('&', $sandwich_input);
```

The first argument to this function specifies the pattern on which to split the string, and the second is the string to be split. The value of **$name_value_pairs[0]** is **protein=Roasted+Tofu**, **$name_value_pairs[1]** is **oz=6.5**, and so on.

**Parsing Each *name=value* Pair into a Name and a Value**    You can use the **split** function again to separate a *name=value* pair into a separate name and value (this time splitting on '**=**'), but now you have to do it for each entry in the **@name_value_pairs** array. The best way to go through and change everything in an array is to use a **foreach** loop, as in

```
foreach $pair (@name_value_pairs) {
  ($name, $value) = split('=', $pair);
}
```

Here the variable **$pair** is successively set to equal each element in the array **@name_value_pairs** before the statement(s) in the loop's body are executed; the loop terminates only when all of the array's elements have been so processed. This **foreach** loop is actually a good start, but before you close its body with the final **}**, you've got to perform several other tasks, such as storing the separated names and values for later use.

## Decoding the Parsed Names and Values

Once you've parsed the query string into individual names and values, the next task is to reverse the effects of URL encoding. (Recall that browsers encode all submitted form data to make it ready for transmission as part of a URL.)

**Translating the Plus Signs Back into Spaces**    The first step in the decoding process is to translate any plus signs in the names and values back into spaces. None of the names used for input fields in sandwich.html contain any spaces, so we'll perform this translation only on the values. For this, you can use Perl's **tr** operator. In general, the statement

```
$string =~ tr/searchlist/replacementlist/
```

in which both *searchlist* and *replacementlist* are lists of characters, tells the program to replace the string contained in the variable **$string** with a character-by-character translation: Each character in the search list that is found in **$string** is replaced by the corresponding character in the replacement list. Hyphenated ranges are also allowed between the slashes, so

```
$string =~ tr/A-Z/a-z/
```

translates the contents of **$string** to lowercase.

The translation of plus signs to spaces is simple; there is only one character in both the search list and the replacement list:

```
$value =~ tr/+/ /;
```

You translate only the *value* side of the former *name=value* pair, because there shouldn't have been any spaces in *name* in the first place.

**Converting Hexadecimal Codes Back into Characters**    Next you have to undo the encoding of any characters that were translated into their hexadecimal equivalents during the URL encoding process. URL encoding is defined in the HTTP 1.0 specification; it's done so that URLs can be represented in a standard way on practically any hardware and software platform. The specification requires that all characters with ASCII values less than 33 (hexadecimal 21) or greater than 127 (hexadecimal 7F), as well as characters that have special meanings inside query strings (such as **?**, **&**, **%**, **+,** and **=**) must be *escaped*. That is, the character must be replaced by a percent sign and the two-digit hexadecimal number representing its place in an extended ASCII character set. Thus the space character (ASCII 32, hexadecimal 20) will be represented as %20. (The plus sign that represents a space is left over from an earlier convention—that's why you had to translate it first.) And if you want to include a question mark (ASCII 63, hexadecimal 3F) in a name appearing as part of a URL, it will have to be encoded as %3F when it is sent as part of a GET request to an HTTP server (otherwise it would be interpreted as the marker at the beginning of a query string).

You can translate back from escaped hexadecimal codes with a single line in Perl:

```
$value =~ s/%(..)/pack("C", hex($1))/eg;
```

**Substituting the Decoded Characters Back into the Value Strings** Perl's substitution operator, **s**, also known as a search and replace function and written symbolically as **s/*search*/*replace*/**, is much more powerful than the simple translation operator (**tr**) shown previously. The search pattern between the first two slashes is actually a *regular expression*. The symbols and syntax used to search for and replace substrings using regular expressions are extensive enough to form their own language. I will discuss them more fully in Chapter 8, but here I will concentrate only on this single line of code to show how hexadecimal translation is accomplished in Perl.

As a search pattern, the regular expression **/%(..)/** matches any string that begins with a percent sign followed by any two characters. Each period (**.**) matches any single character except a newline. The parentheses are there not to be matched themselves but to mark whatever is matched by the pattern inside them for future reference.

### The Decoding Process Applied to an Example

For instance, let's say that the user entered **Jack & Jill** in your form's name field. The query string would have originally contained the pairing **name=Jack+%26+Jill**. You have already changed the plus signs back into spaces, so **$value** contains the string **Jack %26 Jill**.

Now the search pattern **/%(..)/** matches the substring **%26**, and the effect of the parentheses is to save the two-letter substring **26** as the match to the pattern **..** inside them. Where does it put the **26**? The **26** goes in the special variable **$1**.

The replacement pattern appears between the **s** operator's second and third slashes. This is actually not a regular expression, but a function. Perl's **hex()** function returns the decimal value of any valid hexadecimal number contained in its argument string. Here its argument is the special variable **$1**, which contains the first substring matching the search pattern **/%(..)/**. In this example, the value of **$1** as a string is **26**, which causes **hex($1)** to return decimal **38**.

### Converting Individual Characters Using Perl's pack Function

Is this progress? Well, the function call **hex($1)** is itself only the second argument to the Perl **pack** function, so now **pack** will go to work on **hex**'s return value, meaning that, in this example,

```
pack("C", hex($1))
```

is equivalent to **pack("C", 38)**. The **pack** function takes an array or list of values and packs it into a string whose binary format is specified by its first argument; it is often used to convert numerical values from one binary type to another. In this example, the format **"C"** specifies a string of unsigned (full 8-bit) characters. You've given it only one number, **38**, and this becomes—lo and behold—the ampersand character. Thus the entire replacement pattern **/pack("C", hex($1))/**, two function calls and all, evaluates to a single **&**.

Finally, the **s/search/replace/** operator replaces the matched search string, **%26**, with the fully evaluated contents of the replacement string, namely **&**. Thus you arrive, full circle, at **Jack & Jill**. All of this is accomplished with only a single line of Perl:

```
$value =~ s/%(..)/pack("C", hex($1))/eg;
```

The substitution operator's last argument, **eg,** specifies a pair of options. The **e** option stands for *evaluate*; this tells Perl to treat the replacement argument as a function instead of as a string. The **g** option stands for *global replacement*; this tells Perl to replace all occurrences of the search pattern with the results of the evaluation of the replacement expression.

## Assigning the Values to Named Variables

So far, you've been able to parse, split, and decode the query string back into the form's original names and values. Can you now simply turn these names into variables and assign them their original values? Almost, but not quite. There are two reasons why you can't do that. One has to do with multiple values assigned to the same name; the other has to do with security.

**Handling Names with Multiple Values**   Some names might be paired with multiple values. Back in the form, the same NAME=*name* attributes may have appeared inside more than one INPUT or SELECT tag in a form. In the case of a SELECT tag with the MULTIPLE attribute, multiple values paired with the same name are both valid and unavoidable. If you turn one of these multiply paired names into a variable, which of the values should be assigned to it? The answer is: "All of them." That is, to these variables you'll attach a string of values separated by a character that is (almost) impossible to enter through a form, namely the null character (ASCII 0). (If you've been following closely, you already know one way to fake it—just type **%00** into a query string inside your browser's Go To or Visit Location box.)

**Security Issues in Processing Form Input**   Before you go any further, take a minute to consider the security implications of allowing your script to execute assignment statements when not only the values but even the names of the variables come in off the Net. True, the names of these variables would supposedly be supplied by the NAME attributes you gave to your form's elements, but I've told you how you can essentially forge a query string. Suppose that a dishonest user found out that one of your scripts used a global variable named **$refund_owed_user**. Surely you wouldn't want him or her to be able to change its value simply by calling your script with a fake query string such as **$refund_owed_user=99,999.99**, would you?

The solution that CGI programmers have almost universally adopted also has much to recommend it in terms of programming style. The answer is to isolate all these named variables and (possibly multiple) values in their own associative array. That way the form-supplied or user-supplied variables can't trample on your script's general name space, and you can operate on all of them as one group. Of course, you can still access them individually as well, referencing them within the array by their names.

Here is the code for placing named variables and their possibly multiple values into a single associative array called **%order**:

```
if (defined($order{$name})) { # If $order{$name} already exists,
   $order{$name} .= "\0";       # append \0 as a separator
}                               # before appending the new value;
$order{$name} .= $value;        # always append (new) value
```

In this code fragment, the key **$name** in the associative array **%order** is always associated with the contents of **$value**; the separator precedes this new value only when **%order** already has a value defined for this particular key.

This assignment of each name and value into the associative array is the last task you need to perform inside the **foreach** loop, and this concludes the process of getting and decoding the form's input data. It may be a lot to absorb if you are new to programming, but the rest of the script is downhill from here on. Later in the chapter, this script is listed in its entirety, with many comments (see Listing 3.6). Here is a listing of just the input and decoding stage. Stripped of comments, and with the **if** statement slightly rearranged, it's fairly short:

```
$sandwich_input = $ENV{'QUERY_STRING'};
@name_value_pairs = split('&', $sandwich_input);
foreach $pair (@name_value_pairs) {
   ($name, $value) = split ('=', $pair);
   $value =~ tr/+/ /;
   $value =~ s/%(..)/pack("C", hex($1))/eg;
   $order{$name} .= "\0" if (defined($order{$name}));
   $order{$name} .= $value;
}
```

The first three lines could actually be combined into the single line

```
foreach $pair (split('&', $ENV{'QUERY_STRING'})) {
```

but not every shortcut is worth taking. In the next chapter, I'll put the comments back in and turn this piece of code into a reusable subroutine.

## Processing the Input Data from the Form

Now that you've taken in the form's raw input and placed it into your associative array, **%order**, you're ready to process this information to accomplish the form's original purpose, which is to solicit sandwich orders.

Unlike the code in the previous section, which was quite general and could be used with any form submitted with the METHOD=GET attribute, the code in this section is peculiar to this particular form. Listing 3.4 shows the complete code for this portion of the form-handling process.

**LISTING 3.4**   **The code for processing the sandwich form's input (the second part of sandwich-reply.cgi)**

```
############## STEP 2: PROCESS THE INFORMATION FROM THE FORM: ##############

$name = 'No-Name' unless $name = $order{'name'};
$date = `date +"%D at %T"`;


if ($veggie_list =  $order{'veggies'}) {
    $veggie_list =~ s/\0/, /g;
} else {
    $veggie_list = 'no veggies';
}


if ($order{'mayo'})    { $condiments .= 'mayonnaise, '; }
if ($order{'butter'})  { $condiments .= 'butter, '; }
if ($order{'mustard'}) { $condiments .= 'Dijon mustard, '; }
if ($order{'ketchup'}) { $condiments .= 'ketchup, '; }
$condiments = 'no condiments, ' unless $condiments;


$sandwich_order = sprintf(
    "%s (%s oz.) on %s %s with %s, %s and a complimentary toothpick.\n"
    , $order{'protein'}
    , $order{'oz'}
    , $order{'toasted'}
    , $order{'bread'}
    , $veggie_list
    , $condiments
);
```

You might recognize the format of the first two lines from the examples in Chapter 1. Line 1 assigns the default value **'No-Name'** to the scalar variable **$name** unless a name entry was found in the form's **%order** array. In Line 2, **$date** receives as its value the output of the backticked Unix **date** command.

What's new is the search of the string **$veggie_list**, which may contain none, some, or all of the selections from the form's veggies menu, and the replacement of each null character (used to separate multiple values) with a comma and a space:

```
$veggie_list =~ s/\0/, /g;
```

This is a simpler usage of the same search-and-replace operator you used in the input section; here the search string is the single character **\0**, denoting the null character as an octal 0, and the replacement string is literally **,** —a comma and a space.

The condiments are handled in a very similar way: All of the condiment options that the user checked are added to the list, followed by a comma and a space. If none were checked, **$condiments** receives the default value **'no condiments, '**.

Finally, the **sprintf** function prints all of the chosen sandwich ingredients in one formatted string and then returns this interpolated string in the variable **$sandwich_order**. (The name *sprintf* is a sort of Unix-like abbreviation of "string-print-function.") Here each **%s** in the format string (**sprintf**'s first argument) is replaced, in order of appearance, with the value of one of the subsequent arguments. Like many other functions in Perl, **sprintf** can take one or more arguments. Since Perl ignores white spaces outside of quotation marks, the function call with all its arguments can be spread over multiples lines. The net result is that **$sandwich_order** now contains the entire sandwich design in one string. That's all you want; now you're ready to output your reply.

## Replying to the Form's User by Outputting a New Document

The final phase is the easiest. You'll simply output the usual header, Content-type: text/html, and then send back the submitted name, the current date and time, and the formatted sandwich order, all as variables embedded within a basic page of HTML. Listing 3.5 shows the code for this part of the process.

What's new here is the **print <<***UNTIL_TERMINATOR*** construct (shown in Listing 3.5 as **print <<EOF**), a line-oriented form of quoting that Unix programmers refer to as the "here document" syntax. It allows you to quote (or print) many lines of text without worrying about embedded quotation marks or line

termination characters except at the very beginning and end. It works like this: In any context in which you could place a quoted string, such as

```
$my_output = " Uh...\nDid you say \"what\"?";
```

you instead place your own single-word terminator string right after a **<<**, as in

```
$my_output = <<END_OF_MY_OUTPUT;
Uh...
Did you say "what"?
END_OF_MY_OUTPUT
```

**LISTING 3.5**    **The code for outputting the sandwich form's reply (the last part of sandwich-reply.cgi)**

```
############# STEP 3: REPLY BY OUTPUTTING A NEW DOCUMENT: #############

print "Content-type: text/html\n\n";  # output HTML header

print <<EOF; # Print lines below up to EOF on a line by itself...
<HTML>
<HEAD><TITLE> Sandwich Reply </TITLE></HEAD>
<BODY BGCOLOR="#AACCAA">
<H2><CENTER> Thanks for Designing Your Own Sandwich! </CENTER></H2><B>

Dear $name,<P>

On $date, we received your order for...<P>

<BLOCKQUOTE> $sandwich_order </BLOCKQUOTE>

Excellent choices! Unfortunately, the robot that would have
built you this delicious treat and downloaded it to your
browser is out to lunch.<P>

Better luck <A HREF="../sandwich.html">next time</A>!

</B></BODY></HTML>
EOF
# OK, stop printing now.
```

The same string is assigned to the variable **$my_output** either way, but the "here document" method is much easier to read. You can output entire HTML pages this way. If you include double or single quotes around the *UNTIL_TERMINATOR* string after the **<<**, all the lines up to the ending *UNTIL_TERMINATOR* string will be treated as if they were quoted the same way. For example, if you place double quotes around your terminator, as in

```
print <<"EOF";
   My name is $name
EOF
```

the current value of **$name** will be substituted in and printed. If you use single quotes, as in

```
print <<'EOF';
   My name is $name
EOF
```

the line will be printed as is, without interpolation. If you do not include quotes at all, the result is the same as if you use double quotes; in other words, substituting values for variables is the default behavior. As you can see in Listing 3.5, the reply to the user in the design-your-own-sandwich example includes three variables that will be replaced by their values at print time. This construct works only if the terminating string is flushed all the way left on a line by itself.

Outputting an HTML file from a CGI program can thus be as easy as writing the HTML. You cannot only write all of your document's HTML with Perl, you can also use Perl to embed strings that are evaluated at runtime and that can reflect user-entered data or other dynamic information. Figure 3.3 shows the reply page that is sent back when the form is submitted with the choices shown in Figure 3.2.

## A Brief Review: The sandwich-reply.cgi Script as a Whole

You set out to write a script that would accomplish three things: get and decode the input from a form, process it, and send back a reply. This was a fairly simple project, and the code quite naturally broke down into three sections to accomplish these tasks. Later examples in this book will be much more complicated. I hope you have learned from this simple example that putting in the effort to design your scripts so that each section focuses on a particular problem will almost certainly save you time in the long run.

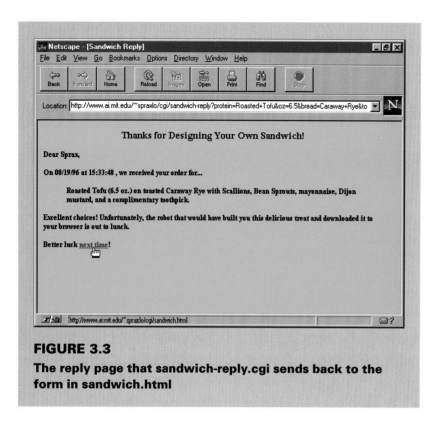

**FIGURE 3.3**
**The reply page that sandwich-reply.cgi sends back to the
form in sandwich.html**

Listing 3.6 shows the sandwich-reply.cgi script in its entirety, annotated with
sufficient comments so that the trees can be seen through the forest, and vice versa.

**LISTING 3.6    The complete sandwich-reply.cgi script for processing input from
sandwich.html**

```perl
#!/usr/local/bin/perl
# sandwich-reply.cgi

############## STEP 1: GET AND DECODE THE INPUT FROM THE FORM: ##############

$sandwich_input = $ENV{'QUERY_STRING'};          # Get the query string

@name_value_pairs = split('&', $sandwich_input); # Split it into pairs

foreach $pair (@name_value_pairs) {              # Convert each pair...

  # Split the pair into a name and a value:
  ($name, $value) = split ('=', $pair);
```

**LISTING 3.6    The complete sandwich-reply.cgi script for processing input from sandwich.html (Continued)**

```perl
# Translate any plus signs in the value string into spaces:
$value =~ tr/+/ /;

# Translate escaped hex numbers back into characters:
$value =~ s/%(..)/pack("C", hex($1))/eg;

# Convert the names and values into named, assigned variables;
# that is, use each name as a key in an associative array and associate
# it with all the values originally paired with that name, separating
# multiple values for the same name with the null character...

if (defined($order{$name})) { # If %order{$name} already exists,
    $order{$name} .= "\0";       # append \0 as a separator
}                                # before appending the new value

# Now append the value to the named entry in the associative array:
$order{$name} .= $value;     # If %order didn't already have a value
}                            # for the key $name, it does now

############# STEP 2: PROCESS THE INFORMATION FROM THE FORM: #############

$name = 'No-Name' unless $name = $order{'name'};
$date = `date +"%D at %T"`;

if ($veggie_list = $order{'veggies'}) {
    $veggie_list =~ s/\0/, /g;
} else {
    $veggie_list = 'no veggies';
}

if ($order{'mayo'})    { $condiments .= 'mayonnaise, '; }
if ($order{'butter'})  { $condiments .= 'butter, '; }
if ($order{'mustard'}) { $condiments .= 'Dijon mustard, '; }
if ($order{'ketchup'}) { $condiments .= 'ketchup, '; }
```

**LISTING 3.6** **The complete sandwich-reply.cgi script for processing input from sandwich.html (Continued)**

```perl
$condiments = 'no condiments, ' unless $condiments;


$sandwich_order = sprintf(
    "%s (%s oz.) on %s %s with %s, %s and a complimentary toothpick.\n"
    , $order{'protein'}
    , $order{'oz'}
    , $order{'toasted'}
    , $order{'bread'}
    , $veggie_list
    , $condiments
);



############## STEP 3: REPLY BY OUTPUTTING A NEW DOCUMENT: ##############

print "Content-type: text/html\n\n";  # output HTML header

print <<EOF; # Print lines below up to EOF on a line by itself...
<HTML>
<HEAD><TITLE> Sandwich Reply </TITLE></HEAD>
<BODY BGCOLOR="#AACCAA">
<H2><CENTER> Thanks for Designing Your Own Sandwich! </CENTER></H2><B>

Dear $name,<P>

On $date, we received your order for...<P>

<BLOCKQUOTE> $sandwich_order </BLOCKQUOTE>

Excellent choices! Unfortunately, the robot that would have
built you this delicious treat and downloaded it to your
browser is out to lunch.<P>

Better luck <A HREF="../sandwich.html">next time</A>!
```

**LISTING 3.6    The complete sandwich-reply.cgi script for processing input from sandwich.html  (Continued)**

```
</B></BODY></HTML>
EOF
# OK, stop printing now.


############ END OF sandwich-reply.cgi ##########
```

# The Varieties of CGI Input

# Obtaining CGI Input Using Perl

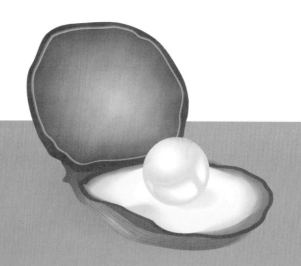

# Chapter 4
# Input through the Common Gateway Interface

This chapter goes into some detail about the various techniques used to input data to Common Gateway Interface (CGI) programs. It is intended to be used as both a tutorial and a reference. I'll explain many small examples along the way, but I'll also go far enough into the gory details that you'll probably want to refer back to this chapter when you're working through the later parts of this book or when you're out there writing your own programs.

## The Varieties of CGI Input

A CGI program can receive input in several different ways, and this input can originate from a number of different sources. The exact definition of *input* depends on your vantage point. As you have seen in the previous chapters, the nature of a networked client/server interface is that each of the entities involved—user, document, browser, server, and program—has its own role to play, in input as well as in everything else.

From a user's point of view, input to CGI might be simply a matter of filling out forms and clicking on buttons. To the browser, CGI input basically comes down to whatever is sent by the GET and POST methods of sending a request to a server. To the server, input is the HTTP and other information it receives as bits and pieces of requests. The server, after translating some of the information into local terms, encapsulates all of the data in environment variables, which it passes to the CGI program. Finally, from the program's point of view, there are exactly three ways to get CGI input: through environment variables, through the standard input stream, and (rarely) through command-line-style arguments.

All of these vantage points are important, and I'll discuss each one of them in turn, starting with the document/browser combination. Along the way, we'll look at input from the point of view of the CGI programmer using Perl.

## How Browsers Send Input to Servers: GET, POST, and Extra Path Information

There are three ways in which a browser can send data to a server as input to a CGI program:

▶ As a query string appended to the URL in a GET request

▶ As data posted inside the message body of a POST request

▶ As extra path information in the URL (GET or POST)

Browsers generally send requests to Web servers by using either of two HTTP methods, GET or POST. Data sent via the POST method is usually URL-encoded just like a query string, but instead of being appended to the URL as a GET request is, it's sent inside a message body (like an e-mail message). *Extra path information* is not a separate method; it is directory-like information included inside the URL itself, immediately following the name of the CGI program. For instance, if bowdlerize is an executable file in /cgi-bin, a GET or POST request for the URL http://www.site.dom/cgi-bin/bowdlerize/droll/lurid.html will invoke /cgi-bin/bowdlerize as a CGI program with the extra path information **/droll/lurid.html** passed to it in an environment variable. Presumably, bowdlerize will use this extra path information to hunt down the file named lurid.html and send back an expurgated version of its contents. I'll discuss each of these input mechanisms in the following three sections.

### Sending Input Using the GET Method: Query Strings

GET is the default method for sending form data and is the *only* method for retrieving static Web documents such as saved images and HTML files. Input sent via the GET method is always appended to the CGI program's URL, either as extra path information, as a URL-encoded query string, or both, as shown here:

```
GET /cgi-bin/bowdlerize/movies/flick.avi?rating=G HTTP/1.0
```

Here the server would pass both the extra path information **/movies/flick.avi** and the query string **rating=G** to /cgi-bin/bowdlerize as environment variables.

Browsers generate and send query strings from three different kinds of HTML documents—or more precisely, from three kinds of HTML *elements*, since a single page may contain several of each. These are

▶ **Forms in which the METHOD attribute is either GET or not specified**
The URL-encoded query string takes the form *name1=value1&name2=value2*.

▶ **Searchable indexes**   A *searchable index* is any HTML file that contains an ISINDEX element. The URL-encoded query string takes the trivial form *query*, with no *name=value* pairs separated by ampersands, as in

```
GET /cgi-bin/vote-tallies?CDA+1996 HTTP/1.0
```

The ISINDEX element is still supported in HTML 3, but most programmers consider it to be obsolete.

▶ **Server-side image maps**   A *server-side image map* is an IMG element with the ISMAP attribute or a FIG element with the IMAGEMAP attribute (in HTML 3). The query string is not encoded but takes the simple form *x,y*, where *x* and *y* are integers representing a pixel location in the active image, as in

```
GET /cgi-bin/imagemap/data/mymap.txt?45,65 HTTP/1.0
```

Searchable indexes and server-side image maps are rarely used anymore, because forms and client-side image maps are much more useful. I'll come back to these three kinds of query-string-generating HTML elements later in this chapter.

For now, notice that the query string's encoding alone is enough to tell servers which of these element types gave birth to it. Servers actually scan query strings for unencoded equal signs in order to determine how to pass their contents to CGI programs.

Query strings can also be entered manually (in a browser's Go To Location field, for example) or sent from hypertext links with a reference attribute, as in

```
HREF=URL?query_string
```

In these cases, however, the browser will not URL-encode the query string for you, so it is recommended (although not always necessary) that you encode it yourself. Alternatively, once you've pointed your browser at some location using the correct query string, you can copy it from the browser's location field or save it in a bookmark or Internet shortcut file.

## Sending Input Using the POST Method: Message Bodies

POST is used almost exclusively to send input data from forms. Extra path information can still appear in the URL, but the browser sends all of the user-entered data inside a message body. You're probably familiar with message bodies that follow sets of MIME-type headers; often the bodies of e-mail messages are sent this way. If the earlier request were sent using the POST method, it would look like this:

```
POST /cgi-bin/bowdlerize/movies/flick.avi HTTP/1.0
Content-type: application/x-www-form-urlencoded
Content-length: 8

rating=G
```

Notice that the contents of the message body are still URL-encoded, just like a query string. The blank line between the HTTP headers and the message body is mandatory. The number of bytes specified in the content-length header must be correct because it will be passed to the CGI program in an environment variable, and most CGI programs will attempt to read exactly this much data from STDIN. Of course, you don't have to worry about the encoding or content length if the POST is coming from a form submission, because the browser generates the message automatically.

## Sending Input Using Extra Path Information: The Path Apparent

A piece of extra path information (EPI) always looks like a pathname, and most often it is one. It must begin with a forward slash because it's tacked onto the end of some CGI program's URL, and aside from a space or a question mark, the / character is the only means the server has of discerning where the name of the CGI program ends and something else begins. The server always interprets an EPI line as a relative path, with the reference path being its own document root directory (the directory it serves up to the Web as /). It passes the extra path information to the CGI program in two environment variables: PATH_INTO contains the EPI in its original form, whereas PATH_TRANSLATED contains the EPI as translated into an absolute path on the machine (which, for security reasons, usually isn't given out to clients).

For example, if the server uses /etc/httpd/web as its document root directory and it receives a request for /cgi-bin/bowdlerize/two/backed/beast, PATH_INFO will be **/two/backed/beast** and PATH_TRANSLATED will be **/etc/httpd/web/two/backed/beast**. Having both variables is somewhat redundant, because a server will also put the path of its own root document directory in another environment variable called DOCUMENT_ROOT, so PATH_TRANSLATED is always the same as DOCUMENT_ROOT/PATH_INFO.

Extra path information is typically used to identify an auxiliary file or directory to be used by a CGI program that acts like a general utility. For example, most server-based image maps are not given their own custom-made CGI programs just to match image locations with URLs. Instead, they call the nearly ubiquitous /cgi-bin/imagemap program with an extra path such as **/data/mymap.txt** to identify the text file that contains the coordinates of the ISMAP image's active areas.

But an EPI string's initial resemblance to a pathname doesn't mean that it has to be a pathname. After the initial **/**, it can be an arbitrary string. Since it is part of a URL, however, it should in principle be URL-encoded, and since the only way to send EPI from a form or other HTML document is as the value of an ACTION, HREF, or SRC attribute, you'll have to encode it yourself. For example, if the inline image tag

```
<IMG SRC="http://www.site.dom/cgi-bin/make-calendar/¬
1997/April%26May/images/risqu%E9/Hawaii">
```

is inserted into an HTML document, the program /cgi-bin/make-calendar on www.site.dom will be called every time the resulting page is loaded (or reloaded) into a browser, and the extra path information

```
/1997/April%26May/images/risqu%E9/Hawaii
```

will be passed to this program in the PATH_INFO environment variable. You can expect any CGI program to translate the **%26** into an ampersand (**&**) and the **%E9** into an acute-accented lowercase **e** (**é**), but whether it then treats the whole thing as one long directory path or as a set of options depends on the particular program.

## How Web Servers Forward Input to CGI Programs

Just as there are three standard ways for browsers to send CGI input to servers, so are there three standard ways for servers to forward this input to CGI programs. The general mechanisms servers use to pass data to programs are defined in the CGI specifications, and from a technical point of view, these are the only means whereby programs receive input from the Common Gateway Interface.

All three standard mechanisms derive from the common praxis of programming under Unix, where the World Wide Web and CGI started. They are

- ▶ **Environment variables**  The server puts everything the browser sends, except for posted message bodies, into environment variables that are freely available to the CGI program. In particular, any query string is passed as the value of QUERY_STRING.

- ▶ **Standard input**  The CGI program reads the contents of a posted message body from its own STDIN filehandle, which is actually connected to the server's STDOUT as a pipe (see the "Runtime Environments and Standard

Input/Output" sidebar in Chapter 1). The message can be of any length; there is no minimum or maximum. Its size is given by the environment variable CONTENT_LENGTH.

▶ **Command-line arguments**   The server parses and decodes a simple ISMAP-type or ISINDEX-type query string and passes the results to the CGI program in a special predefined array called **@ARGV** as if they were arguments entered on a command line. (The original query string is still passed in QUERY_STRING.) Environment variables are thus ubiquitous.

In the present incarnations of HTTP and CGI, standard input is used only to obtain posted form data, but since POST has become the preferred method for submitting forms, STDIN already plays a major role in CGI input. As standards are developed that allow browsers to upload greater volumes of data to servers (for example, as MIME attachments), the role of standard input is bound to grow. Command-line arguments, on the other hand, are on their way out, because server-side image maps and searchable indexes (which can send only a single input string) are becoming increasingly scarce. The simpler types of query strings will be left hanging around only as a legacy.

# Obtaining CGI Input Using Perl

Input is essential to most CGI programs; without it, they cannot tailor their output to specific users and requests. Receiving input means not only getting the raw information but also converting it into data that the program can use. Since CGI input is usually not sent in an ongoing process but instead exists as a fixed amount of data that is all there and available from the server when the program starts up, the input phase can be isolated from the rest of the program.

Also, since the initial processing is almost always generic, it's most often encapsulated in subroutines that can be reused in other programs. In fact, many such subroutines that handle CGI input in Perl are already freely available on the Web in example scripts and libraries. In this section, you'll write a subroutine named **getFormData** and put it into its own Perl library file.

## Accessing Environment Variables

When a Web server invokes a CGI program, it places a set of environment variables into the program's runtime environment. Programs written in different programming languages access these variables in different ways, but inside a Perl script, all the environment variables are contained in a predefined associative array called **%ENV**. Thus you don't need a special function to input environment variables into a CGI script; they are already there for the taking. All you have to do is reference them by name in **%ENV**.

None of this is peculiar to CGI. When you run a Perl script from a Unix or DOS command line, the **%ENV** array will be loaded up in the same way, except that it will then contain the environment variables already defined in the command shell. As explained in Chapter 1, environment variables provide a way for one process (the *parent*) to pass information to a program that it starts up as another process (its *child*). When a Web server or a command shell (the parent process) runs a script as a Perl program (the child process), it can either define a new set of environment variables for the running program to use or pass on its own set of environment variables. You can use this fact to test your Perl scripts in a shell before installing them on a server; just set the environment variables in the shell to whatever values you're testing, and the shell will pass them on to any Perl script you start up in that shell.

### The Most Common CGI Environment Variables

When a Web server receives a client request for a CGI program, it puts practically everything it knows about the client and the request into environment variables. The variables that are defined, however, vary among different servers and clients. Some environment variables, such as SERVER_NAME and REQUEST_METHOD, are always defined. Others, such as PATH_INFO and HTTP_ACCEPT, are defined only if the request contained extra path information or Accept headers, respectively. Many servers define QUERY_STRING even when its value is the empty string.

Tables 4.1 through 4.3 list the most commonly defined CGI environment variables (and some typical values). They fall into three main categories:

▶ **Server-specific variables**   The CGI specification requires that the GATE-WAY_INTERFACE, SERVER_NAME, and SERVER_SOFTWARE server-specific variables always be defined. These don't change while a server is running. Other server information is optional.

▶ **Request-specific variables**   Request-specific variables can change with every request. REMOTE_ADDR, REQUEST_TYPE, and SCRIPT_NAME always have values. QUERY_STRING is usually defined even if its value is nothing, and CONTENT_LENGTH is defined only if the request included a content-length header and a message body.

▶ **Client-specific variables**   Any header line that is received from the client and that follows the request header can be placed into the environment as a

## TABLE 4.1    SERVER-SPECIFIC ENVIRONMENT VARIABLES

| Variable | Description | Example |
|---|---|---|
| DOCUMENT_ROOT | The root directory from which the server serves documents | /usr/etc/httpd/web |
| GATEWAY_INTERFACE | The version of the Common Gateway Interface used by the server; always defined | CGI/1.1 |
| SERVER_ADMIN | The e-mail address or other information about the systems administrator | webmaster@site.dom |
| SERVER_NAME | The server's (virtual) host name, DNS alias, or IP address as it would appear in a self-referencing URL; always defined | www.site.dom |
| SERVER_PORT | The server host port number to which the client sent the request (or which received the request) | 80 is the default; 8000, 8001, and 8080 are common |
| SERVER_SOFTWARE | The name and version of the server program answering the request and running the gateway; always defined | Apache/1.2 |
| TZ | The time zone in which the server resides | EST5EDT |

## TABLE 4.2    REQUEST-SPECIFIC ENVIRONMENT VARIABLES

| Variable | Description | Example |
|---|---|---|
| AUTH_TYPE | The protocol-specific authentication method used to validate the user; defined only if the server supports user authentication and the script is protected; goes with REMOTE_USER. | password |
| CONTENT_FILE | The DOS path and filename of a temporary file to hold the client's complete request (Windows HTTPd server only). The file's size is CONTENT_LENGTH bytes. | |
| CONTENT_LENGTH | The length in bytes of any content sent by the client as an attachment or message body; goes with CONTENT_TYPE. | |
| CONTENT_TYPE | The MIME type of any data attached to an HTTP query such as POST or PUT; defined only if such information is sent. | application/x-www-form-urlencoded |
| OUTPUT_FILE | The DOS pathname of the temporary file (on the server) that is to receive the CGI script's output (Windows HTTPd server only). | |
| PATH | The default command path for the CGI program. | /bin: /usr/bin: /usr/local/bin: |
| PATH_INFO | The extra path information, as given by the client. | /~me/index |
| PATH_TRANSLATED | The server-translated version of PATH_INFO: an absolute ("physical") rather than relative ("virtual") path. On a DOS or Windows system, slashes may be replaced by backslashes. | /usr5/web/me/public_html/index.html |

**TABLE 4.2    REQUEST-SPECIFIC ENVIRONMENT VARIABLES (Continued)**

| Variable | Description | Example |
|----------|-------------|---------|
| QUERY_STRING | Query information from an HTTP GET request header; any string appended to the URL after a ? and not decoded. | |
| REMOTE_ADDR | The IP address of the host making the request; always defined. | 128.52.40.148 |
| REMOTE_HOST | The Internet host name of the client's host; defined only if DNS lookup is enabled. | bzrq.ai.mit.edu |
| REMOTE_IDENT | The remote user name retrieved from the server; defined only if the HTTP browser and server support RFC 931 identification (rare). | |
| REMOTE_USER | The authenticated user name; defined only if the server supports user authentication and the script is protected; see AUTH_TYPE. | |
| REQUEST_LINE | The full line of the HTTP request header; rarely implemented. | GET / HTTP/1.0 |
| REQUEST_METHOD | The method of the information request. | For HTTP: GET, HEAD, POST, etc. |
| SCRIPT_FILENAME | The absolute pathname of the CGI program. | /usr5/web/me/public_html/tryit.cgi |
| SCRIPT_NAME | The relative pathname, also called the partial URL, of the CGI program being executed; used for self-referencing URLs; always defined. | /~me/tryit |
| SERVER_PROTOCOL | The name and version of the protocol identified in the client request. | HTTP/1.0 |

**TABLE 4.3    CLIENT-SPECIFIC ENVIRONMENT VARIABLES (FROM HTTP HEADERS)**

| Variable | Description | Example |
|----------|-------------|---------|
| HTTP_ACCEPT | MIME types the client will accept, ordered by preference. Per HTTP/1.0, this should be one comma-separated list. | image/jpeg, image/gif, */* |
| HTTP_AUTHORIZATION | The encryption scheme and (encrypted) user authentication data. The format is scheme data. | |
| HTTP_CONNECTION | The preferred HTTP connection type. | Keep-Alive |
| HTTP_PRAGMA | A directive to the server. Currently the only widely supported pragma directive is no-cache, which instructs a proxy server to retrieve the document from the original server instead of retrieving the locally cached copy. | |
| HTTP_REFERER | The URL of previous document loaded by the client. | |
| HTTP_USER_AGENT | Client software (the browser sending the request); defined if the client sent a user-agent header. The format is browser/version library/version. | Mozilla/3.0b4 (X11; I; SunOS 4.1.4 sun4m) |

variable. The variable will take its name from the header name (uppercased) and will be prefixed with HTTP_. For example, the header line

```
User-agent: Mozilla/3.0b4 (X11; I; SunOS 4.1.4 sun4m)
```

would result in an environment variable named HTTP_USER_AGENT, and everything to the right of the colon would be its value. Redundant information might be ignored, although the data from multiple headers of the same name would be combined into one value as a comma-separated list. For example,

```
Accept: video/quicktime
Accept: video/x-msmovie
```

should translate into HTTP_ACCEPT with the value **video/quicktime, video/x-msmovie**.

SERVER_PROTOCOL is a slight misnomer; it's often described as a server-specific variable, but its value is usually whatever the client sent in as the third part of the HTTP request header.

For example, if the request were

```
GET /cgi-bin/printenv Dove-Cum-Olive-Branch-Protocol/3000BC
```

most servers would dutifully set SERVER_PROTOCOL to **Dove-Cum-Olive-Branch-Protocol/3000BC**, even though both server and client are actually using HTTP/1.0.

## Printing Out All the Environment Variables

Associative arrays such as **%ENV** are very convenient for storing an indefinite number of paired names and values all in one place and for referring to those values by their arbitrary names instead of by a fixed set of numbers. Looping through an associative array's contents in a predefined order, however, is a different story, even if all you want to do is print them out. The lack of a numerical index means that you can't use a simple **for** or **foreach** loop, as you can to iterate through the contents of an ordinary array.

To remedy this situation, Perl provides several operators that allow you to create lists containing each of an associative array's keys and/or values; not too surprisingly, these operators are named **each**, **keys**, and **values**. The next few sections explain how to use these operators and others to loop through the entries in an associative array.

**Using Perl's each, keys, and values Functions**    In Perl, the closest thing to a numerical index for stepping through the contents of an associative array is actually not a number at all, but a function, **each**. This function returns a two-element list containing the "next" key/value pair in an associative array. The pair that is "next" depends on Perl's internal representations, but the **each** function will not repeat itself until the entire associative array has been read, and then it returns an empty list before starting over again. This allows you to iterate over the array, as in

```
while (($key, $value) = each %ENV){
   print "$key = $value\n";
}
```

However, the **each** function is rather limited; it doesn't give you any control over the order in which the environmental variables are printed.

To refer to a specific value in an associative array, you have to know its key. In the case of **%ENV**, the keys are the names of all the environment variables, as in

```
$query_string = $ENV{'QUERY_STRING'}
```

You can place all of the keys into an ordinary array using the Perl **keys** function, as in

```
@keys = keys( %ENV );
```

Likewise, you can get all the values at once using the **values** function:

```
@values = values( %ENV );
```

These two functions return the keys or values in an apparently random order, but unless you change the array between the two calls, the elements will be the same order. (You might guess that an associative array would be stored with its keys always in alphabetical order, but this would be very inefficient. The order returned by **each**, **keys**, and **values** is actually based on Perl's internal storage of the associative array, which uses a hash table.)

Now if you knew how many keys (and values) there were, you could print them out by iterating through either of the ordinary arrays these functions return. In Perl, there are two ways to get this number. In a scalar context, the name of an ordinary array itself evaluates to the number of elements it contains, as in

```
$number_of_elements = @name_of_array;
```

The other option uses the expression **$#array_name**, which always gives the numerical index of the last entry in the array. Since arrays in Perl begin with 0 as the first index, the last index is usually 1 less than the number of elements:

```
$#name_of_array = @name_of_array - 1;
```

(You can actually change the initial array offset to be any number you like by setting the value of the special variable **$[**. For example, die-hard Fortran programmers might like **$[ - 1;**.)

Thus an elementary way to print all of the environment variables and their values would be to use the **keys** and **values** functions and a **for** loop:

```
@env_var_names = keys( %ENV );
@env_var_values = values( %ENV );
for ($j = $#env_var_names; $j >= 0; $j-) {
  print $env_var_names[$j], " = ", $env_var_values[$j], "\n";
}
```

**Using Perl's foreach and sort Operators**   In Perl, you don't really need to know the length of an array in order to iterate through it. A more elegant way to print out the contents of **%ENV** is to use a **foreach** loop: You can use the keys themselves as the index, eliminating the need for both **@env_var_values** and **$j**. This way, you can also sort the keys (the names of the environment variables, in this case) and still get the right value for each one:

```
@env_var_names = sort(keys(%ENV));
foreach $name (@env_var_names) {
  print $name, " = ", $ENV{$name}, "\n";
}
```

Notice that you can apply the **sort** function immediately to whatever is returned by **keys**, without saving any intermediate results.

**Using printf instead of print**   Actually, you don't need to store the keys in **@env_var_names**, either. Here is the code I recommend for printing all the environment variables and their values:

```
foreach $name (sort(keys(%ENV))) {
  printf("%20s = %s\n", $name, $ENV{$name});
}
```

The **printf** function is more flexible than the simple **print** operator and is almost as easy to use. This **printf** statement prints its first argument, **"%20s = %s\n"**, as a format string, with the two remaining arguments substituted for the two string-replacement symbols **%20s** and **%s**. The **20** in the first symbol means that its re-placement string should be printed as a field at least 20 characters long (more if the actual string is longer). If the string is shorter than 20 characters, it will be right-justified in the 20-character field. Thus the output will look something like this:

```
       DOCUMENT_ROOT = user/etc/httpd/web/docs
   GATEWAY_INTERFACE = CGI/1.1
         HTTP_ACCEPT = image/gif, image/jpeg, */*
     HTTP_CONNECTION = Keep-Alive
           HTTP_HOST = www.site.dom
 . . .
     SERVER_SOFTWARE = Apache/1.2-dev RSThreads/0.1
                  TZ = EST5EDT
```

## Example 4A: A Scripts That Prints Out Its Own Environment

Listing 4.1 shows the printenv.cgi program, a CGI Perl script that uses the **keys**, **sort**, **foreach**, and **printf** operators to print out its entire environment in a plain text Web page.

Giving away some of this information on the Net, however, is generally consid-ered a security risk. In particular, systems administrators are touchy about divulging the value of DOCUMENT_ROOT or the absolute pathname of any Web document

---

**LISTING 4.1    A simple CGI script that prints out its own environment**

```perl
#!/usr/local/bin/perl
# printenv.cgi
print "Content-type: text/plain\n\n";

print "Hi, I'm $0\n";  # $0: pathname of this script
print "and here are my runtime environment variables:\n";
foreach $var (sort(keys(%ENV))) {
   printf("%20s = %s\n", $var, $ENV{$var});
}
```

(which is given in SCRIPT_FILENAME and PATH_TRANSLATED). Depending on your installation of Perl, the special variable **$0** may evaluate to the absolute pathname of the script itself or to only the relative pathname. Thus, if you install a script such as this for testing purposes, you should remove it as soon as you're done. Alternatively, you can print only the environment variables you actually need to know or explicitly test for and skip the ones you don't want printed, as shown in Listing 4.2.

The effect of the line

```
$script = __FILE__ unless $script = $ENV{'SCRIPT_NAME'};
```

is to assign to **$script** the value of the server-created environment variable SCRIPT_NAME, if this is defined and non-null; if SCRIPT_NAME is undefined or null it will assign to **$script** the value of **__FILE__**. Perl will translate **__FILE__** into the pathname used to invoke the running script; this is not a variable but a *special literal*, also known as a *pseudo-literal* or *built-in macro*. This either/or assignment allows you to use the same script either as a CGI program or as a command-line program and thus see how its environment varies.

The effect of a **next** statement in a loop is to skip the rest of the statements in the body of the loop and go to the next index, which in this case is the next sorted name of an environment variable.

**LISTING 4.2    A CGI script that prints out its own environment and skips over absolute path information**

```
#!/usr/local/bin/perl
# printenv-part.cgi
print "Content-type: text/plain\n\n";

$script = __FILE__ unless $script = $ENV{'SCRIPT_NAME'};
print "This is $script\n";
print "Here is *part* of my runtime environment:\n";
foreach $var (sort(keys(%ENV))) {
  next if $var eq 'DOCUMENT_ROOT';
  next if $var eq 'SCRIPT_FILENAME';
  next if $var eq 'PATH_TRANSLATED';
  printf("%20s = %s\n", $var, $ENV{$var});
}
```

## Reading the Posted Message Body from STDIN

When a browser uses the POST method to send a request to a Web server, any accompanying data is sent in a message body, much like the body of an e-mail message.

The size of the message body in bytes must be given by a *content-length* header; the content itself is whatever follows all the HTTP headers and the blank line that terminates them. In particular, when a browser submits a form, the data is all strung together as **&**-separated *name=value* pairs and URL-encoded in exactly the same way that a query string is. But instead of being appended to a URL after a **?**, the string is sent as the message body, as shown here:

```
POST /cgi-bin/printall HTTP/1.Ø
Content-type: application/x-www-form-urlencoded
Content-length: 25


name1=value1&name2=value2
```

When a Web server receives such a request, it doesn't put the contents of the message body into an environment variable such as QUERY_STRING but instead makes the data available to the CGI program so that the program can read it from its standard input filehandle, STDIN.

## Reading Input from the STDIN Filehandle

In Perl, reading from a filehandle is very easy. The function

```
read (FILEHANDLE, scalar_variable, number_of_bytes)
```

attempts to read the given number of bytes from the specified *FILEHANDLE* and store the bytes as the value of the scalar variable. Here *number_of_bytes* can be

## Naming Perl Variables and Filehandles

All names in Perl must consist entirely of letters and/or numbers and must begin with a letter; a name can be a single character (although most single-character names in Perl have predefined significance). It is also important to note that Perl considers the underscore character (_) to be a letter. In order to distinguish filehandles from other variables and words that are part of Perl itself (such as **if** and **for**), it is customary to give filehandles all-uppercase names, such as STDIN or INPUT.

either a literal number (such as 25) or an expression that evaluates to a number in a number context (such as 17 + 8 or **$length**, if its value looks like a number).

Since *scalar_variable*'s contents will be modified by the call to the **read** function, it must be a variable (such as **$string**), not a literal constant (such as **"string"**). Finally, *FILEHANDLE* is neither a variable nor a number, but a literal *name*. (See the sidebar entitled "Naming Perl Variables and Filehandles" for more information.)

STDIN and STDOUT are the default input and output filehandles; they are already open for reading and writing, respectively, whenever a Perl script begins execution. Thus if you know that your CGI script's input is coming from a posted form, you can get the form's data using this single **read** statement:

```
read (STDIN, $query_string, $ENV{'CONTENT_LENGTH'});
```

The result will be the same if you know that the input is coming from a form submitted using METHOD=GET and your script begins with

```
$query_string = $ENV{'QUERY_STRING'});
```

To handle either case, you can check the value of the environment variable RE-QUEST_METHOD, as shown in Listing 4.3.

Usually it's best to write your code so that it covers both cases. Even though the METHOD attribute in a form's opening FORM tag specifies whether the form is to be submitted via GET or POST, it's easy enough for somebody to modify a downloaded copy of the form and submit that. Also, you'll probably want to wrap this code up in one general subroutine and use it for parsing the input from all of your forms.

On the other hand, GET and POST are the only two methods currently allowed for submitting form data. What do you do if you get a request that uses some other method, such as PUT or DELETE? Outputting an error message and quitting is probably the best answer. That way you've covered all the bases, and that's

**LISTING 4.3    A code fragment for recovering the query information from a GET or POST request**

```
$request_method = $ENV{'REQUEST_METHOD'};
if ($request_method eq 'GET') {
  $query_string = $ENV{'QUERY_STRING'};
} elsif ($request_method eq 'POST') {
  read (STDIN, $query_string, $ENV{'CONTENT_LENGTH'});
}
```

what you'll do in the following example, which demonstrates a subroutine for han-dling input from forms.

## Creating the Library File

Parsing form data in the general case is simply a matter of merging the REQUEST_ METHOD-checking code of the previous section with the input code in a CGI file. This example will use the sandwich-reply.cgi file (Listing 3.6) from Chapter 3. You'll go one step further and wrap this merged code up into a subroutine called **getFormData**. Once this subroutine has been written, you can cut and paste it into any CGI script that backends a form and then call that local copy to parse and decode the form's data. Even better, you can put **getFormData** into a library file and then include that file in any script that calls the subroutine. That way you won't have to copy it manually every time.

In Perl, the preferred way to include a simple library of subroutines is to place a **require** directive near the top of the script; after that, any subroutines in the in-cluded file can be called by name, as shown here:

```
require "FormData.pl";
&getFormData(*FormData);
```

The effect of this subroutine call is to load an associative array named **%FormData** with the paired names and values from a form's query data. Here the **&** identifies **&getFormData** as a subroutine call, just as **$**, **@**, and **%** identify scalar, array, and associative array variables. You might guess that the prefixed ampersand is used to distinguish subroutine calls from calls to Perl's built-in functions, such as **print** or **split**, but that's not quite true. You can call **getFormData** either way:

```
$query = getFormData();
```

is basically equivalent to

```
$query = &getFormData;
```

However, both of these function calls have the unfortunate side effect of making **%FormData** a global variable. This means that it can be accessed and modified anywhere in the program, with potentially harmful results. The preferred way of calling **getFormData** is to pass it a single argument by its glob name, as in

```
$query = &getFormData(*Name);
```

(A **\***-prefixed name in Perl is called a *type glob* because it globs together all the ob-jects of the same name. Globs will be described in detail later in this chapter.) Inside the function, *Name* will be used as the name of an associative array, which is either created from scratch or modified in place. (To see how these different ways of calling **getFormData** work, you'll have to look inside the subroutine.)

So there really isn't much difference in Perl between a subroutine and a function. Functions usually take arguments and return values, but they don't have to, and Perl blurs the distinctions between empty, null, and undefined (nonexistent) values anyway. The rule in Perl is that if it looks like a function call, it is a function call, but if it doesn't, it still might be one (and in some other programming languages, even **&getFormData**; might look like a function call). The preferred way of calling a function in Perl, however, is to use both the **&** prefix and an argument list.

**A Library Routine for Parsing Froms: getFormData** Listing 4.4 shows the file FormData.pl, which contains only the **getFormData** subroutine. Since this file won't be executed as a standalone Perl script, it doesn't need to begin with the usual pound-bang command line (**#!/usr/local/bin/perl**). But since it will be included in other scripts, it does need to end with a nonzero value on a line by itself. This last expression will be evaluated as the return value of the file-inclusion operator inside these other scripts. You won't actually use this value; Perl just needs it to be there for internal checking purposes.

---

**LISTING 4.4  The getFormData() function, defined in its own library file, FormData.pl**

```perl
# FormData.pl - Perl library file containing getFormData, a
# CGI subroutine for parsing and decoding any submitted form
# Usage: $original_query_string = &getFormData( *name_for_assoc_array );

sub   getFormData {
  local(*FormData) = @_ if @_; # Make *FormData an alias for the argument
  local($QueryInfo, $request_method, $name_value, $name, $value);

  # Get the query string as appropriate for the request method: if GET,
  # extract it from the environment; if POST, read it from standard input:
  $request_method = $ENV{'REQUEST_METHOD'};
  if ($request_method eq 'GET') {
    $QueryInfo = $ENV{'QUERY_STRING'};
  } elsif ($request_method eq 'POST') {
    read (STDIN, $QueryInfo, $ENV{'CONTENT_LENGTH'});
  } else {
    print "Content-type: text/html\n\n";
```

**LISTING 4.4**    The getFormData() **function, defined in its own library file, FormData.pl**
                   **(Continued)**

```perl
    print "<TITLE>Error parsing form</TITLE>\n";
    print "<H2>Error parsing form</H2>\n";
    print "Request method must be GET or POST, not ``$request_method''\n";
    die("$0: Bad request method: [$request_method]\n");
}


  # Split $QueryInfo into name=value pairs and convert each pair:
  foreach $name_value (split('&', $QueryInfo)) {

    # Translate any plus signs in the pair strings into spaces:
    $name_value  =~ tr/+/ /;

    # Split the name=value pair into a separate name and value:
    ($name, $value) = split ('=', $name_value);

    # Translate escaped hex numbers back into 8-bit characters:
    $name  =~ s/%(..)/pack("C", hex($1))/eg;
    $value =~ s/%(..)/pack("C", hex($1))/eg; # It's OK if a value is null

    # Now convert the names and values into named, assigned variables;
    # i.e., use each name as a key in an associative array and associate
    # it with all the values originally paired with that name, separating
    # multiple values for the same name with the null character:

    if (defined($FormData{$name})) {  # If %FormData{$name} already has a
      $FormData{$name} .= "\0$value"; # value, append '\0' as a separator
    } else {                          # before appending the new value.
      $FormData{$name}  =   $value;   # Otherwise, just assign the new
    }                                 # value to %FormData{$name} as is.
  }
  $QueryInfo; # Return the original query string or posted message body
}


1; # Library functions must end with the statement "1;" to satisfy the require¬
operator
```

Inside the definition of **getFormData**, the only thing that's really new is the **local** operator, used at the very beginning to name and localize variables. I'll explain the use of **local** in the next section.

**The Return Value: True If There Is Any Data** At the very end of the subroutine, the variable containing the original query information appears on a line all by itself:

```
$QueryInfo; # Return the original query string or posted message¬
body
```

This bare statement makes **$QueryInfo** the *return value* of **getFormData** when the subroutine is used as a function. At a slight cost in overhead, you can also use an explicit return statement to return a value from anywhere inside a function body, as in

```
if ($request_method eq 'POST') {
        print "POST no forms here, please!\n";
        return 0;
    }
```

But if *control* (the current execution point) reaches the end of a function without coming across an explicit return statement, the return value of the function is the value of whatever expression was last evaluated.

**Creating Local Variables Using Perl's local Operator** The first thing the **getFormData** subroutine does is name its parameters and other variables using the **local** operator. A subroutine's *parameters* are just the arguments that appear in the actual subroutine call; they can be variables or literal values of any data type, as in

```
&subroutine( 1, "arg2", ARG3, $arg4, @arg5, %arg6);
```

The purpose of using **local** at the beginning of a subroutine is threefold:

▶ To create new variables that are local to the subroutine—that is, variables that exist only until the subroutine finishes executing.

▶ To copy the values of the subroutine's parameters, which all come in through the special array variable **@_**, into new, local variables. The local copies can then be changed without affecting the originals.

▶ To name the subroutine's parameters and variables all in one place. This is mainly for the sake of clarity.

**Variables of Global and Local Block Scope**   By default, all variables in Perl are *global*; that is, they can be evaluated or changed anywhere in the script, even inside files included with the **require** operator. This makes it easy to create and call subroutines without even bothering to name their parameters or create new variables, but such sloppy practices can end up costing you a lot of time when things go wrong. The main thing that can go wrong is that you'll accidentally modify a global variable, causing unforeseeable damage in another routine far away.

The fundamental purpose of the **local** operator is to create new variables whose existence is limited to a single *block* (a chunk of code delimited by a pair of curly braces). The body of a subroutine definition is one instance of a block, but a block can appear anywhere. For example, the output of the code fragment

```
$string = "outward frenzy";
{
  local( $string ) = "inner serenity";
  print "$string, ";
}
print "$string\n";
```

would be

```
inner serenity, outward frenzy
```

Inside the block, the local variable **$string** is created and initialized with the value **"inner serenity"** and then printed. When the block ends, that variable is destroyed, and **$string** regains its former value. Or, rather, the variable that was named **$string** outside the block, and then *hidden* by the local variable of the same name inside the block, again becomes *visible*. Another way of saying the same thing is to say that a variable created with **local** has only local or block scope. The *scope* of a variable is the block in which it is defined; it is *visible* in the portions of code in which it can be accessed by name. The fact that a variable can remain in scope even when temporarily invisible (locally hidden) means that, technically speaking, Perl has *dynamic local scoping*. (And as long as we're speaking technically, variables in Perl are not actually global but are always localized within a *package*. Everything you're doing at present, however, lies within the scope of one big package called *main*.) The **local** operator thus temporarily hides variables of outer scope at the same time that it creates new ones local to a block. Variables that are created using **local** at the beginning of a subroutine are limited in scope to the local block of the subroutine's body.

**The uppercase Function**    The second purpose of the **local** operator—to copy all of a subroutine's parameters into new, local variables—is actually a special case of the first. It's an important special case, because another default in Perl is that variables appearing as arguments in function calls are always *passed by reference* rather than *by value*. This means that the function can modify the *original* variables, not just its own local copies of the values. In the code fragment shown in Listing 4.5, the **uppercase** function does an efficient job of converting all of its argument strings to uppercase; the problem is that it does the conversion *in place*, converting the original strings instead of local copies.

The net result of running the code in Listing 4.5 would be to translate all the strings in both **@lower** and **@upper** to uppercase, giving the following output:

```
lower upper: BELL HOOKS - NOT!
```

This outcome is probably not what you want.

A better way to implement this function would be

```perl
sub uppercase {
  @strings = @_;        # Beware of global side effects!
  foreach $string (@strings) {
    $string =~ tr/a-z/A-Z/;        # Here, too!
  }
```

---

**LISTING 4.5    Code fragment showing a first attempt at defining** uppercase()

```perl
sub uppercase {
  foreach $_ (@_)    { $_ =~ tr/a-z/A-Z/; }
  return @_;
}


$string = "- not!";
@lower = ("bell", "hooks");
@upper = &uppercase(@lower, $string);
print "lower upper: $lower[0] $upper[1] $upper[2]\n";
```

```
    return  @strings;
  }
```

All of the arguments here are copied into the array **@strings,** and then only the copies are modified.

The only problem with this version of **uppercase** is that it assigns values to both **@strings** and **$string** as global variables. If an array called **@strings** is already defined somewhere else in the script, all of its values will be clobbered in one fell swoop by the line

```
    @strings = @_;
```

If **@strings** doesn't already exist, it will be created and will linger on after the function finishes executing. The scalar variable **$string,** on the other hand, will be left holding whatever string was last uppercased inside the **foreach** loop.

The **local** operator can be used to make a version of **uppercase** that neither modifies its parameters nor spills out global side effects. Listing 4.6 shows one such version.

For those inclined to minimize keystrokes (or maximize hackery), here is an alternative to the routine shown in Listing 4.6. This one-liner compiles only under Perl 5. (To make it work in Perl 4, enclose the first **@_** in parentheses.)

```
    sub uppercase { local @_ = @_; for (@_) { y/a-z/A-Z/; } @_}
```

Here the **local** operator makes the **@_** on the left-hand side of the assignment a different variable from the same-named variable on the right-hand side. The keyword **for** is actually a synonym for **foreach**; and **$_,** as the default variable both in **for** loops and for any pattern matching operator, need not be written. The **y** is a synonym for **tr,** provided for devotees of the Unix **sed** command; and finally, a terminating semicolon can be omitted at the end of a block. Believe it or not, this

---

**LISTING 4.6    A corrected version of the** uppercase() **function**

```
sub uppercase {
  local ( @strings ) = @_;
  local ( $string );
  foreach $string (@strings)    { $string =~ tr/a-z/A-Z/; }
  return  @strings;
}
```

one-liner is functionally equivalent to the 6-line version of **uppercase** shown in Listing 4.6 and might actually run a microsecond or so faster. In terms of readability, though, it leaves something to be desired.

**Naming Variables**   That brings us to the third reason for enclosing all the parameters and variables in **local** statements at the beginning of a subroutine. Using **local** in this way has the effect of *naming* your variables, and the purpose this serves is clarity. Perl will let you create local and global variables anywhere you like, but if you name all of your variables at the beginning of each subroutine, your scripts will be much easier to read.

Many programming languages require you to list the names and types of every one of a subroutine's parameters as part of its definition; these declarations of *formal* parameters provide the names by which your subroutine refers to the *actual* parameters. Such stringency is great for purposes of runtime efficiency, general error-checking, and, in particular, closely monitoring variables and memory usage. The downside is that it has a way of making you worry about very low-level issues, such as how many bytes you should use to represent a number.

Perl is just the opposite. Perl subroutines require no such formal argument list, because all the arguments are passed in the special array variable @_, which grows or shrinks to hold only the actual arguments. You can call the same function with different kinds of parameters and manipulate them as you please. The other side of all this freedom is that it's fairly easy to misname a variable or lose track of your own subroutine-calling conventions and end up wondering how code that was so easy to write could run so wrong. But if you adopt the custom of localizing all your variables at the beginning of each subroutine, you'll be far less likely to clobber, alias, or otherwise mangle your data.

**Creating a Local Alias**   Finally, there will be times when you *do* want a subroutine to modify your original variables or arrays, not just local copies of them. You could try to do this using global variables, but the variables' names must be the same both inside and outside the subroutine. That would make the subroutine inflexible and defeat much of the basic purpose of using subroutines, which is to reuse the same code in different situations and on different data. You could also try taking advantage of Perl's call-by-reference parameter passing, but in the case of multiple or array arguments, writing everything in terms of the @_ array would soon become cumbersome and obscure. Faced with this situation in low-level programming languages such as C, you might pass to the subroutine pointers to your original variables. (*Pointers* are symbolic variables whose values are the addresses of your original variables' locations in memory.) But even in Perl 5, the facilities for using pointers (which in Perl are called *references*) are rather limited and difficult to use. What you really want inside the subroutine are local, symbolic *names* that you can use exactly as if they were the names of your variables outside the subroutine. Such symbolic names are also known as *aliases* because they serve as new, temporary names for the subroutine's original arguments.

To create a local alias in Perl, you make an assignment like this:

```
local( *alias_name ) = *original_name;
```

The effect of this statement is not to copy any data that's referred to by a variable called **\*original_name**, but rather to make **alias_name** an alternate name for *any* variables named **original_name**, regardless of their types. This means that **$alias_name** is now a synonym for **$original_name**, **@alias_name** is a synonym for **@original_name**, and so on, even if these variables haven't (yet) been defined. As mentioned earlier, a **\***-prefixed name in Perl is called a *type glob* because it globs together all the objects of the same name. You can think of the star symbol (**\***) as a wildcard that represents all the other characters that prefix variables (**$**, **@**, and **%**), but a type glob also collects any filehandle, directory handle, or subroutine that bears its name or one of its aliases. What a type glob actually refers to is a binary structure of symbol table entries; so you can't simply print it out or copy all of its contents into a variable, you can only pass its name around as a catch-all alias. But that's exactly the point. Using type globs and aliases is the only practical way to pass a filehandle or two separate arrays to a subroutine, and it's definitely the preferred method for using a function to create or modify an associative array, as you do in **getFormData**.

As a simple example, Listing 4.7 shows one more version of **uppercase**, which this time modifies its original arguments by design.

In this new version of **uppercase**, the effect of the line

```
local ( *string ) = @_;
```

is not to create local variables named **$string**, **@string**, or **%string**, and not to copy anything out of **@_**, but only to identify the name **string** as a local alias for whatever type glob appears as the argument in the function call, which just happens to be **\*change**:

```
@return = uppercase( *change );
```

It also so happens that **@change** is already initialized before this function call, whereas variables named **$change** and **%change** don't exist. Inside **uppercase**,

**LISTING 4.7    A version of** uppercase() **that (intentionally) modifies its arguments in place**

```perl
#!/usr/local/bin/perl

sub uppercase {
  local ( *string ) = @_; # Use "string" as an alias for arguments
  foreach $string (@string)   { $string =~ tr/a-z/A-Z/; }
  return  @string;
}


$string = "lower case";
@change = ("bell", "hooks");
@return = uppercase( *change );

print "change is now $change[0] $change[1]\n";
print "return is now $return[0] $return[1]\n";
print "and string is still $string\n";
```

then, **$string** is created as a new variable the first time it is used. Since this doesn't happen inside a **local** statement, it might appear that **$string** is global, but since the name **string** has been localized to **uppercase**, this variable is local, too, and is destroyed when the subroutine ends. The array **@string**, on the other hand, is not created inside **uppercase**, but is just a local alias; modify **@string** and you directly modify **@change**. And when **uppercase** returns **@string**, it is only returning **@change**. So if you wanted to use **uppercase** only as a subroutine, the return statement would be redundant; it's only there so that **uppercase** can also be used as a function. (But remember, you can omit the keyword **return**.) The output of the above script is thus

```
change is now BELL HOOKS
return is now BELL HOOKS
and string is still lowercase
```

Now, finally, let's look at the first line in **getFormData**:

```perl
local(*FormData) = @_ if @_;
```

This means that if the subroutine is called with a type glob name as an argument, as in

```
&getFormData(*input);
```

the name **FormData** will serve as the local alias for any outside variables globbed under **input**. But if **getFormData** is called with no arguments (or with anything but a type glob), **%FormData** will be created as a global variable the first time it's used in the subroutine. So if you don't mind letting a subroutine create a global variable and you happen to know the name of this variable, you can also call it in these ways:

```
&getFormData();        # Call with an empty argument list

&getFormData;          # Call with no argument list whatsoever

getFormData();         # Call function-style with an empty argument list
```

Because of **getFormData**'s last line, which is just

```
$QueryInfo; # Return the original query string or posted message¬
body
```

the subroutine can also be called as a function, with or without arguments. Here are two more possibilities:

```
$query = &getFormData;         # Call as a function with no argument¬
list
```

```
$query = getFormData(*input); # This is not redundant
```

The first of these still creates **%FormData** as a global variable, whereas the second does not. So the very first and last examples above are the preferred ways of calling **getFormData**, with the return value assigned to **$query** only if you intend to use it later. And that's almost everything you'll ever need to know about localizing variables.

## Example 4B: Listing the Data Recovered from a Form

Now that you have **getFormData** safely stored away in its own library file, you can practically forget about the actual code it contains. As long as you understand how to call it with a type-glob parameter and get back its return value, you can call **getFormData** from any script by inserting just two lines: the **require** directive to include the file FormData.pl and the subroutine call itself. The example test script shown in Listing 4.8 takes advantage of this. It replies to form input by listing all the decoded names and values. It also displays any command-line arguments it receives—there shouldn't be any if the query string or posted message body actually came from a form. Finally, it lists its own environment, minus a few absolute directory paths. You might find it useful when developing or debugging a form.

**LISTING 4.8    ShowData.cgi, a CGI script that displays all of its input**

```perl
#!/usr/local/bin/perl
# ShowData.cgi - display all CGI input data as text
require "FormData.pl";

$script = $ENV{'SCRIPT_NAME'} || $0;

print "Content-type: text/plain\n\n";
print "Hi, I'm $script\n";

if (&getFormData(*input)) {
  print "Here's the data I got from getFormData:\n";
  foreach $key (sort(keys(%input))) {
    if (@_ = split(/\0/, $input{$key})) {
      foreach $_ (@_) {
        printf("%24s = %s\n", $key, $_);
      }
    } else {
      printf("%24s ! [defined, but with null value]\n", $key);
    }
  }
}

if (@ARGV) {
  print "\nHere are my command-line arguments:\n";
  for ($j = 0; $j < @ARGV; $j++) {
    printf("%24d = %s\n", $j, $ARGV[$j]);
  }
}
```

**LISTING 4.8    ShowData.cgi, a CGI script that displays all of its input (Continued)**

```perl
print "\nAnd here are all my environment variables:\n";
foreach $_ (sort(keys(%ENV))) {
  next if $_ eq 'DOCUMENT_ROOT';
  next if $_ eq 'SCRIPT_FILENAME';
  next if $_ eq 'PATH_TRANSLATED';
  printf("%24s = %s\n", $_, $ENV{$_});
}
```

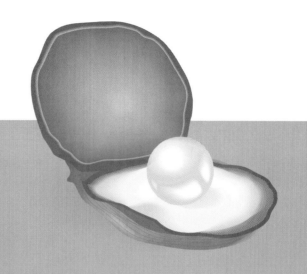

# The Varieties of CGI Output

# Redirecting the Client to a Different URL

# Sending Static Files

# Chapter 5
# Output through the Common Gateway Interface

Common Gateway Interface (CGI) output can be any kind of data—images, audio clips, movies, executable code, raw or encrypted database files, HTML code, SGML code, VRML code, you name it. The only constraint is that, if a client browser is to display this output as a document, the data must be preceded by the proper HTTP headers. In addition to sending data to STDOUT, which the server pipes through to the client, a CGI program might open local files or other data channels and send output to them. Saving a record of a transaction or relaying information to some other local resource is often just as important as replying to the client. I'll turn to applications that make use of such local output in later chapters. This chapter focuses on CGI output proper, which always goes through STDOUT and is usually just what the browser/user sees and/or hears.

## The Varieties of CGI Output

Output through the Common Gateway Interface can be divided into three basic categories:

- ▶ **Redirection headers** that output different URLs for the client browser to look up

- ▶ **Static files** (existing documents) that are piped through STDOUT

- ▶ **New documents** that are generated on the fly

All of the output from the example programs I've explained up to now would fall into the third category, because those programs generate new HTML documents at runtime. In this chapter, I'll cover output that falls into the first two categories. I'll turn to creating new images and other kinds of documents besides HTML in Chapter 6.

# Redirecting the Client to a Different URL

One very simple way in which a CGI program can reply to a client browser is to redirect it to a different URL. The redirected browser can then retrieve this other URL without further input from the user. The browser will display the new URL's contents or output as if that, and not the original CGI program, had been the object of its original request. To accomplish such automated redirection, your program need only output the new URL in a Location response header such as this:

```perl
#!/usr/local/bin/perl
print "Location: http://www.alternative.edu/different.html\n\n";
```

The server will parse this incomplete header (which must be followed, as ever, by a blank line) and will add an initial status code as well as other response headers before sending it on to the client browser.

When it receives this reply, the browser should not display it but should immediately send out a request for the new URL given in the Location header. If everything works correctly, the browser will load the new document without your CGI program's own URL even going into the browser's history of links. (Consequently, the user can't "go back" to it.) To accommodate browsers that don't support automatic redirection, however, most servers also send a short HTML document that contains an explanation and a link to the new URL, which the user can then click on manually. Thus the whole reply sent from such a program would typically look like the one given in Listing 5.1.

As you can see in Listing 5.1, the server sends the status code 302 ("Document Found") as part of a complete set of headers and follows that with a message that includes the link. In fact, the whole reply is exactly the same as if the server had found the other URL by itself, without invoking any CGI program. (Servers typically "find" documents and return a 302 status header when the original URL is missing a trailing **/** or file extension; most can also be configured to automatically redirect requests for specific documents or directories.) With CGI-based redirection, however, you have much greater control over the whole process. When you use CGI, it's easy to make your script send different URLs depending on the client's browser type, the (authenticated) user's identity, or any other available information. Moreover, these URLs can reference other CGI programs or information gateways and can include extra path information and/or query strings. The following examples are just a few of the many possibilities.

---

**LISTING 5.1    A typical redirection response from a Web server**

---

```
HTTP/1.0 302 Found
Server: CERN/3.0A
Date: Sat, 31 Aug 1996 02:08:45 GMT
Location: http://www.alternative.edu/different.html
Content-Type: text/html
Content-Length: 359


<HTML>
<HEAD>
<TITLE>Redirection</TITLE>
</HEAD>
<BODY>
<H1>Redirection</H1>
This document can be found
<A HREF="http://www.alternative.edu/different.html">elsewhere.</A><P>
You see this message because your browser doesn't support automatic
redirection handling. <P>
<HR>
<ADDRESS><A HREF="http://www.site.dom">CERN-HTTPD 3.0A</A></ADDRESS>
</BODY>
</HTML>
```

## Example 5A: Different Pages for Different Browsers

The script in Listing 5.2 redirects any client browser that requests it to one of three different documents, depending on the kind of browser that made the request. The script simply copies the browser information from the environment variable HTTP_USER_AGENT into the string **$browser** and then searches this string for substrings known to distinguish Microsoft Internet Explorer and Netscape Navigator from all other types of browsers. As soon as **$browser** matches one of the expressions (which are contained between forward slashes), the script sends the appropriate Location header and exits.

Depending on your server's configuration, you may be able to place this script and the documents it refers to in their own directory, name the script index.cgi, and then just give out the URL of this directory. Of course, you can put the script

---

**LISTING 5.2    A script that redirects a request based on the browser type**

```perl
#!/usr/local/bin/perl
# Name this script mydoc.cgi or mydoc/index.cgi

$browser = $ENV{'HTTP_USER_AGENT'};

if      ($browser =~ /Explorer/) {
  print "Location: mydoc-floating-frames.html\n\n";
} elsif ($browser =~ /Mozilla/) {
  print "Location: mydoc-netscape-frames.html\n\n";
} else {
  print "Location: mydoc-no-frames.html\n\n";
}
```

---

anywhere you need to, as long as the relative URLs are correct. The main advantage of using a script like this is that different browsers can request the same URL and yet get the document appropriate to their type.

Redirection can thus be used to serve up multiple versions of the same document, each one taking advantage of features specific to a particular browser or platform. For instance, only Internet Explorer currently supports free-floating frames, and the Microsoft method of encoding such frames makes no provision for other browsers to display their contents. Netscape introduced frames in such a way that non-frame-parsing browsers should still be able to view the default content (in other words, whatever the author puts between the NOFRAMES tags) of frame-bearing pages, but it is often more convenient to place the default content in a separate page and use that as the source for one of the frames. The script in Listing 5.2 shows an efficient way to implement multiple, client-dependent versions of a document, each with its own unique URL. All of the versions can be obtained through one common URL, but if you use redirection you can also allow each to be accessed via its own unique URL.

## Example 5B: Redirection Using Extra Path Information and Query Strings

You can also redirect input from one CGI script to another based on the input, the origin of the request, or other factors. In this way you can divide the labor among different scripts or even different machines.

The script bowdlerize.cgi, shown in Listing 5.3, redirects each incoming request to one of four more specialized scripts—bowdlerize_audio, bowdlerize_image, and so on—based on extra path information. It also ensures that every request it redirects includes a rating assignment as part of the query string. If there is no query string, it creates a new one. And if the request originates from a host outside of the Internet domains 128.52 or 18., the script sets this rating to G by appending this new specification to the existing query string. (Presumably, the last rating prevails.) Finally, the name of the specialty script, the original extra path information, and the possibly modified query string are put back together and issued as the URL in a Location header.

**LISTING 5.3    The bowdlerize CGI script, which acts as a front end to other CGI programs**

```perl
#!/usr/local/bin/perl
# /cgi-bin/bowdlerize - a front end for dividing up labor based on input


$extra = $ENV{'PATH_INFO'};


if    ($extra =~ m!^/(audio)/!) { $media = $1; }
elsif ($extra =~ m!^/(image)/!) { $media = $1; }
elsif ($extra =~ m!^/(movie)/!) { $media = $1; }
else                            { $media = 'text'; }


# The above statement is equivalent to:
# ($media) = ($extra =~ m!^/(audio|image|movie)/!) || 'text';


if ( ! ($query  =  $ENV{'QUERY_STRING'})) {
        $query  =  'rating=PG-13';
} elsif ($query !~  /rating=[^&]+/) {
        $query .= '&rating=R-18';
}


if ($ENV{'REMOTE_ADDR'} !~ /^(128\.52|18\.)/) {
    $query .= '&rating=G';
}


print "Location: /cgi-bin/bowdlerize_$media$extra?$query\n\n";
```

For example, if the incoming request header is

```
GET /cgi-bin/bowdlerize/movie/pasolini/100days.avi?mode=derez HTTP/1.0
```

from remote host 128.52.40.148, the script's output will be

```
Location: /cgi-bin/bowdlerize_movie/movie/pasolini/¬
100days.avi?mode=derez&rating=PG-13
```

This redirects the client to request a different CGI program on the same server, with the same extra path information but with an altered query string.

## How the Script Works

Gaining an understanding of how /cgi-bin/bowdlerize works in detail is largely an exercise in regular expression matching and logical negation. For a definition of regular expressions and a tutorial on using Perl's **m//** and **s///** operators, see Appendix A. The following explanation assumes that you have at least a basic understanding of how to use regular expressions.

### Using Regular Expression Matching to Pull a Substring Out of the Extra Path Information   In the example above, the request header includes the extra path information

```
/movie/pasolini/100days.avi
```

which matches the regular expression **^/(movie)/** in the **m**-operator construct

```
m!^/(movie)/!
```

Here the exclamation points are not part of the search pattern but are used only to delimit it. Regular expressions are usually delimited by forward slashes (as in **/pattern/**), in which case the initial **m** is optional. If you include the optional **m**, however, you can delimit the pattern with any pair of identical non-alphanumeric characters. A pair of exclamation points is often a good choice for delimiting pathnames, because it avoids any confusion about slashes and because the exclamation point has no special meaning inside regular expressions.

In this example, then, the regular expression proper is **^/(movie)/**, where the caret or "hat" symbol (**^**) represents the very beginning of a string and the forward slashes are not delimiters but literal characters to be matched.

The parentheses specify which parts of a matching string Perl should "remember" for later use. Perl "remembers" by placing any substring that matches the first parenthetical subexpression in the special variable **$1**, any substring that matches the second in **$2**, and so on. In this case, there is only one subexpression in parentheses, namely, the literal string **movie.** If **$extra** matches this expression, **$1** must be assigned the value **movie**, since no other match is possible. The whole line

```
elsif ($extra =~ m!^/(movie)/!) { $media = $1; }
```

is thus equivalent to the more elementary rendering

```
elsif ($extra =~ m/^\/movie\//) { $media = 'movie'; }
```

If **$extra** matches the pattern, the value of **$media** becomes **movie**. Other possible values for the extra path information are tested similarly, and if none of the patterns match, **$media** is assigned the value **text** as a default.

If you use the single regular expression **audio|image|movie** to match any of the three alternatives, you can replace the three branches of the if-else statement with only one, as in

```
if ($extra =~ m!^/(audio|image|movie)/!) { $media = $1; }
else                                     { $media = 'text'; }
```

In a scalar context, an expression such as **($extra =~ m!^/(audio|image| movie)/!)** evaluates to the scalar value true or false (**1** or **''**), but in an array context, it evaluates to the list of substrings that match the parenthesized subexpressions in the pattern. In the following statement, an array context is created by placing parentheses around **$media**; this makes it into a list containing one element. Thus

```
($media) = ($extra =~ m!^/(audio|image|movie)/!);
```

is equivalent to

```
$extra =~ m!^/(audio|image|movie)/!; $media = $1;
```

and the above if-else statement is equivalent to

```
$media = 'text' unless (($media) = ($extra =~¬
m!^/(audio|image|movie)/!));
```

But this can be written more succinctly as

```
($media) = ($extra =~ m!^/(audio|image|movie)/!) || 'text';
```

Here the II symbol is the "logical OR" operator. The value of an expression such as **A II B** is **A** if **A** is true, otherwise it is **B**; the **B** part is evaluated only if **A** evaluates as false (0). Thus you can read an expression such as **A II B** as "*A* or *B*," in the sense of "Give me liberty or give me death!" It really means "unless *A, B*." In this particular case, the right-hand side of the assignment evaluates to **audio**, **image**, or **movie** if **$extra** matches one of the alternatives in the regular expression; otherwise it evaluates to **text**.

**Regular Expression Matching and Logical Negation**   Next the script checks the query string to make sure that it includes a rating—that is, a substring of the form **rating=*something***. If a request comes in with no query string at all, the script creates a new one, namely **rating=PG-13**, as shown here:

```
if ( !  ($query  =  $ENV{'QUERY_STRING'})) {
        $query  =  'rating=PG-13';
}
```

The exclamation point in the construct above signifies logical negation, so that the whole expression

```
(! ($query = $ENV{'QUERY_STRING'}))
```

evaluates as true if and only if

```
($query = $ENV{'QUERY_STRING'})
```

is false—in other words, if the result of the assignment is that **$query** contains the empty string. Otherwise, **$query** is not empty, so the code searches it for a rating. If none is found, the script appends a new one (following an ampersand as separator, of course), as shown here:

```
elsif ($query !~  /rating=[^&]+/) {
        $query .= '&rating=R-18';
}
```

Here the exclamation point again denotes negation; the symbol **!~** is the opposite of **=~**, so

```
($query !~ /rating=[^&]+/)
```

evaluates as true if and only if the string in **$query** does *not* match the pattern in **/rating=[^&]+/**.

But what kind of rating would look like **[^&]+**? In regular expressions, square brackets are used to enclose a list of characters, any one of which can match a single character in the string being searched. Thus **[?=&]** would match exactly one instance of **?**, **=**, or **&**. If the first character in the list is the caret (**^**), however, this entire list is negated. Thus **[^?=&]** will match any single character *except for* **?**, **=**, and **&**. A plus sign appended right after the closing bracket is a quantifier; it means that the character or grouped object preceding it in the pattern must match one or more instances in the search string. (By way of contrast, the quantifier **\*** matches zero or more instances.) Thus **[?=&]+** would match any non-empty string composed entirely of the three characters inside the brackets.

In Example 5B, with **^** negating the single character **&** in the list, the **[^&]+** matches any string of one or more characters *up to but excluding* the first **&**. Thus the whole expression **/rating=[^&]+/** will match **rating=R18**, for instance, but it won't match **rating=** by itself or **rating=&mode=blackbox**, neither of which specifies a value for the rating. Finally, the negative pattern-binding operator **!~** negates the whole thing, so

```
($query !~  /rating=[^&]+/)
```

is true exactly in those cases in which the query string contains no rating. To such query strings, including the one in the original request, **mode=derez**, the script appends **&rating=R-18**.

At this point you know that the query string contains a rating, and you're assuming that the last rating in the string will prevail. So to effectively change the rating, all you have to do is append a new one. That's exactly what the program does next if the client browser's host lies outside the Internet domains 128.52 and 18 (which happen to belong to the Massachusetts Institute of Technology). To accomplish this, the program checks the IP address in the environment variable REMOTE_ADDR against the regular expression **/^(128\.52|18\.)/**, where the caret again represents the beginning of a string, the vertical bar separates alternative match patterns, and the parentheses group these alternatives together as one subexpression:

```
if ($ENV{'REMOTE_ADDR'} !~ /^(128\.52|18\.)/) {
    $query .= '&rating=G';
}
```

In the event of a match, **$1** would be set to 128.52 or 18., but the remainder of the script doesn't use it for anything; the parentheses are just there to make the whole expression a little easier to read and edit than **/^128\.52|^18\./**. The net effect is that any queries from outside of MIT's domains get (re)assigned a rating of G.

Finally, the script outputs a single string in which the values of **$media**, **$extra**, and **$query** are interpolated into the URL in a Location header. What will bowdlerize_movie do with the extra path information **/movie/pasolini/100days.avi** and the query string **mode=derez&rating=PG-13**? I imagine it will output a movie by Pier Pasolini in which the resolution in certain parts of certain frames has been sufficiently degraded for the whole to merit a rating of PG-13. Its actual implementation is left as an exercise for the reader.

# Sending Static Files

The second major type of CGI output this chapter discusses is the sending of static files to a browser. In this section, you'll learn how to send different types of static files to clients.

## Other Content Types, Other Headers

Outputting content other than HTML code or plain text is almost as easy as outputting the proper HTTP headers. To output a GIF image, for instance, all you have to do is print **"Content-type: image/gif"**, a blank line, and then the contents of a GIF file. To send a previously saved image, you can even use a backticked external command such as the Unix **cat** command or the DOS **type** command, as in this one-liner:

```
print "Content-type: image/gif\n\n", `cat my_image.gif`;
```

HTTP sends data as a binary stream, so there's no special encoding or anything else you have to do to the contents of a file before you print it to STDOUT. You can just send it down the wire as is. The most straightforward way to send the contents of a particular GIF image file in Perl is shown here:

```
#!/usr/local/bin/perl
print "Content-type: image/gif\n\n";
open ( IMAGE, "my_image.gif" );
print <IMAGE>;
```

The **open** function opens the file my_image.gif for reading and assigns it a filehandle called **IMAGE**. Then the special input symbol **<IMAGE>**, formed by enclosing the name of the filehandle in angle brackets, tells Perl to read in every line in the file as the list of arguments for the print function.

You can do the same thing with a JPEG image, a Wave audio clip, or any other kind of file. Just be sure to start with the right content-type header (image/jpeg, audio/x-wav, and so on). One fast way to find the right MIME type for a file is to look in the preferences window for your browser's helper applications. Another way is to look at the headers sent by your favorite Web server in reply to an ordinary

HTTP GET request for that kind of file. (For instance, use **telnet**, as shown in Chapter 1.)

## How to Send a Header that Specifies the Correct Content Length

While downloading a document, most browsers indicate the document's size and the percentage already received in a status line. But how does a browser know how big a file is before it has finished downloading it? Also, instead of retrieving a remote document from the Web, a browser will sometimes only reload a locally cached copy. How does it decide when to request a new copy instead of reloading the locally cached copy?

If you look at the headers that Web servers send in advance of the static files they serve, you'll see the answers to both questions. Most servers send out a content-length header, which specifies the size in bytes of the document that follows, and they also often include a last-modified header. Many also send out a header of the form Expires: *date*. Browsers routinely use this information to provide feedback to users and to decide whether and when to (re)retrieve documents. All three types of headers are shown in Listing 5.4 (note the various dates).

Servers make system calls to get this information about static files, but when the output to be relayed to a client is coming from your CGI program, the server has no way of knowing in advance how long it will be. (In other words, servers don't usually save your CGI output to a file, compute its size, and then send it to the client; they avoid such overhead by streaming it right through.) Out of consideration for your users, then, you should make sure that your scripts output such headers themselves.

Actually, you needn't worry much about the last-modified or expires headers because both servers and browsers should handle a CGI program as if it always output a new document. Some servers automatically add an Expires: *date* header to the output of a CGI program, where *date* is the date and time when the output begins.

Outputting a content-length header that specifies the right number of bytes, however, can help ensure that the browser will correctly receive the file. It's not always strictly necessary, but in general, it's the right thing to do.

**LISTING 5.4    A full HTTP header sent by a Web server**

```
HTTP/1.1 200 OK
Date: Fri, 18 Oct 1996 20:46:34 GMT
Server: Apache/1.2
Connection: close
Content-type: image/gif
Content-length: 4367
Expires: Fri, 18 Oct 1996 20:46:34 GMT
Last-Modified: Tue, 28 May 1996 21:09:31 GMT
```

**Using File Test Operators to Get the Size of a File**  The easy way to get the size of a file in Perl is to use the *file test operator* **-s**, as in

```
$size = (-s filename);
```

Another useful operator is **-r**, which returns **1** if the file is readable by the process running your script and **0** if it is not. In the same way, the operators **-e**, **-w**, **-x**, and **-T** respectively test whether a file exists, whether it is writable, whether it is executable, and whether it is a plain text file. Thus an easy way to output the right content-length header is like this:

```
print "Content-length: ", (-s "my_image.gif"), "\n\n";
```

The hard way find out a file's size is to use Perl's **stat** function, which returns a 13-element array of numbers that represent the usual Unix-style statistics for a named file or filehandle, as in

```
($device, $inode, $mode, $links, $userid, $groupid, $rdev,
 $size, $acctime, $modtime, $creatime, $blksize, $blocks)
= stat($filename);
```

I include this here because when you are looking at Perl scripts from the Unix world, you'll quite often run into a line such as

```
$bytes_in_file = (stat($filename))[7];
```

which extracts the file's size as the eighth element in the array returned by **stat**. An even more cryptic piece of code you could encounter looks something like this:

```
require "stat.pl";  # library module included at beginning
@file_statistics = &Stat($filename);
$file_size = $file_statistics[$st_size];  # Calling Stat creates
$fmod_time = $file_statistics[$st_mtime]; # ref vars $st_size, etc.
```

The capitalized version **Stat**, defined in the library file stat.pl, returns the same 13-element array and also defines the offset variables **$st_size**, **$st_mtime**, and so forth, for referencing the elements of this array.

You'll encounter the **stat** function again in later chapters, because it can be very useful for seeing exactly when a file was created, last accessed, or last modified. File test operations such as **-M**, which returns the number of days between the date of a file's last modification and the date the current script started up, are less precise. And besides, when you use any file test operator, Perl actually performs the equivalent of the Unix system call **stat**, obtaining all the statistics above whether you need them or not. The good news is that Perl automatically stores these statistics until they are replaced by the next file test (or the next call of a **stat** function). To access this saved information without incurring the overhead of another system call, you can test (or **stat**) the special filehandle that consists of a solitary underscore character, as in

```
if (-r $file && -w _) { print "$file is readable and writeable\n"; }
```

where the _ in the conditional refers to **$file** because it was just tested. Here's another example:

```
if (-T $file) { @file_statistics = stat(_); }
else {   print "$file is not a plain text file!\n"); }
```

Here the **-T** test causes Perl to **stat** the file as a side effect, and then it goes beyond that information and actually examines the file's contents for non-ASCII characters. When used in this way, **-T** can distinguish a text file from practically any image or other binary file, even when the operating system (and thus **stat**) does not.

To send a GIF image complete with the right headers, then, you could use a script such as the one in Listing 5.5. This script is of no practical use as a CGI program, because a request for its URL would give basically the same result as a request for the URL of the image it's hardwired to send. Still, it can give you a good starting point for writing other scripts, and it can be useful for showing you what's going on.

If you request the URL of this script by itself, the image my_image.gif will be displayed in its own window (either by a helper application or on a blank page, depending on your browser). And if this URL appears in the SRC attribute of an IMG tag, the file this script sends will appear as an inline image—unless, of course, it can't find the file or the file is unreadable.

**Returning an Error Code**   If the file is not found or is unreadable, the script outputs a 404 or 403 status code in order to be totally HTTP-compliant, just as a server does in such situations. Normally you won't worry so much about sending error codes, but this example shows you how to do it when the server won't do it for you. (A 404 code sent directly from the server in this case would not mean that it couldn't find my_image.gif, but rather that it couldn't find sendagif.cgi.)

Finally, if all else fails, the script outputs status code 500 with a comment about what happened. This comment would be recorded in the server's log file but would probably never be seen. Formally, code 500 is meant to mark a server "internal error," but it's used as a kind catch-all. For example, if this script were to output

**LISTING 5.5    The sendagif.cgi script, which is hardwired to send a particular GIF image file**

```perl
#!/usr/local/bin/perl
# sendagif.cgi  —  requesting the URL of this script is
# almost the same as requesting the URL of my_image.gif

print "Content-type: image/gif\n";
$Image = 'my_image.gif';

if (open(Image, $Image)) {
  $size = ( -s  $Image);
  print "Content-length: $size\n\n";
  print <Image>;
  close (Image);
} elsif (! (-e $Image)) {
  print "Status: 404 Not Found\n\n";
} elsif (! (-r _)) {                      # _ refers to $Image
  print "Status: 403 Forbidden\n\n";
} else {
  print "Status: 500 CGI Error reading $Image\n\n";
}
```

nothing at all, not even the image/gif header, the server would send a code 500 status header and the message "Content-type: application/x-httpd-cgi."

## Example 5C: A Subroutine for Sending Image Files

Sending a file as an HTTP document is a common task in CGI programming, and the details vary little from file to file. Therefore, it's convenient to generalize the code and to wrap it up in a subroutine such as **sendFile** (see Listing 5.6). The main body of **sendFile** is similar to that of the sendagif.cgi script shown in Listing 5.5. The most significant difference is that **sendFile** can send different kinds of files and thus different MIME content-type headers. Since **sendFile** outputs a content-type header only upon successfully opening the file, it doesn't concern itself with outputting any 400-series HTTP status codes for file access errors. Instead, it reports problems locally, using some of Perl's internal error-handling mechanisms and the **die** routine.

**LISTING 5.6** **The sendFile.pl script, which is a library file that contains the definition of** sendFile

```
# sendFile.pl - a program that defines a library routine for sending a file¬
through CGI

sub sendFile {
  die("$0: sendFile called w/o File\n") unless my $File = $_[0];
  die("$0: sendFile called on $File, no type\n") unless my $type = $_[1];
  my $size = 0;
  if ( open( File, $File)) {
    $size = (  -s  $File);
    print "Content-type: $type\n";
    print "Content-length: $size\n\n";
    print <File>;
    close (File);
  } else {
    print "Status: 500 CGI Error\n\n";
    die("$0: sendFile died on file \"$File\" (", (0+$!), " - $!)\n");
  }
  $size;    # return size of $file or 0 (if still alive)
}


1; # This statement is here to make "require 'sendFile.pl';" work
```

The **sendFile** function expects two arguments, a filename and a MIME type for the named file. If it doesn't get both arguments, it calls **die** to output an error message and terminate the script's execution.

`Fatal Errors and Dying Gasps: die and $!` Perl's **die** routine never returns. It prints all its arguments to the special filehandle STDERR and then calls **exit** with a system error number (the current value of **$!**) or a backticked `` `command` `` status number (the current value of **$?**). When Perl encounters an error while evaluating a system call (usually inside one of its own built-in or library functions), you can usually check the value of the special variable **$!** to find out what happened. In a numerical context, **$!** evaluates to the number of the error; in a string context, it evaluates to an error message. To see both, you could use

```
print STDERR "Errno: ", (0 + $!), " Errmsg: $!\n";
```

System calls are typically used to open, read, write, and close files. They are not the same as Perl's functions of the same names, but they underlie them, at least on a Unix system. However, since the value of **$!** is not set unless a system error has actually occurred, you should not depend on the value of **$!** unless a function that relies on system calls has already returned an error value. In other words, **$!** can be used only to diagnose an error after the fact, not to determine whether a file operation succeeded or failed. Thus

```
die("$0: Error opening file $File: $!\n") unless open(FILE,$File);
```

is a useful statement, whereas the following construct may call **die** even when the **open** succeeds:

```
$! = 0;     # A misguided attempt to clear $! beforehand
$returnValue = open(FILE, $File);
if ($!) {  # Depending on $! by itself is always a mistake!
  die("$0: open($File) returned $returnValue, error: $!\n");
}
```

The major mistake here is that this code tests **$!** instead of **$returnValue.** You don't want to do this, because some implementations of Perl's **open** function change **$!** even when there is no error.

Furthermore, calling your own subroutine with the wrong arguments is not an error that **$!** can diagnose for you. In such cases, your own error messages should give you enough information to track down the problem. Outputting fatal error messages with **die** is often more useful than simply calling **print** and/or **exit**. If **die**'s last argument does not end in a newline (**\n**), Perl appends the filename and line number where **die** was called in your script, as well as the current input line number (if any). In the case of a library routine such as **sendFile**, however, the filename and script line number refer to the library file, not the calling script file. Your own error messages can and should be more helpful than that, especially if you begin them with the special variable **$0**, which is always set to the name of the currently executing script.

## Using warn **instead of** die

You can use **warn** in exactly the same way as **die** to output messages to STDERR without aborting execution.

The only difference is that **warn** does not call **exit** when it finishes outputting the message.

### Redirecting Diagnostic Output from STDERR to STDOUT or to a File

Output to STDERR can be redirected independently from output to STDOUT, and in the context of CGI, it's usually appended to one of the Web server's log files. Thus it is generally safe to print diagnostic messages to STDERR that you don't want Web users to see. The problem might be getting to see them yourself.

On Unix Web servers, the logs quite often are world-readable, which means that you can view your error messages if you have a shell or an FTP account. On other kinds of servers, viewing your own diagnostic output might not be so easy. Although many service providers will e-mail your logs to you if you ask, that is not exactly real-time feedback.

A useful alternative when you are debugging a script is to redirect all of the output that would normally go to STDERR so that it instead goes to STDOUT (and thus to the Web client) or to your own log file. To redirect output from STDERR to STDOUT, use

```
open(STDERR,">STDOUT");
```

This **open** statement closes the previously opened filehandle identified by STDERR and opens a new one that sends its output to the filehandle currently identified as STDOUT. In effect, STDERR is merged with STDOUT.

The following code fragment saves the filehandle currently pointing at STDERR, temporarily redirects STDERR's output to a file, and then restores the original STDERR:

```
$myBad = "/home/me/private/myBad.txt";
open(SAVERR, ">&STDERR") || print "Error saving STDERR: $!"\n;
open(STDERR, ">>$myBad") || print "Error opening myBad: $!"\n;
print STDERR "STDERR here... "; warn "Are you there, $myBad?\n";
open(STDERR, ">&SAVERR") || print "Error restoring STDERR: $!\n";
```

The ampersand in **>&** tells **open** to create SAVERR as a duplicate filehandle for STDERR. The original filehandle is closed when the identifier STDERR is reused in the next call to **open**. After this second call to **open**, STDERR points to the file named by $myBad, but SAVERR still points to the original STDOUT. To restore it, the program opens STDERR again, this time as a duplicate of SAVERR, and this last **open** simultaneously closes $myBad.

### Example 5D: A One-Armed Bandit

A more practical example of using CGI to send inline images, the one_arm.cgi script in Listing 5.7 implements a simple one-armed bandit (shown in Figure 5.1).

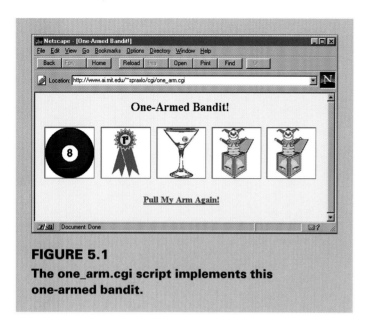

**FIGURE 5.1**
The one_arm.cgi script implements this one-armed bandit.

This script behaves like two different programs that share the same URL: One program executes when the script is called with a query string, and the other executes when it is called without a query string.

## Calling one_arm.cgi with a Query String: Seeding the Random Number Generator

When called with a query string, one_arm.cgi randomly draws a filename from an array called **@files** and then calls the subroutine

---

**LISTING 5.7    The one_arm.cgi script, which implements an electronic one-armed bandit, sans coin slot**

```perl
#!/usr/local/bin/perl5
# one_arm.cgi - implements a simple one-armed bandit, sans coin-slot
# Copyright 1996 by Stephen Lines (spraxlo@ai.mit.edu)
require "sendFile.pl";

############# If called with query string, output an image from @files:

if ($query = $ENV{'QUERY_STRING'}) {

    my @files = qw( 8ball.jpg apple.jpg cherries.jpg grapes.jpg
                    jacknbox.jpg lemon.jpg martini.jpg orange.jpg
                    ribbon1.jpg sponge.jpg tomatoes.jpg );
    my $seed = $$;
    $seed = $1 if ($query =~ /(\d+)/);
    $seed = $seed + rand(time|$$);
    srand($seed);
    my $image = $files[rand(@files)];
    sendFile("icons/$image", "image/jpeg");
    exit 0;
}
```

**LISTING 5.7**    **The one_arm.cgi script, which implements an electronic one-armed bandit, sans coin slot (Continued)**

```perl
############ No query string, so output the page:

print "Content-type: text/html\n";
print "Pragma: no-cache\n\n";

print <<EOF;
<HTML><HEAD><TITLE> One-Armed Bandit! </TITLE></HEAD>
<BODY BGCOLOR="beige"><CENTER>
<H2> One-Armed Bandit! </H2><B>
<TABLE CELLSPACING="5">
<TR ALIGN=MIDDLE>
EOF

## $ENV{'SCRIPT_NAME'} = '/cgi-bin/one_arm.cgi'; # <- for testing only
my $selfURL = $ENV{'SCRIPT_NAME'};
my $seed = rand(time|$$);
srand($seed);

for (1..5) {
  $seed = rand(time);
  print <<ENDFOR;
<TD>
<A  HREF="$selfURL">
<IMG SRC="$selfURL?$seed"></A>
</TD>
ENDFOR
}

print <<EOF;
</TR></TABLE>
<H3><A HREF="$selfURL">Pull My Arm Again!</A></H3>
</CENTER></BODY></HTML>
EOF
exit 0;
```

**sendFile** to send the chosen file. In this case, the script acts as little more than a wrapper for automating calls to **sendFile**: The script supplies the filenames and then **sendFile** does all the work. The only trick is to try to make sure that the drawing really is random by seeding Perl's random number generator with an unpredictable number.

The first thing the script does is search the query string for a number using the regular expression **/(\d+)/**, where **\d** matches a digit. If a number is found, the script doesn't wholly trust it to use as is but combines it with its own system process number (**$$**) and the current time (the number of seconds since midnight, December 31, 1970, as returned by Perl's built-in function **time**). Only then does it seed the random number generator, by feeding the resulting number to **srand**. The **rand** function itself returns a (more-or-less) random fractional number between 0 and the value of its argument. To pick an item from an array, you need any whole number from 0 up to the last index in the array, namely **$#files**, which is 1 less than the number of elements it contains. But in a numerical context, the name of the array itself, **@files**, evaluates to the number of elements it contains, and in the integer context (the context in which arrays are indexed), the fractional number returned by **rand** will be truncated to a whole number value.

Thus, assuming that **rand** has been properly seeded, the statement

```
my $image = $files[rand(@files)];
```

will give you exactly what you want, a random element from **@files**.

**Calling one_arm.cgi without a Query String**   When called without a query string, on the other hand, this script outputs an HTML page that displays a row of five inline images as the elements in a table. Listing 5.8 shows the complete output.

Whence come these images? From the same script called with a query string, of course. The source of each image is given by the SRC=*URL* attribute inside its IMG tag. In this case it just so happens that all five URLs are the same as that of the page surrounding them, albeit with five different embedded query strings, such as

```
<IMG SRC=/cgi-bin/one_arm.cgi?714010452.3836749</A>
```

These query strings are just random numbers that the script generates and appends to its own relative URL, as given by the environment variable SCRIPT_NAME. When a browser downloads the generated page, it automatically issues five requests to one_arm.cgi in order to retrieve the content specified by these IMG tags. As explained above, these query strings do not uniquely determine which image

**LISTING 5.8   The output of one_arm.cgi as it appears when it is called with no query string**

```
HTTP/1.0 200 OK
Date: Thu, 05 Sep 1996 14:45:07 GMT
Server: Apache/1.2-dev RSThreads/0.1
Content-type: text/html
Pragma: no-cache

<HTML><HEAD><TITLE> One-Armed Bandit! </TITLE></HEAD>
<BODY BGCOLOR="beige">
<CENTER>
<H2> One-Armed Bandit! </H2><B>
<TABLE CELLSPACING="5">
<TR ALIGN=MIDDLE>
<TD>
<A  HREF=/cgi-bin/one_arm.cgi>
<IMG SRC=/cgi-bin/one_arm.cgi?714010452.3836749</A>
</TD>
<TD>
<A  HREF=/cgi-bin/one_arm.cgi>
<IMG SRC=/cgi-bin/one_arm.cgi?759619239.38941491</A>
</TD>
<TD>
<A  HREF=/cgi-bin/one_arm.cgi>
<IMG SRC=/cgi-bin/one_arm.cgi?98919272.714563325</A>
</TD>
<TD>
<A  HREF=/cgi-bin/one_arm.cgi>
<IMG SRC=/cgi-bin/one_arm.cgi?39156038.718735546</A>
</TD>
<TD>
<A  HREF=/cgi-bin/one_arm.cgi>
<IMG SRC=/cgi-bin/one_arm.cgi?142968595.03362611</A>
</TD>
</TR></TABLE>
<H3><A HREF=/cgi-bin/one_arm.cgi> Pull My Arm Again! </A>
</B></CENTER>
</BODY></HTML>
```

will be sent; they only help seed the random number generator. All of this makes it fairly difficult for a user to cheat, since the actual names of the image files are never sent and the files effectively all share the same URL.

On the other hand, judging when a user has won (when the same image appears in all five windows) is a different problem! The only place where this information actually exists is in the loaded page itself, on the user's screen and not in the page's HTML source. (Reloading the same source file should produce a different page.) But if there are ten images to draw from, the theoretical chance of winning is one in 10,000, so let's not sweat it just yet!

Sending out random numbers only to get them back again as query strings is thus a compromise between calling the script with no input information, which may make it hard to keep the random number generator from repeating itself, and calling it with too much information, which might let the user gain control over the outcome. The script embeds query strings in its output pages like this to save some information about its own history. Otherwise, it would have to handle each new request by starting from scratch. To take this script one step further, you could encrypt these random numbers in such a way as to be able to tell later whether they really came from a previous call to this script. I'll explain some other methods for saving state in Chapter 7.

### Example 5E: CGI Animation Using Server Push

A request for a single URL generally retrieves a single document, but with the *server push* mechanism the server can send multiple documents in succession, each separated by a common, preset boundary string. You might have noticed such boundaries when reading your e-mail; the protocol is similar to that used when multipart MIME messages are attached to an e-mail message. The difference is that with server push the succeeding documents are not appended onto one message; instead, each new document entirely replaces the preceding one. This mechanism lets you animate inline images or, in theory, any combination of HTTP-transportable documents. It certainly works with sounds and plain or HTML text, if you're willing to stretch the meaning of "animation" to fit such cases.

To use server push from a CGI script, all you have to do is send a MIME-type header such as

```
Content-type: multipart/x-mixed-replace;boundary=BOUNDARY
```

where *BOUNDARY* is an arbitrary ASCII string you'll combine with hyphens to form your own document separator. Here's how it works: Before each document, you send the string **--*BOUNDARY*** on a line by itself, followed immediately by the appropriate HTTP headers for that particular document. After the last document, you can send *--BOUNDARY--* to let the client browser know you're finished. (In some cases you might want to omit this final boundary string, to make sure that the last document remains on display and does not disappear.)

The nph-animate.cgi script (see Listing 5.9) illustrates this mechanism and also provides another example of sending the contents of files rather than their URLs.

This program sends all the files listed in **@files** one or more times, using nested **for** loops. (Recall that **for** and **foreach** are actually synonyms; the first form in nph-animate.cgi implicitly uses **$_** as its index variable.) Here's the code:

```
for (1..$loops) {
  foreach $file (@files) {
    print "\r\n-$bound\r\n";  # Output separator before each part
    sendFile($dir.$file, $type);
    sleep($delay) if $delay;
  }
}
```

The body of the inner loop sends the proper separator formed from the string in **$bound,** and then it calls **sendFile** to send the content-type and content-length headers as well as the contents of the file represented by **$dir.$file**. The dot operator (**.**) concatenates the strings in **$dir** and **$file** (so unless **$dir** is the empty string, it should end with a slash or, on Windows, possibly a double backslash). The outer loop controls the number of times the script sends the entire sequence in **@files**.

It would be fairly easy to convert this code into a subroutine, but since the bulk of the script is concerned only with configuration issues, as explained in its comments, it would probably not be worth the trouble. You would either be stuck using the same parameters every time or you'd have to pass all the configuration parameters to the subroutine as arguments. Here they're all set up and explained in one place. Only the name of the script, nph-animate.cgi, is a little overly abstract. The best way to create animations of different images or sounds, then, is to edit copies of this script and name them after their contents. The names should always begin with **nph-** unless you also comment out the non-parsed-header status line

```
print "HTTP/1.0 200 OK\r\n";
```

The particular instance of the script shown in Listing 5.9 sends a number of GIF icons that are distributed with some versions of the Apache Web server software. (Other servers come with other icons.) It sets STDOUT to "binary" data transfer

**LISTING 5.9** **The nph-animate.cgi script, a modifiable script for animating images, sounds, or whole pages**

```perl
#!/usr/local/bin/perl
# nph-animate.cgi - a program that animates a list of image (or other) files
# Animate inline images using <IMG SRC="nph-animate.cgi">
# or change the script and use <A HREF="nph-animate.cgi">sounds</A>
# to send a series of sounds — you might want to set $delay > 0

require "sendFile.pl";

# Below is the list of files to animate; they must all be
# of the same type, e.g. image/gif. Here qw makes a quoted
# list of its literal arguments; exclude commas and comments.
@files = qw (
  broken.gif burst.gif comp1.gif comp2.gif
  compressed.gif continued.gif default.gif
  dir.gif dir2.gif forward.gif generic.gif
  generic2.gif generic3.gif image.gif image2.gif
  index.gif movie.gif sound.gif sound2.gif
  tar.gif text.gif transfer.gif unknown.gif
);                    # End of qw-quoted list of files
$type  = "image/gif"; # MIME type for files: "image/jpeg" for JPEG, etc.
$dir   = "../icons/"; # Directory for files, relative to this script
$loops = 2;           # Number of times to loop through list of files
$|     = 1;           # Unbuffer STDOUT by making $| != 0 (recommended)
$delay = 0;           # Time to wait between sending files (ymmv)
$bound = "WhAtEvEr";  # Arbitrary string to separate files (but not —)
binmode(STDOUT);      # On PCs, turns off translation of \n to \r\n
                      # Neither binmode nor \r's should affect Unix

print "HTTP/1.0 200 OK\r\n";
print "Content-type: multipart/x-mixed-replace;boundary=$bound\r\n\r\n";

for (1..$loops) {
  foreach $file (@files) {
    print "\r\n-$bound\r\n";  # Output separator before each part
```

> **LISTING 5.9** **The nph-animate.cgi script, a modifiable script for animating images, sounds, or whole pages (Continued)**
>
> ```
>     sendFile($dir.$file, $type);
>     sleep($delay) if $delay;
>   }
> }
>
>
> print "\r\n-$bound-\r\n";    # Indicates end of multipart document
> ```

mode by calling **binmode**. This is to prevent any instance of the ASCII newline character (**\n**) that appears as image data inside the GIF files from being translated into a carriage-return/newline (CRLF) combination (**\r\n**), although this usually isn't necessary even on a Windows system. (In Unix, the mode is always "binary," and the extra **\r**'s shouldn't bother any servers or browsers.) The particular value of **$bound** set in this script should be fine, as long as the string **"—WhAtEvEr"** doesn't happen to appear as a comment or data inside any of the GIF images.

Some more general tips for using nph-animate.cgi are listed here:

▶ Keep inline images small (in terms of load time). GIFs usually work better than JPEGs. Otherwise, you may need to introduce a delay between images.

▶ HTML 3 does not make any explicit provision for "inline audio," and you cannot use an IMG tag such as <IMG SRC="nph-anim-snd.cgi"> to call an audio-animating version of this script. However, some browsers support extensions to HTML that do provide for "inline" sounds. You may be able to use these and make the execution of browser-specific code depend on the value of HTTP_USER_AGENT. Or, at the cost of an extra mouse-click, you can play an "animated" sequence of sounds using a link such as <A HREF="nph-anim-snd.cgi">sounds</A>.

▶ Browsers usually call external applications in order to play sounds, and some of these are capable of playing many sounds at once. So you may (or may not) want to introduce a delay when sending a series of longish sounds.

▶ You can change **$type** to **"text/html"** and use this script to present a "slide show" of Web pages. Each page can have its own (possibly animated) inline images, hyperlinks, and so forth. Remember to set a reasonable delay, and omit the final multipart document terminator string if you don't want the final "slide" to go blank. Also, the entire slide show will end as soon as the user clicks on any link in one of the pages.

▶ Alternating HTML documents with sounds is quite possible (if you modify this script), but if you really want to show a movie and not a slide show, consider using a movie format such as Quicktime or MPEG2.

If you do want to mix different image types, or if you want to mix text with sounds, make the following two changes to a copy of nph-animate.cgi. First, change **$files** to alternate filenames with their respective file types and viewing/listening times, so that it becomes a list of triplets, as in

```
@files = qw (
    amazon01.html    text/html      7
    birdcall.aiff    audio/aiff     0
    amazon02.html    text/html      9
    mesozoic.snd     audio/basic    0
); # No commas, quotes, or comments inside qw's list
```

The **qw** operator is just a convenience device that was introduced in Perl 5. It takes a list of strings or numbers separated by white spaces (not commas) and turns it into an ordinary array.

Second, change the inner **foreach** loop to a **for** loop with explicit indices, as in

```
for ($j = 0; $j < @files; $j += 3) {
    print "\n-$bound\n";
    sendFile($dir.$files[$j], $files[$j + 1]);
    sleep $files[$j + 2] if $files[$j + 2];
}
```

This **for** loop steps through the **@files** array three entries at a time, and every third entry is treated as the MIME type for the preceding filename or the number of seconds to delay before sending the next file. (Recall that in a scalar context, **@files** stands for the number of entries in the array, and that **$j += 3** is the same as **$j = $j + 3**) To run the list forever forward and backward without repeating the endpoints, change the outer **for (1..$loop)** to **for(;;)** and then duplicate the inner loop, changing the beginning of this second inner loop to

```
for ($j = @files - 6; $j > 0; $j -= 3) {
```

If you are animating inline images rather than presenting a slide show, you might also need to use a nonzero delay when sending larger images or mixing GIFs with JPEGs. CGI was not originally designed for sending multipart documents or performing animations, so your mileage may vary. The most important thing is to experiment with your particular Web server.

# Reading, Writing, and Creating Files

# Using the GD Library to Provide Dynamic Graphical Output

# Creating a Dynamic Interface

# Chapter 6
# Creating Dynamic Documents and Interfaces

There are times when sending a saved document or a plain form is not enough. You may need to generate a graph, chart, or other graphical element that reflects changing, time-sensitive data, or you might want to replace a one-size-fits-all form with an application interface that users can customize for their own use. The previous chapter showed you how to create CGI programs to redirect requests or directly send the contents of any file. You needn't stop there, however: Any file on a computer is the output of some program, and there's nothing to say that this program couldn't be—or at least interface with—a CGI program. This chapter continues the theme of CGI output by showing you how to generate documents on-the-fly and create dynamic interfaces through CGI. In the examples presented in this chapter, you'll get to practice what you learn by making a graphical access counter, a dynamic pie chart, and a "self-modifying" interface (in other words, a user-configurable form). Along the way, I'll explain how to read and write files safely in a multiuser environment, how to run external programs from within Perl, how to redirect input and output, and how to use a simple but powerful graphics library. The examples here are probably not exactly the applications you want or need to program into your own Web pages, but the principles they illustrate are likely to prove valuable when you are creating just about any advanced CGI application.

## Reading, Writing, and Creating Files

The previous chapter presented examples that showed you how to open files and read their contents using Perl's **open** function and the angle-bracketed input symbol <FILEHANDLE>. And back in Chapter 4, you used Perl's **read** function on the special filehandle STDIN to obtain a message body posted from a form. The special filehandles STDIN, STDOUT, and STDERR are already open when a script begins execution. The examples in this section demonstrate how to read, write, and create files using these and other filehandles.

**155**

File input/output is an important part of almost any CGI application that does more than send a document. Even doing something as simple as keeping track of the number of times a certain page has been accessed requires writing that number to a file. That's because computer programs run as *processes*. When a program finishes executing, its process is destroyed, and all the memory into which its data and instructions were loaded is reclaimed by the system. Writing to a disk file is just about the only means a program has of saving information beyond the termination of its process. Later, another instance of the same program (or a different program) can recover the saved information by reading this file.

## The Problem: Sharing Files among Multiple Processes

When multiple instances of a single program (or different programs) read from and write to the same file at the same time, you've got to figure out how to coordinate them so that they share the file nondestructively. For instance, word processors typically read a file in whole or in part for editing and then rewrite the file in whole or in part when the user chooses to "save" it. If several different word processors (or several simultaneously running instances of a single word processor) happen to be editing the same file at the same time, the file on disk will usually be whichever version was last saved, regardless of whether this version is the "right" one. But it's also possible for two word processors to rewrite different parts of a document (with a "Fast Save" option, for example) or even to write to the same file at the same time. The results can range from undetectable errors to obvious gibberish or a completely unusable file. The same kind of thing can happen even to the lowly text file in which a CGI access counter stores its count.

### The Standard Solution: File Locking

The standard solution to the problem of file sharing is to use file locking. The term *file locking* means the use of any mechanism that allows one process to gain read and/or write access to a file while simultaneously shutting out all others.

One might suppose that only write access needs to be restricted—in other words, that it doesn't matter how many processes (that is, concurrently running programs) have a file open for reading, as long as only one of them is allowed to write to it. But such a scheme is a sure recipe for data loss, especially on a multitasking system that performs asynchronous (buffered) file input/output. For example, if you are always allowed to open a file for reading, regardless of whether someone else has it open for writing, how can you be sure that what you are reading or have already read is (still) the latest version? If you know that some other process has temporarily opened the file for reading and writing, one obvious strategy would be to wait for that other process to finish up and close the file, whereupon any changes made during that process would have to be saved to disk. Conversely, if you are the one whose process currently has the file open for reading and writing, one way to ensure that other users and processes get any changes you make would be to prevent them from even reading the file until you have saved your changes to disk. This would also prevent other people or processes from reading the file under the (possibly mistaken) premise that they would later be able to save their own edited versions to disk.

Most file-locking schemes allow you to do at least these three basic things: lock a file, wait for a locked file to become unlocked, and unlock a file you've locked. Many such schemes, including the one built into Perl, also distinguish between *shared* and *exclusive* locks. The shared lock and exclusive lock concepts correspond very loosely to read-only and read/write access to a file, respectively, but they are by no means the same things. The main point of holding onto a shared lock is to prevent some other process from gaining an exclusive lock (and then possibly changing the file's contents behind your back). Conversely, the main point of retaining an exclusive lock is to prevent some other process from gaining even so much as a shared lock (and then reading the file as if it were the latest version).

**Perl's Advisory File-Locking Mechanism: flock**   The file-locking mechanism built into Perl is *advisory only*, which means that a process does not gain exclusive access to a file per se but only to a systemwide lock on the file. A process is

## File Sharing and the Golden Rule, or Do Unto Other Processes...

"Where do all these processes come from," you might ask, "and why do they all want to access my files?" In the context of CGI programming, all the processes contending for access to your files are likely to be simultaneously running instances of your own CGI program(s). You are thus stuck with a kind of golden rule: Let your process do unto other processes as you would have them do unto your process. In particular, don't use any file locking or modification schemes that you wouldn't want another process to use against you. You can expect a CGI program to spend just as much time waiting for a locked file as it makes other programs wait. In the case of multiple concurrent instances of the same program, this rule becomes a tautology.

"advised" of a file's locked status only when it attempts to gain the lock for itself. At that point, the process may wait for the lock to become available or go on about its business. In fact, it might read and write the file without ever bothering to check for locks in the first place. Under advisory file locking, then, processes must cooperate. To avoid overwriting each other's changes to a file, each process must always lock the file before reading and changing its contents. Any process that does not cooperate with the advisory file-locking mechanism can still change the file at any time.

Perl's **flock** function is called like this:

```
$ret = flock(FILEHANDLE, lockmode);
```

where the value of *lockmode* is a bitwise combination (obtained using the inclusive OR) of the following four requests (which are the same as in the underlying **flock** function in C):

▶  **1**: **Obtain a shared lock**  Multiple processes can hold a shared lock simultaneously; this simply prevents another process from gaining an exclusive lock.

▶  **2**: **Obtain an exclusive lock**  Only one process can hold an exclusive lock at any given time. Any other process must wait to obtain the lock (which happens when its call to **flock** returns).

▶  **4**: **Don't block**  If the file is already locked, **flock** shouldn't wait for it but should just return **-1** and put an error message in **$!**.

## Non-Unix Workarounds for flock

Unfortunately, the **flock** function is not implemented in the current HIP Communications ports of Perl for Windows 95 or Windows NT or in MacPerl for the Macintosh. If your server is running on one of these platforms, calling **flock** will result in a fatal error. One alternative would be to comment out the calls to **flock** and hope that the operating system sorts out contentious file accesses in a sensible way on its own. Another alternative would be to use a temporary file as a semaphore, as explained later in this chapter. The best alternative would be to find a platform-specific equivalent to **flock** for your system. I'm not aware of any simple and complete workarounds for Windows 95 or MacOS, but they probably exist.

▶ **8**: **Release any locks this process holds on the file**  The system should give the lock to the next process that requests it or that is already waiting for it.

Sufficient to our purposes are the lockmode values **2** and **8**, which are used to gain an exclusive lock and release it. These can be used to guarantee that each process reads in the latest version of the file (even if it has to wait for it) and writes out any changes it makes to the file before the next process takes over.

The following example shows you how to use file locking to read and write files safely. If you don't have **flock** on your system, comment out the calls to **flock;** the method shown below will probably still be the safest way to read from and write to a text file within Perl, as least for quick changes to small files.

## Example 6A: A Plain Text Access Counter

Web page access counters can be used to display the number of times a page has been requested and to record client information in a log file. They serve two main purposes: to show users how popular a page is, and to show site administrators how popular a page is. Not all users are convinced by numbers, of course, and if you have access to your Web server's main log files, you might find them more than adequate to the second purpose. Yet there are two more reasons for installing a counter that can hardly be gainsaid: access counters are easy and fun to implement, and they promise to make your pages "cool."

The scheme behind Web page access counters is very simple. Every time the page is accessed, the counter program must

1  Read the current count from a file

2  Increment this count

3  Write the new count back into the file

When it comes to implementing this scheme, you need to make sure that you use the correct access mode to open the file. In order to handle nearly simultaneous requests from different Web clients, you should also lock the file before reading and then unlock it after writing. The number of steps this actually takes varies with the programming language and operating system. For instance, most flavors of Unix, and thus of Perl, require one function call to open a file and another to lock it. (In programming parlance, the operation of opening a file for exclusive use is not *atomic.*)

## The Problem: How Not to Implement a Counter

Here is one elementary algorithm that can be implemented in Perl:

1 Open the count file for reading.

2 Read the count from this file.

3 Close the count file.

4 Open the file again for writing. This instantly destroys all the contents of the old file.

5 Increment the count.

6 Write the incremented count into the otherwise empty count file.

7 Close the count file.

Minor variations of this algorithm drive probably the majority of access counters on the Web today, and yet the algorithm makes no provision for counting simultaneous or overlapping accesses. Some versions even add exclusive file locking and unlocking operations after steps 1 and 2, and then again after 4 and 6, but to no avail. If one instance of this program reads the count from the file and a second instance reads the file before the first has written it out again, the least that could go wrong is that the second instance will have read the same count as the first. Worse, if there is no file locking at all, the second instance may have attempted to read from an empty file (which could happen any time between the first instance's steps 4 and 6), and in this case it might have taken 0 as the current count. Either way, the instance of the program that writes its new count last prevails. At best, one access goes uncounted, and at worst, the count is started over from scratch.

The flaw in this algorithm lies in closing the file the first time before opening it again to write the incremented count to it. Even if the first process locks the file after step 1, the second process will be waiting specifically for that lock to clear, which it will do as soon as the first process releases it or closes the file. The second process is then likely to gain the lock for itself.

## The Solution: How to Read and Write a File Without Destroying It

To correct this problem, the program must be able to open a file for both reading and writing and keep it locked from start to finish. Table 6.1 displays most of the ways you can open a file using Perl's **open** function and describes the resulting access modes. Clearly what you want is to open the file for reading and writing

**TABLE 6.1    THE MOST COMMON WAYS TO OPEN A DISK FILE IN PERL**

| Function Call | Effect If the Call Is Successful |
| --- | --- |
| open(FH, "fn") | Opens the file named **fn** for reading only and associates it with the filehandle **FH**. (This is the default.) |
| open(FH, "<fn") | Opens **fn** for reading only. |
| open(FH, ">fn") | Opens **fn** for writing only. (This destroys any prior contents.) |
| open(FH, ">>fn") | Opens **fn** for appending only. (This is nondestructive because you can't back up.) |
| open(FH, "+>fn") | Opens **fn** for both writing and reading. (This always destroys the file's prior contents but lets you back up over what you've already written since opening.) |
| open(FH, "+<fn") | Opens **fn** for both reading and writing. (This is destructive only when and where you overwrite prior contents. It lets you seek forward and backward.) |

without destroying its prior contents (the access mode specified by **+<**). Once you've read the current count from the beginning of the file, you can back up to the beginning and overwrite it with the incremented count and then close the file.

All you need to add to this is file locking. In order to ensure that you read in the latest version of the count file, you should attempt to lock it right before your first read from it. If another instance of the program has already locked the file, you'll have to wait until it finishes writing to the file and relinquishes the lock. In order to keep other processes from reading an out-of-date version, you should keep the lock until after your last write, and then immediately close the file. On many systems, closing the file automatically releases the lock as a side effect, but it's better not to rely on this. Also, calling **flock** on a closed filehandle is meaningless, so you can't lock a file before opening it or unlock it after closing it. If **flock** is not implemented on your system, see the sidebar titled "Do-It-Yourself File Locking."

These constraints practically dictate the correct algorithm for you. The right way to read and write the count to a file is given by the following steps:

1 Open the count file for reading and writing.

2 Obtain an exclusive lock on this file.

3 Read the count from the first line of the file.

4 Increment the count.

5 Back up to the beginning of the file and write the new count into the first line.

6 Release the lock.

# Do-It-Yourself File Locking

If you are using a port of Perl that does not implement the **flock** function, you might want to use something such as the following subroutine as a somewhat impoverished substitute:

```
sub myflock {             # creates/deletes $LockFile as a semaphore
local ($LockFile, $mode, $retries) = @_;
  if ($mode == 8) {                    # To release the lock, just
    unlink($LockFile);                 # delete the lock file
  } elsif ($mode & 3) {                # The 1 or 2 bit is on
    $retries = 0 if ($mode & 4);       # 4 = no blocking = no retries
    while (-e $LockFile) {             # Test whether lock file exists
      return  0 if (!($mode & 2) && -z _);# Shared lock OK if file size 0
      return -1 if (-$retries < 0);    # Don't wait forever...
      select(undef,undef,undef,0.2);   # Sleep for 0.2 seconds
    }                                  #
    open( LockFile,">$LockFile");      # Create the lock file
    print LockFile $mode if ($mode & 2); # nonzero size = exclusive
    close(LockFile);                   # Close it again
  }
  0;                                   # return 0 (success)
}
```

This function uses a temporary file as a semaphore to signal whether a lock is set or not. (The temporary lock file must be in a directory in which the Web server is able to create and destroy files.) To set the lock, it creates the file; to release the lock, it deletes the file. A file size of 0 indicates a shared lock. A nonzero size means that some process has obtained an exclusive lock. One way to call this subroutine to request a lock would be

```
warn("$0: couldn't get lock") if &myflock("/tmp/mycount.lock", 2, 50);
```

If an exclusive lock is requested and the lock file already exists, **myflock** can wait and test the file again. If the file eventually disappears (that is, if some other process deletes it or releases the lock), **myflock** re-creates it and returns **0** (success). After a specified number of retries (**0** if **$mode**'s nonblocking bit is set), **myflock** returns **-1** (failure).

If a shared lock is requested, **myflock** returns **0** if the lock file exists and its size is 0. If the lock file doesn't exist, **myflock** creates a new one.

Probably the worst bug in the file-locking scheme this function implements is that when any one process relinquishes a shared lock it destroys the lock for all processes that shared it. Trying to fix this bug brings you right back to the problem of file sharing, to which file locking is supposed to be the solution! However, for exclusive (one-process-at-a-time) file sharing, **myflock** should work just fine.

**7** Close the count file.

This algorithm is implemented as the subroutine **countf** in Listing 6.1.

Whenever you open a file for reading, writing, or both, the system keeps track of your current location in the file so that you don't read the same lines twice or overwrite what you've already written. In this case, you actually do want to overwrite part of the file's contents—namely, the count. To make it easy and efficient both to read and to rewrite the count, store the count all by itself on the first line of the file. Perl's **seek** function can then be used to "rewind" the filehandle to the beginning of the file. More generally, **seek** is called like this:

```
seek(FILEHANDLE, offset, origin)
```

where *offset* specifies the new read/write position relative to *origin* and *origin* is **0** for the beginning of the file, **1** for the current position, and **2** for the end of the file. (Thus *offset* can be negative.) The function returns **1** on success and **0** on failure, but for any open file, **seek(FILEHANDLE, 0, 0)** should always succeed.

**Implicit Conversions between Numbers and Strings** It's worth noting in Listing 6.1 that **countf** returns **$count** as a number, not a string. Let's follow it through the function. When **$count** is first named and localized as a scalar variable using

```
my $count;
```

its value is undefined. You could set it to a default value such as **0** or **-999**, but this wouldn't make any difference. If the call to **open** succeeds, **$count** will be assigned to the first line read in from the file:

```
$count = <FILE>;              # count = first line of FILE, a ¬
    string
```

Or rather, if the file is empty, **$count** remains (or would become) undefined; if the file isn't empty, **$count** becomes a string consisting of any and all characters in the file up to and including the first newline, if there is one. In any event, the next line in **countf** has the side effect of converting **$count** into a number:

```
$count = $count + 1;
```

The arithmetic operator **+** makes the right-hand side of the assignment a numerical context, and Perl evaluates anything in a numerical context as a number if at all possible. If **$count** is undefined or has a string value such as **"um, 23?"**, it will

**LISTING 6.1    The countf.pl library file, which defines the function** countf

```perl
#!/usr/local/bin/perl
# countf.pl - a counter function with read/write file locking
# Usage: $count = &countf("file"), where file is the path of the
# text file containing the count as its first line
# NB: The flock function is not implemented in NTPerl or MacPerl

sub countf {
  die("$0 called countf w/o a filename\n") unless my ($cFile) = @_;
  my $count;                          # Localize count to this function
  if (open(FILE, "+<$cFile")) {       # Open countFile for reading and writing
    flock( FILE, 2);                  # 2 means exclusive lock
    $count = <FILE>;                  # count = first line of FILE, a string
    $count = $count + 1;              # Increment the count & convert to a number
    seek(  FILE, 0, 0);               # Rewind to beginning of FILE
    print  FILE $count, "\n";         # Write incremented count to FILE
    flock( FILE, 8);                  # 8 means release lock
    close( FILE );                    # Close right after unlocking
  } else {                            # Don't try to create file, just die!
    die("$0: error opening $cFile for read/write ($!)");
  }    # NB: The server shouldn't be able to create files in your directories
  $count;                             # Return the count
}

1; # This statement is here to make "require 'countf.pl';" work
```

evaluate to **0**, because it begins with letters. A string value such as **"0123huh45what\n\n"** may result in a warning printed to STDERR (if Perl was invoked with the **-w** switch), but this string actually evaluates to **123**, because it begins with numbers. The net result is that on the left-hand side of the assignment, **$count** is assigned a numerical value (**0 + 1**, if nothing else), and this is the number that **countf** returns, if it returns at all. If the **open** fails, **countf** calls **die** and never reaches the last line.

**When to chop, chomp, or Change Nothing**   Unlike Unix shells and other scripting languages, Perl does not automatically strip off the trailing newline from an input line. The statement

```
$string = <FILEHANDLE>;
```

copies into **$string** the next line from the filehandle FILEHANDLE, newline and all. To remove the newlines, many beginning Perl programmers get into the habit of calling Perl's **chop** function on every line they read from a file, as in

```
$string = <FILEHANDLE>;
chop($string);
```

or, equivalently,

```
chop($string = <FILEHANDLE>);      # NOT: $string = chop(<FILEHANDLE>);
```

The **chop** function removes the last character from each of the strings in its argument list (whether it is a newline or not) and returns the last chopped character. The above statements are thus also equivalent to

```
$string = <FILEHANDLE>;
$string =~ s/.$//;        # remove the last character
```

If the file doesn't end with a newline, its last character is lost. If the file happens to contain only a count on a line by itself, this use of **chop** can quickly truncate the count to nothing. The naive programmer might then resort to something such as

```
$count = <FILE>;
if ($count =~ /\n$/) {
  chop($count);
}
```

These statements are actually equivalent to

```
$count = <FILE>;
chomp($count);
```

The **chomp** function is similar to **chop**, but it removes the last characters from the strings in its argument list only if the characters are line endings. It then returns the total number of characters removed.

Thus, if you do need to remove the newlines from your input, use **chomp** instead of **chop**. But if your input lines will only be inserted into ordinary HTML text, you don't usually need to remove newlines, because browsers ignore them anyway. (Lines break on <BR>, not on **\n**.) And if you are inputting only a number, you also don't need to **chop** or **chomp** the input line, because when a scalar value is automatically converted from a string into a number, all trailing newlines are ignored.

## Setting Up a Text File to Store the Count

Before you can use the **countf** function, you need to set up a text file to store the count. Create the file using any editor, put **0** (or any other starting count) on the first line, and save it as text. Other lines in the file won't be read or changed, so you can include a note if you like, as in

```
0
This is count.txt, which stores the access count for counted.shtml
```

## Setting the Count File's Access Permissions

On a Unix system, you'll also need to set the file's permissions so that the Web server can read from and write to it. This can be done by issuing the command

```
chmod 666 count.txt
```

Unlike many other access counters, the **countf** function does not try to create a new count file if one does not already exist. That would require the Web server to have write permission in the directory in which it is to create the file, which would be something of a security hole. For one thing, if a server can create files in a given directory, it can also delete them. And if the server did create the file, the server—not you—would own it. In that case, you might find that you lack the permissions to modify the file yourself!

## Adding the Counter to a Web Page

Using the **countf** function, it's extremely easy to add a text-only access counter to any page. If the page has already been generated from a Perl script, just require the countf.pl library file into this script and call **countf** with the path of the count file as its argument:

```
require  "countf.pl";
$count = &countf("mydir/count.txt");
print "<H5>This page has been accessed $count times.</H5>\n";
```

If the page is static HTML, you can turn it into a CGI script-generated page (see Figure 6.1) by enclosing the whole thing in a "document here" **print** statement, as in

```
$count = &countf("mydir/count.txt");
print <<END_OF_PAGE;
```

```
<HTML><HEAD>Thebeginning of the BODY of your page
<H5>This page has been accessed $count times.</H5>
The rest of your page</BODY></HTML>
END_OF_PAGE
```

Alternatively, if your Web server is configured to enable Server Side Include (SSI) directives, including the **exec** command, you can insert a text counter into a static page using an SSI **exec cgi** command. Just put the call to **countf** into its own script, as in

```
#!/user/local/bin/perl
# countsuch.cgi - counter for such-and-such static page(s)
require  "my/perl/lib/countf.pl";
print &countf("my/log/count.txt");
```

Then call the script using an SSI directive embedded in the page:

```
<H5>This page has been accessed <!--#exec cgi="countsuch.cgi" --> ¬
times.</H5>
```

You'll also have to change the page's filename extension from html to shtml, or whatever extension your server uses to distinguish server-parsed files.

**Efficiency: SSI vs. CGI**   You might guess that the SSI version is more efficient, but that isn't necessarily so. For the SSI version to work, the server must scan every line of the SHTML source file, execute any commands it finds (such as a command to start Perl to run countsuch.cgi as an independent CGI process), and send the resulting text to the client. For the non-SSI version to work, the server must start Perl to run one CGI process, which in effect scans every line of the script, executes all the code, and sends the resulting text through the server to the client. With only the one variable, **$count**, to be inserted into the page's otherwise static text, the two versions are very similar. The greatest overhead in either case will be starting up a copy of Perl. But if there are two or more SSI directives that call an external CGI program in this way, using SSI may be much more computationally expensive than using pure CGI.

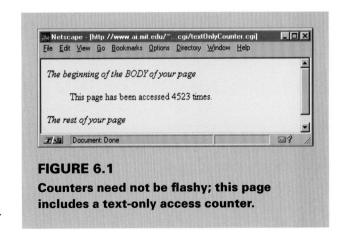

**FIGURE 6.1**
**Counters need not be flashy; this page includes a text-only access counter.**

## Example 6B: A Graphical Access Counter

As Web access counters go, the text-only counter of the previous example is minimal, giving it the advantages of speed and efficiency. More fully featured counters let you screen access, log every access to a file, or even present the count as a graphical image. One advantage of a graphical access counter is that it can be called from within an IMG tag, without resorting to SSI or converting the text of an entire page into CGI output. The main disadvantage is the overhead of generating a new image for every access. Since by definition the count is different every time the page is accessed, the image must be generated "in real time" or "on-the-fly." (Another disadvantage is that inside a static page the count won't be available as text for the IMG tag's ALT attribute.)

Generating images is computationally expensive in general, and Perl is particularly slow and unsuited for it. Nevertheless, there are two common workarounds. One is to start an external graphics program and issue it commands from within Perl. The other is to link Perl with an external library of graphics subroutines, typically written in C (as is Perl), and then call these subroutines from within Perl. Either way, the resulting image is sent back to the client browser as a stream of binary data, the same as if it had been read from a previously saved image file.

The countfly.cgi script (see Listing 6.2) uses the first method to implement a full-featured graphical access counter. It screens the URL of the calling page, calls **countf** to update the count file and return the new count, and then either directs the client to a canned image or starts an external program named fly to generate a GIF image that shows the count (see Figure 6.2). This program sends the new image directly to STDOUT, which it shares with the calling script. (There are other ways to trap or redirect the output of an external program called from Perl, but we'll get to those later.) When the image has been sent, countfly.cgi logs the client's remote host name and other information to a file and exits.

---

**LISTING 6.2    The countfly.cgi script, which implements a graphical access counter**

```
#!/usr/local/bin/perl5
# countfly.cgi - an inline image access counter

require "countf.pl";


############## CONFIGURATION VARIABLES ##############
```

**LISTING 6.2**    **The countfly.cgi script, which implements a graphical access counter (Continued)**

```
$countFile    = "counts.txt"; # File storing the count as its first line
$accessLog    = "access.log"; # File for logging accesses (may be same file)
$errorLog     = "errors.log"; # File for logging "errors" (may be same file)
$useLog       = 1;            # To turn off logging, change this to 0
$digitDir     = "digits";     # Holds GIF images for digits 0.gif - 9.gif
$digitWidth   = 44;           # All digit images must be of equal width
$digitHeight  = 36;           # Ditto their height
$frameSize    = 6;            # Extra space around the number, in pixels
$frameColor   = "255,0,255";  # RGB, so "255,255,0" is yellow, etc.
$flyProg      = "myprog/fly"; # (Relative) path of the fly program
$otherImgURL  = "";           # URL of image to send INSTEAD of count
$transColor   = "";           # Set to "0,0,0" to make black transparent.
$interlace    = 1;            # Create counter image as interlaced
$|            = 1;            # Unbuffer STDOUT before opening a pipe

# To prevent other Web pages or sites from using this counter, put only
# the trusted URL(s) or Web server(s) in $referers, separated by |'s.
# If you're counting hits to one page only, put in its whole URL.
$referers = "www.mysite.com|localhost|127.0.0.1";


############## THE MAIN PROGRAM #########################


&checkReferer if ($referers);     # Reject bad referers


$count = &countf($countFile);     # Get the new count


if ($otherImgURL) {               # Redirect to some constant image
  print "Location: $otherImgURL\n\n"
} else {                          # Send the MIME header for new image
  print "Content-type: image/gif\n\n";
  &sendGifCount($count);          # Subroutine creates and sends image
}


&appendLog($accessLog);           # Log access (if useLog is true)
```

**LISTING 6.2    The countfly.cgi script, which implements a graphical access counter (Continued)**

```perl
exit;                              # Outta here


############## GENERAL SUBROUTINES ######################


sub appendLog {
  if ($useLog ) {
    local ($logFile, $message) = @_;
    local ($sec,$min,$hour,$mday,$mon,$year) = localtime(time);
    local  $date = sprintf("%02d.%02d.%02d %02d:%02d:%02d"
                           , $year, $mon, $mday,  $hour, $min, $sec);
    open( LOG,">>$logFile") || die("$0: error opening logfile $logFile: $!");
    flock(LOG, 2);                 # Get exclusive lock on the log file
    print LOG "$date $ENV{'HTTP_REFERER'} from ";
    print LOG "$ENV{'REMOTE_HOST'} using $ENV{'HTTP_USER_AGENT'}";
    print LOG $message if $message;
    print LOG "\n";
    flock(LOG, 8);                 # Release the lock
    close(LOG);
  }
}


sub checkReferer {
  unless ($ENV{'HTTP_REFERER'} !~ /$referers/) {
    appendLog($errorLog, " - bad referer");
    die("$0: bad referer $ENV{'HTTP_REFERER'} from $ENV{'REMOTE_HOST'}\n");
  }
}


########### GRAPHICS SUBROUTINES ######################


sub sendGifCount {
  local  ($count) = @_;
  local  @digits = split(//, $count);  # Split string into array of chars
```

**LISTING 6.2    The countfly.cgi script, which implements a graphical access counter (Continued)**

```
# Compute width & height of output image:
$imgWidth  = $digitWidth * @digits  + ($frameSize * 2);
$imgHeight = $digitHeight           + ($frameSize * 2);


# Open a pipe to send commands to the fly program (-q for quiet)
# NB: flyProg will write to STDOUT, which should be flushed (set $| = 1):
open( FLY,"|$flyProg -q") || die("$0: error opening pipe to $flyProg: $!");
print FLY "new\n";
print FLY "size $imgWidth,$imgHeight\n";
print FLY "rect 0,0,$imgWidth,$imgHeight,$frameColor\n" if $frameSize;


# Commands to copy individual digit images into the frame:


$insertX = $insertY = $frameSize;
foreach $digit (@digits) {
   print FLY "copy $insertX,$insertY,-1,-1,-1,-1,$digitDir/$digit.gif\n";
   $insertX = $insertX + $digitWidth;
}


print FLY "transparent $transColor\n" if ($transColor =~ /\d+,\d+,\d+/);
print FLY "interlace\n"                 if $interlace;
close(FLY);                             # Ahem...  Thanks for closing it.
}


############################# NOTES #######################
# Fly was written by Martin Gleeson for Unix; his online documentation
# (http://www.unimelb.edu.au/fly/fly.html) says:
# All x,y values are in pixels measured from the top left of the image.
# For a 128x256 image, top left is 0,0 and bottom right is 127,255.
# All x1,y1,x2,y2 pairs must specify the top left and bottom right of the
# shape, where appropriate. (And -1 means min or max possible value.)
```

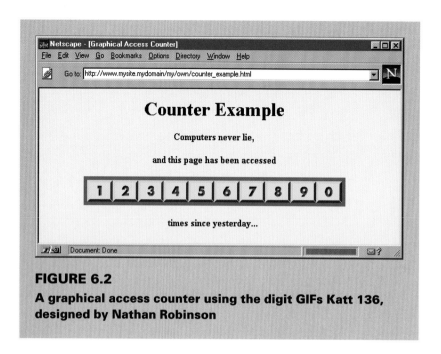

**FIGURE 6.2**
**A graphical access counter using the digit GIFs Katt 136, designed by Nathan Robinson**

## Installing countfly.cgi in Your Web Pages

To install countfly.cgi as part of an access counter, you'll need to complete the following six steps:

1  Get the fly program, which is available from the University of Melbourne at http://www.unimelb.edu.au/fly/fly.html. Its author, Martin Gleeson, wrote it in C for Unix and has promised a port for the Macintosh. At present, you can download precompiled versions for Windows/DOS and many different flavors of Unix/Linux.

2  (Optional) If you have access to a C compiler for your Web server, you might want to get the source distribution (from the same Web site) and build the binary executables yourself. In that case, you may also need to get and compile libgd, a C library by Thomas Boutell. At present, this comes bundled with the fly sources. You can also download it from www.boutell.com.

3  Download a set of equally sized GIF digit images. One excellent source is Digit Mania (http://www.digitmania.holowww.com). You can also look at Yahoo! (http://www.yahoo.com/Computers_and_Internet/World_Wide_Web/Programming/Access_Counts/) or create your own. The images need to be renamed 0.gif through 9.gif.

**4**  Set up the text file for **countf** as you did in Example 6A.

**5**  Change the configuration variables at the top of countfly.cgi to reflect the locations of everything installed in steps 1 through 4. The script is fairly self-explanatory on this.

**6**  Use this script's URL as the source of an inline image in the page(s) for which you want to count accesses, as in

```
Access count: <IMG SRC="countfly.cgi" ALIGN=MIDDLE>
```

## How countfly.cgi Works as a Perl Script

The code for maintaining a graphical access counter could be written in all kinds of ways, but I've tried to structure countfly.cgi in such a way as to reflect the logic of the task and make its own algorithm clear. The main program is basically a sequence of four subroutine calls (one of them conditional), and each subroutine isolates one subtask from the rest.

It's especially important to separate the graphics-generating code from the rest, because if fly is not available or if you would rather use some other program or graphics library, you might want to replace that code entirely. This kind of modular design allows you to modify or replace one subroutine without affecting the rest of the script.

Let's take the subroutines not in the order that they are called but in the order that they are defined.

**Maintaining a Log File with appendLog**   The first subroutine, **appendLog**, takes two arguments: the path of the log file to be appended and an optional message to append to it.

In any assignment to a list, such as

```
local ($logFile, $message) = @_;
```

the variables on the left-hand side are assigned the corresponding values on the right-hand side in order of occurrence. If there are not enough values on the right-hand side to correspond to those on the left, the last variables of the left-hand side are left (or become) undefined. Thus the optional arguments always appear last in a subroutine's parameter list; **appendLog** dies if it isn't called with **$logFile** set to the path of a log file it can open for appending, but it doesn't complain if it is called with no **$message**.

Conversely, if there are more entries in the list on the right-hand side than on the left, these extra values are discarded. Perl's **localtime** function actually returns a nine-element array of numbers that represent a date and time corrected for the local time zone, but you won't use the last three (day of the week, day of the year, and daylight saving time), so the program doesn't bother to "catch" them on the left-hand side of the assignment:

```
local ($sec,$min,$hour,$mday,$mon,$year) = localtime(time);
```

The usual (and default) argument to **localtime** is the current time, as measured in seconds since the beginning of 1970 Greenwich mean time, and as returned by the function **time**.

The remainder of **appendLog** is fairly straightforward; **sprintf** is used to reformat the date and time with leading zeros, as in

```
96.09.07 01:34:02
```

and this value is then appended along with several environment variables as the next line in the file. The reason for including HTTP_REFERER, which should always be the URL of the page that refers to countfly.cgi as the SRC for an inline image, is to allow the same file to be used to log accesses to as many pages as you like. In fact, all the files that countfly.cgi reads and writes could actually be one master file for counting and logging accesses to every page in your site. Most of the advantages, however, are on the side of using several smaller files. This reduces contention (and thus possible loss or corruption, if you don't have **flock**), and it also makes it easy to spot problems at a glance (for example, a nonzero size for a file that logs errors only).

**Who's That Calling My Access Counter?**  The **checkReferer** subroutine is called only if **$referers** is set to a regular expression that represents one or more trusted URLs or sites, and then it does nothing unless **$ENV{'HTTP_REFERER'}** fails to match this expression. (Recall that a regular expression made up of a number of patterns separated by pipes will match any one of the patterns in the search string.) If someone were to type in countfly.cgi's URL by hand, for instance, they could request it with an HTTP_REFERER set to an arbitrary value (such as whatever page just happened to be loaded in their browser window) or even no value at all. In either case, **checkReferer** would reject their request without further notice to the client. You could change it to send back an error message or your favorite GIF of disapproval, but why bother? As implemented, **checkReferer** calls **appendLog**

to record the faulty referring URL in **$errorLog** and dies with a similar message for the server's error log.

**The Conditional Statement at the Center of the Script**  We've already discussed **countf** above, and Location headers in Chapter 5, but before turning to **sendGifCount**, let's consider the script's main conditional. If you want to use countfly.cgi only for logging, you don't need to call the fly program at all. If you just set **$otherImgURL** to the URL of an alternative image source, clients will be redirected there to retrieve an image for the referring IMG tag. This URL could be to anything: a transparent one-pixel dot, a company logo, an inline image that the page would contain anyway, or even another CGI program. Whatever **$otherImgURL** is set to, if the item is non-null, countfly.cgi will output a Location header and then skip to **&appendLog($accessLog)** and exit.

**Generating and Sending the Image: sendGifCount**  Finally we arrive at the subroutine that encapsulates all the graphics. The first thing **sendGifCount** does is take the count as a scalar parameter and split it up into an array of individual digits:

```
local   ($count) = @_;
local   @digits = split(//, $count);  # Split string into array of¬
    chars
```

The null pattern **//** matches anything, so **split** simply splits its string argument up into separate characters. (See the sidebar entitled "How to Get At the Individual Characters in a String.") The resulting array of digits will be used to form the pathnames of the GIFs that will be copied into the output image, but first you use the number of these digits to determine this output image's size. Its total width should be the width of each digit times the number of digits, plus the extra width of the frame on either side. The height is computed similarly:

```
$imgWidth  = $digitWidth * @digits  + ($frameSize * 2);
$imgHeight = $digitHeight           + ($frameSize * 2);
```

**Running an External Program and Redirecting Its Input/Output**
To generate the actual image that contains the count, you can run fly from within Perl. fly is a good example of a program whose input and output can both be redirected, so I'll use it to illustrate several different techniques for running an external

# How to Get At the Individual Characters in a String

Many programmers new to Perl are stumped by the question of how to reference or modify the individual characters that constitute a string. In many other programming languages, a string is nothing but an array of characters, and programmers are accustomed to being able to subscript these arrays. In Perl, however, **$string[2]** does not usually mean the third (or second) character in a string named **$string**, but rather the third element in an array named **@string**.

You can try to do all your string manipulation using regular expressions with search and replace, but that can become very tricky. To extract a number of characters from a given starting point within a string, it's more straightforward to use Perl's **substr** function, like this:

```
$chars3thru5 = substr($string, 3, 2);
```

To modify substrings according to position, you can also use **substr** as an "*lvalue*" (the left-hand side of an assignment statement), like this:

```
substr($string, 5, 4) = $newChars5678;
```

But to a C or BASIC programmer, calling any function may seem overly indirect.

If you do want to manipulate strings like arrays, you can convert any string into an array using **split**, and even keep the same name, as in

```
@string = split( //, $string);
```

After this statement, **$string[2]** will refer precisely to the character at position **2** in the string **$string**, and the unsubscripted form retains its former value as the whole string.

Another useful wildcard expression for **split** is **∧n*/**, matching zero or more occurrences of the newline character. Since **split** discards the part of the string that matches the splitting pattern, this particular pattern causes **split** to return the array of all the string's characters *except* for newlines. (You don't need it in **sendGifCount** because the **$count** returned by **countf** is already just a number, not a string. In fact, Perl would automatically convert a number into a string so that **split** could work on it.)

program from within Perl. In the end, I'll settle on the one that best achieves the goal of sending the new image to the client as quickly and efficiently as possible.

All of fly's options and the flexibility they provide for redirecting input and output are quite typical of programs designed to run in a Unix shell-like environment, and most of these options are also common among DOS programs. Thus, most of what I tell you here about fly also applies to the general case of running an external command from within Perl. (To learn more about fly itself, see Martin Gleeson's online documentation at http://www.unimelb.edu.au/fly/fly.html.)

The standard manner of invoking the fly program from a command line is

```
Unix%  fly -i input.txt -o output.gif
```

where the **-i** option is used to specify an input file containing directives for creating the image and the **-o** option specifies a pathname for the output image file. If you omit the **-i** option, you can type in commands directly from the terminal. That is, in the absence of any other input file, fly takes its input from STDIN. These input directives are just simple commands for creating shapes and copying images that already exist. If you don't specify a path for the output image, fly will send the image straight back to the terminal, via STDOUT. Although you probably don't want binary image data splattered across your terminal screen, you can use this feature to redirect the image to any other file or filehandle.

Before outputting the image itself, fly also outputs status information before or after executing almost every command. If an output image file was specified using **-o**, these status lines are printed to STDOUT; otherwise, fly prints them to STDERR. By default, both of these output streams go right back to the terminal. If you run fly interactively (that is, with no input file), these status lines can provide useful feedback as you go (see Listing 6.3), but when you're running fly automatically, you'll usually want to get this diagnostic output out of the way. You could redirect it to yet another file or output device like this:

```
Unix%  fly -i input.txt -o output.gif >>&! /dev/null
```

Once you know that the directives in input.txt work, however, it's best to turn these messages off entirely, using fly's **-q** option (quiet mode). This suppresses all output except for the image itself. The original command is thus equivalent to using both input and output redirection, as in

```
Unix%  fly -q < input.txt >! output.gif
```

> **LISTING 6.3** **An interactive session with fly, in which the user (boldface) copies the digit GIFs 1, 2, and 3 into a 144-by-48-pixel magenta rectangle**

```
UNIX% myprog/fly -o output.gif
new
size 144,48
Creating new 144 by 48 gif, <output.gif>
rect 0,0,144,48,255,0,255
## Rectangle ## drawn from 0,0 to 144,48. (colour: 255, 0, 255 = 0)
copy 6,6,-1,-1,-1,-1,digits/1.gif
Copying GIF from existing file: digits/1.gif
Copying digits/1.gif to coordinates 6,6
copy 50,6,-1,-1,-1,-1,digits/2.gif
Copying GIF from existing file: digits/2.gif
Copying digits/2.gif to coordinates 50,6
copy 94,6,-1,-1,-1,-1,digits/3.gif
Copying GIF from existing file: digits/3.gif
Copying digits/3.gif to coordinates 94,6
transparent 0,0,0
## Make transparent [colour: 0, 0, 0 = 39]
interlace
Image is interlaced
^D
EOF: fly finished.
UNIX% ls -l output.gif
-rw-r--r--   1 spraxlo   user           1184 Sep 12 10:59 output.gif
```

(The **!** tells the Unix shell to overwrite the file if it already exists; in DOS, that's the default.) Another equivalent is to feed fly its input commands by piping the contents of a file to it using the I symbol:

```
Unix%  cat input.txt | fly -q >! output.gif
```

Or, if you had a program (such as the one called gifcount in the code line below) that takes in a number and automatically generates fly commands, you could use

```
Unix%  gifcount 123 | fly -q
```

to run fly and send the output image directly to STDOUT. This last way is the closest to what **sendGifCount** does as a subroutine.

Let's turn now to the problem of redirecting fly's input and output from within the CGI script.

## Running an External Program from within Perl

There are many different ways to run an external program from within Perl, and some of the differences among them are subtle. In the next section, I'll discuss how to call an external program using backticks, and I'll continue to use fly as an example. If you are interested only in how **sendGifCount** actually works, you can safely skip to the section on using pipes.

**Invoking an External Program Using a Backticked Command**  One way to execute any shell command or command-line-invokable program from within Perl is to use backticks. If the script had already written all the right fly commands into a temporary file with a unique name such as tmp/fly_*count*.txt (where *count* is replaced by the actual count), you could use something such as

```
$info = `fly -o tmp/fly_$count.gif -i tmp/fly_$count.txt`;
send_file_cgi( "tmp/fly_$count.gif", "image/gif");
`rm -f        tmp/fly_$count.gif    tmp/fly_$count.txt`;
```

to create the GIF as a temporary file, send it with the proper HTTP headers, and then remove both temporary files. Note that just writing the new GIF to disk and returning its URL as part of a Location header would be a very bad idea, because in that case, instead of deleting it right away, you'd have to leave it in a directory where the client could retrieve it. At any rate, creating and deleting two temporary files per access is not very efficient.

You could reduce the overhead by creating only the command file, using a technique such as

```
$image = `myprog/fly -q -i tmp/fly_$count.txt`;  # catch STDOUT
print "Content-type: image/gif\n\n";
print($image);
unlink("tmp/fly_$count.txt");                # delete the temp image
```

The first statement assigns the entire contents of the GIF image to **$image** as a scalar value (or as a binary string, if you like). This technique avoids the overhead of creating two files, but it does so at the price of loading the whole image into your program's memory space before sending it.

In Perl, the scalar value of any backticked command is whatever the execution of that command sends to STDOUT; anything it sends to STDERR, on the other hand, will still go to STDERR. Most Web servers redirect STDERR data from the CGI programs they run into their own log files, but a few non-Unix servers actually send it to the client browser. Thus, inside a CGI program you should always run fly with the **-q** option.

If you want to dispense with the input file, you could put all the directives to fly into the backticked command itself, like this:

```
$flycommand = <<END_COM
myprog/fly -q
new
size $imgWidth,$imgHeight
rect 0,0,$imgWidth,$imgHeight,$frameColor
    . . . further directives here . . .
END_COM;
$image = `$flycommand`;
```

The "document here" syntax works the same way in assignments to strings as it does in **print** statements, preserving newlines and interpolating values for variables. In sum, this technique disposes of both temporary files but incurs an extra cost in memory. This is about the best you can do using backticks, because the output of a program cannot be redirected inside a backticked command. That is, something such as

```
`$flycommand > STDOUT`;
```

won't work no matter what file or device you use in place of STDOUT. Your only choice using backticks inside a Perl script is to "catch" the standard output results of a command as a scalar value (or, optionally, as a list value, if the output is more than one line).

**Opening a Pipe for Sending Input to an External Program**   There is a way to make fly share the same STDOUT as your Perl script and thus send the output image back to the client browser with no need for temporary files or extra memory. This technique is to *open a pipe* to the external program:

```
open( FLY,"|$flyProg -q") || die("$0: error opening pipe to $flyProg:¬
$!");
```

The I symbol at the beginning of **open**'s file argument directs it to open a pipe to a program specified by **$flyProg**. More precisely, this function call attempts to open a filehandle named FLY that can be used to send input directly from the Perl script into the external program fly, as specified by **$flyProg**. For this **open** to succeed, Perl must find the fly program and start it up to await further input. If it can do so, **open** returns **1**, and the second half of the disjunction—the call to **die**—is not executed. (Read the whole statement as **open *OR* die**.) Once the pipe is open, anything printed to FLY will go to the waiting fly program exactly as if fly had been invoked from a terminal and was accepting input line by line:

```
print FLY "new\n";              # First line of input to fly
print FLY "size $imgWidth,$imgHeight\n";  # Second line...
    . . . print further input to FLY here . . .
```

In particular, for each  digit in the **@digits** array, you can send fly a command line to make it copy part of an image from a GIF file in your digit directory into the output image; actually, the subimage coordinates **-1,-1,-1,-1** direct the program to copy the entire source image:

```
foreach $digit (@digits) {
    print FLY "copy $insertX,$insertY,-1,-1,-1,-1,$digitDir/$digit.¬
gif\n";
    $insertX = $insertX + $digitWidth;
}
```

The image of each digit is copied in at the current insertion point **$insertX,$insertY**, which is then shifted to the right by the width of one digit.

Finally, closing the filehandle to fly is the equivalent of terminating its input by typing Ctrl-D (also known as an EOF or end-of-file character; DOS uses Ctrl-Z), as shown here:

```
close(FLY);                    # terminate input to fly
```

This is when fly actually generates the image and sends it as a binary stream of data to STDOUT. Opened through a pipe in this way, fly actually shares the same standard output stream as the calling process, countfly.cgi. (Internally, the fly program's STDOUT filehandle is a duplicate of the parent program's.)

Since fly will temporarily take control of STDOUT, you need to make sure that anything that countfly.cgi has already printed prior to this point has actually made it through STDOUT's buffering system. That's why you need to set **$l = 1**, to unbuffer STDOUT. Otherwise, the image may be sent out ahead of the content-type header.

Until the pipe is closed, fly merely waits for further input and does not actually generate the image. If you forget to close the filehandle FLY, Perl will close it for you when the script ends, just as it would close any filehandle to an open file. In this example, that would keep the client browser waiting until after the call to **appendLog**, violating the goal of designing the program to give the speediest possible return.

The fly program is capable of more than creating colored shapes and superimposing images over them. You can also use it to draw lines and arcs, paint with saved images as brushes, and add lettering with some basic built-in fonts. With a list of fly's directives in front of you, you'll find it fairly easy to plot a graph or draw the shapes that make up a bar chart. You can also draw on top of a pre-existing image. In a duel between two directives that affect the same output pixel, the last draw wins. (And thus our old friend bowdlerize.cgi may not be so far-fetched after all, at least for GIFs.)

# Using the GD Library to Provide Dynamic Graphical Output

The GD library is much more elaborate than the simple library files that have been presented as parts of the examples in this book. The GD library must be installed as a complete object-oriented *package module* in your site's Perl 5 lib directory before you can use it. (To download the GD library and the instructions for installing it under Unix, see http://www.genome.wi.mit.edu/ftp/pub/software/WWW/GD.html; at this time, there are no ports to non-Unix platforms.) The syntax of the GD library's function calls, or object-oriented *methods*, is quite similar to that of fly's directives, because both GD and fly are based on the same underlying C library (libgd by Thomas Boutell). Although GD is not inherently more powerful than fly, using its methods within Perl is often more convenient than exporting directives to an external program.

## Example 6C: Drawing a Pie Chart Using GD

Drawing a pie chart is a little more complex than drawing a bar chart or plotting a graph. Instead of drawing different-sized rectangles or lines from one data point to the next, you need to divide up a circle and fill the resulting slices with colors. This involves a little bit of trigonometry and a lot of calculation, especially if you include a legend with color labels, titles, and percentages. The pieGD.cgi script (shown in Listing 6.4) shows how to do this in a fairly general way, with the bulk of its operations spent in an attempt to make the output image resizeable.

---

**LISTING 6.4    The pieGD.cgi script, which creates a pie chart**

---

```perl
#!/usr/local/bin/perl5
# pieGD.cgi - a program that generates a pie chart from data in $File


use GD;


$radius = 170;              # Radius of pie graph
$border =  10;              # Border around graph
$legend = 210;              # Width of legend
$oY     = $radius + $border; # y-origin: usually vertically centered
$oX     = $radius + $border; # x-origin: usually = $oY
$height = $oY * 2;          # Pie graph + borders
$width  = $height + $legend; # Pie graph + borders + legend
$bX     = 370;              # Legend box's starting X-coordinate
$bW     = 25;               # Legend box width
$bH     = 25;               # Legend box height
$font   = gdLargeFont;      # Literal, no quotes; 1 of 4
$fW     =  8;               # Font width (see the GD docs)
$fH     = 16;               # Font height (i.e., GD.html)
$padW   = $border/2;        # Padding around boxes


$im = new GD::Image($width,$height);        # Create new image
# Allocate ten colors, even if you won't use all of them:
$white =    $im->colorAllocate(255, 255, 255);  # First color is bkgrnd
$black =    $im->colorAllocate(  0,   0,   0);  # Outline of slices
@clrs  = (  $im->colorAllocate(255,   0,   0),  # $red
            $im->colorAllocate(  0, 255,   0),  # $green
            $im->colorAllocate(  0,   0, 255),  # $blue
            $im->colorAllocate(255, 255,   0),  # $yellow
            $im->colorAllocate(  0, 255, 255),  # $cyan
            $im->colorAllocate(255,   0, 255),  # $magenta
            $im->colorAllocate(255, 140,   0),  # $orange
            $im->colorAllocate(250, 128, 114),  # $salmon
            $im->colorAllocate(160,  32, 240),  # $purple
```

```
              $im->colorAllocate(240, 230, 140),   # $khaki
        );                                         # end w/ comma ok
```

**LISTING 6.4    The pieGD.cgi script, which creates a pie chart (Continued)**

```
$File = "franchises.txt";
readFields2(*titles, *shares, $File);

if (@shares > @clrs) {
  warn("$0: More items than colors - TRUNCATING DATA from $File!\n");
  @shares = @clrs;
}
$totalShares = 0;
foreach $_ (@shares) {  $totalShares += $_; }

$strLen   = int (($legend - $bW - $padW - $fW*8 - $border)/$fW);
$strColor = $im->colorAllocate(20, 40, 120);   # a dark blue
$im->rectangle(0, 0, $width-1, $height-1, $strColor);


# Draw the circle (360-degree arc) and the first radius at 0:
$totalRadians = 0;
$im->arc( $oX,$oY, $radius*2 + 2, $radius*2 + 2, 0, 360, $black);
$im->line($oX,$oY, $oX + $radius*cos($totalRadians)
                 , $oY + $radius*sin($totalRadians), $clrs[0]);

# For each share: increment total angle, draw new radius,
# color slice from within, then add color box & string to legend:
$twoPi   = atan2(1,1)*8;     # Arctan of 1 is 45 degrees = pi/4
for ($j = 0; $j < @shares; $j++) {
  $relativeShare = $shares[$j]/$totalShares;
  $sliceRadians  = $relativeShare * twoPi;
  $totalRadians += $sliceRadians;
  $im->line($oX,$oY, $oX + $radius*cos($totalRadians)
                   , $oY + $radius*sin($totalRadians), $clrs[$j]);
  $im->fill( $oX + ($radius - 5)*cos($totalRadians - $sliceRadians/2)
           , $oY + ($radius - 5)*sin($totalRadians - $sliceRadians/2)
```

```
                , $clrs[$j]) if ($sliceRadians > 2.0/(radius - 5));
    $bY = $oY  +  ($j - @shares/2)*($bH + $border) + $padW;
```

**LISTING 6.4    The pieGD.cgi script, which creates a pie chart (Continued)**

```
    &drawBoxFramed($bX, $bY, $clrs[$j]);
    &drawBoxString($bX, $bY, $titles[$j], $relativeShare*100);
}


# $im->interlaced('true');   # Make interlaced GIF
# $im->transparent($black);  # Make pie's edges disappear
print "Content-type: image/gif\n\n";
print $im->gif;
exit 0;



sub drawBoxFramed {
  local ($bX, $bY, $color) = @_;
  $im->filledRectangle( $bX, $bY, $bX + $bW, $bY + $bH, $color);
  $im->rectangle(       $bX, $bY, $bX + $bW, $bY + $bH, $black);
}


sub drawBoxString {
  local ($bX, $bY, $title, $percent) = @_;
  local ($string);
  $string = sprintf("%-${strLen}.${strLen}s %5.2f%%"
                    , $title, $percent);
  $im->string($font, $bX +  $bW + $padW
                    , $bY + ($bH - $fH + 1)/2, $string, $strColor);
}


sub readFields2 {
  local(*titles, *shares, $File) = @_;
  local($title,  $share);
  if (open(File, $File)) {
    flock( File, 1);                  # 1 means get shared lock
    while ($_ = <File>) {
      if ($_ =~ /\t/ ) {
```

```
      ($title, $share) = split(/\t/, $_);
      push(@titles, $title);    # Push title onto end of array
```

**LISTING 6.4**

**The pieGD.cgi script, which creates a pie chart (Continued)**

```
      push(@shares, $share);
    }
  }
  flock( File, 8);                # 8 means release lock
  close( File );                  # Close right after unlocking
} else {
  die("$0: error opening $File ($!)");
}
}
```

The program reads in a data file named franchises.txt. You can assume that this file is frequently updated and is formatted as follows, using tabs:

```
# franchises.txt - format is city<tab>count
```

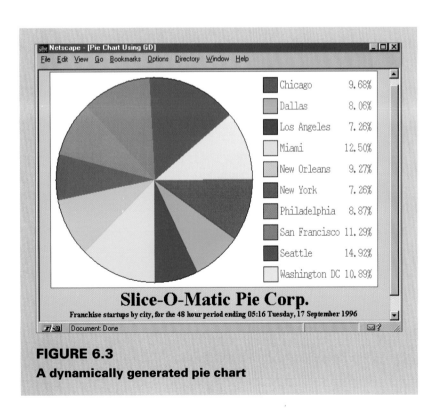

**FIGURE 6.3**

**A dynamically generated pie chart**

```
# Any line without
tabs is a comment
Chicago 24
Dallas  12 # Anything
after two fields is
also a comment
```

The first loop in pieGD.cgi splits each tab-separated line into a title and a number representing a raw count, up to a maximum of ten lines. (To allow more items, you'd have to allocate more colors and change the sizes.) Then it draws each item's slice of the pie in proportion to its share of the total count and enters its title and percentage into the graph's legend (see Figure 6.3).

The script represents the common case in small-scale graphics programming. You start with a library of subroutines for drawing very elementary shapes, and then you combine those shapes to build more complex shapes. Most of the variables are global to the whole script, and many are constant, set at the beginning just to initialize some parts of the graphics system or to get all the interdependent sizes right. (When you're using GD, you always create a new image object and allocate colors for it, with the first color automatically becoming the background color.)

If you'll be drawing the same shape many times, you can write a short subroutine for drawing just that shape and pass to it only the parameters that actually vary or those that help make the code more readable. In pieGD.cgi, **drawBoxFramed** is an example of this. It could have been written with no parameters at all, but giving a subroutine access to a loop-index variable (**$j**, in this case) is generally poor practice. The main reason for defining the routine is for clarity, assuming that one call to a subroutine named **drawBoxFramed** is easier to understand than two lower-level calls to the methods **filledRectangle** and **rectangle** (which, by the way, must be called in the order shown).

The subroutine **drawBoxString** is similar; most of the variables it evaluates are constants set at the beginning of the script. Its main purpose is to make the script more readable by separating all the string manipulation out of the main loop. The format string in the call to **sprintf**,

```
"%-${strLen}.${strLen}s %5.2f%%"
```

can be broken down as follows: **%s** causes the corresponding argument to be printed as a string, and **%f** causes its argument to be printed as a floating-point number. Both format fields take an optional size specifier of the form **m.n**, where **m** and **n** evaluate to numbers. For strings, **n** is the maximum length; longer argument strings will be truncated. For floating-point numbers, **n** specifies the decimal precision. For either, **m** is the minimum length of the output field; a negative value will left-justify the field. The formula for the y-coordinate of the inserted string,

```
$bY + ($bH - $fH + 1)/2
```

is just an attempt to center the title string vertically with respect to the corresponding box in the legend: the starting level of the box plus half the height of the box minus half the height of the font plus one half for rounding off. (The GD methods, like those for fly and the underlying libgd, measure vertical distance from the top, and fractional numbers are subject to losing their fractional parts when converted to absolute pixel coordinates.)

The work of drawing the pie graph itself is left inside the main loop, because this is the place where it is easiest to understand. The details of drawing the legend are abstracted and moved out of the way by subroutine calls, leaving only the actual pie chart and its slices. The bounding circle is already drawn before the loop begins, as is the first radius (the line from the circle's center to its edge), at 0 degrees. Now for each item added to the graph, you have only to draw a new radius whose angle from the previous one is proportional to that item's share of the whole pie. The whole pie is 360 degrees around, which is actually 2 pi (2π) in radians. So whatever share that item gets of the pie, that's how much it gets of the total angle, **$twoPi**:

```
$relativeShare = $shares[$j]/$totalShares;
$sliceRadians  = $relativeShare * twoPi;
```

If you ever need to get the value of pi (or convert angles between degrees and radians), the standard trick to remember is this: The short sides of a triangle with two 45-degree angles are both the same length, so the tangent of 45 degrees is 1; but 45 degrees is also pi over 4 (π/4), so the arctangent of 1 is π/4, and 8 times that is 2π:

```
$twoPi    = atan2(1,1)*8;      # Arctan of 1 is 45 degrees = pi/4
```

The program also keeps a running total of the size of the angle of all the slices you've already added:

```
$totalRadians += $sliceRadians;
```

With this much information, you'd be all set, except for the fact that GD doesn't have a method for drawing a line from one point to another based on angles and distances. It only understands absolute Cartesian coordinates. Figuring out where to draw the next line is thus a matter of converting the angle and the length of the circle's radius into the next xy coordinate pair. The answer to this is found through trigonometry: the x-distance from the origin of the circle to a point on its circumference is always the radius times the cosine of the angle, and the y-distance is the sine of the angle times the radius. All along, we've measured the angle in radians just because that's what Perl's sine and cosine functions need:

```
$totalRadians += $sliceRadians;
$im->line($oX,$oY, $oX + $radius*cos($totalRadians)
               , $oY + $radius*sin($totalRadians), $clrs[$j]);
```

Once you've drawn the line defining the boundaries of the next slice, you need to fill the resulting empty wedge with color. GD's fill method works like the paint-bucket tools in many interactive graphics applications. It floods an area pixel-by-pixel until it reaches a bounding line that is a different color than the pixel at which the paint bucket was originally "dropped." Therefore, to fill each wedge, you can back up to position yourself in the middle of the wedge you just created, and then you can call the fill method on a point there that's just a few pixels inside the circle boundary:

```
$im->fill( $oX + ($radius - 5)*cos($totalRadians - $sliceRadians/2)
         , $oY + ($radius - 5)*sin($totalRadians - $sliceRadians/2)
         , $clrs[$j]) if ($sliceRadians > 2.0/(radius - 5));
```

On a slice of negligible size, however, this could spill the color all over the adjacent slices; that's the reason for sneaking in the conditional

```
    if ($sliceRadians > 2.0/(radius - 5));
```

This check ensures that the wedge is at least 2 pixels wide at the fill point before "dropping the bucket."

Finally, the y-coordinate for each item's color box is calculated in an appropriately ad hoc manner, and that item's title and percentage of the pie is added to the legend:

```
$bY = $oY  +  ($j - @shares/2)*($bH + $border) + $padW;
&drawBoxFramed($bX, $bY, $clrs[$j]);
&drawBoxString($bX, $bY, $titles[$j], $relativeShare*100);
```

That ends the loop, and thus ends the example. Any other chart or graphical element you want to create using fly, GD, or a similar graphics resource is just a matter of building visible structures from these very primitive elements.

## Creating a Dynamic Interface

As a change of pace, let's turn now to a different kind of dynamic output. The example script in this section generates a page that changes not to reflect external events such as the number of prior accesses or the current trends in the widget industry, but to reflect ongoing user input.

### Example 6D: A Dynamic Interface (a User-Modifiable Form)

**LISTING 6.5    The changeMe.cgi script, which generates a self-modifiable form**

```perl
#!/usr/local/bin/perl5
# changeMe.cgi - an interactively changeable form
require "FormData.pl";
require "ctime.pl";
$date = &ctime(time);        # "Converted" time
$maxOptions = 24;


$query = &getFormData(*Form) if ($script = $ENV{'SCRIPT_NAME'});


$SUBMIT_S    = "Submit Shown Values";
$SUBMIT_D    = "Submit Default Values";
$SUBMIT      = $Form{'SUBMIT'}          || $SUBMIT_S;
undef %Form if $SUBMIT ne $SUBMIT_S;  # Revert to default values
$TITLE       = $Form{'TITLE'}          || 'Fix Me';
$BGCOLOR     = $Form{'BGCOLOR'}        || '#207050';
$TEXT        = $Form{'TEXT'}           || '#FFFF00';
$GIF         = $Form{'GIF'}            || 'red';
$LINK        = $Form{'LINK'}           || '#FF2244';
$VLINK       = $Form{'VLINK'}          || '#CC4422';
$ALINK       = $Form{'ALINK'}          || 'blue';
$BACKGROUND  = $Form{'BACKGROUND'}     || 'None';
$BGI_URL     = $Form{'BGI_URL'}        || 'http://';


$BGDIR = "bg";
if ($BACKGROUND eq 'None') {
    $BGS = '';    # No background specification at all
} else {
    $BGS = "BACKGROUND=$BGDIR/$BACKGROUND";
    $bgURL[0] = 'None';    # Make 'None' the first alternative
}


# Heuristic regular expressions for weeding out invalid URLs:
$isaURL = '^http://\w+[.:]\w+[.:@/]?';
$notURL = '[\s"<>[\b]^`{|}]';
```

**LISTING 6.5    The changeMe.cgi script, which generates a self-modifiable form
(Continued)**

```perl
# Check user-entered URL for background image:
if (length($BGI_URL) > 7) {   # longer than the default 'http://'?
    if ($BGI_URL =~ /$isaURL/ && $BGI_URL !~ /$notURL/) {
        if ($BGI_URL =~ /.*\.(gif|jpe?g)$/) {
            $BGS = "BACKGROUND=$BGI_URL";
        } else {
            $BGI_URL = "Sorry, unusable URL: $BGI_URL";
        }
    } else {
        $BGI_URL = 'Sorry, invalid URL: to edit it, go back.';
    }
}


# Generate a list of background image options:
if (opendir(DIR, $BGDIR)) {                    # open the directory
    push(@bgURL, grep(!/^\./, readdir(DIR))); # read list of files
    closedir(DIR);
    @bgURL = &randpick($maxOptions, @bgURL) if @bgURL > $maxOptions;
    @bgURL = sort(@bgURL);
}


&regenerate;
exit 0;


###############################################################
sub randpick {
    local ($picks, @fromList) = @_;
    local (@picked);
    srand(time|$$);
    while ($picks > 0) {
        push(@picked, splice(@fromList, rand @fromList, 1));
        $picks--;
    }
    @picked;
}
```

**LISTING 6.5** **The changeMe.cgi script, which generates a self-modifiable form (Continued)**

```perl
################################################################################

sub regenerate {
print "Content-type: text/html\n\n";
print <<EOF;
<HTML>
<HEAD><TITLE> $TITLE </TITLE></HEAD>
<BODY $BGS  BGCOLOR="$BGCOLOR"
TEXT="$TEXT" LINK="$LINK" VLINK="$VLINK" ALINK="$ALINK">

<FORM METHOD=POST>

<TABLE CELLSPACING=5>
<TR ALIGN=right>
<TD> <STRONG> Title: </STRONG> </TD>
<TD COLSPAN=6><INPUT TYPE=TEXT SIZE=60 MAXLENGTH=255 NAME=TITLE VALUE=$TITLE></TD>
</TR>
<TR ALIGN=right>
<TD ROWSPAN=2 VALIGN=center><STRONG> Colors: </STRONG></TD>
<TD>                Bkgrnd:        </TD><TD><INPUT TYPE=TEXT SIZE=10 NAME=BGCOLOR
    VALUE=$BGCOLOR></TD>
<TD><FONT COLOR=$TEXT>  Text:</FONT></TD><TD><INPUT TYPE=TEXT SIZE=10 NAME=TEXT
    VALUE=$TEXT></TD>
<TD><FONT COLOR=$GIF>    GIF:</FONT></TD><TD><INPUT TYPE=TEXT SIZE=10 NAME=GIF
    VALUE=$GIF></TD>
</TR>
<TR ALIGN=right>
<TD><FONT COLOR=$LINK>  Link:</FONT></TD><TD><INPUT TYPE=TEXT SIZE=10 NAME=LINK
    VALUE=$LINK></TD>
<TD><FONT COLOR=$VLINK>Vlink:</FONT></TD><TD><INPUT TYPE=TEXT SIZE=10 NAME=VLINK
    VALUE=$VLINK></TD>
<TD><FONT COLOR=$ALINK>Alink:</FONT></TD><TD><INPUT TYPE=TEXT SIZE=10 NAME=ALINK
    VALUE=$ALINK></TD>
</TR>
```

**LISTING 6.5     The changeMe.cgi script, which generates a self-modifiable form (Continued)**

```
</TABLE>


<TABLE>
<TR ALIGN=left>
<TD ROWSPAN=2 VALIGN=center><STRONG> Bkgrnd: </STRONG></TD>
<TD COLSPAN=2 NOWRAP> Choose an image here: </TD>
<TD COLSPAN=2>
<SELECT NAME=BACKGROUND>
<OPTION> $BACKGROUND
EOF


foreach (@bgURL) {  print "<OPTION> $_\n";  }


print <<EOF;
</SELECT>
</TD>
<TD COLSPAN=2> or enter a URL below: </TD>
</TR>
<TR ALIGN=left>
<TD COLSPAN=6><INPUT TYPE=TEXT SIZE=60 MAXLENGTH=255 NAME=BGI_URL VALUE=$BGI_URL>
</TD>
</TR>
</TABLE><P><CENTER>
<INPUT TYPE=SUBMIT NAME=SUBMIT VALUE="$SUBMIT_S">
<INPUT TYPE=SUBMIT NAME=SUBMIT VALUE="$SUBMIT_D">
<INPUT TYPE=RESET                VALUE="Reset Current Values">
</CENTER></FORM><CENTER>
[<A HREF="$script">     START OVER - Constant link back</A>]
[<A HREF="$script?$query">RESUBMIT - Changing link back</A>]<BR>
<SMALL>Generated $date by the script $script with Perl version $]
</SMALL></CENTER></BODY></HTML>
EOF
}
```

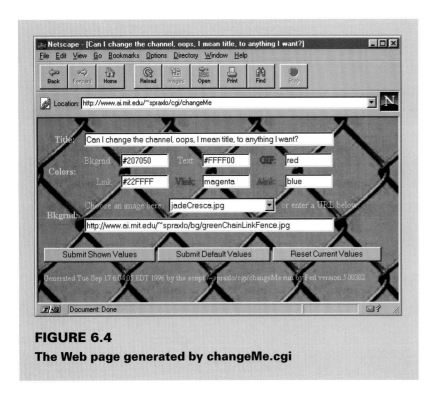

**FIGURE 6.4**
**The Web page generated by changeMe.cgi**

The changeMe.cgi script (shown in Listing 6.5) generates a form that accepts input regarding its own properties and outputs a modified copy of itself (see Figure 6.4). Its title, background colors and images, and the colors of ordinary text and links are all changeable, although it would be more accurate to say that input to one instance determines the appearance of the next. In one sense, then, this is a self-modifying form, in that it is both changeable and self-referential. However, it's really a user-modifiable form. This may seem like a novelty, but in fact this is the way in which many application interfaces work, on the Web and off. The difference is that changeMe.cgi doesn't simultaneously modify something other than itself—a spreadsheet, for instance. You can think of this example as a test form; you might even find it useful for testing out backgrounds and color combinations.

This program also shows how to perform several other useful tasks, such as obtaining a directory listing directly by reading in a directory file and picking a random subset from a list. More importantly, it illustrates a simple method for keeping track of previous user input, which will become increasingly useful in the remaining chapters of this book. As I explain how the script works, I'll highlight only those features and functions of Perl that haven't already appeared in earlier scripts.

## Reading a Directory to Obtain a List of Its Files and Subdirectories

In Perl, reading all the filenames from a directory is very similar to reading all the lines from a single file. The semantics of Perl's **opendir**, **readdir**, and **closedir** functions are nearly the same as those of **open**, **read**, and **close**, except that the directory functions entertain far fewer options and variations. For instance,

**opendir** always opens a directory handle for reading only. It returns **1** on success and **0** otherwise, as in

```
opendir(DIR,$DIR) || die("$0: Error opening DIR $DIR: $!\n");
```

Directory handles enjoy their own namespace, and Perl distinguishes a directory handle from a filehandle of the same name by context alone. That is partly why the angle brackets don't work as input operators for directory handles. You have to use **readdir** instead, as in

```
$nextEntry = readdir(DIRHANDLE); # (NB: $nextEntry = <DIRHANDLE> ¬
doesn't work)
```

In an array context, **readdir** returns a list of all the entries in the directory that haven't already been read:

```
@remainingEntriesInDir = readdir(DIRHANDLE);
```

This is just like using **<FILEHANDLE>** to read all the remaining lines in a file:

```
@remainingLinesInFile = <FILEHANDLE>;
```

You can also use Perl's built-in **grep** function to keep only the entries in the returned list of filenames that match a regular expression or pass the test of some other operator. For example,

```
@imageFiles = grep( /\.([gt]iff?|jpe?g)$/i, readdir(DIR));
```

keeps only the entries in DIR that have a filename extension of gif, giff, tif, tiff, jpg, or jpeg (ignoring capitalization).

Directories, like associative arrays, may hash and compact their entries, so the entry names are not guaranteed to be stored in any particular order. To obtain an alphabetically sorted list of directory names that do not begin with a period, you could use

```
@visibleDirectories = sort(grep( -d && !/\./, readdir(DIR)));
```

To back up to the beginning of a directory, use **rewinddir(DIR)**, and to close it, use **closedir(DIR)**.

## Picking a Random Subset from a List or an Array

The subroutine **randpick** implements a standard method for randomly picking a specified number of elements from its parameter list. All the interesting action takes place in one statement, which calls **rand**, **splice**, and **push**, in that order:

```
push(@picked, splice(@fromList, rand @fromList, 1));
```

Once **srand** has seeded the random number generator (as explained in Chapter 5), the expression **rand @fromList** returns a number between **0** and the number of elements in **@fromList**.

The **splice** function is called like this

```
@removed = splice(@source, offset, N, list);
```

where *N* elements are removed from the array **@source**, starting at the position specified by *offset*, and replaced with the entries in *list*, if any. It returns the excised elements and grows or shrinks the **@source** array as necessary. If *N* is omitted, it removes all the elements from *offset* onward.

The **push** function is called like this

```
$size = push(@stack, list);
```

where the values in *list* are pushed onto the end of the array **@stack** (as if they were plates being added to a spring-loaded stack in a cafeteria). It returns the resulting number of elements in **@stack**.

The **randpick** function uses these functions together in one iterated statement to remove random elements from **@fromList** and add them to **@picked**. It's worth noting that although **splice** requires its first argument to be an actual array (as opposed to a literal list), Perl automatically converts all the scalar and ordinary array arguments to a subroutine into one array, namely **@_**. Thus you could also call **randpick** with a statement such as

```
@oneSuitDraw = &randpick(5, 1 .. 10, 'J', 'Q', 'K');
```

The changeMe.cgi script reads all the filenames from a specified directory, and if there are too many to fit comfortably into a pull-down menu, it calls **randpick** to return a random subset of them.

## Maintaining the State of a User-Modifiable Interface

The changeMe.cgi script always outputs the same form, but some of the parameters that affect its appearance change to reflect the values a user has input in previous submissions of this same form. To implement this feedback loop, many of the script's variables appear in the output page more than once. The background color,

**$BGCOLOR**, is typical. It appears once in a context in which the browser will translate it into a displayed color,

```
<BODY $BGS  BGCOLOR="$BGCOLOR"
TEXT="$TEXT" LINK="$LINK" VLINK="$VLINK" ALINK="$ALINK">
```

and once in a context that makes it a default input value for the next submission of the form,

```
<INPUT TYPE=TEXT SIZE=10 NAME=BGCOLOR VALUE=$BGCOLOR>
```

Both the displayed color and the string that represents the color's name or RGB number are part of the interface's current state. It is not the CGI program or the Web server that keeps track of them between requests, but the downloaded page as stored or displayed in the remote browser.

In this way, the CGI program is able to simulate a closed feedback loop. It appears as if the program were always there, waiting to take in further user input and use it to modify previously entered values, whereas, in fact, it exists only for a few fractions of a second at a time and never "remembers" anything between incarnations. The next chapter explains several other methods a CGI program can use to simulate a feedback loop with a user—or, more generally, to maintain some "memory" of a browser's current state from one invocation to the next.

Overcoming the
Statelessness of
CGI

Maintaining a
Persistent Context
in Multiple-Page
Applications

Maintaining State
with Magic Cookies

# Chapter 7
# Maintaining State in Multiple-Page Applications

One of the basic decisions you'll face as a CGI programmer is how to maintain context between pages, which is necessary if you want your programs to be able to pass user-entered information from one form to the next. Another decision, which often overlaps the one above, is how to keep track of individual users, either for the duration of one session or more permanently, across multiple sessions. If you are developing a transaction-based application such as an on-line catalog that uses "shopping carts" or multistage order forms, your program must be able to keep track of a user and a set of form responses at least throughout one session. If you have users who are frequent shoppers, or if your application is an order-tracking system, you might also want to store user profiles or account histories across multiple sessions. For instance, you might want to let the user retrieve a previous order, check on its current shipping status, and edit it in its original onscreen order form so that he or she can submit it as a new order. If your application is more like an interactive game than a catalog, you might want the user to be able to start it up in a previously saved state or even join others in an ongoing, multiplayer session.

For all of these scenarios, a CGI programmer's options are limited by the fact that the current HTTP standard does not include any built-in mechanisms for tracing a history, saving a context, or reliably identifying a user. Nor does the CGI standard, which requires external programs to run as new processes every time they are requested, provide any obvious solutions. Indeed, the concepts of history, state, context, and a stable identity may seem antithetical to a hypermedia world of random-access links and networked channel surfing.

This chapter introduces several different CGI programming techniques for maintaining context from one page to another and, more generally, for saving information between different invocations of a CGI program by the same user. These techniques include the use of hidden fields in forms, self-referential links with embedded query strings (*call-backs*), and CGI-inserted "cookies."

**199**

# Overcoming the Statelessness of CGI

One of CGI's biggest limitations is its statelessness. As discussed in earlier chapters, every time a CGI program is requested, it runs as a new process in a separate environment, starting with only the information contained in the request itself or in a generic set of environment variables. In other words, its starting *context* includes no history of previous requests or their results. When the program exits, this context and any other information it has accrued in memory—that is, its *internal state*—is entirely lost. The Web server, which actually waits for the CGI process to exit as a normal part of handling a request, then closes the connection to the client and "forgets" everything it knew about both the CGI program and the client browser that requested it. And browsers, although they may keep track of their own histories, have no access to a server-resident CGI program apart from what it outputs in each separate instance. Thus it is up to the CGI program itself to save state between instances, and it must do so within this very limited framework.

## Some Familiar Examples of Maintaining State

Even without any help from the server or browser, there are several different ways for a CGI program to save state between requests. In fact, you've already encountered some of these methods in earlier chapters. For instance, the "self-modifying form" example (Example 6D) at the end of Chapter 6 takes in user-entered values from one instance of the form and embeds them as the default values for the same input fields in the next instance. The current state of the form's background color variable, **$BGCOLOR**, for instance, is manifest as the background color itself or can at least be viewed as a number in the input field when you hit the Reset button. This is similar to what many word processors and other complex applications do: The settings that determine how a document will look in one of the application's windows are stored inside the document itself rather than inside the application (or in one of its own resource files), and yet to change these settings you must use the original application. In the case of changeMe.cgi, the document's variable settings are stored as VALUE fields inside HTML INPUT tags.

## Using Call-Back Links with Embedded Query Strings to Maintain Context

The one-armed bandit script in Chapter 5 (Example 5D) illustrates a different way for an application to save state information inside its output documents instead of within its own local files. The one_arm.cgi script outputs an image if it is called with a query string; otherwise it outputs an HTML page containing a number of automatically generated *call-backs* to itself—that is, IMG elements that request the same script again with random numbers as query strings. As a means of preventing the random number generator from repeating itself in subsequent call-backs, the one_arm.cgi script inserts previously generated numbers into its outgoing HTML page. It inserts these random numbers as query strings appended to its own URL inside the IMG tags that call it back; for example:

```
<IMG SRC=/cgi-bin/one_arm.cgi?98919272.714563325>
```

Thus it sends out bits of state information only to get them back again as part of a later request. Or, to be more precise, one instance of the running program sends them out and a later instance gets them back, probably after the first instance has died and vanished from the system's memory.

Because they are embedded as the SRC attributes of IMG tags, the call-backs that this particular program outputs are always executed right away. But CGI call-backs can also be embedded within HTML documents as ordinary links; these can contain any valid query string, including one from a previously submitted form. Clicking on a link that contains an embedded query string is similar to entering a URL and query string by hand in a browser's Go To field or Visit Location box; you have to make sure that the query string is already encoded, because the browser won't do it for you. If you're using a previously submitted query string, of course, this isn't an issue.

Call-backs with embedded query strings can thus be used to maintain context even between pages that include no forms, as long as all the links connect to CGI programs that can make sense of the attached query strings. A noteworthy exception is any script that handles only POST requests. Although it's easy from a technical point of view to handle both an appended query string and a message body as part of the same posted request, browsers don't submit the data from forms this way, and most CGI programs first examine the REQUEST_METHOD environment variable and then process only one or the other. The subroutine **getFormData**, explained in Chapter 4, is a typical example of this either/or processing strategy. CGI programmers are accustomed to taking advantage of the dichotomy between the GET and POST methods, and a great many scripts installed on the Web depend on it. The upshot is that unless your CGI script is designed to handle query strings as part of GET requests (possibly in addition to posted message bodies), you're basically stuck with forms and SUBMIT buttons instead of links, and this may severely impair your navigational freedom.

The flexibility that can be attained using embedded query strings is in fact one of the few good reasons for continuing to use the GET method instead of POST for submitting forms. Nor is it necessarily the fate of a call-back link to drag behind itself the entire history of your application as one great chain of query strings. Instead of including all the context information in its original form, you can embed short query strings that serve only as identifiers, and then use these as keys for accessing the full context that is stored back on the server. This is the basic idea behind cookies, as you shall see. I'll provide examples of how to use cookies later in the chapter.

## Using Hidden Fields to Maintain Context

Hidden fields are simply INPUT elements in HTML forms that have the special attribute TYPE=HIDDEN. Although they are not displayed, their NAME and VALUE attributes are submitted just like the *name=value* pairs from other INPUT fields. Thus you can use them to create a form that will submit any predefined information you like, in addition to whatever the user enters. This makes it very easy to maintain context from one automatically generated form to another. Hidden fields were in fact invented to obviate the need for multipage forms that keep soliciting the same information on every page, and this is still how they are most often used. They are invisible not because the information they contain is meant to be secret, but

## WARNING! Hidden Fields Are Not Very Hidden

Hidden fields are not displayed, but neither are they secret. Any user can see their contents by choosing an Edit or View Source command in the browser, and users can even change their values before submitting the form. (With some browsers, they'll have to save the source HTML as a file before editing it.) So don't use hidden fields to "hide" sensitive information, such as real passwords or credit card numbers, and don't think that users can't change the information—prices, item numbers, or any other terms of sale—that you store in them. As with embedded query strings, you might want to replace explicit information with codes, but even encrypted strings can be cracked or simply exchanged. Hidden fields provide convenience, not security.

because it is meant to be saved and not changed by the user. (See the sidebar entitled, "WARNING! Hidden Fields Are Not Very Hidden.")

## Example 7A: Using Hidden Fields and Call-Backs

The SaveText.cgi script, shown in Listing 7.1, provides a simple example that uses hidden fields to save previously entered data, and it illustrates some of the differences between using hidden fields and using call-back links that contain embedded query strings. It always outputs the same HTML form (shown in Figure 7.1), with only the values of three embedded variables varying between instances. Each of these variables is embedded in a different way: as the displayed VALUE field of a text input element, as the invisible VALUE field in a hidden input element, and as the (usually) invisible query string in a call-back link. The functions tied to the various submit buttons only work on two of these variables, **$EntryText** and **$SavedText**, either by copying the value of one to the other or interchanging them. These two internal variables and their attendant operations are sufficient to let the user enter, save, or recall a line of text, or switch back and forth between the current (displayed) and saved (hidden) text.

In addition to the submit buttons Enter, Save, Recall, and Switch Entry/Saved, there is a Start Over submit button, which posts a form submission back to the same script, but without any data other than SubmitBtn=Start+Over. Hitting this button has the same effect as clicking on the self-referential Start Over link, which sends back a GET request without any query string.

Finally, the Back Up link does contain an embedded query string, which is just the most recently received query information (submitted using either GET or POST), minus the name of any submit button. Depending on what was in the previous submission, clicking on this call-back button usually serves to undo the previous operation. For example, alternately clicking on the Recall button and Back Up link lets the user go back and forth between the most recently saved and entered text; this is like having separate redo and undo functions. The Switch Entry/Saved button, on the other hand, is a toggle switch; the attached operation is its own inverse.

This example is admittedly a toy, kind of like a see-through plastic watch: it's main purpose is just to show you how its inner workings work. The next few sections explain the code step by step.

### Using `getFormData` to Get All the Input

The SaveText.cgi program can be invoked by either a GET or a POST request, with or without any query information—that is, an appended query string in the case of GET or a form-submitted message body in the case of POST. Rather than checking

**LISTING 7.1    The SaveText.cgi script, which saves and recalls text using a hidden field and a call-back link**

```perl
#!/usr/local/bin/perl
# SaveText.cgi - example using a hidden field and a call-back link
# Copyright (C) 1996 Stephen Lines <spraxlo@ai.mit.edu>

require 'FormData.pl';

# Names for all the submit (and reset) buttons:
$Enter  = 'Enter';
$Save   = 'Save';
$Recall = 'Recall';
$Switch = 'Switch Entry/Saved';
$Reset  = 'Reset';
$Start  = 'Start Over';

if ($QueryInfo = &getFormData( *FormData )) {
    $QueryInfo =~ s/&SubmitBtn=[^&]*//;  # Remove button name unless
} else {                                 # it comes first in query.
    $QueryInfo = 'EntryText=I%27m+hiding+now%2C+call+back+later%21';
}

$EntryText = $FormData{'EntryText'} || 'Default Entry Text';
$SavedText = $FormData{'SavedText'} || 'Default Saved Text';
$SubmitBtn = $FormData{'SubmitBtn'} || $Enter;

if    ($SubmitBtn eq $Save)   { $SavedText = $EntryText;  }
elsif ($SubmitBtn eq $Recall) { $EntryText = $SavedText;  }
elsif ($SubmitBtn eq $Switch) { ($EntryText , $SavedText) =
                                ($SavedText , $EntryText); }

print  "Content-type: text/html\n\n";
print <<END_OF_PAGE;
<HTML><HEAD><TITLE> Example of Saving Text in a Hidden Field
</TITLE></HEAD><BODY BGCOLOR="#55DCBA" TEXT="#864210">
<H1> Saving Text in a Hidden Field</H1>
<FORM METHOD=POST>
```

**LISTING 7.1    The SaveText.cgi script, which saves and recalls text using a hidden field and a call-back link (Continued)**

```
<INPUT TYPE=TEXT    NAME=EntryText VALUE="$EntryText" SIZE=65>
<INPUT TYPE=HIDDEN NAME=SavedText VALUE="$SavedText">
<P><TABLE><TR><TD>
<INPUT TYPE=SUBMIT NAME=SubmitBtn VALUE="$Enter" ></TD><TD>
<INPUT TYPE=SUBMIT NAME=SubmitBtn VALUE="$Save"  ></TD><TD>
<INPUT TYPE=SUBMIT NAME=SubmitBtn VALUE="$Recall"></TD><TD>
<INPUT TYPE=SUBMIT NAME=SubmitBtn VALUE="$Switch"></TD><TD>
<INPUT TYPE=RESET                 VALUE="$Reset" ></TD><TD>
</FORM><FORM METHOD=POST>
<INPUT TYPE=SUBMIT NAME=SubmitBtn VALUE="$Start" ></TD>
</FORM></TR></TABLE>
<P>
[<A HREF="$ENV{'SCRIPT_NAME'}"><B>Start Over:</B> This self-referring
link resets everything by sending back a plain GET request</A>]
<BR>
[<A HREF="$ENV{'SCRIPT_NAME'}?$QueryInfo"><B>Back Up:</B> This call-back
link sends the following URL-encoded query string:<BR><DD>$QueryInfo</A>]
</BODY></HTML>
END_OF_PAGE
```

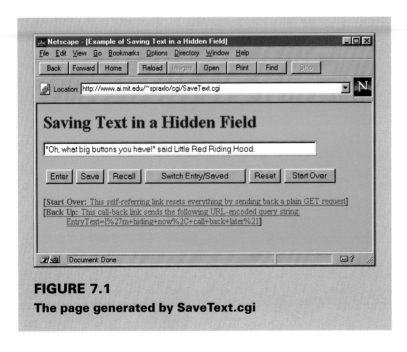

**FIGURE 7.1**
**The page generated by SaveText.cgi**

these conditions itself, the program simply calls the subroutine **getFormData** (defined in Chapter 4) to do all the dirty work for it:

```
if ($QueryInfo = &getFormData( *FormData )) {
```

If a client browser does send query information as part of its request, **getFormData** will parse and decode it, loading the resulting name and value pairs into an associative array named **%FormData**. It will also return the original query information as a string, here assigned to **$QueryInfo**. This return value lets you use **getFormData** for testing purposes, as illustrated by the following code fragment:

```
if (&getFormData(*parsedData)) {
  &doSomethingUsefulWithTheSubmittedData(*parsedData);
} else {
  &outputSomeNewFormWithNoPriorStateInformation;
}
```

## Preparing the Call-Back Query String

Once you've got all of a form's data parsed and loaded into an associative array, the original query information is seldom useful; in the code fragment above, it's simply discarded. In SaveText.cgi, however, you want to keep it around to use as an embedded query string, so you'll store it in **$QueryInfo**. Before sending it back out to the browser, however, the script should modify it slightly. If it came from a submission of the form output from a prior invocation of SaveText.cgi, it's likely to contain a *name=value* pair of **SubmitBtn=*ButtonName***, where *ButtonName* is the value field from one of the form's three submit buttons. You need to snip this pair out to make sure that the embedded query string will work properly in call-backs:

```
$QueryInfo =~ s/&SubmitBtn=[^&]*//;
```

Here the **s/*pattern*/*replacement*/** operator is used to excise any substring in **$QueryInfo** that begins with **&SubmitBtn=** and continues either to the next ampersand or to the end of the string. It's worth noting that this operation will not affect any user-entered text because **$QueryInfo** is still URL-encoded. If a user were to enter the string **&SubmitBtn=**, the ampersand would be encoded as **%26** and the equal sign as **%3D**; the resulting string, **&26SubmitBtn%3D**, does not match the search pattern.

If a client browser does not send any query information as part of its request, **$QueryInfo** will be null, so you assign it a default value. The complete conditional statement is

```
if ($QueryInfo =  &getFormData( *FormData )) {
    $QueryInfo =~ s/&SubmitBtn=[^&]*//;  # Remove button name unless
} else {                                 # it comes first in query.
    $QueryInfo = 'EntryText=I%27m+hiding+now%2C+call+back+later%21';
}
```

You need to URL-encode a query string before embedding it in a link, because when a user clicks on the link, the browser will request the embedded URL exactly as written.

## Extracting or Initializing the Text and Button Values

Next, the variables **$EntryText**, **$SavedText**, and **$SubmitBtn** are extracted from **%FormData.** If any these is not defined, it is assigned a default value (see the sidebar, "The Importance of Your Program's Internal Consistency"):

```
$EntryText = $FormData{'EntryText'} || 'Default Entry Text';
$SavedText = $FormData{'SavedText'} || 'Default Saved Text';
$SubmitBtn = $FormData{'SubmitBtn'} || $Enter;
```

Recall that an expression of the form **A** II **B** is evaluated as **A** or else **B**. Here, for example, **$EntryText** is assigned the value **Default Entry Text** only if **%FormData** has no value defined for the key **EntryText**.

## Implementing the Save, Recall, and Switch Buttons

The heart of the script is contained in the three conditional statements that implement the Save, Recall, and Switch Entry/Saved buttons:

```
if    ($SubmitBtn eq $Save)   {  $SavedText = $EntryText;  }
elsif ($SubmitBtn eq $Recall) {  $EntryText = $SavedText;  }
elsif ($SubmitBtn eq $Switch) { ($EntryText , $SavedText) =
                                 ($SavedText , $EntryText); }
```

At this point in the script, the two strings $EntryText and $SavedText are always defined, and the effect of the user's clicking on the Save or Recall button is simply to replace one of these strings with the other. In conjunction with the form's hidden field, which always contains $SavedText as its value, this is all it takes to save or recall a string, or, in other words, to move a string into or out of the form's single hidden field. The Switch Entry/Saved button uses a list assignment to swap these two strings in-place.

# The Importance of Your Program's Internal Consistency

You might ask, "Are all these default values really necessary? And why test these variables individually—either they are all defined by the submitted form data or none of them are, right?"

My answer to the first question is no, not all of these tests and default value assignments are really necessary, but if you want your CGI program to maintain state with clients, you should at least make sure that its internal state is well-defined and predictable. Keeping all of its variables defined is easy and goes a long way toward ensuring consistent results. For example, giving **$SubmitBtn** a default value has no effect on SaveText.cgi's actual output (as long as that default value is neither **"Save"** nor **"Recall"**), but it does add to the consistency of the program's internal state, and makes the programmer's intentions clear. As SaveText.cgi is actually implemented, **$SubmitBtn**'s default value of **"Enter"** is inconsequential, because entering the text currently displayed in the form's input field is already the script's default action. However, if you ever wanted to change the default action (to make it, for example, append the current text to the saved text), then **$SubmitBtn**'s default value would suddenly matter very much.

My answer to the second question is also no; you should never count on the data submitted to your script being exactly what you expect from the form. Just because your output form includes a certain name or a predefined set of values in its input fields doesn't mean that this name or one of these values must appear in the data submitted back from it, or that other names and values cannot be inserted. Web users actually do save and edit local copies of forms, and then use them to submit data to the original form-processing CGI program. (This is one way of getting rid of advertisements.)

In the example at hand, the data submitted from the form output by SaveText.cgi will not necessarily include a name=value pair from any of its submit buttons. Since it only includes one text input field, many browsers will submit this form even when the user only hits the Enter key. Also, this particular program accepts arbitrary query strings as part of GET requests, and these strings need not conform to the prescribed form's input fields. Thus the only way to ensure that all the names from the form really do receive values is to check them individually.

## The Output Form with Its Visible and Hidden Input Fields

The SaveText.cgi program always outputs the same HTML page, using the "document here" construct **print <<END_OF_PAGE**. The form contained in this page is rather straightforward, and it contains only two embedded variables. It should be no surprise that these two are **$EntryText** and **$SavedText** and that they appear (or don't appear) as the values of the text input and hidden fields, respectively:

```
<FORM METHOD=POST>
<INPUT TYPE=TEXT   NAME=EntryText VALUE="$EntryText" SIZE=60>
<INPUT TYPE=HIDDEN NAME=SavedText VALUE="$SavedText">
```

The opening FORM tag contains no ACTION attribute; therefore, this form is always submitted back to the same URL from which it originated. When this form ends, another one immediately begins, which contains no input elements other than a submit button for starting over:

```
</FORM><FORM METHOD=POST>
<INPUT TYPE=SUBMIT NAME=SubmitBtn VALUE="$Start" ></TD>
</FORM></TR></TABLE>
```

Hitting this button issues a POST request back to the same script but with none of the data from the other form. The changeMe.cgi script presented at the end of Chapter 6 also had a button for resetting everything to its default value, only it worked by calling the **undef** operator to undefine **%Form**. Including an empty "mini-form" like the one here is just another method for doing the same thing.

As a trick to keep all of the buttons displayed on one line, the end of the first form and the beginning of the second are enclosed inside the same table element. Ordinarily, a <FORM> or </FORM> tag breaks the line.

## The Output Page's Two Call-Back Links: Restart and Undo

The page output by SaveText.cgi also includes two self-referential links that can be used to call the program back again. Both links use the value of the environment variable SCRIPT_NAME as their basic URL:

```
[<A HREF="$ENV{'SCRIPT_NAME'}"><B>Start Over:</B> This self-referring
link resets everything by sending back a plain GET request</A>]
<BR>
[<A HREF="$ENV{'SCRIPT_NAME'}?$QueryInfo"><B>Back Up:</B> This ¬
call-back
link sends the following URL-encoded query string:<BR><DD>$QueryInfo¬
</A>]
```

Clicking on the first link does just what it says: By calling SaveText.cgi with a plain GET request, it starts a new session, losing any state information formerly saved in a query string or in the downloaded copy of the form itself.

The second link appends **$QueryInfo** to the call-back URL as an embedded query string. As explained above, **$QueryInfo** is nothing more than the query string or posted message body sent by a browser as part of the current request, albeit with the *name=value* pair corresponding to the SUBMIT buttons removed. The effect of clicking on the Call Back link will be interesting only if the form was last submitted with the Save Entered button or the Recall Saved button. In these cases, respectively, the value of **$SavedText** or **$EntryText** as a variable substituted into the form's input fields may be different from the value of **SavedText** or **EntryText** that appears as a name in the embedded query string. Otherwise, clicking on this call-back link will have the same effect as clicking on the Enter Current Text button or simply hitting your keyboard's Enter key.

Both of these links appear at the very end of the page, but they could have been placed anywhere after the call to **getFormData** on the second line of the program. The effect of clicking on either of them depends only on its embedded query string (or lack thereof). In particular, they need not appear inside a form and can even be placed in a separate page and still provide identical results.

## For the Few Browsers that Can't Handle Multiple SUBMIT Buttons....

Their numbers are dwindling, but some people still use browsers that cannot handle multiple SUBMIT buttons. If you are worried about backward compatibility of this kind, try using the following code fragment as a workaround:

```
if ($ENV{'HTTP_USER_AGENT'} =~ /Lynx|CERN-LineMode/) {
  <INPUT TYPE=RADIO NAME=Submit VALUE="Do it this way" CHECKED>
  <INPUT TYPE=RADIO NAME=Submit VALUE="Do it that way">
  <INPUT TYPE=SUBMIT NAME=DontLookAtMe_LookAtSubmit VALUE="Do It">
} else {
  # Code for the rest of the world (multiple SUBMIT buttons)
}
```

Another possible workaround is to replace multiple SUBMIT buttons with single or multiple image maps, but some of the same browsers also can't handle image maps.

So you see that a call-back link with an embedded query string can have some of the same functionality as a submit button, but not all. On the other hand, call-backs are in some ways more flexible. In particular, an embedded query string is self-contained. This means that it can appear anywhere, but it also means that the values that it submits to a CGI program are already determined when it it is inserted into a page, and cannot interact with the values of any form input elements.

# Maintaining a Persistent Context in Multiple-Page Applications

Hidden fields and/or call-back links with embedded query strings are often sufficient for maintaining state throughout a single session with a single page, but what about multiple pages?

One problem that any multiple-page Web application must address is how to maintain context when the user is navigating among its various pages. Hyperlinks provide the most common means of getting from one page to another on the Web, but these pose special problems when maintaining state is an issue. Links with embedded query strings are at best only a partial solution, because query strings are limited in their absolute length, and clicking on a link that is on the same page as a form will cause that form's present contents to be discarded. (You can actually use one embedded query string in conjunction with POST-submitted form data, but this provides no advantage over hidden fields, because the query string can be appended to the URL only in the FORM element's ACTION attribute.) Thus links do not provide a generally viable mechanism for navigating among multiple forms when you need to preserve state information.

Apart from information that resides outside of the pages and the short-lived CGI process itself, such as server-side or client-side cookie mechanisms, that leaves us with only the information submitted from the form itself. Hidden fields can be used to contain information about where the client browser has already been and where it should go next, but because they are hidden, these do not offer the user any choice in the matter.

One approach to this problem of navigation is to present a number of choices via the usual input elements of forms and let the user decide for him- or herself where to go and how to get there. It is generally a good idea to devote some part of any multiple-page forms interface to explicit navigational information such as this.

The opposite approach is to automate navigation as much as possible, using some behind-the-scenes mechanism in the CGI program. The simplest way to accomplish this is to cycle through a predefined sequence of pages. You can generalize this strategy by implementing a lookup table that returns the next page to visit as a function of the current and/or previously visited pages.

In many cases, it is a good idea to provide the user with either option: a choice of destinations as well as an automatically selected default next page. The examples that follow illustrate several different navigational strategies.

## Example 7B: Using One Script to Generate Multiple Pages with No Hidden Information

Although hidden fields and call-backs can be very helpful for maintaining a persistent context between multiple pages, they are not indispensable. The script www-mart.cgi (shown in Listing 7.2) implements a shopping cart that can be "carried" from page to page using only displayed input fields and the standard mechanisms of form submission and processing (see Figures 7.2 and 7.3). One of the advantages of this kind of shopping cart is that its contents are always available for review and possible deselection; the user doesn't have to visit any special page to review the contents of the cart or change the selections. One of the disadvantages is that it places some restrictions on the possible means of navigating from one page to another. Links, for example, must be avoided, because to follow one would be to leave the shopping cart behind. Another constraint is that a single back-end CGI script must be used both for moving to the next page and for transferring the shopping cart between pages. In this example, that same script is also used to generate all the pages themselves.

**LISTING 7.2    www-mart.cgi: a script that generates multiple pages, all of which share one shopping cart**

```perl
#!/usr/local/bin/perl
# www-mart.cgi - Simple shopping cart example (no cookies/hidden fields)
# Copyright (C) 1996 Stephen Lines <spraxlo@ai.mit.edu>
require "FormData.pl";
require "MailForm.pl";

$owner    = "checkout\@www-mart.com";
$BGCOLOR  = "#ABDDBA";
$CheckOut = "Checkout Counter";
$Payment  = "Process Payment";
$AddVideo = "<P>Add this video to your shopping cart: \n";
$Price    = 2.50;
```

**LISTING 7.2    www-mart.cgi: a script that generates multiple pages, all of which
share one shopping cart (Continued)**

```
############### Data: Names and texts for the pages: ##########
$num = -1;


$PageNames[++$num] = 'The Apartment';
$PageTexts[  $num] = <<END_OF_PAGE;
Starring Jack Lemmon, Shirley MacLaine, and Fred MacMurray<BR>
Directed by Billy Wilder.<BR>1960 USA, 125 min.
$AddVideo <INPUT TYPE=CHECKBOX NAME=videos VALUE="$PageNames[$num]">
END_OF_PAGE


$PageNames[++$num] = 'Apartment Zero';
$PageTexts[  $num] = <<END_OF_PAGE;
Starring Hart Bochner, Colin Firth, and Fabrizio Bentivoglio.<BR>
Directed by Martin Donovan.<BR>1988 UK, 124 min.
$AddVideo <INPUT TYPE=CHECKBOX NAME=videos VALUE="$PageNames[$num]">
END_OF_PAGE


$PageNames[++$num] = 'The Landlord';
$PageTexts[  $num] = <<END_OF_PAGE;
Starring Beau Bridges, Lee Grant, Diana Sands, and Pearl Bailey.<BR>
Directed by Hal Ashby.<BR>1970 USA, 112 min.
$AddVideo <INPUT TYPE=CHECKBOX NAME=videos VALUE="$PageNames[$num]">
END_OF_PAGE


$PageNames[++$num] = 'The Tenant (Le Locataire)';
$PageTexts[  $num] = <<END_OF_PAGE;
Starring Isabelle Adjani, Roman Polanski, and Shelley Winters.<BR>
Directed by Roman Polanski.<BR>1976 France, 125 min.
$AddVideo <INPUT TYPE=CHECKBOX NAME=videos VALUE="$PageNames[$num]">
END_OF_PAGE


#################### The checkout page must be last: ##########
$LastNum = ++$num;
```

**LISTING 7.2**   **www-mart.cgi: a script that generates multiple pages, all of which share one shopping cart (Continued)**

```perl
$PageNames[  $num] = $CheckOut;
$PageTexts[  $num] = <<END_OF_PAGE;
<P>Account Name:
<INPUT TYPE=TEXT SIZE=40 NAME="AccName" VALUE="$Form{'AccName'}">
<P>5-Digit Account Number:
<INPUT TYPE=TEXT SIZE=10 NAME="AccNum"  VALUE="$Form{'AccNum'}">
END_OF_PAGE


######### Main Program: Check out or output next page: #######


print "Content-type: text/html\n\n";


#### Algorithm: a "goal-driven loop": check all criteria
#### leading up to the main objective, and if they're met, exit;
#### otherwise, determine the next page to display...


if (($ENV{'REQUEST_METHOD'} eq 'POST')  && &getFormData(*Form)) {
  if (( $PageName =  $Form{'PageName'}) &&
      ( $PageName eq $CheckOut || $PageName eq $Payment)) {
    if ($PageName eq $Payment  && &ProcessPayment(*Form)) {
      &mailForm(*Form, $owner, $owner, $0, $ENV{'HTTP_REFERER'});
      &Thankyou;
      exit;
    }
    $PageNum  = $LastNum;         # stay on checkout page
  } else {
    for ($PageNum = $LastNum - 1; $PageNum > 0; $PageNum--) {
      last if ($PageName eq $PageNames[$PageNum]);
    } # If the name isn't found, the loop ends at $PageNum == 0.
  }
} else {
  $PageNum  = 0;                  # default page num is 0
}
```

---

**LISTING 7.2** **www-mart.cgi: a script that generates multiple pages, all of which share one shopping cart (Continued)**

---

```perl
# Now use PageNum to determine next and previous pages:
  $NextName = $PageNames[($PageNum + 1) % $LastNum];
  $PrevName = $PageNames[($PageNum - 1) % $LastNum];
# warn("$0: num=$PageNum next=$NextName prev=$PrevName\n"); #debug


############### Haven't exited, so output the next page: #####


print <<EOF;
<HTML><HEAD><TITLE>
WWW-Mart $PageNum: $PageNames[$PageNum]
</TITLE></HEAD><BODY BGCOLOR="$BGCOLOR">
<FORM METHOD=POST><H1>
$PageNames[$PageNum]</H1>
$PageTexts[$PageNum]
<P><HR><INPUT TYPE=RESET                 VALUE="RESET this Page">
Next:  <INPUT TYPE=SUBMIT NAME=PageName VALUE="$NextName">
Back:  <INPUT TYPE=SUBMIT NAME=PageName VALUE="$PrevName">
EOF


############### Display the cart's contents, if any: #########


if ($videos = $Form{'videos'}) {
  @videos = split(/\0/, $videos);
  $numvid = @videos;
  print "<HR><H2>Your Shopping Cart</H2><P>\nCurrent selections:\n";
  print "<SELECT NAME=videos MULTIPLE SIZE=", 1 + $numvid, ">\n";
  foreach $_ (@videos) {
    print "<OPTION SELECTED> $_\n";
  }
  print "</SELECT><BR>\n";
  $Total = $Price * $numvid;
# print  "That's $numvid video rental", ($numvid > 1) && 's', "\n";
  print  "That's $numvid video rental", ($numvid > 1) ? 's' : '', "\n";
  printf(" at \$%.2f each, for a total of \$%.2f.\n", $Price, $Total);
```

**LISTING 7.2    www-mart.cgi: a script that generates multiple pages, all of which share one shopping cart (Continued)**

```
  if ($PageNum == $LastNum) {
    print "Order these now:\n";
    print "<INPUT TYPE=SUBMIT NAME=PageName VALUE=\"$Payment\">\n";
  } else {
    print "Take these to the:\n";
    print "<INPUT TYPE=SUBMIT NAME=PageName VALUE=\"$CheckOut\">\n";
  }
}
print "</FORM></BODY></HTML>\n";



############### Local Subroutines: ##########################

sub ProcessPayment {
  ((length($Form{'AccName'}) > 2) && ($Form{'AccNum'} =~ /^\d{5,5}$/));
}


sub Thankyou {
print <<EOF;
<HTML>
<HEAD><TITLE> WWW-Mart Thanks You </TITLE></HEAD>
<BODY BGCOLOR="$BGCOLOR"><CENTER><H3>
W-w-we at WWW-Mart are st-stuttering with excitement about your order!
</H3><H1> THANK YOU!</H1>
</CENTER></BODY></HTML>
EOF
}
```

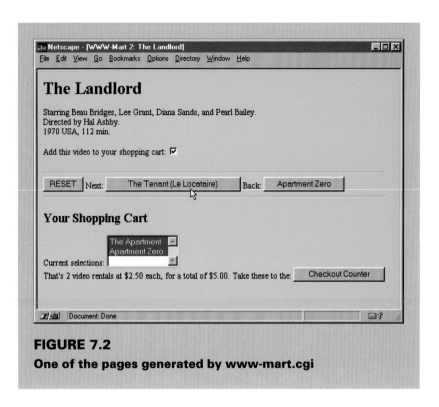

**FIGURE 7.2**

**One of the pages generated by www-mart.cgi**

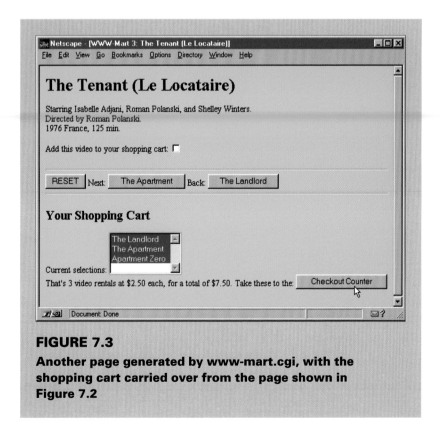

**FIGURE 7.3**

**Another page generated by www-mart.cgi, with the shopping cart carried over from the page shown in Figure 7.2**

### Initializing the Page Data

The first half of www-mart.cgi initializes the data structures needed for serving multiple pages, navigating among them, and servicing any possible input from them. The Perl interpreter compiles the script's contents and resolves symbols sequentially, so these structures need to be defined before they can be referenced later on in the program.

The very first section sets configuration variables. For example, it defines the application owner, to whom final orders will be e-mailed:

```
$owner    = "checkout\@www-mart.com";
```

Perl 5 requires the backslash before the at sign to disambiguate between the literal string **"\@www"** and the array name **@www**. (Perl 4 silently guesses at the meaning of an at sign inside a double-quoted string. Here, if an array named **@www** had already been defined, it would interpolate the array elements into the string, separated by spaces; otherwise, it would treat **"@www"** as a literal string.)

Following that are the names and texts of the pages themselves, for example:

```
$PageNames[++$num] = 'The Apartment';
$PageTexts[  $num] = <<END_OF_PAGE;
Starring Jack Lemmon, Shirley MacLaine, and Fred MacMurray<BR>
Directed by Billy Wilder.<BR>1960 USA, 125 min.
$AddVideo <INPUT TYPE=CHECKBOX NAME=videos VALUE="$PageNames[$num]">
END_OF_PAGE
```

Each page is given its own name—which happens to be the name of the movie that the page advertises for rental—and this name is placed in the array **@PageNames**. The order in which the pages are defined will also be the order in which they are displayed, so the array indices also serve as page numbers. The main text of each page, a blurb about the videotape it offers for rental, is placed in an array named **@PageTexts**, which is indexed with the same numbers, as given by **$num**. Ordinary arrays whose indices are in exact correspondence are said to be *parallel*. Using two parallel arrays may seem less elegant than using one associative array, but ordinary arrays are much more suitable for storing data in a predefined order. The reason for using a symbolic index with an auto-increment operator (**$num** and **++$num**) instead of literal numbers is to make it easy to add or delete page entries and to prevent typos. Any mistake you made when typing in the literal page numbers would throw the arrays out of their parallelism.

**Using Prefixed and Postfixed Increment Operators**   In Perl, as in C++ and several other programming languages, double plus signs are used as the *unary increment* operator. Unary operators operate on only one argument, or *operand*; in contrast, binary operators such as **+** or **-** require two operands. The **++** operator can be applied only to a variable that evaluates to a number in a scalar context, and its meaning depends on whether it is prefixed or postfixed to its operand. When **++** is prefixed to a variable, the value of the resulting expression is incremented before it is referenced, whereas in the postfix position, **++** increments its operand only after it is referenced. For example,

```
$PageNames[++$num] = 'The Apartment';
```

is equivalent to

```
$num = $num + 1;
$PageNames[$num] = 'The Apartment';
```

whereas

```
$PageNames[$num++] = 'The Apartment';
```

is equivalent to

```
$PageNames[$num] = 'The Apartment';
$num = $num + 1;
```

The same prefix and postfix rule applies to the unary decrement operator (—).

**The Form Contents of Each Page**   Every entry in **@PageTexts** contains its own form input elements. The first four entries define catalog pages; they each contain a checkbox that takes **videos** as its NAME attribute and the name of the page as its VALUE, as in

```
$AddVideo <INPUT TYPE=CHECKBOX NAME=videos VALUE="$PageNames[$num]">
```

Here **$AddVideo** will be replaced at runtime by its initial value, *"<P>Add this video to your shopping cart: \n."* Since there is only one video title to add to the cart, why is the input name field "videos" instead of "video"? Because this same NAME attribute will be shared by input elements in all of the catalog pages, as well as in the shopping cart itself. The standard convention for handling multiple input fields with the same name is to join all the values together in one null-separated string. In this script, getFormData does that automatically.

The last page, which serves as the WWW-Mart application's "checkout counter," contains a pair of text fields for entering an account name and an account number. In the pages that www-mart.cgi actually outputs, these particular input elements will be supplemented by several elements common to all the pages—namely, two or three SUBMIT buttons and a scrollbox that displays the current contents of the shopping cart.

The strategy for maintaining a shared context between multiple pages is simply to interpolate the individual page names and texts into one master page, which serves as a template. Most of www-mart.cgi's context information is kept inside this common template.

### Navigating among the Pages in a Loop

This example adopts a very simple method for navigating among pages. All navigation is performed using submit buttons, and all of them share the same NAME attribute, namely, PageName, but have different VALUE fields. Every time the script serves a page, it binds the name of the following page to a submit button, and the name of a previous page to another submit button, as in:

```
Next:   <INPUT TYPE=SUBMIT NAME=PageName VALUE="The Landlord">
Back:   <INPUT TYPE=SUBMIT NAME=PageName VALUE="The Apartment">
```

If the form is submitted using METHOD=POST, as specified in its FORM tag, then the form's input data should always include exactly one PageName=value pair (but just in case it doesn't, a PageName will be assigned by default). As a result, the user can break out of the predefined sequence of catalog pages only by hitting another such submit button to jump to the checkout page. If the user keeps clicking on the "Next:" or "Back:" button, the pages will eventually loop full circle. A more flexible version might provide alternate navigational options in separate input elements, but then there would also have to be provisions for resolving conflicts between the different navigational methods, since (unlike video selections) there can really only be one next page.

The application's approach to "turning the page" is implicit in its basic algorithm for handling a request. Although each instance of the running program handles only one request, the state information saved between instances makes it quite natural to characterize the total operation in terms of a loop, and this loop repeats until either of two terminal conditions is met: Either the user terminates the loop (for example, by leaving a page with a shopping cart on it and never coming back) or the user goes to the checkout counter and has his or her payment method approved, in which case the application terminates the loop.

Loosely speaking, you could characterize this algorithm as a "goal-seeking" loop. The goal is to get the customer to go to the checkout counter with one or more videos to rent and pay for them. Accordingly, the center of the program is a compound conditional statement starting with

```
if (($ENV{'REQUEST_METHOD'} eq 'POST')  && &getFormData(*Form)) {
   if (( $PageName =  $Form{'PageName'}) &&
      ( $PageName eq $CheckOut || $PageName eq $PayNow)) {
    if ($PageName eq $PayNow   && &ProcessPayment(*Form)) {
```

If all of these conditions are satisfied, there's really nothing left to do but finish processing the request and exit:

```
&mailForm(*Form, $owner, $owner, $0, $ENV{'HTTP_REFERER'});
&Thankyou;
exit;
}
```

In this case, the script e-mails all the contents of **%Form** to the recipient, **$owner**. An implementation of this function follows this example.

Failing that, the script must get ready to output a new page. Exactly which page it will output next depends on how many of the above conditions were met, but the main point is that the loop between the application and the user's browser will continue with all previous state information intact. If the particular request made it all the way to **&ProcessPayment(*Form)** and then failed, the new page number will still be **$LastNum**, which is the number of the "checkout counter" page. If the submitted form data includes a new value for PageName other than **$CheckOut** or **$PayNow**, then this value should specify the name of the next page to output. However, this value is first placed in **$PageName** and compared with the names in **@PageNames** to obtain the corresponding index number as the value of **$PageNum**:

```
for ($PageNum = $LastNum - 1; $PageNum > 0; $PageNum—) {
   last if ($PageName eq $PageNames[$PageNum]);
} # If the name isn't found, the loop ends at $PageNum == 0.
```

Finally, if the request contained no form data or wasn't even a POST request, the next page defaults to page 0.

**Validating and Assigning Page Names and Page Numbers**  Once the value of **$PageNum** is set, it can be used with the modulus operator **%** to obtain the names the of the next and previous pages for the output page's Next and Back buttons:

```
$NextName = $PageNames[($PageNum + 1) % $LastNum];
$PrevName = $PageNames[($PageNum - 1) % $LastNum];
```

The value of the expression **N % M**, where **N** and **M** are integers and **M** is positive, is **N** modulo **M**—that is, the smallest positive integer **R** such that **N = Q\*M + R** for some integer **Q**. If **N** is positive, **R** is just the remainder left from dividing **N** by **M**. This value will always lie in the range **0** to **M - 1**, inclusive, and thus, **$PageNames[($PageNum + 1) % $LastNum]** will always be a valid page name, no matter what value **$PageNum** has.

Besides finding the index number, which can be used to reference the entries in **@PageTexts** as well as **$PageNames**, the little loop above also serves to validate the submitted request. Every submission that comes back from one of the pages output by www-mart.cgi should include a PageName=*VALUE* pair, where *VALUE* is exactly the value of **$CheckOut**, **$PayNow**, or one of the entries in **@PageTexts**. Moreover, this *VALUE* is not typed in, but comes directly from the VALUE attribute of a submit button. Shouldn't the program simply accept this *VALUE* as the legitimate name of the next page? My answer is no way! You should never blindly trust user-submitted data, even if it isn't ordinarily user-entered. There are simply too many things that can go wrong, accidentally or otherwise.

This particular script is fairly fail-safe, at least in the matter of correctly outputting the next page, and the extra step of mapping the incoming page name to a page number and then back again is a big part of that. But if it were blindly to accept a user-submitted value for **$PageNum**, say, then it could be fooled into outputting an almost blank page. Due to the modulus operations in the lines that assign values to **$NextName** and **$PrevName**, the Next and Back buttons would still be correctly labeled and restore order on the next submission, but that is small consolation. If a compiled C program were to accept a bad value for a variable used like **$PageNum**, it would most likely crash, or possibly even open up a security hole. In this instance, Perl is more forgiving, and in some ways more safe. I will return to these issues of validation and security for multiple-page applications in the next example.

As www-mart.cgi is actually written, it maps a bad value for PageName to page number **0**, which gives the same output as an initial GET request that contains no submitted form data.

## Outputting the New Page

Once all the data has been initialized and the next page chosen, outputting this new page is exceedingly simple. The main part of it is accomplished with a single **print** statement, in whose output the values of several variables, most notably **$PageTexts[$PageNum]**, are interpolated. In this way, all the content that distinguishes one of www-mart.cgi's output pages from another is inserted into a common framework. An alternative approach, which you shall see in a later example, would be to insert the generic, state-maintaining information into separate HTML files. Either way, the page that ends up being downloaded and displayed by the remote browser will contain a mixture of original, static content and the new, dynamically generated information that marks the current state between the browser and the CGI program.

## Generating, Displaying, and Re-inputting the Shopping Cart

Generating a representation of the shopping cart for display is an easy exercise in constructing a suitable set of input elements. *Input* elements? Yes, because its contents must be input again with every submission of a new form. If you also stow all the cart's contents in hidden fields, of course you are free to display copies of these contents any way you like, but the hidden fields are still input elements.

However you choose to display the video titles in the shopping cart, you will have to split them apart. Since they all originate from the VALUE attributes of INPUT tags bearing the same **NAME=videos** attribute, the **getFormData** function places them all in **$Form{'videos'}**, joined together by null characters (ASCII 0). To separate them into the distinct elements of an ordinary array, you can use the split function:

```
@videos = split(/\0/, $videos);
```

Their number is then given by the name of the array as evaluated in a scalar context:

```
$numvid = @videos;
```

This step isn't necessary if you'll only be using the number in a scalar context (such as **1 + @numvid**), but in a list context—for example, among the arguments of the **print** statement

```
print  "That's $numvid video rental", (($numvid > 1) ? 's': ''), ¬
    "\n";
```

the array name **@numvid** in place of **$numvid** would evaluate to all of **@numvid**'s elements joined as one long string. For the meaning of the expression **(($numvid > 1) ? 's': '')**, see the sidebar, "Perl's A ? B : C Construct."

In this example, I've chosen a scrollbox (see Figures 7.2 and 7.3) because it easily grows or shrinks to hold all of the items in the cart and makes each item available for review and immediate deselection:

```
print "<SELECT NAME=videos MULTIPLE SIZE=", 1 + $numvid, ">\n";
foreach $_ (@videos) {
   print "<OPTION SELECTED> $_\n";
}
print "</SELECT><BR>\n";
```

## Perl's A ? B : C Construct

That odd expression that appears as an argument in one of the example's **print** statements,

```
($numvid > 1) ? 's': ''
```

evaluates to the single **s** character if the value of **$numvid** is greater than **1**; otherwise, it evaluates to the empty string. In general, a conditional construct of the form **A ? B : C** evaluates to **B** if the **A** is true (non-null and non-zero), and **C** otherwise, where **C** is evaluated only if **A** is not true.

In Perl 5, the special case where **A** is an assertion and C is null is synonymous with the conjunction **A && B**. In general, the value of a compound expression as a whole is the value of its last evaluated subexpression; in an assignment statement, for example, this would always be the value assigned to the variable on the left-hand side. In **A && B**, **B** is evaluated if and only if **A** is true. Otherwise, evaluation stops with the value of **A** as null (the empty value **''**). Thus **(($numvid > 1) ? 's': '')** is logically equivalent to **(($numvid > 1) && 's')**.

In Perl 4, however, *false* has a different meaning. An assertion or other purely logical expression evaluates not to **1** or **''**, but to **1** or **0**. Thus **(($numvid > 1) && 's')** would evaluate to either **"s"** or **0**, and the **print** statement would output **"rental0"** when **$numvid** is **1**. This subtle difference in the semantics of true/false can thus lead to tangible portability problems between Perl 4 and Perl 5, and this example uses the full **A ? B : C** construct instead of **A && B** for the sake of backwards compatibility.

(In keeping with the program's "goal" of renting videos, maybe it shouldn't be so easy to pull up to the checkout counter and then dump out the cart's entire contents just before hitting the final "Process Payment" button!)

## A Library Function for Mailing Form Data

In the example above, the final action of the script before it thanks the user and exits is to call a function named **mailForm**, which e-mails all of the submitted form data along with some context information to an address specificed by **$owner**. Although the details of such routines vary with the platform and installation you use, they are often very simple and are readily available on the Internet. Listing 7.3 shows an implementation that will work on most Unix machines, where /usr/lib/sendmail is still one of the most commonly used mailers. For PCs, two Simple Mail Transfer Protocol (SMTP) mailers that are similar to sendmail are Blat (http://gepasi.dbs.aber.ac.uk/softw/Blat.html) and wSendmail (http:/home.sol.no/jgaa/cgi-bin.htm).

### How It Works

The way **mailForm** works is very simple: It opens a pipe to the e-mail–sending program identified by **$Mailer** and feeds it a stream of data:

```
open (MAIL,"|$Mailer") ||
  die("$0: error opening mailer $Mailer: $!\n");

print MAIL "To: ",    $To || $ENV{'SERVER_ADMIN'}, "\n";
print MAIL  . . . et cetera . . .
close(MAIL);
```

The mailer should parse this stream, create the appropriate headers for your site, and send the mail on its way. This technique of opening a pipe to a program is very similar to Example 6B, the graphical access counter in Chapter 6, which opened a pipe to the fly program.

The last expression in **mailForm** is a call to Perl's built-in **close** function. Because the **close** function returns 1 on success and 0 otherwise, **mailForm** will do the same (if it hasn't already died on the call to **open**).

### Unix Mailers and Security Holes

The most important things to know about using a Unix mailer such as sendmail or UCB mail are the potential security holes that such a mailer may open. Some Unix mailers support *tilde-escapes*, which are special commands that may appear at the beginning of any line in the e-mail message. For instance, the sequence ~! at the beginning of a line in some mailers will start up a Unix shell. From there, a malicious user could issue a command such as **rm -rf /** (which means "recursively remove all files and subdirectories starting at the root directory, and don't stop, complain about failures, or ask any questions along the way"). The following three lines in **mailForm**

```
$value =~ s/~!/ ~!/g;           # remove tilde-escapes
$value =~ s/<!-(.|\n)*->//g;  # remove SSI directives
print MAIL " $key:  $value\n"; # print space before key
```

are an attempt to remove a few of the security risks that are present in some mailers. The removal of SSI directives is important only if you might redisplay the contents of the e-mail as part of a server-parsed Web page.

**LISTING 7.3    MailForm.pl, a library function for mailing data that was obtained with getFormData**

```
# MailForm.pl - library function for mailing form data
# Usage: mailForm(*FormData, To, ReplyTo, Subject, Message, Mailer);
# where all parameters after To are optional.
# Note: Designed to be compatible with getFormData (in FormData.pl).

sub  mailForm {
  local(*FormData, $To, $ReplyTo, $Subject, $Message, $Mailer) = @_;
  local($key, $value);

  # Path of a mailer that sends formatted mail it reads from STDIN:
  $Mailer = $Mailer || '/usr/lib/sendmail -t -oi';
  # For sendmail, -t means take the headers from the lines following
  # the initial command — don't ever put a user-entered value for
  # the recipient in the command itself! The -oi options means don't
  # interpret a line beginning with a period as ending the input.

  open (MAIL,"|$Mailer") ||
    die("$0: error opening mailer $Mailer: $!\n");

  print MAIL "To: ",    $To || $ENV{'SERVER_ADMIN'}, "\n";
  print MAIL "Reply-To: $ReplyTo\n"   if $ReplyTo;
  print MAIL "Subject:  $Subject\n\n" if $Subject;
```

# Maintaining State with Magic Cookies

One way for a CGI program to maintain a persistent context with a browser is for it to embed state information in the pages it sends to the browser, in such a way that it can get the information back again as part of subsequent requests. In all of the examples presented so far, the embedded information was used for keeping some kind of history of what the CGI script had already input or output. In the case of one_arm.cgi, it was previously generated random numbers, and in the case of www-mart.cgi, it was previously selected movie titles. These example scripts did not save any state information locally, on the server, but instead they entrusted its safekeeping to their remote clients.

**LISTING 7.3    MailForm.pl, a library function for mailing data that was obtained with getFormData (Continued)**

```
print MAIL $Message                          if $Message;
print MAIL "\n_____ FormData follows:\n";


if (%FormData) {
  foreach $key (sort(keys(%FormData))) {
    foreach $value (split(/\0/, $FormData{$key})) {
      $value =~ s/~!/ ~!/g;                # remove tilde-escapes
      $value =~ s/<!-(.|\n)*->//g;  # remove SSI directives
      print MAIL " $key: $value\n";  # print space before key
    }
  }
} else { print MAIL "The form was empty!\n"; }


  print MAIL "\n_____ MailData follows:\n";
  print MAIL "Server protocol: $ENV{'SERVER_PROTOCOL'}\n";
  print MAIL "Remote host name: $ENV{'REMOTE_HOST'}\n";
  print MAIL "Remote IP address: $ENV{'REMOTE_ADDR'}\n";
  close(MAIL);      # makes mailForm return 1 on success, 0 on error.
}


1; # return 1 to make "require 'MailForm.pl';" work.
```

A different approach would be for the CGI program to keep a local record of past or pending transactions, and to have remote browsers identify themselves every time they request a new transaction. Browsers, however, do not automatically identify themselves in any unique or reliable way. The same IP address, for instance, as reflected in the environment variable REMOTE_ADDR, is shared by all the different browsers and/or browser windows on a given host computer, regardless of their individual session histories. And if a browser is using proxy servers to go through a firewall, its IP address may even change within the course of retrieving the documents that comprise a single page. The other common environment variables are no better; for an environment variable to serve as an adequate identifier, this functionality would have to become integrated as a mandatory part HTTP itself.

One solution is for the CGI program itself to create a unique identifier and send it to the browser; the browser must then send it back again as part of every request for the remainder of the session (or at least until the CGI program gives it a new identifier). In computer parlance, such a unique identifier is known as a *cookie*.

A cookie's particular contents usually serve only as an identifier, not as a value with which to perform computations. (Exceptions to this rule are often called *magic* cookies; one example is a number that "magically" changes its value depending on the byte order of the machine that evaluates it.) In the context of CGI, cookies are not magic, but can be any string or random number, as long as the one sent to each browser is unique. It is quite common to use the exact time of the first transaction as part of the cookie, because that is one identifier that won't be repeated.

**cookie**. *n*. A handle, transaction ID, or other token of agreement between co-operating programs. "I give him a packet, he gives me back a cookie." The claim check you get from a dry-cleaning shop is a perfect mundane example of a cookie; the only thing it's useful for is to relate a later transaction to this one (so you get the same clothes back).

—*The New Hacker's Dictionary*, edited by Eric S. Raymond (MIT Press), http://www.ccil.org/jargon/

The browser's original IP address also makes a good candidate for *part* of a cookie (the address may change, but the cookie remains the same). Yet another approach would be to use a function like **countf**, defined in Chapter 5, to assign each browser the next number in an absolute sequence, but this is actually a bad idea, because it would then be easy for a malicious user to steal somebody else's cookie just by guessing a valid ID number.

## Short-term and Persistent Cookies

Cookies vary in their uses and durations, as well as their contents. Some cookies are instantaneous; they are used to enable only a single transaction, then discarded. CGI programs usually reuse the same cookie for all the pages they output in a sequence to one browser. The cookie itself is passed back and forth between the Web server and the browser, typically as the same hidden field placed in a series of forms. Since the cookie is stored in pages that are only temporarily loaded in the browser, it is lost when the browser application is shut down. If the browser is pointed again at the same application the next day, it will receive a new cookie and start all over again. Such a cookie is said to be a *short-term* cookie; it lasts at most for the duration of one browser-user session.

A *persistent* cookie has a defined lifetime, which may be specified to last longer than a single session. Like short-term cookies, a persistent cookie is created by a server-side program, such as a CGI application, and then sent to the client side, where it actually resides. The difference is that short-term cookies are stored inside HTML pages, whereas persistent cookies are stored in a file controlled by the client browser. For the cookie to endure beyond the end of a browser session, the browser must save this cookie file and reload it whenever it starts up again.

For many purposes, such as a video-rental application that employs a shopping cart metaphor, short-term state maintenance is everything you'd need or want as a user. When you check out or quit, your shopping cart is emptied, and if you come back the next day, you pick up a new, empty cart. If you're like me, however, you've probably held a video box in your hand, read the blurb on the back, and still been unable to remember whether you had ever seen that movie before. Perhaps you told a checkout teller your name and address and asked them to look up your past rentals in their database—and perhaps, if you are hoping to be nominated for the U.S. Supreme Court, you were chagrined to find out that they actually could look it up!

A persistent cookie could very easily serve as a membership ID card and be used as a key into a database that associates your name with any other information recorded from your previous transactions. Several proposals have been made for standardizing the implementation and use of persistent cookies, but at present, only Netscape's specification is in widespread use.

### Short-term Cookies

By embedding a cookie in every HTML page that it outputs, a CGI program can maintain context throughout a user session. A hidden field within a form makes an excellent place to embed a cookie, because then any submission of the form will send back the cookie. CGI programs can also send out and retrieve cookies as part of query strings attached to URLs in call-back links. Changing all the links in an output page is more work than adding one INPUT field of type HIDDEN, but links tend to be more convenient for navigation. Either way, since the cookie is stored inside HTML pages, it lasts only as long as the browser caches those pages, and is only available for transactions that start from those pages. When the user quits the browser application, and the cached pages are flushed from the client host's memory, the cookie is gone forever.

The cookie, however, is only an identifier. The actual state information must be kept on the server side. CGI programs typically store the state information either in a shared database, to which the cookie serves as a key, or in a plain, temporary file, which is labeled for use only with that one particular cookie. Every time the CGI program receives a cookie back from a browser, it has to reopen this file and retrieve the saved state information. The next example script implements such a short-term cookie scheme using a Unix DBM-style database.

## Netscape Persistent Cookies

Netscape has developed a specification for persistent cookies that relies client-specific extensions to HTTP, and has (correctly) implemented it in its own browsers since Navigator version 1.22. These extensions are not a part of the HTTP 1.1 proposed standard, and are likely to be revamped or even completely replaced in the not too distant future, whether they are incorporated into a new HTTP standard or not. Netscape still labels its own specification as preliminary, and advises that it be used with caution (http://home.netscape.com/newsref/std/cookie_spec.html). This section is based mainly on Netscape's public specification.

The scheme itself is very simple. In addition to the usual HTTP response headers such as "Content-type: text/html" and the current date and time in Greenwich Mean Time (GMT), the Web server sends a browser an HTTP "Set-Cookie" header. This header specifies one name/value pair along with several other attributes, such as a domain name for the Web site and a pathname for the subdirectory of documents to which the cookie applies. If the browser doesn't understand this header, it should simply discard it; browsers ignore unrecognized headers all the time. But if the browser *accepts* the cookie, it saves all of the cookie's specifications in a text file. Then, whenever the browser sends a request for a document inside the cookie's area of application, it should also send an extra HTTP request header back to the server. This "Cookie" header contains the same name/value pair that was originally sent from the server side. It's up to the server—or rather, the CGI program that actually creates and keeps track of the cookie's associated contexts—to make this name/value pair meaningful. The browser's role is always passive with regard to setting the cookie's contents.

To set a cookie on a client browser, the Web server sends a header of the following format:

```
Set-Cookie: NAME=VALUE; Expires=GMT standard-format DATE; Path=¬
PATHNAME; Domain=DOMAIN; Secure
```

From a CGI Perl script, you can simply print a header of the above form along with the "Content-type" and any other headers. (Just remember to follow the last header with a blank line). From a static HTML document, you can send a Netscape persistent cookie using a META HTTP-EQUIV tag, as in

```
<META HTTP-EQUIV="Set-Cookie" CONTENT="Customer=Wile_E_Coyote;
Expires=Expires=Fri, 31-Dec-1999 23:59:59 GMT;
Path=/~me/cgi/ck; Domain=www.my.site.com">
```

The attributes are separated by semicolons, and the attribute names are all case-insensitive. The individual fields should not be enclosed in quotation marks, and are not required to be URL-encoded, although the Netscape specification recommends that you avoid semicolons, commas, and white space inside the *VALUE* field.

When the browser requests a document inside an accepted cookie's area of application, it should follow the initial request-method (GET or POST) header with a header of the format

```
Cookie: NAME=VALUE
```

Or, if more than one cookie applies, then the browser should combine their values into one Cookie header line of the following format:

```
Cookie: NAME1=VALUE1; NAME2=VALUE2 . . .
```

Any Web server will convert such a header into the client-specific environment variable HTTP_COOKIE, following the usual HTTP conventions (see Chapter 4). It's then up to the CGI program to parse and (possibly) decode the value of this variable.

A server may send multiple Set-Cookie headers in a single response, and a browser may send more than one value for the same name in a single request header. At any time, cookie instances of the same name and path will overwrite each other on the browser. This implies that between two instances with the same name and path but different expiration dates, the last-set date prevails. Instances where either the name or the path is different should be able to coexist, rather than replace each other, and setting the path to a higher-level value should not override other, more specific path mappings. Thus if there are multiple matches for a given cookie name, but with separate paths, all the matching cookies should be sent. However, all the cookies with a more specific path mapping should be sent before cookies with less specific path mappings, where / is the most inclusive path, and /sub, for instance, is more specific. You can also delete a cookie at any time by sending a Set-Cookie header with the exact same name and path, but an expiration time that is already past.

The Netscape specification stipulates limitations on cookie sizes and the number of cookies that a client can store at any one time. A client should be prepared to receive and store a minimum of 300 cookies total, where the name and value fields combined do not exceed 4 kilobytes per cookie. There is also a limit of 20 cookies per server or domain, although completely specified hosts and domains are treated as separate entities and have a 20-cookie limitation for each one, not combined. The specification further states that servers, i.e., CGI programs, "should not expect clients to be able to exceed these limits. When the 300 cookie limit or the 20 cookie per server limit is exceeded, clients should delete the least recently used cookie. When a cookie larger than 4 kilobytes is encountered, the cookie should be trimmed to fit, but the name should remain intact as long as it is less than 4 kilobytes."

Despite this simple specification, there have been some problems and variances in various implementations of such persistent cookies. Netscape's own implementations have not wholly complied with this specification, and there are some known bugs, especially in Navigator version 1.1. Other browsers, including Microsoft's Internet Explorer and Quarterdeck's Mosaic (both starting with their versions 2.0) have implemented almost the same scheme, but with some minor differences. As implemented in Netscape's browsers, for example, only the Name=*value* attribute is actually required. Default values are assumed for any missing attributes or fields, as described below. Internet Explorer, however, and possibly other browsers as well, accept only fully qualified "Set-Cookie" headers. Many other browsers do not support persistent cookies at all, or may have only partial or buggy implementations (as did Netscape Navigator 1.1).

`Netscape Persistent Cookie Attributes`   The following list describes Netscape persistent cookie attributes, both as originally specified, and as actually implemented, features, bugs, and all.

   ▶ **NAME=VALUE.** Both *NAME* and *VALUE* are arbitrary strings of characters, excluding semicolons. The specification also excludes white space and commas, but in at least Netscape's present implementation, they do no harm. To avoid potential ambiguities, you should at the very least encode semicolons that might otherwise appear inside the *VALUE* field. All the encoding and decoding must be done in your CGI program, so you are free to choose whatever methods or conventions you like. (If you use URL-style hexadecimal escape codes, the code for ; is %3B, and the code for % itself is %25.)

▶ **Expires=*DATE***. The expires attribute specifies an expiration date and time for the cookie. Once the expiration date has been reached, the cookie should no longer be stored or given out. The date string is formatted as

```
Day, DD-Mon-YY HH:MM:SS GMT
```

where *Day* is a day of the week in English (and may be abbreviated to Sun, Mon, Tue, Wed, Thu, Fri, or Sat), *DD* is a 2-digit day-of-month, *Mon* is the month name in English (which may also be abbreviated to its first three letters), YY is a year, with or without the century, but starting with 1970 (so, for example, 23 means 2023, not 1923), and the time is always specified for the GMT time zone.

For Netscape's browsers, the Expires field is optional, and defaults to the end of the current session. This is a very useful feature, because it places the burden of managing short-term cookies almost completely on the client, and a context can be maintained even when the sequence of cookie setting and receiving transactions is broken (by intermediate visits, say, to a site on the browser's hot list).

If the weekday doesn't match the date in an Expires attribute, a browser should reject the expiration date and accept the cookie as expiring at the end of the session (the default). However, even Netscape's browsers have strayed from the specification in matters of the date's format, specified time zone, and actual behavior upon acceptance and/or expiration of cookies that include an Expires attribute. Also, many computers' clocks are wrong. So it is best not to rely too heavily on the specifics of the expiration date's value or format. You should always use the same format, and if your application will allow it, set the expiration date at least one day later than you really need.

▶ **Path=*PATH***. The *PATH* field specifies a single hierarchy of paths for which the cookie is valid. The root path "/" is the most general; it includes all objects in the specified server domain. Pathnames need not have any particular endings, and comparisons start from the left, so that /foo matches both /foobar and /foo/bar.html.

There is a bug in Netscape Navigator version 1.1 and earlier, which prevents the browser from saving cookies between sessions unless the path attribute is set explicitly to "/". This limits the usefulness of persistent cookies with these browsers.

On browsers that comply with Netscape's specification (for example, Navigator 1.22 and later), the path attribute defaults to the path of the object currently being served (which follows the complete, blank-line-terminated header in the normal fashion).

▶ **Domain=*DOMAIN*.** The DOMAIN field specifies a hierarchy of Internet domains for which the cookie is valid. Only hosts within a given domain may set a cookie for that domain, and matching is performed from the tail end of the domain name. Thus a server (i.e., CGI program) at www.acme.com may set a cookie with the *DOMAIN* of acme.com, and this cookie will be modifiable by servers at home.acme.com, but not by servers at www.ajax.com. If the cookie is originally set with the full domain name of www.acme.com (the default setting for Netscape browser's), then a server at home.acme.com would also be excluded from receiving or changing it.

There are also some built-in safeguards to prevent a server from setting a cookie for a top-level domain such as .com or .va.us. Any specified domain that falls within one of the seven top-level domains .com, .edu, .net, .org, .gov, .mil, or .int must include at least two periods. Any other domain requires at least three. This rules out short domain names like nba.com or cern.ch (the birthplace of the World Wide Web). Most servers are accessible via one or more aliases, such as www.nba.com, but www.cern.ch still does not qualify).

On browsers that comply with Netscape's specification, the domain attribute defaults to the IP host name of the server that generates the cookie response.

▶ **Secure.** If a cookie is marked secure, it should only be transmitted back to the server over a secure communications channel. Currently this means that secure cookies will only be sent to HTTPS servers, that is, to HTTP servers that communicate over a Secure Sockets Layer (SSL) channel. If the Secure attribute is not specified, a Netscape-compliant browser would consider it safe to send the cookie over ordinary, unsecured channels.

## When To Use Short-term and Persistent Cookies

Despite the qualifications and problems described above, persistent cookies can significantly extend the capabilities of Web-based applications. They could be even more useful if their implementation adhered to a standard specification like the proposed HTTP 1.1. For some purposes, the extra functionality they can provide may be outweighed by the current limitations on their compatibility.

Another limitation is that persistent cookies are only exchanged at the beginning of each transaction, so that their contents tend to lag one step behind the current state of the application. It's quite possible to store even large amounts of state information in client-side persistent cookies, but just as when you use state information stored in a server-side database, you must give precedence to the data received from the latest form submission.

As the next example shows, a short-term cookie passed in hidden fields and/or embedded query strings is more than adequate for the purpose of transferring a list of selected items from page to page, as in a "shopping cart" application. However, if you need to track users across multiple visits to your site, whether they submit any input or not, then you need to use persistent cookies.

The following example serves nearly the same function to pages as the previous one, but its use of a hidden cookie and a back-end database afford it much greater navigational flexibility. It also keeps track of all the pages a user visits, whether the user ever adds any selection to a shopping cart or not. The short-term cookie it uses to identify the customer could be replaced by a persistent cookie simply by changing a few lines of code in one subroutine.

## Example 7C: Maintaining State with a Cookie and Inserting Dynamic Information into Static Files

The script in this example, www-cart.cgi, assigns each client browser a unique short-term cookie, and keeps track of its current state by using the cookie as part of a key into a database. It outputs pages that are very similar to those output by www-mart.cgi in the previous example; one of the only differences is that you can jump between www-cart.cgi's output pages by following links (see Figure 7.4). Its method for generating dynamic pages, however, is the reverse of the one used by www-mart.cgi. Whereas www-mart.cgi interpolates constant, movie-specific information into a dynamically generated HTML form, www-cart.cgi inserts dynamically generated text and form elements into static, movie-specific HTML files. It accomplishes this by defining and calling a function named **sendParsedFile**, which reads a file from disk and sends its contents to the client browser, transforming them on-the-fly. It actually parses files in much the same way that a Web server parses .shtml files on their way to a client browser and replaces Server-side Include directives with their computed values. The "checkout counter" form also sits in its own separate HTML file, and is parsed on-the-fly by **sendParsedFile**. Listings 7.4 and 7.5 show a catalog file and the checkout counter form, wApartment.html and wzCheckOut.html. Listing 7.6 shows the script, www-cart.cgi. The following sections explain the script in detail.

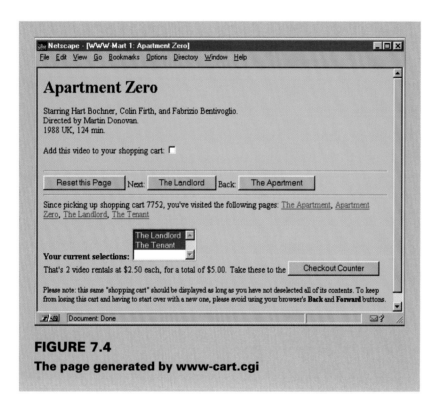

**FIGURE 7.4**
**The page generated by www-cart.cgi**

---

**LISTING 7.4    wApartment.html, a catalog file for use with www-cart.cgi**

```
<HTML><HEAD><TITLE>
WWW-Mart: The Apartment
</TITLE></HEAD><BODY BGCOLOR="#99AA77">
<FORM METHOD=POST ACTION="www-cart.cgi">

<H1> The Apartment </H1>
Starring Jack Lemmon, Shirley MacLaine, and Fred MacMurray<BR>
Directed by Billy Wilder.<BR>
```

**LISTING 7.4    wApartment.html, a catalog file for use with www-cart.cgi (Continued)**

```
1960 USA, 125 min.

<P>Add this video to your shopping cart:
<INPUT TYPE=CHECKBOX NAME=videos        VALUE="The Apartment">
<P><HR><INPUT TYPE=RESET                VALUE="Reset This Page">
<!-#Insert Next->Next: <INPUT TYPE=SUBMIT NAME=NextName VALUE="Apartment¬
Zero">
<!-#Insert ShoppingCart->
</FORM></BODY></HTML>
```

**LISTING 7.5    wCheckOut.html, the "checkout counter" for use with www-cart.cgi**

```
<HTML><HEAD><TITLE>
WWW-Mart Checkout Counter
</TITLE></HEAD><BODY BGCOLOR="#99AA77">
<FORM METHOD=POST ACTION="www-cart.cgi">

<H1> WWW-Mart Checkout Counter </H1>

<!-#Insert ShoppingCart-> Oops! <INPUT TYPE=SUBMIT VALUE="Start Here">
<P>Account Name:   <INPUT TYPE=TEXT SIZE=40 NAME="AccName">
<P>Account Number: <INPUT TYPE=TEXT SIZE=10 NAME="AccNum">

<P><HR>
<INPUT TYPE=RESET VALUE="Reset this Page">
<!-#Insert Next->Next: <INPUT TYPE=SUBMIT NAME=NextName VALUE="The ¬
Apartment">
</FORM></BODY></HTML>
```

**LISTING 7.6    www-cart.cgi, a script that filters static HTML files and maintains state using a database and a cookie**

```perl
#!/usr/local/bin/perl5
# www-cart.cgi - example shopping cart script that parses HTML
# files (catalog pages) and inserts hidden fields, including a
# cookie that serves as a key into a DBM-style database.
# Copyright (C) 1996 Stephen Lines <spraxlo@ai.mit.edu>
require 'FormData.pl';
require 'MailForm.pl';

# NB: The Web server must have read/write/search access to the directory
# containing $DBMF if openDBM is to handle any necessary file creations.
$DBMF         = '../my/safe/place/videoDB'; # The glob symbol DBMF is
              # used to name both the database file and the hash array.
$Price        = 2.50;
$owner        = 'checkout@www-mart.com';
$CheckOut     = 'Checkout Counter';
$PayNow       = 'Pay Now From This Account';
$Script       = $ENV{'SCRIPT_NAME'};
%Files2Names = ( "wApartment.html"      => "The Apartment"
               , "wApartmentZero.html"  => "Apartment Zero"
               , "wLandlord.html"       => "The Landlord"
               , "wTenant.html"         => "The Tenant"
               , "wzCheckOut.html"      => $CheckOut
               ); # Make checkout file alphabetically last.
$FileNum = 0;
foreach (sort(keys(%Files2Names))) {
  $ValidFiles[ $FileNum ] = $_;
  $ValidNames[ $FileNum ] = $NextName = $Files2Names{$_};
  $Names2Numbs{$NextName} = $FileNum++; # Used to validate names.
}

unless ($Script) {                    # Must be testing in the shell...
  $ENV{'SCRIPT_NAME'}    = $0;
  $ENV{'REQUEST_METHOD'} = 'GET';
  $ENV{'QUERY_STRING'}   = 'NextName=wApartment.html';
  $ENV{'CONTENT_LENGTH'} = length($ENV{'QUERY_STRING'});
```

**LISTING 7.6   www-cart.cgi, a script that filters static HTML files and maintains state using a database and a cookie  (Continued)**

```perl
}

if (&getFormData(*Form) && ($NextName = $Form{'NextName'})) {
  $NextName  = &PayNow(*Form) if ($NextName eq $PayNow);
  $NextName  = $Files2Names{$NextName} if ($NextName =~ /\.html$/);
  #   Now simultaneously get $NextName's number and validate it:
  $FileNum   = $Names2Numbs{$NextName} || 0;
} else {
  $FileNum   = 0;
}


&sendParsedFile( *Form, $FileNum );
exit;


############### Local Subroutines: ############################

sub  sendParsedFile {
  local ( *Form, $FileNum ) = @_;
  my    ( $line, $File, $NextName, $PrevName );
  $File  = $ValidFiles[ $FileNum ];
  $Cookie = &getCookie(*Form);            # Get cookie first, and...
  print "Content-type: text/html\n\n"; # ...then output header.
  open(File, $File) || die("$0: sendParsedFile died on $File ($!)\n");
  while ($line = <File>) {
    if ( $line =~ /^<!-#insert\s+(\w+)\s*->/i) {
    # $_ = $1; # Leave match to (\w+) in read-only variable $1.
      if ($1 eq 'Next') {   # Found an <!-insert Next-> directive.
        &insertNames(*Form, $FileNum,  $Cookie);
        &trackVisits(*Form, $File,     $Cookie);
      }
      elsif ($1 =~ /^ShoppingCart$/i) {
        &displayCart(*Form, $File);
      }
    # else { print $line; } # Don't output any insert directives.
    }
```

**LISTING 7.6** **www-cart.cgi, a script that filters static HTML files and maintains state using a database and a cookie (Continued)**

```perl
      else { print $line; }    # Do output all other lines unchanged.
    }
    close (File);   # returns 1 on success
}


sub  insertNames {
  local ( *Form, $FileNum, $Cookie ) = @_;
  my    ( $ThisFile, $NextName, $PrevName );
  $ThisFile = $ValidFiles[ $FileNum ];
  $NextName = $ValidNames[($FileNum + 1) % $#ValidFiles];
  $PrevName = $ValidNames[($FileNum - 1) % $#ValidFiles];
# $PrevName = $Files2Names{$Form{'ThisFile'}};
# $PrevName = $ValidFiles[($FileNum - 1) % $#ValidFiles]
#   unless ($PrevName && ($PrevName ne $NextName));
  print "<INPUT TYPE=HIDDEN NAME=Cookie   VALUE=\"$Cookie\">\n";
  print "<INPUT TYPE=HIDDEN NAME=ThisFile VALUE=\"$ThisFile\">\n",
  "Next: <INPUT TYPE=SUBMIT NAME=NextName VALUE=\"$NextName\">\n",
  "Back: <INPUT TYPE=SUBMIT NAME=NextName VALUE=\"$PrevName\">\n";
}


sub getCookie {
  local(*Form) = @_;
  local($Cookie);
  $Cookie = &newCookie
    unless (($Cookie = $Form{'Cookie'}) && $Cookie =~ /\d_\d\d\d_\d/);
  $Cookie;
}


sub newCookie {
  srand(time^$$);
  local($ck) = 100 + int(rand(899));   # Get a 3-digit random number.
  $ck = join('_', $ENV{'REMOTE_ADDR'}, $ck, time);
# print "<DD><FONT COLOR=RED>New Shopping Cart ID: $ck</FONT><BR>\n";
```

**LISTING 7.6** **www-cart.cgi, a script that filters static HTML files and maintains state using a database and a cookie (Continued)**

```perl
      $ck;
}


sub trackVisits {           # Usually called *before* displayCart.
  local (*Form, $File, $Cookie) = @_;
  my    ($visits, $number, $previous, $pageName);

  &openDBM(*DBMF) || die("$0: error opening DBMF=$DBMF ($!)\n");
  # Replace the database entry with Form values, or vice versa:
  if ($ENV{'REQUEST_METHOD'} eq 'POST') {
    if (defined($Form{'videos'})) {
      $DBMF{$Cookie, 'videos'} = $Form{'videos'}
    } else {
      delete $DBMF{$Cookie, 'videos'};
    }
  } else {
    $Form{'videos'} = $DBMF{$Cookie, 'videos'} || undef;
  }
  # Keep track of all pages visited by a browser with this cookie:
  if ($visits = $DBMF{$Cookie, 'visits'}) {     # Extract DB entry.
    $DBMF{$Cookie, 'visits'} .= "\0".$File;     # Append to DB entry.
  } else {
    $DBMF{$Cookie, 'visits'} =      $File;      # Create new DB entry.
  }
  &closeDBM(*DBMF);

  if ($visits) {
    $number = substr($Cookie, -4);         # returns last 4 characters
    print "<HR>Since picking up shopping cart $number, \n";
    print "you've visited the following pages:\n";
    $previous = '';
    foreach $_ (sort(split( /\0/, $visits))) {
      if ($_ ne $previous) {
        $pageName = $Files2Names{$_};
```

**LISTING 7.6    www-cart.cgi, a script that filters static HTML files and maintains state using a database and a cookie  (Continued)**

```perl
        last if ($pageName eq $CheckOut);  # Checkout sorts last.
        print ",\n" if $previous;
        print qq(<A HREF="$Script?NextName=$_&Cookie=$Cookie">\n);
        print $pageName, "</A>";
        $previous = $_;
      }
    }
  }
  $visits;   # return visits
}


sub  openDBM {
  local(*DBM) = @_;
  unless (dbmopen(%DBM, $DBM, undef)) {
    # warn("$0:  Creating new DBM: $DBM\n");
    local($umask) = umask(0);  # change umask to 0, save old umask in $umask
    dbmopen(%DBM,$DBM,0666) || die("$0: open $DBM ($!)\n");
    umask($umask);             # restore old umask
    # warn("$0: Created new DBM file: $DBM,  umask was $umask\n");
  }
  # warn("$0: Opened existing DBM file: $DBM\n");
  1; # Return 1 on success, because that's what dbmopen does.
}


sub closeDBM {
  local(*DBM) = @_;
  dbmclose(%DBM); # Close bound hash array as if it were a filehandle.
}


sub displayCart {               # Display the cart's contents, if any.
  local (*Form, $File) = @_;
  local ($videos, @videos, $numvid, $total);
  return 0 unless ($videos = $Form{'videos'});
  @videos = split( /\0/, $videos);
```

**LISTING 7.6    www-cart.cgi, a script that filters static HTML files and maintains state using a database and a cookie  (Continued)**

```perl
  $numvid = @videos;
  $total  = $numvid * $Price;
  print "<P><B>Your current selections:</B>\n";
  print "<SELECT NAME=videos MULTIPLE SIZE=", 1 + $numvid, ">\n";
  foreach $_ (@videos) {
    print "<OPTION SELECTED> $_\n";
  }
  print  "</SELECT><BR>\n";
  print  "That's $numvid video rental", (($numvid > 1) ? 's' : ''), "\n";
  printf("at \$%.2f each, for a total of \$%.2f.\n", $Price, $total);
  if ($Files2Names{$File} eq $CheckOut) {
    print "<INPUT TYPE=SUBMIT NAME=NextName VALUE=\"$PayNow\">\n";
  } else {
    print "Take ", (($numvid > 1) ? 'these' : 'it'), " to the ",
          "<INPUT TYPE=SUBMIT NAME=NextName VALUE=\"$CheckOut\">\n";
    print <<EOF;
<P><SMALL>Please note: this same "shopping cart" should be displayed
as long as you have not deselected all of its contents.  To keep from
losing this cart and having to start over with a new one, please
avoid using your browser's <B>Back</B> and <B>Forward</B> buttons.
EOF
  }
  $numvid;
}


sub PayNow {
  local (*Form) = @_;
  if (&ProcessPayment(*Form)) {
    &mailForm(*Form, $owner, $owner, $0, $ENV{'HTTP_REFERER'});
    &Thankyou;
    exit;
  }
  $CheckOut;   # Stay on check out page.
}
```

---

**LISTING 7.6** **www-cart.cgi, a script that filters static HTML files and maintains state using a database and a cookie (Continued)**

---

```
sub ProcessPayment {
  ((length($Form{'AccName'}) > 2) && ($Form{'AccNum'} =~ /^\d{5,5}$/));
}


sub Thankyou {
  print <<EOF;
<HTML>
<HEAD><TITLE> WWW-Mart Thanks You </TITLE></HEAD>
<BODY BGCOLOR="#A9BA87"><CENTER><H3>
W-w-we at WWW-Mart are st-stuttering with excitement about your order!
</H3><H1> THANK YOU!</H1>
</CENTER></BODY></HTML>
EOF
}
```

## Initializing the Mappings between Names, Files, and Numbers

The first thing that www-cart.cgi does, after setting a few configuration variables, is to initialize several arrays that contain the names of all the files it can parse and serve to a browser. Like www-mart.cgi, www-cart.cgi labels the pages or objects it serves in three different ways: by number, by name, and by content. Corresponding to www-mart.cgi's **$PageNum**, **@PageNames**, and **@PageTexts**, www-cart.cgi has its **$FileNum**, **@ValidNames**, **@ValidFiles**. But whereas **@PageTexts** contained the actual movie-specific text that went into the page, **@ValidFiles** contains only the names of the files that contain this text. The contents of the output pages are largely the contents of these files, as shown in Listings 7.4 and 7.5.

Another difference between the two scripts is that www-cart.cgi creates more mappings between its various sets of page labels. In www-mart.cgi, the only pre-computed mappings were from numbers to page names and texts. That is, the ordinary arrays **@PageNames** and **@PageTexts** were used to do what ordinary array always do: they mapped an index *number* to something else. There were no preset inverse mappings, from names or texts to numbers, nor was there an easy, one-step method for getting the text that corresponded to a page name. Instead, there was a loop in the main program that explicitly compared a fixed name, **$PageName**, against **$PageNames[$PageNum]** for all valid values of **$PageNum** until an exact match was found (or the loop terminated at **$PageNum** equal to **0**):

```
for ($PageNum = $LastNum - 1; $PageNum > 0; $PageNum-) {
    last if ($PageName eq $PageNames[$PageNum]);
} # If the name isn't found, the loop ends at $PageNum == 0.
```

Since all the pages www-mart.cgi could serve were numbered from **0** to **$LastNum - 1**, this loop necessarily mapped **$PageName** to a valid **$PageNum**, which in turn guaranteed that **$PageNames[$PageNum]** was a valid page name. The same page number could then be used to access the corresponding text, as **$PageTexts[$PageNum]**. To get from a page name to a page text, then, you first had to obtain the corresponding page number, and then rely on the fact that the arrays **@PageNames** and **@PageTexts** were parallel to each other.

The present script changes all that. In addition to the two ordinary arrays **@ValidNames** and **@ValidFiles**, which map page numbers to page names or filenames, there are two associative arrays, **%Files2Names** and **%Names2Numbs**, which map filenames to page names and page names to page numbers, respectively.

The **%Files2Names** array is initialized as a list of explicitly paired filenames and page names, using the **=>** operator:

```
%Files2Names = ( "wApartment.html"     => "The Apartment"
             , "wApartmentZero.html" => "Apartment Zero"
             , "wLandlord.html"      => "The Landlord"
             , "wTenant.html"        => "The Tenant"
             , "wzCheckOut.html"     => $CheckOut
             ); # Make checkout file alphabetically last.
```

The **=>** operator is actually just a convenient visual device; it is defined only in the context of initializing an associative array, where its meaning is the same as that of a comma.

The mapping from page names to page numbers, **%Names2Numbs**, is defined in the same loop that initializes **@ValidFiles** and **@ValidNames**:

```
$FileNum = 0;
foreach (sort(keys(%Files2Names))) {
    $ValidFiles[ $FileNum ] = $_;
    $ValidNames[ $FileNum ] = $NextName = $Files2Names{$_};
    $Names2Numbs{$NextName} = $FileNum++; # Used to validate names.
}
```

The keys and values in **%Files2Names** thus serve as the master lists of filenames and page names, respectively.

Altogether, these mappings form a triangle: from names to numbers to files and back again to names. Only the mapping from name to numbers, as defined by **%Names2Numbs**, has a precomputed inverse, namely, **@ValidNames**. This lets you go from a number directly to a name in one step. For all the other inverse mappings, you have to go two steps the other way round the triangle. For instance, to obtain a filename from a page name to a filename, you would have to use something like

```
$FileName = $ValidFiles[$Names2Numbs{$PageName}];
```

If there were a **%Names2Files** array, defined as the inverse to **%Files2Names**, then this construct involving two layers of subscripting could be replaced by a one-step subscript, as in

```
%Names2Files = reverse %Files2Names;
$FileName = $Names2Files{$PageName};
```

To invert a large associative array is a fairly expensive operation, however, and to make this program scale well, unnecessary operations should be avoided. The way www-cart.cgi is actually written, this particular mapping isn't needed. With one exception, the program always uses the mappings that go around the triangle in the other direction, from files to names, and the triangle is set up so that all array subscripting is one-step only. (If you examine the scheme's subtleties, you'll see that starting from a **%Names2Files** array and reversing the orientation of the triangle would be a mistake.)

## Determining the Next Action

The main control algorithm in www-cart.cgi is very simple, and very similar to that in www-mart.cgi. Both algorithms are organized around a scalar variable whose value may literally be the name of an object, but which is actually used to name the main transaction of the current program instance. In www-mart.cgi, this variable was **$PageName**; its value could be one of the names in **@PageNames**, but it could also be **$CheckOut** or **$PayNow**, which are better thought of as actions than as page labels. In www-cart.cgi, this additional variable is **$NextName**, and although its value can be any one of the entries in **@ValidNames** or **@ValidFiles**, it too can take on the values **$CheckOut** and **$PayNow**, with these values indicating the same actions as in the earlier script. The script is designed so that every action it takes, whether it's processing  a payment or serving the next page, is channeled through **$NextName** as a single bottleneck. Running everything through a bottleneck like this makes it much easier to monitor and understand what the script is doing in the center, and this in turn makes it easier to design and modify the rest of the program. It can also be very helpful for answering security concerns.

Since the central action of either script is almost always to output a new page (or file), both of them must have a method for mapping this variable to the next page's (or file's) index, which is just a number. As discussed above, www-mart.cgi implemented this method by way of a loop that explicitly compared **$PageName** with the entries in **@PageNames**. In www-cart.cgi, this method takes the form of two precomputed mappings that reference the associative arrays **%Files2Names** and **%Names2Numbs**.

First, the value of **$NextName** is assigned from the submitted form data, if there is any, and if it happens to be **$PayNow**, the **PayNow** subroutine is called to process the payment:

```
if (&getFormData(*Form) && ($NextName = $Form{'NextName'})) {
    $NextName  = &PayNow(*Form) if ($NextName eq $PayNow);
```

The **PayNow** function implements the same actions that www-mart.cgi took when payment information was submitted: it "checks" the entered account name and number, and if they pass muster, it mails the current order to **$owner** using **mailForm**, and terminates execution. (A real-world application for processing electronic payments is, I'm afraid, beyond the scope of this book.) If the payment information does not pass, then **PayNow** returns **$CheckOut** as the value for **$NextName**, and execution proceeds.

If the value **$NextName** ends in the extension .html, the **%Files2Names**: array is used to map what is assumed to be a filename to a page name:

```
$NextName  =  $Files2Names{$NextName} if ($NextName =~ /\.html$/);
```

Then the **%Names2Numbs** array is used to convert the name to a page/file number and at the same time check **$NextName**'s validity. If **$NextName** was not one of the original values in the **%Files2Names** array, then **$Names2Numbs{$NextName}** will be null, and **$FileNum** will default to **0**, the same as if no form data were submitted at all:

```
#   Now simultaneously get $NextName's number and ensure its ¬
validity:
    $FileNum   =  $Names2Numbs{$NextName} || 0;
} else {
    $FileNum   = 0;
}
```

The net result is that **$FileNum** is always assigned a valid file number, which in turn ensures that **$ValidFiles[$FileNum]** will be a valid filename. Besides simplifying the algorithm, the policy of translating every request for a new page into a valid file number is also important for security reasons. A function like **sendParsedFile** is capable of serving any file that the Web server can access, whether the file is in the Web document tree or not. If the script did not take such precautions, a clever user might be able to trick it into sending the system password file.

Once an incoming request has been funneled down to a valid file number, the script calls **sendParsedFile** with **$FileNum** as a parameter, and the rest of the processing is handled by various subroutines. I'll discuss the more important of these subroutines in the order in which they are usually called.

## sendParsedFile: Filters, Parsers, and CGI-Side Includes

The **sendParsedFile** function reads a static file from disk and sends it to the client browser, replacing lines that contain certain directives with other, dynamically generated contents. In general, such an on-the-fly transformation of a data stream is called *filtering*, and the transformation itself is called a *filter*. When the filter assumes the particular shape of searching for and replacing a predetermined set of patterns in the contents of a file, such filtering is referred to as *parsing* the file. The term "parsing" is often used to describe other operations in information processing and the linguistic sciences, but in the context of serving files on the Web, this has become the common meaning. Web servers parse SHTML files to replace SSI directives of the form

```
<!-#COMMAND ARGUMENT ->
```

with dynamically computed values on output, and **sendParsedFile** works in the same way. If you implement your own filters as CGI programs and/or functions, it's easy to emulate and even go far beyond any of the capabilities of SSI. The comparison with SSI has led some CGI programmers to dub such filtering techniques as parsing "CGI-side includes," or *CSI*.

This particular script's implementation of **sendParsedFile** searches every line of a file for matches to the regular expression **^<!—#insert\s+(\w+)\s*—>**:

```
open(File, $File) || die("$0: sendParsedFile died on $File ($!)\n");
while ($line = <File>) {
  if ( $line =~ /^<!-#insert\s+(\w+)\s*->/i) {
```

This pattern matches strings that start at the beginning of a line and whose basic format is

```
<!-#insert ARGUMENT->
```

Here *ARGUMENT* can be any word composed entirely of alphanumeric characters (including the underscore character), and extra white space characters may appear around both "insert" and *ARGUMENT*. Also, the case of the letters in "insert" is ignored. Let's agree to refer to strings in this format as *Insert* directives.

Any line that does not begin with an Insert directive is sent on to the client browser exactly as it was read in from the file. But whenever a line is found that does begin with an Insert directive, it is replaced. First, Perl automatically places the *ARGUMENT* substring, that is, whatever matches the regular expression's parenthesized subexpression **(\w+)**, in the special "memory" variable **$1**. As the value of **$1**, the argument from the Insert directive can then be compared against any number of predefined values, and if it matches one of these, the appropriate action can be taken. The point of dividing the search up into two stages like this is mainly for efficiency. Each line is searched only once, and for a pattern that must appear at the very beginning of the line. As soon as one character in the line fails to match the pattern, the line is sent on to the browser, and the search moves on to the beginning of the next line.

The present implementation of **sendParsedFile** looks for Insert directives with two different arguments: "Next," which must match exactly as shown, and "ShoppingCart," which can be written in any combination of upper- and lowercase letters. When it finds an "Insert Next" directive, it calls a pair of functions:

```
if ($1 eq 'Next') {    # Found an <!-insert Next-> directive.
    &insertNames(*Form, $FileNum,  $Cookie);
    &trackVisits(*Form, $File,     $Cookie);
}
```

Any output these functions send to STDOUT will take the place of the entire matching line in the output sent to the client browser.

Likewise, any line that begins with an "Insert Shopping Cart" directive will be replaced by the output resulting from a call to **displayCart**:

```
elsif ($1 =~ /^ShoppingCart$/i) {
    &displayCart(*Form, $File);
}
```

The **displayCart** function outputs basically the same text, scroll box, and submit button that appears as the "shopping cart" of the previous example.

Any other line that begins with an Insert directive will also be omitted from the output stream, even though its *ARGUMENT* is not recognized. In the present application, omitting the matching lines from the output is quite convenient, because it means that the HTML files can contain lines like the following:

```
<!—#Insert Next—>Next: <INPUT TYPE=SUBMIT NAME=NextName VALUE="The ¬
Tenant">
```

This allows the same file to be used as parsed or unparsed. If a browser downloads the page as a plain HTML document, it will display this line as only the word "Next:," followed by a submit button with "The Tenant" as its value. The browser will treat the Insert directive just as it would any other HTML comment. As sent through **sendParsedFile** and replaced by the output of **insertNames** and **trackVisits**, however, this line would be replaced by two other submit buttons, two hidden fields, and a varying number of links.

Overall, this implementation of **sendParsedFile** is not meant to be general, but to serve the specific needs of www-cart.cgi. There is of course nothing special about the arguments "Next" or "ShoppingCart." I chose them just because they were easy to remember while I was editing the HTML files wLandlord.html, wTenant.html, and so forth. This function's "line-swallowing" behavior, too, can and should be changed to suit any particular application that makes use of it. Web servers replace SSI directives within the line, and there is no limit on how may directives a single line may contain. On the other hand, this implementation of **sendParsedFile** does much more than simply filter files. Based on the Insert directives it finds, it calls functions that produce permanent side effects, such as updating a database. Because of these side effects, the kinds of operations that **sendParsedFile** performs might be more properly referred to as *generalized filtering*. I will return to a discussion of filtering techniques in Chapter 9.

## newCookie and getCookie: Creating and Retrieving a Unique Identifier

Before it even opens the file it is going to parse and send to a browser, **sendParsedFile** calls **getCookie** to get the cookie that uniquely identifies that browser. If the browser has already received a page from www-cart.cgi, then it will have received a valid cookie as a hidden field inside that page, and this same cookie should be part of its submitted form data. Otherwise, **getCookie** calls **newCookie** to create a new cookie for that browser:

```
$Cookie = &newCookie
   unless (($Cookie = $Form{'Cookie'}) && $Cookie =~ /\d_\d\d\d_\d/);
```

In turn, **newCookie** calls **time**, **srand**, **rand**, and **join** to create a new cookie that is practically certain to be unique:

```
srand(time^$$);
local($ck) = 100 + int(rand(899));   # Get a 3-digit random number.
$ck = join('_', $ENV{'REMOTE_ADDR'}, $ck, time);
```

The format of the resulting cookie,

```
{IP address}_{3-digit random number}_{time in seconds since 1970}
```

always matches the regular expression **/\d_\d\d\d_\d/**, which **getCookie** uses as a rudimentary validity test.

The point of making the cookie unique is to prevent browsers from accidentally accessing and/or overwriting each other's records on the server. The point of making it hard to guess is to prevent users from intentionally accessing each other's records. Verifying the format (or contents) of a cookie is usually not as important, and probably shouldn't be: using a generic cookie to authenticate access to sensitive information (like credit card numbers) is not a good idea. However, you might want to check the cookie's format just to be sure that it originated from the present application, and if this application is subject to large scale changes, it might be wise to include its name and version number in either the name or the value of the cookie. Such controls are of course more important for persistent cookies than for short-term, form-based cookies like the one used here. The last section in this chapter explains how to add a Netscape persistent cookie to www-cart.cgi.

### insertNames: Adding Buttons and Embedding the Cookie

The **insertNames** subroutine performs one simple task. As called by **sendParsedFile**, it replaces a line that contains an "Insert Next" directive with a pair of submit buttons and two hidden fields. First it obtains the filename for the page currently being sent and the page names for the next and previous pages:

```
$ThisFile = $ValidFiles[ $FileNum ];
$NextName = $ValidNames[($FileNum + 1) % $#ValidFiles];
$PrevName = $ValidNames[($FileNum - 1) % $#ValidFiles];
```

These last two statements are actually the only place in the script where the **@ValidNames** array is used. The alternative would be to use the pair of mappings that go in the other direction around the triangle:

```
$NextName = $Files2Names{$ValidFiles[($FileNum + 1) % $#Valid¬
Files]};
```

```
$PrevName = $Files2Names{$ValidFiles[($FileNum - 1) % $#Valid¬
Files]};
```

If there were a great many pages with long names, using this alternative and completely eliminating **@ValidNames** from the script would save memory and probably time as well. The triangle of mappings makes it somewhat redundant. For any small, simple application, however, the overhead of running the Perl interpreter itself will far outweigh the memory and CPU requirements of the script.

Once **insertNames** has obtained the correct file and page names, it outputs them along with the cookie in two hidden fields and a pair of submit buttons:

```
print "<INPUT TYPE=HIDDEN NAME=Cookie   VALUE=\"$Cookie\">\n";
print "<INPUT TYPE=HIDDEN NAME=ThisFile VALUE=\"$ThisFile\">\n",
"Next: <INPUT TYPE=SUBMIT NAME=NextName VALUE=\"$NextName\">\n",
"Back: <INPUT TYPE=SUBMIT NAME=NextName VALUE=\"$PrevName\">\n";
```

This step serves to automate the procedure of creating and maintaining an important part of the application's consistent forms interface. When new HTML files are added, references to a next or previous page in the old files may become out of date, but the automatically inserted Next and Back buttons will continue to show the correct values.

## trackVisits: Using a Database to Record a Browser's History and State

The **trackVisits** function uses a database to keep track of all of a browser's page accesses and any videos currently in its shopping cart. Perl can treat several different styles of database files and front ends as if they were associative arrays. This particular function uses a standard Unix DBM- or NDBM-style database, mainly because it's simple and very widely available. (DBM stands for Data Base Management, and the standard Unix implementation is a set of C library routines that provide random access to a set of records stored in a pair of specially formatted files. Many flavors of Unix have transparently replaced DBM with the New DBM library, which provides better support for shared use.) Perl includes several built-in functions for manipulating DBM-style databases, but there are also library functions that allow Perl to access database records stored in Oracle, Sybase, and many other popular database formats.

This function begins by calling **openDBM**, which opens the DBM file named by the configuration variable **$DBMF** and binds it to the associative array **%DBMF**:

```
&openDBM(*DBMF) || die("$0: error opening DBMF=$DBMF ($!)\n");
```

As soon as it is finishes manipulating the records bound to **%DBMF**, **trackVisits** closes the database by calling **closeDBM**, which has the effect of saving any changes to disk.

While the database is open, **%DBMF** can be treated in almost the same way as any other associative array. The cookie parameter is combined with the literal strings **'videos'** and **'visits'** to form keys into **%DBMF**, and the values associated with these keys are just strings. For instance, the assignment

```
$DBMF{$Cookie, 'videos'} = "The Landlord\0The Tenant";
```

would associate the string consisting of the two null-separated movie titles to a key of the format

```
"128.52.40.148_543_847473340106\034videos"
```

where the octal character **\034** (also known as Ctrl-\, FS, and ASCII 28) is Perl's default subscript separator. To change the default separator, you can just change the value of Perl's special variable **$;**. In fact, any reference to an associative array element such as

```
$foo{ $a, "b", 'c' }
```

is really a just shorthand expression for

```
$foo{ join($; , $a, "b", 'c') }
```

Combining keys in this way is a standard technique for emulating multidimensional arrays in Perl, and it makes the current task of maintaining two different database records keyed on **$Cookie** quite simple.

The actual maintenance algorithm is a little trickier. If the current request brings in new data from the browser, that data should be used to update the database. On the other hand, if the current request is missing some previously recorded data, then database records should be used in at least some circumstances to fill in the blanks. Such might be the case if the browser sent in a GET request that included its assigned cookie but no video selections. If the database contains a video list for that cookie, then the browser might have left its old shopping cart behind on some other page. If so, the shopping cart's former contents should be restored from the database. But it might just be that the user deselected everything in the cart before resubmitting the form, in which case its contents should not be restored.

There are actually a number of different scenarios that could account for missing information, but to simplify the maintenance algorithm, **trackVisits** gives precedence to any data submitted as part of a POST request, and reloads a shopping cart from the database only when the request method is not POST:

```
if ($ENV{'REQUEST_METHOD'} eq 'POST') {
  if (defined($Form{'videos'})) {
    $DBMF{ $Cookie, 'videos'} = $Form{'videos'}
  } else {
    delete $DBMF{$Cookie, 'videos'};
  }
} else {
  $Form{'videos'} = $DBMF{$Cookie, 'videos'} || undef;
}
```

## Slight Differences Between Null, Undefined, and Nothing At All

You may have noticed a small discrepancy between the treatments of **%DBMF** and **%Form**. The database record **$DBMF{$Cookie, 'videos'}** is assigned the value of **$Form{'videos'}** only when the value is known to be defined:

```
if (defined($Form{'videos'})) {
  $DBMF{$Cookie, 'videos'} = $Form{'videos'}
}
```

On the other hand, **%Form{'videos'}** is blindly assigned either the value of **$DBMF{$Cookie, 'videos'}** or the return value of the **undef** operator:

```
$Form{'videos'} = $DBMF{$Cookie, 'videos'} || undef;
```

By definition, the value of **undef** is the undefined value, which is Perl's closest approximation to nothing at all. If you assign **$Form{'videos'}** the null string **''**, it will still be defined, but if you assign it **undef**, then **defined(%Form{'videos'})** will evaluate to *false* (that is, to **''** in Perl 5, and to **0** in Perl 4). In the case of an associative array bound to a database, however, **undef**'s approximation of nothing is not close enough. An assignment of **undef** to **$DBMF{$Cookie, 'videos'}** will actually define a database record that takes up disk space and passes the test of the **defined** operator. Thus there really are slight differences between defining something as undefined and not defining it at all.

For this scheme to work, all of the application's HTML FORM tags must contain a METHOD=POST attribute, since GET is the default, and GET requests never update the database's video records.

There is also another advantage to using the POST method for all form submissions. It makes it easy to recognize when the incoming request has resulted from the user's clicking on a link with the cookie embedded in a query string. This is definitely a case where the CGI application should reload the browser's shopping cart from the database. In fact, the capacity to handle this kind of request is one of the major reasons for using cookies and databases in the first place. It gives the user the freedom to navigate by clicking on links instead of always having to turn the page by submitting a form.

The rest of **trackVisits** puts this freedom to use. It maintains the complete sequence of file accesses for each cookie, and it uses this history list to create hyperlinks back to previously visited pages. Unlike the list of currently selected videos, the history list can only grow, and so it is much easier to maintain, at least so far as www-cart.cgi is concerned. If the database grows very large, you'll probably want to write a separate Perl script to delete the oldest entries. Since the time of the original access is part of each cookie, expiring them from the database should be easy.

The history list is copied from the database into **$visits** before the current file access is appended to **$DBMF{$Cookie, 'visits'}**, so that only past visits are converted into links:

```perl
if ($visits = $DBMF{$Cookie, 'visits'}) {      # Extract DB entry.
    $DBMF{$Cookie, 'visits'} .= "\0".$File;     # Append to DB entry.
} else {
    $DBMF{$Cookie, 'visits'}  =       $File;     # Create new DB entry.
}
```

The links are created by splitting the null-separated history list into individual filenames, and then **%Files2Names** is used to map filenames to page names. To prevent more than one link to the same page, the list of visited files is sorted, and then each entry is used only if it is different from the previous one:

```perl
$previous = '';
foreach $_ (sort(split( /\0/, $visits))) {
    if ($_ ne $previous) {
        $pageName = $Files2Names{$_};
```

To keep users from revisiting the checkout counter with an empty cart, any visits to wzCheckout.html are also omitted from **trackVisit**"s output. Since this filename was chosen so that it would always sort last during the initialization of **@ValidFiles**, **trackVisits** takes its appearance as a sign to quit outputting links:

```
            last if ($pageName eq $CheckOut);  # wzCheckOut sorts last.
            print ",\n" if $previous;
            print qq(<A HREF="$Script?NextName=$_&Cookie=$Cookie">\n);
            print $pageName, "</A>";
            $previous = $_;
        }
    }
```

In each of these links, the embedded query string contains two items: a NextName field, whose value is the name of one of the HTML files as saved in the database, and a Cookie, whose value is of course that of the present cookie. These two values are all that's needed for the browser to jump to another page and recover its saved state from the database when it gets there.

That navigational flexibility is the biggest advantage of using a short-term cookie. A persistent, browser-resident cookie provides even more flexibility. For if the cookie is stored in and sent by the browser itself, instead of having to be embedded in every one of the application's links, then the browser's state can be recovered even when it follows a completely static link to another of the application's pages.

## Adding Netscape Persistent Cookies to www-cart.cgi

To convert www-cart.cgi into using Netscape persistent cookies instead of short-term, form-based cookies, all you would have to do is replace a few lines of code in the **getCookie** function. A better idea would be to add persistent cookies for browsers that support them, and still use the form-based method for browsers that do not. More browsers are adding support for Netscape-style cookies all the time, and some browsers allow the user to turn cookies acceptance on and off. So instead of comparing the HTTP_USER_AGENT environment variable with the names of browsers that are known to support (or not support) persistent cookies, it would be reasonable to send a Set-Cookie header to all browsers, in addition to a form-based hidden field that contains the same cookie.

If a particular remote browser is accepting such cookies, it should send back a Cookie header with the next request, as in

```
Cookie: Cookie=128.52.40.148_543_847473340106
```

The CGI program's Web server will automatically place this header's contents (everything after the colon) in an environment variable named HTTP_COOKIE. (This behavior actually has nothing to do with cookies per se, but is a standard part of HTTP.) Thus to retrieve the cookie in a Perl CGI script, all you have to do in Perl is extract it from the value of **$ENV{'HTTP_COOKIE'}**.

If the remote browser is not accepting and sending back cookies, your application can still use the **'Cookie'** value submitted with the rest of the form data, if there is one. The following code fragment implements this strategy.

```
if (($_ = $ENV{'HTTP_COOKIE'}) && /Cookie=([^;]+)/) {
  $Cookie = $1;
} else {
  $Cookie = $Form{'Cookie'} || '';
}
$Cookie = &newCookie if ($Cookie !~ /\d_\d\d\d_\d/); # Verify ¬
format.
```

To add Netscape persistent cookies to www-cart.cgi, you could simply replace its **getCookie** function with **getAndSetNSCookie**, shown in Listing 7.7. The only call to **getCookie** is located in **sendParsedFile**, where it sits, conveniently enough, just ahead of the line that outputs the Content-type header:

```
$Cookie = &getCookie(*Form);         # Get cookie first, and...
print "Content-type: text/html\n\n"; # ...then output header.
```

That is exactly where the modified program should output the Set-Cookie header, as in

```
print "Set-Cookie: Cookie=$Cookie";
print "; Expires=Fri, 31-Dec-1999 23:59:59 GMT";
print "; Path=",   $ENV{'SCRIPT_NAME'};
print "; Domain=", $ENV{'SERVER_NAME'};  # No "Secure".
print "\n"; # End of "Set-Cookie" header, "Content-type" to follow.
```

Here the expiration date is somewhat arbitrary; you might want to make it into a configuration variable or even set it dynamically, using Perl's built-in **gmtime** function (see the sidebar, "Netscape Persistent Cookie Time"). Also, according to the Netscape specification, the values assigned here to Path and Domain are actually the defaults, and may therefore be omitted. They may still be required, however, by Microsoft's Internet Explorer and some other browsers. Since the specification itself is subject to change, it's best to make the Set-Cookie header as compatible as possible.

**LISTING 7.7    getAndSetNSCookie, a function that handles both persistent and short-term cookies**

```perl
sub getAndSetNSPCookie {
  local(*Form) = @_;
  local($Cookie);
  if (($_ = $ENV{'HTTP_COOKIE'}) && /Cookie=([^;]+)/) {
    $Cookie = $1;
  } else {
    $Cookie = $Form{'Cookie'} || '';
  }
  $Cookie = &newCookie if ($Cookie !~ /\d_\d\d\d_\d/); # Verify format.
  print "Set-Cookie: Cookie=$Cookie";
  print "; Expires=Fri, 31-Dec-1999 23:59:59 GMT";
  print "; Path=",   $ENV{'SCRIPT_NAME'};
  print "; Domain=", $ENV{'SERVER_NAME'};  # No "Secure".
  print "\n"; # End of "Set-Cookie" header, "Content-type" to follow.
  $Cookie;
}
```

## Netscape Persistent Cookie Time

To set the expiration date of a Netscape Persistent Cookie dynamically, you need a function that can convert a time parameter, as offset from the present moment, into a date string in one of the formats given in the Netscape Persistent Cookie specification (see the section on "Netscape Persistent Cookie Attributes" for details). One such function, **NSPCtime**, is defined as follows:

```perl
sub NSPCtime {
    my($time)  = $_[0] || time;
    my(@wkday) = qw(Sun Mon Tue Wed Thu Fri Sat);
    my(@month) = qw(Jan Feb Mar Apr May Jun Jul Aug Sep Oct Nov Dec);
    my($sec, $min, $hour, $mday, $mon, $year, $wday) = gmtime($time);
    sprintf("%s, %02d-%s-%02d %02d:%02d:%02d GMT", $wkday[$wday]
            , $mday, $month[$mon], $year % 100, $hour, $min, $sec);
    }
```

**NSPCtime** converts a specified local time to Greenwich Mean Time and returns this as a date string in the following Netscape-cookie-compatible format:

```
Day, DD-Mon-YY HH:MM:SS GMT
```

To perform the conversion, **NSPCtime** calls Perl's built-in function **gmtime**. In a scalar context, **gmtime** returns a date string formatted like

```
Sat Nov  9 00:02:11 1996
```

(Unfortunately, this format is not allowed by the Netscape Persistent Cookie specification.) In a list context, **gmtime** returns a 9-element array of integers, which may be assigned to a list as follows:

```
($sec, $min, $hour, $mday, $mon, $year, $wday, $yday, $isdst) = ¬
gmtime(time);
```

The time parameter is to be specified as a local machine time, as returned by Perl's built-in **time** function. If called with no argument, **NSPCtime** actually uses the current value of **time** (as does **gmtime**). This is always the number of seconds since the beginning of the present epoch. In Unix, it's the number of seconds since the end of 1969; on a Macintosh, it's the number of seconds since the end of 1903.

To obtain a valid expiration date one year from the present time, call **NSPCtime** as follows:

```
$expires = &NSPCtime(time + 365*24*60*60);
```

To delete a cookie that was accepted by a remote browser more than a week ago, you can send the same Set-Cookie header that was originally used to set it, but with an expiration date obtained from the following call:

```
$expires = &NSPCtime(time - 7*24*60*60);
```

Due to the fact that a 32-bit signed integer can only hold about 68.1 years worth of seconds, **NSPCtime** will fail, at least on a Unix system, if you try to obtain an expiration date later than Tue, 19-Jan-2038 03:14:07 GMT. But perhaps by then, the Web will have changed . . . ■

# Chapter 8
# Searching, Indexing, and Reorganizing Information

This chapter discusses some of the major issues and strategies for designing and implementing search engines. It also provides three example scripts that cover the basics of building a custom search facility for a low- to medium-volume Web site.

## Search Engines Large and Small

The volume and variety of data on the Web have given new meaning to the issues involved in searching, indexing, and reorganizing electronic information. Searching is one of the most studied issues in the information sciences, but the best algorithms vary greatly depending on the amount and format of the data to be searched, and the growth of the amount of diverse data on the Web is unprecedented. Even with the most sophisticated algorithms and the fastest hardware at their disposal, high-volume search sites such as AltaVista, HotBot, Infoseek, Inktomi, Lycos, WebCrawler, and Yahoo! are far from providing complete solutions.

Although a search facility limited to one small site may be able to get away with exhaustively searching all of its pages for matches to each new query, a larger one definitely cannot. Global Web search facilities such as AltaVista and Yahoo! must rely on precompiled indices that might take weeks for a robot or humans to update—and even then the index will be from a very limited point of view. Because of the overhead involved in building the index, global search engines cannot compete with well-designed site-specific search facilities in terms of speed, completeness, and contextual relevance. Nevertheless, if you want to provide users with the ways and means to search your own site, you will have to confront some of the same problems that AltaVista and Yahoo! address. Thus it may be worthwhile to review what the big, global Web search engines do before you add search facilities to your own site.

# How Global Search Engines Work

Most of the global search engines search documents for keywords, although there are a few that attempt to locate documents within hierarchies of concepts or categories. AltaVista, Infoseek, Inktomi, Lycos, WebCrawler, and many others use variations of keyword searching that make use of indices.

## How Indices Facilitate Searching

The basic idea behind using indices to accelerate searches is very simple. Instead of searching through the entire text of each document, you search only its index, which, like the index of a book, is an ordered list of its keywords. If you use the same list of keywords for all the documents to be searched, the indices can all be stored together in one big table, where each row corresponds to one document and each column represents a keyword. The presence of keyword $y$ in document $x$ is indicated by a 1 (or possibly the total number of its occurrences) in row $x$, column $y$ of the table. Then, to find all documents containing a given keyword, you have only to scan for nonzero values in the corresponding column. Such a table is called an *inverted index*, because although it is constructed by the addition of a new row for each indexed document, you will want to search it by descending columns, not by traversing rows.

AltaVista, for example, claims that its spider downloads 3 million pages a day, so in order to enable this search method, its indexer must essentially create and add 3 million rows a day to its master table. The number of keywords indexed, however, and thus the length of each row in the table, is likely to be considerably less than the number of entries in a large dictionary. If you use an inverted table such as this as your index, it is straightforward to implement Boolean functions for multiple keywords; you could then find, for example, all the documents containing the words "English" and "dictionary" or "Dictionary" but not "Webster."

### Scoring Matches and Ranking Results

An easy enhancement to this method is to assign a score to each match of a keyword. The score can be based on criteria such as the occurrence of the keyword in the document's title, its nearness to the beginning, or the total number of occurrences. Then, instead of placing only a 0 or a 1 in that keyword's table entry, you can store its total score and rank the search results accordingly. This is one step beyond Boolean searching, which can test only for the presence or absence of individual words. It is easy to add this kind of scoring because the table's basic form remains the same. Virtually all of the high-volume search engines on the Web use some method for scoring matches and ranking results.

## Word Order, Location, and Proximity

A bigger enhancement to inverted-index searching is to keep track of word proximity and/or word order so that groups of words can be searched for as phrases or proper names. (The alternative, treating all commonly occurring phrases and names as indivisible keywords, would result in a combinatorial explosion of the number of keywords.) Keeping track of word proximity and/or word order requires each table entry to contain information about the location of the keyword's occurrences in the document and/or the nearby occurrences of other keywords. Thus each nonzero table entry must become in itself a list or mini-table (or a pointer to a list or mini-table). Note that once you have stored the locations of all the keywords that occur in each document, you can compute the scores for ranking found documents on-the-fly. If generic occurrences of a keyword are represented by their offset in the number of words from the beginning, special locations such as the title or the inside of a META tag might be indicated by a set of reserved numbers. This is probably closer to the way AltaVista and Inktomi actually do store indices of tens of millions of pages.

# Searching for Concepts

At the other end of the spectrum is Yahoo!, in which all pages submitted by authors or found by Yahoo!'s spider are reviewed, classified, and cross-linked by Yahoo!'s staff of humans as the pages are added to the database. This staff is headed by a full-time "ontologist," whose job is partly to formulate guidelines to ensure consistency. The URLs of the pages so classified can then be found by descending the tree of categories. One side effect is that Yahoo! can always present its catalogued URLs within a humanly constructed context of URLs that point to related content, even if, internally, Yahoo! too uses keyword indexing to search across or outside of its own categories.

## Synonymy, Homonymy, and Dynamic Taxonomies

Conceptual searching techniques are meant to address the two opposing problems of synonymy and homonymy. If you try to find information on a given topic by searching only on words, you are liable to miss some relevant information unless you include all of the words' synonyms. However, if you expand your search to include all of a word's synonyms, too, you are likely to get back many unwanted matches, especially if that word is a homonym—that is, a word with more than one meaning. Synonymy reduces your chances of finding relevant information via a keyword search, whereas homonymy increases your chances of retrieving irrelevant information. If a search engine had some representation of the meaning of the words, it should in principle be able to expand and reduce search terms to cover more-or-less similar *meanings*, not mere words. In general, these problems are far from being solved, but even the existing concept-based search engines have taken some steps in the right direction.

One refinement on conceptual searching is to allow for synonyms when matching the names of categories in the hierarchy. This does solve the problems of synonymy and homonymy.

Another modification is to create the categories automatically, as the Excite search engine claims to do, using techniques from statistics and data compression. Oracle's ConText software uses machine "understanding" of text to automate the classification of documents according to a huge, humanly devised concept hierarchy. The future in global search engines will probably be a merging of keyword and conceptual search techniques.

# How to Implement a Local Search Facility

The Web now offers a wide variety of site-specific search facilities, but despite their differences in appearance, all of them must perform some of the same tasks. A local search facility for your site will need to do the following three things:

**1** Obtain and interpret queries; that is, translate queries from user-entered words to the appropriate search commands

**2** Perform searches efficiently, possibly with the aid of a precompiled index

**3** Present an orderly and informative summary of the search results, complete with links to the relevant sources of information

In all of this, the user interface may be just as important as the search engine in the back end.

## Obtaining and Interpreting Queries

Obtaining search queries is no different from obtaining any other form data, but the way the queries are treated once they've been input depends on what kind of search is to be done. The simplest thing to do would be to take in plain strings of text and search for exact matches. Allowing the user to enter combinations of individual keywords adds one level of complexity, and allowing him or her to choose between these two methods or to choose other options such as matching or ignoring case and finding substrings or whole words only adds another. All of these features can be fairly easy to implement, however, and the examples in this chapter demonstrate these options and more.

Formatting tags and inline protocol elements pose special problems when HTML text is searched. Should text enclosed within arbitrary HTML tags be searched just like any other text? A naive search algorithm may produce a great many matches for keywords such as "body" and "head," all of them coming from HTML <HEAD> and <BODY> elements. This is not usually what the user wants. However, the text inside some HTML elements—for instance, the ALT attribute of an IMG tag—may bear genuinely useful information. And what about text that appears inside comments or a JavaScript applet? The answer is not entirely obvious. Relevant information can be contained in image captions or even in text strings that are printed only by the applet. In most cases, it is probably better to ignore any text inside HTML tags, but even some of the global search sites include it in their indices. This can result in supposedly matching documents in which the "found" keyword is nowhere to be found. Ideally, users should be able to choose whether to search inside of tags or not. (In this chapter, Example 8B implements such an option.)

Interfaces to search facilities already vary greatly in their ease of use and in their power to discriminate potential matches from each other. There is no such thing as a standard search interface, so as a search provider, you are faced with tradeoffs between intuitiveness, precision, and completeness (or all the bells and whistles). Keep in mind the objectives and expectations of your users; the search habits of PC users, Unix hackers, journalists, academics, and casual surfers will all be different.

## Implementing Your Search Engine

The form interface shown in Figure 8.2, later in this chapter, searches the text files in only one directory. To allow your engine to search sites with multiple directories, you can use similar search functions to search all the documents in a directory tree by means of iteration or recursion. On a site that contains many directories and documents, searching all of the text to satisfy each new query rapidly becomes inefficient. That's when an index becomes useful. Duplicating the sophisticated indexing methods of an engine such as AltaVista, however, would be massive overkill for any particular site, and such a fully automated approach wouldn't use the knowledge of the site managers or content authors to its greatest advantage anyway.

The opposite extreme might be an approach similar to Yahoo!'s: Formulate a hierarchy of concepts relevant to your site, and then manually classify all the documents accordingly. The user's interface to this scheme will probably appear as a multiply linked hierarchy of lists, each entry showing its classification(s) as well as providing hyperlinks to the relevant documents. Constructing something like this, of course, is a lot of work. First of all, you've got to create the classifications, which must be general enough to cover all possible documents that your site provides and yet specific enough to let the user find what he or she wants. Second, you'll have to maintain this scheme by classifying every new document. Unless you are eternally vigilant, your catalog may fail to keep in step with your documents—or even worse, the concepts themselves may become outdated as your site's contents grow or change.

One compromise between fully automatic and fully manual search methods is the placement of keywords within named META tags or similarly designated places throughout HTML documents. (An example is the use of the NAME attribute as generalized in HTML 3.) Such a scheme makes it much easier for automated indexing programs to find the keywords deemed appropriate by the document's original authors or editors. Given an awareness of the conventions behind such a scheme, and only a little added effort on the part of search interface designers and implementers, the user can search for these marked keywords explicitly. Of the global Internet search engines, Infoseek, with its roots in journalism and library services, is currently the one that makes the greatest use of keywords and other information enclosed within META tags. Some of the features of Infoseek's actual interface, however, have a reputation for not being immediately obvious to novice users. In the future, look for—or help create—more conventions and more intuitive interfaces to local as well as global search facilities.

## Presenting Search Results

Once your search function has found matches to the user's queries, it should present an orderly and informative summary of these search results, complete with links to the matching documents. Ideally, the appearance of this presentation should vary depending on what the user is trying to do—generate a comprehensive list of all articles by a particular author, for example, or navigate as quickly as possible from the symptoms of poisoning to remedies.

For instance, you may want to allow the user the option of sorting search results according to closeness of match (assuming you kept score), the dates of the found documents, or some other criteria. You will probably then want to show the user these dates, scores, or any other criteria used to determine the documents' rankings. As a starting point, you may want to look at how some of the popular search sites present their search results.

The second thing to consider is what to show of the matching documents' actual contents. When it comes to presenting the search results, a site-specific search facility enjoys many advantages over global search pages. Due to the enormity of their task, and their limitations in storage and speed, the existing global search engines are unable to present more than the URLs and the first few lines of text from matching documents. With your own local search facility you can provide much greater depth of response. Although you may wish to present only titles and URLs, you could also show, for example, the total number of matches in each document, or even a few lines from the original context of each match. (Examples 8B and 8C, later in this chapter, implement such enhanced presentations.)

## Example 8A: Searching a Single Document as Text

A simple search facility could be something such as a directory service, where all the information to be searched is contained in one large document. Suppose you had a list of the 440 or so members of the U.S. House of Representatives, formatted as follows:

```
Full Name                       Party Dist.   Room Bldg.   Phone 202-
---- ----                       ----- -----   ---- -----   ----- ----

Abercrombie, Neil                 D     HI01   1233 LHOB    225-2726
Ackerman, Gary                    D     NY05   2243 RHOB    225-2601
        . . . 441 more entries, counting delegates and vacancies ...
Zimmer, Dick                      R     NJ12   228  CHOB    225-5801
```

The US_House.cgi script, shown in Listing 8.1, generates a simple form that allows the user to input a search string and then displays the results in a space below the input elements. If any matches are found, the script will also display information about how to address mail to a House member based on the abbreviated information in the directory listing. Figure 8.1 shows the page as it appears when a search has already been performed.

Practically all of the Perl constructs used in this script have been explained in earlier chapters, so I'll focus mainly on its overall design and highlight only a few details of its actual implementation.

**LISTING 8.1    US_House.cgi, a script for searching a single document as text**

```perl
#!/usr/local/bin/perl
# US_House.cgi - script for searching a pre-formatted text file.
# Copyright 1996 by Stephen Lines (spraxlo@ai.mit.edu)
require "FormData.pl";
$FILE = "US_House.txt";   # Relative path to the data file.

# A conditional block of code like the following is useful for
# testing and debugging your script in a Unix or DOS shell (or
# in MacPerl) before installing it on a server as a CGI program:
unless (defined($ENV{'SCRIPT_NAME'})) {   # this is only a test...
  $ENV{'SCRIPT_NAME'}    = $0;
  $ENV{'REQUEST_METHOD'} = 'GET';
  $ENV{'QUERY_STRING'}   = 'query=Jo.&name2=v2&name2=v2+%26+1%2F2';
  $ENV{'CONTENT_LENGTH'} = length($ENV{'QUERY_STRING'});
}

if (&getFormData(*Form) && ($query = $Form{'query'})) {
  # Escape (most of) the regular expression metacharacters:
  $query =~ s/([\$()*+?\[\\\]^{|}])/\\$1/g;
} else {
  $query = '';
}

print "Content-type: text/html\n\n";
print <<END_OF_FORM;
<HTML><HEAD>
<TITLE>U.S. House of Representatives Directory Search</TITLE>
</HEAD><BODY BGCOLOR=#DDEEFF><H2><DIV ALIGN=CENTER>
U.S. House of Representatives Directory Search</DIV></H2>
<FORM>
Search for information on a House member by entering a string:<BR>
<INPUT TYPE=TEXT SIZE=50 MAXLENGTH=80 NAME=query VALUE="$query">
<INPUT TYPE=SUBMIT VALUE="Submit">
<INPUT TYPE=RESET  VALUE="Reset">
<P>
```

---

**LISTING 8.1    US_House.cgi, a script for searching a single document as text (Continued)**

---

```
For example, enter <B>Kennedy, Joseph</B>, or just <B>Kennedy</B>.<BR>
The \`\`wildcard'' character is \`\`.'' (period);
thus <B>Jo.</B> matches <B>Jos</B>, <B>Joe</B>, <B>Job</B>, etc.
</FORM><HR>
END_OF_FORM


if ($query) {
  print "<B>Results of searching $FILE for $query:</B><PRE>\n",
  "Full Name                       Party Dist.   Room Bldg.  Phone 202-\n",
  "---- ----                       ----- -----   ---- -----  ----- ----\n";
  unless (open(FILE, $FILE)) {
    print(  "Sorry, the program was unable to open $FILE\n");
    die("$0: Error opening $FILE ($!)\n");
  }
  while (<FILE>) {
    # s/<([^>]|\n)*>//g;        # Uncomment this to strip all HTML tags
    # s/<(([^>]|\n)*)>/&lt;$1;$gt;/go;  # this would escape HTML tags
    if (/$query/) {            # search $_ for $query
      $matches++;             # increment match count
      print;                  # print the matching string ($_)
    }
  }
  close(FILE);
  if (! $matches) {
    print "</PRE><B>Sorry, no matching entries were found.</B><BR>\n";
    print "Please check the spelling and try again.<P>\n";
  } else {
    print <<END_OF_ADDRESS
</PRE> Mail should be addressed using the following format:<PRE>
      Honorable (Member Name)
      (Full Name of Building, Room Number)
      Washington, D.C.  20515
</PRE> where the acronyms for the building names in the
      directory listing are replaced as follows:<PRE>
      RHOB  --  Rayburn House Office Building
```

---

**LISTING 8.1    US_House.cgi, a script for searching a single document as text (Continued)**

---

```
        LHOB  --  Longworth House Office Building
        CHOB  --  Cannon House Office Building
</PRE>
END_OF_ADDRESS
    }
}


print <<EOF;
<P><SMALL>(<A HREF=http://www.house.gov/mbr_dir/membr_full_alpha_list.html>
This directory service is based on a list prepared
by The House Information Resources in February, 1996.</A>)
</SMALL></BODY></HTML>
EOF
```

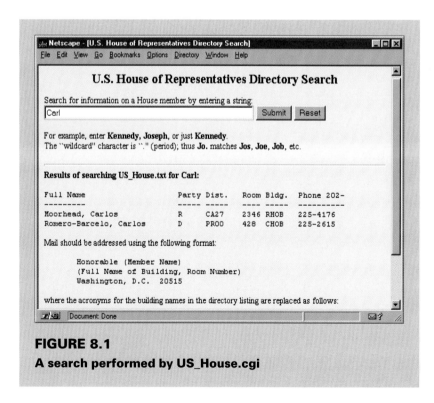

**FIGURE 8.1**

**A search performed by US_House.cgi**

## Obtaining Queries and Displaying the Search Results

This simple interface was designed to be easy to understand and convenient for the user. The form itself is always displayed at the top of the page and provides instructions to the user.

The results of the previous search, if there was one, are clearly labeled and displayed immediately following the form, separated by a horizontal rule (HR) element. If no matches were found, the results include a message to that effect. If there were matches, the page displays some additional information about how to interpret and use the results (in this case, how to convert a directory listing into a proper postal address).

The main reason for redisplaying the form after every search is to allow the user to modify his or her query without starting over. It also provides the user with a constant source of feedback. The user can review the search string in its original setting, and the original search instructions may tell him or her why the query produced the particular results shown.

Finally, because the original source of information is not usually visible in the search interface itself, the script provides a brief explanation of what the user is actually searching. In this case, the original source is one long directory file that doesn't even include the mailing information. This search interface puts all the information in one place and is therefore more convenient for the user.

**Escaping Regular Expression Metacharacters in the Query**   The first thing this script does upon receiving a query is search it for regular expression *metacharacters*. These are non-alphanumeric characters that have special meanings inside regular expressions, such as **$**, which matches not "$," but the end of a string or line. (Many of the same characters also have special meanings in the shell, and should be escaped or even deleted from user-entered strings that are passed to a command shell; see the sidebar, "Regular Expressions vs. Shell Metacharacters." For more information on regular expression matching, see the Appendix.) Whenever this script finds a regular expression metacharacter in the user-entered search string, it "escapes" that character by replacing it with itself preceded by a backslash:

```
if (&getFormData(*Form) && ($query = $Form{'query'})) {
  # Escape (most of) the regular expression metacharacters:
  $query =~ s/([\$()*+?\[\\\]^{|}])/\\$1/g;
}
```

For example, if **$query** were to contain the expression **a\*b+c?**, this search-and-replace statement would convert it into the expression **a\\\*b\+c\?**. Obviously, some of these metacharacters have to be escaped in the very search string that is used to find them (as in **\]**, which does not end the character class, but matches a **]** character in the search string). Some of the other metacharacters lose their special meanings inside the square brackets. One metacharacter that is not touched is the period; instead, the user is informed of its special meaning as a wildcard character.

## Implementing the Back End

US_House.cgi's search algorithm is extremely simple: Read the text file line by line, testing each line as you go. If the line matches the query pattern, print it; otherwise, don't. It could have been implemented in a single line of code, as in

```
while (<FILE>) { print if (/$query/); }
```

Perl's input operator **<FILE>** places each line in the special variable **$_**, which is also the default argument to **print** and to the pattern-matching operator **//**.

## Counting the Matches

As actually implemented, however, the file-input/search loop also keeps a count of matches:

```
if (/$query/) {          # search $_ for $query
    $matches++;          # increment match count
    print;               # print the matching string ($_)
}
```

## Regular Expressions vs. Shell Metacharacters

The reason why you should escape metacharacters in the search string is only to prevent users from entering them unwittingly. Leaving them in would not pose any great threat to security. At most, a clever choice of metacharacters may produce a garbled search pattern that causes the script to abort execution. It is becoming fairly common for high-volume search sites to offer regular expression matching as an option, and even nonprogrammers are learning to take advantage of the advanced features that are standard in the use of regular expressions.

Leaving metacharacters inside strings that are used as external commands, however, is a completely different story. Issuing a remote user-entered string as an external command without first checking it for shell metacharacters is one of the most dangerous (and most common) security holes in CGI programming.

This is the first appearance of **$matches** in the script, but as a scalar variable in a numerical context, it is automatically initialized to 0 on its first use, before the auto-increment operator **++** applies. Thus when the loop finishes, **$matches** will contain the correct number of matching lines. If there were no matches, **$matches** would spring into existence later, as the empty value inside the **if (! $matches)** conditional. This script makes use of **$matches** only as an on/off switch, or "flag." It doesn't need the exact match count to determine whether or not to output the addressing information, but the count is as good (and cheap) a flag as any other. If the search loop were complex enough to merit its own subroutine, the match count would also be useful as a return value.

## Example 8B: Searching All the HTML Documents in a Directory

A CGI interface for searching a single document can be quite useful, but the purpose of a Web search facility is more often to provide a means for searching many different documents at once. The script in this example, tdsearch.cgi, searches all the text files in a given directory for a single string. Its options let the user choose whether to match the case of the search string, match whole words only, and use regular expression searching. The user can also use an option that strips HTML

tags to specify whether to search inside and display HTML tags or to ignore them altogether. As in the previous example, the form itself is always displayed at the top of the page. This persistent interface makes it easy for the user both to understand the results from a previous search and to modify the input string or string-matching options for the next search. Figure 8.2 shows a typical output page.

Listing 8.2 shows the complete script. Much of the code in tdsearch.cgi is similar to that of the previous example, but it's rather more complex, so I'll explain some parts of it in greater detail.

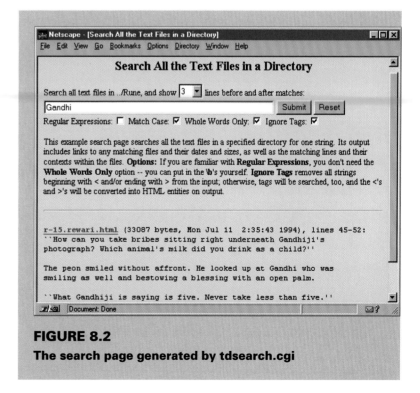

**FIGURE 8.2**

**The search page generated by tdsearch.cgi**

**LISTING 8.2    tdsearch.cgi, a script that searches all the text documents in a directory**

```perl
#!/usr/local/bin/perl5
# tdsearch.cgi - searches all the text files in a directory and
# displays links to matching files as well as context of matching lines.
# This script is based partly on some example code by Larry Wall.
# Copyright (C) 1996 Stephen Lines <spraxlo@ai.mit.edu>

require "ctime.pl";
require "FormData.pl";
$txtdir = "../web/me";            # Relative path to the directory.

unless (defined($ENV{'SCRIPT_NAME'})) {    # this is only a test...
  $ENV{'SCRIPT_NAME'}    = $0;
  $ENV{'REQUEST_METHOD'} = 'GET';
  $ENV{'QUERY_STRING'}   = 'Query=Cologne&StripHTML=CHECKED';
  $ENV{'CONTENT_LENGTH'} = length($ENV{'QUERY_STRING'});
}


&getFormData(*Form);
$Context   = $Form{'Context'}   || 2;
$Query     = $Form{'Query'}     || '';
$RegExp    = $Form{'RegExp'}    || '';    # Options default to "off"
$MatchCase = $Form{'MatchCase'} || '';
$WholeWord = $Form{'WholeWord'} || '';
$StripHTML = $Form{'StripHTML'} || '';

print "Content-type: text/html\n\n";
print <<EOF;
<HTML><HEAD>
<TITLE>Search All the Text Files in a Directory</TITLE>
</HEAD><BODY BGCOLOR=#FFDDAA><FORM><DIV ALIGN=CENTER>
<H2>Search All the Text Files in a Directory</H2></DIV>
Search all text files in $txtdir, and show
<SELECT NAME="Context">
<OPTION> $Context    <OPTION> 1 <OPTION> 2 <OPTION> 3 <OPTION> 4
<OPTION> 5 <OPTION> 6 <OPTION> 7 <OPTION> 8 <OPTION> 9
```

**LISTING 8.2    tdsearch.cgi, a script that searches all the text documents in a directory (Continued)**

```
</SELECT>
lines before and after matches: <BR>
<INPUT TYPE=TEXT SIZE=55 MAXLENGTH=255 NAME="Query" VALUE="$Query">
<INPUT TYPE=SUBMIT  VALUE=Submit>
<INPUT TYPE=RESET    VALUE=Reset><BR>
Regular Expressions:
<INPUT TYPE=CHECKBOX NAME=RegExp    VALUE=CHECKED $RegExp>
Match Case:
<INPUT TYPE=CHECKBOX NAME=MatchCase VALUE=CHECKED $MatchCase>
Whole Words Only:
<INPUT TYPE=CHECKBOX NAME=WholeWord VALUE=CHECKED $WholeWord>
Ignore Tags:
<INPUT TYPE=CHECKBOX NAME=StripHTML VALUE=CHECKED $StripHTML>
<BR>
<P> This example search page searches all the text files
in a specified directory for one string.  Its output includes
links to any matching files and their dates and sizes, as well
as the matching lines and their contexts within the files.
<B>Options:</B> If you are familiar with <B>Regular
Expressions</B>, you don't need the <B>Whole Words Only</B>
option — you can put in the <B>&#92;b</B>'s yourself. <B>Ignore
Tags</B> removes all strings beginning with &lt; and/or ending with &gt;
from the input; otherwise, tags will be searched, too, and the &lt;'s
and &gt;'s will be converted into HTML entities on output.
</FORM><HR><PRE>
EOF

if ($Query) { # Called with at least one argument; search for it.

    unless ($RegExp) { $Query =~ s/([\$()*+.?\[\\\]^{|}])/\\$1/g; }
    if ($WholeWord)  { $Query =  "\\b$Query\\b"; }
    $tags = '<[^>]*?(?:>|$)|(^|\G)[^<>]*?>'; # matches (partial) tags
    $matchOptions = $MatchCase ? 'o' : 'oi';
    $len          = $Context*2 + 1;
    $foundLines   = 0;
```

**LISTING 8.2    tdsearch.cgi, a script that searches all the text documents in a directory (Continued)**

```perl
    $foundFiles   = 0;

    chdir($txtdir);          # cd to the directory to keep it simple...
    opendir(DIR, ".");       # opendir is most portable on current dir (.)
    @txtFiles = grep( -T, readdir(DIR));
    closedir(DIR);

    foreach $file (@txtFiles) {
        open(FILE, $file) || do
            { print "Couldn't open file $file: $!\n"; next; };

        undef @keep;         # Re-initializing @keep is essential!
        for $j (0 .. $Context) {
            $keep[$Context - $j] = ''; # Add blank line before.
            $_ = <FILE>;               # Get next line from FILE.
            s/$tags//go if $StripHTML; # Remove whole and partial tags.
            $keep[$Context + $j] = $_ if $_; # Add next line after.
        }

#       An equivalent initialization, using unshift and push...
#       $_ = <FILE>;                   # Get first line of FILE.
#       s/$tags//go if $StripHTML;     # Must strip every line of input!
#       push( @keep, $_ );             # @keep now holds only 1st line.
#       for (1 .. $Context) {          # Loop to grow @keep outward...
#           unshift(@keep, '');        # Add a blank line to the beginning.
#           $_ = <FILE>;               # Get next line from FILE.
#           s/$tags//go if $StripHTML; # Can't strip matches only!
#           push( @keep, $_ ) if $_;   # Add it to the end of @keep.
#       }

        # Now search with @keep as a silo, shifting old lines out from
        # the beginning and pushing new lines onto the end.  For the
        # sake of efficiency, the whole loop is wrapped inside an eval;
        # only variables escaped with a backslask like \$found can change
        # while eval executes its argument code.  Others, like $Context
```

**LISTING 8.2    tdsearch.cgi, a script that searches all the text documents
in a directory (Continued)**

```perl
# and $Query, are interpolated only once and remain constant
# throughout the loop. A variable whose value is '' (null) would
# be interpolated as nothing at all; to avoid syntax errors such
# as "if ()", its value should be converted to 0, as follows:
$StripHTML = 0 unless $StripHTML;
eval <<ENDLOOP;                       # eval all code up to ENDLOOP.
\$found = 0;
while ( \$keep[$Context]) {
    if (\$keep[$Context] =~ /$Query/$matchOptions) {
        \$beg = \$. - $len;
        print "<A HREF=\\"$txtdir/$file\\"><B>$file</B></A>";
        if (! \$found++) {
            \@file_info = stat("$file");
            \$bytes    = \$file_info[7];
            chop(\$modtime = &ctime(\$file_info[9]));
            print " (\$bytes bytes, \$modtime)";
        }
        print ", lines \$beg-\$.:\n";
        foreach \$line (\@keep) {
            if (\$line) {
                unless ($StripHTML) {   # Can escape tags in
                    \$line =~ s/</&lt;/g; # output only, but must
                    \$line =~ s/>/&gt;/g; # handle < & > separately.
                }
                print \$line;
            }
        }
        print "\n";
    }
    if (\$_) {
        \$_ =  <FILE>;          # Must strip all input or none:
        \$_ =~ s/$tags//go if ($StripHTML);
        # s/<([^>]|\\n)*>//go; # doesn't work on single lines.
    }
    shift(\@keep);                   # out with the oldest line
```

---

**LISTING 8.2**    **tdsearch.cgi, a script that searches all the text documents in a directory (Continued)**

---

```
            push( \@keep, \$_);           # in with the new
        }
ENDLOOP
        die("$0: $@") if $@;              # $@ catches errors from eval.
        close(FILE);
        if ($found) {
            $foundLines += $found;
            $foundFiles++;
        }
    }
    print "</PRE><B>Totals: $foundLines matches in $foundFiles files, ";
    print "out of ", 0 + @txtFiles, " files searched.</B>\n";
}


print "</BODY></HTML>\n";
exit;
```

## Getting and Displaying the Input

The input interface of tdsearch.cgi is very similar to that of US_House.cgi, except that it presents five search options. The search string and the state of all the options' input fields are preserved between requests, giving the user a constant interface.

When you write a single CGI script to output a form and process its input, maintaining the state of that form is very easy. Quite often it's only a matter of choosing meaningful variable names and using them both in the back-end program and in the form itself (the front end). In this script, all of the options work in this way. Consider, for example, the option that allows the user to use regular expression matching. The input field for this option is a checkbox:

```
Regular Expressions:
<INPUT TYPE=CHECKBOX NAME=RegExp    VALUE=CHECKED $RegExp>
```

If the user clicks this checkbox on, **$Form{'RegExp'}** will receive the value **'CHECKED'**, and then the obvious assignment of **$Form{'RegExp'}** back to **$RegExp** completes the loop:

```
$RegExp = $Form{'RegExp'} || '';  # Option defaults to "off"
```

If **$Form{'RegExp'}** is not defined, this statement assigns to **$RegExp** the default value of **''** (the empty string). As a result, the value of **$RegExp** should always be either null or **'CHECKED'**, and the state of the checkbox itself should always reflect the user's most recent choice.

In the back end, **$RegExp** is used only as a *flag*—a true/false value that signals whether the option is on or off. As far as the search algorithm is concerned, the value used to turn an option on might as well be **'CARRY_ON'**, which is why you're free to give the value a double meaning as **'CHECKED'**. It is not always a good idea to use one variable for more than one purpose, but in this case the meanings of **$RegExp** as a flag in the back end and as an attribute value in the front end dovetail quite naturally.

The variable that corresponds to the number of lines to display surrounding a match, **$Context,** is a little different. Its numerical value actually figures in the search algorithm proper, so its meaning is always the same. Still, representing the choices in a pull-down menu makes it easy to preserve the variable's value from one request to the next.

## Connecting the Search Options to the Back End

When you're designing a form-based CGI application, it's often easiest to design the front end first and worry about the back end later, once you've decided on all the user interface's options and features. Also, adding a new feature to an existing program can be as difficult as starting from scratch, so creating the interface first may be the best use of your time. For an application such as tdsearch.cgi, Perl's implementation of regular expression matching and many of the functions for manipulating text make it fairly easy to connect the front and back ends.

The following list enumerates tdsearch.cgi's five options and describes how they are implemented as part of the search engine proper:

▶ **Show *n* lines of context**   The user can choose to display from 1 to 9 lines of text before and after any matching line. The minimum is 1, which results in the display of 3 lines for every match of the search string. A major portion of the script's complexity is spent on maintaining an array of "before" and "after" lines and sifting through it on a first-in, first-out basis as if the lines were in a silo.

▶ **Regular Expressions**   If this option is checked, the user-entered search string is interpreted as a regular expression. If it is not checked, nearly all of the regular expression metacharacters will be escaped, allowing them to be searched for as literal characters.

▶ **Match Case**   If this option is checked, the search is to be performed in a case-sensitive manner. Otherwise, Perl's pattern-matching operator **//** is used with the **i** (ignore case) option.

▶ **Whole words only**   If this option is checked, the search string will match only the text in which it is surrounded by nonword characters such as white space or punctuation marks; to implement this, just add a **\b** to the beginning and end of the string. Otherwise, the string will also match as a substring.

▶ **Ignore Tags**   This option, when checked, tells the search engine not to search inside HTML-like tags (any string that begins with **<** and ends with **>**) and not to output them either. This is implemented by discarding all tags from the file input stream. Otherwise, tags will be searched and escaped to make them visible in the output.

## Bulletproof vs. Quick-and-Dirty Code

To ensure absolute consistency between the state of the **RegExp** checkbox and the true/false value of **$RegExp**, you'd have to replace the above assignment with something such as

```
$RegExp = ($Form{'RegExp'} eq 'CHECKED') ? 'CHECKED' : '';
```

At the other extreme, you could take advantage of the fact that a checkbox is off by default unless its INPUT tag contains the CHECKED attribute, and eliminate **$RegExp** altogether:

```
<INPUT TYPE=CHECKBOX NAME=RegExp VALUE=CHECKED $Form{'$RegExp'}>
```

The approach taken in tdsearch.cgi and, indeed, throughout this book, lies between these two extremes, in what feels to me like a happy medium. In the end, your comfort zone might be different from mine, and on the Web you can certainly find Perl examples that run the gamut, from bulletproof code to quick-and-dirty hacks. As I mentioned in an earlier chapter, one of Perl's slogans is, "There's more than one way to do it." When confronted with a choice in coding the examples in this book, I've generally tried to put clarity first.

## Removing Unwanted HTML Tags

To remove all the HTML tags from a file as it is read in and printed out again line by line, you could use the **s/*pattern*/*replacement*/** operator with a single search expression, as in:

```
while (<FILE>) {
    s/<[^>]*?(?:>|$)|(^|\G)[^<>]*?>//go;
    print;
}
```

The search expression **/<[^>]*?(>|$)|(^|\G)[^<>]*?>/** matches any complete, angle-bracket-delimited tag, or any partial tag that is broken off by the beginning or end of the string itself. It consists of two alternative patterns separated by the vertical bar in the middle. The first pattern, **<[^>]*?(?:>|$)**, matches any substring that begins with **<** and ends with either **>** or the end of the string as a whole (which matches **$**), whichever comes first. The second pattern, **(?:^|\G)[^<>]*?>**, matches any substring that starts at the beginning of the string (which matches **^**) or the place where the last **/g**-modified search left off (which matches **\G**) and ends with the first occurrence of **>**. If you were certain that no tags in the file began on one line and ended on another, you could get away with using the much simpler search expression **/<[^>]*?>/**, but missing even a single partial tag could hide or throw off the rest of the output when it is displayed by a browser.

In the first pattern, the subexpression **(?:>|$)** matches either the **>** character or the end of the string, symbolized by **$**. The parenthese are used only to group the **>** and the **$** together as one element, and not to "remember" the matching sub-string (which in this case could only be **<**) by placing it in the special back-reference variable **$1**. Technically speaking, **>** is an *atom*, and **$** is an *assertion*. An atom is any element of a regular expression that can match only a single character. An assertion is any element that can match only a contextual condition, such as the beginning of the string or a word boundary. It does not match any actual character. If a search string matches a pattern that includes one atom in parentheses, the matching character is copied into the special, read-only "memory" varable **$1**. If there are two such parenthesized atoms, the character matching the second one would be placed in **$2**, and so on. The special symbol **?:**, appearing at the begin-ning of a parenthesized subexpression, disables the back reference mechanism for that subexpression. Thus **(?:>|$)** matches either the end of a tag or the end of a string, without remembering which. This particular subexpression must be used instead of **[>$]** because **$** loses its special meaning inside a character class, and would only match itself, the dollar-sign character. (If you find this explanation hard to follow, now would be a good time to consult the Appendix. But don't worry, this is probably the most complicated regular expression in the entire book.)

In the second pattern, the subexpression **(^\G)** matches the beginning of a line (**^**) or the place (**\G**) where the last **/g**-modified search left off. The **?:** symbol would not make any difference here, because neither **^** nor **\G** is an atom; they are both assertions.

In both patterns, the combination of metacharacters **\*?** is used to quantify a negative character class (**[^>]** or **[^<>]**). In general, an element such as **[ABC]** , called a character class, matches any *one* of the characters **A**, **B**, or **C**, whereas **[^ABC]**, called a negative character class, matches any single character *except* for **A**, **B**, or **C**. A character class is thus a kind of atom.

When the star quantifier is appended to a character class, as in **[ABC]\***, the resulting *quantified atom* matches any string of zero or more characters from the character class—as long a string as possible. When the **\*?** quantifier is appended, as in **[ABC]\***, the resulting quantified atom also matches any string of zero or more characters from the character class, but as *short* a string as possible. Quantification works the same way for negative character classes (because a class defined by exclusion is still a class, of course). In the pattern **<[^>]\*?(?:>|$)**, the class **[^>]** must be quantified using **\*?** instead of **\*** in order to avoid matching two separate tags in the same string as one long tag. In other words, **<[^>]\*?>** would match the individual <B> and </B> tags in "<B>\$100</B>," whereas **<[^>]\*>** would match the whole string, causing **s/<[^>]\*>//g** to discard the "\$100." The **\*?** in **(^\G)[^<>]\*?>** is necessary for similar reasons. (The **?:** symbol, **\*?** quantifier, and **\G** assertion are all new in Perl 5, and are actually tdsearch.cgi's only incompatibilities with Perl 4).

In short, **s/<[^>]\*?(?:>|$)|(^\G)[^<>]\*?>//go** removes all the tags and partial tags from any single-line string to which it is applied.

In tdsearch.cgi, this same regular expression is used in several different places, so to prevent typos and ensure that any changes will be consistent and easy to make, it is assigned to a variable:

```
$tags = '<[^>]*?(?:>|$)|(^|\G)[^<>]*?>'; # matches (partial) tags
```

Here the single quotes are necessary in the assignment, because otherwise **$)** would be interpreted as a variable (in fact, **$)** is the effective group ID number of the running program). If double quotes were used instead of single quotes, the dollar sign would have to be escaped using a backslash.

The script can then use **$tags** as in the following statement:

```
s/$tags//go if $StripHTML;  # Remove whole and partial tags.
```

The net result is no more tags.

## Implementing the Search Engine

A search of all the text files in a directory requires only one extra step beyond those required to search a single text file. Basically, you read the directory to get a list of all the files, and then you search each file individually.

**Reading a Directory to Get a List of Files**  The functions **opendir**, **readdir**, and **closedir** work for directories in just about the same way that **open**, **read**, and **close** work for ordinary files. To avoid the need for an absolute directory path, you can use **chdir** to change to the directory you want to read and open it as **"."** (period):

```
chdir($txtdir);      # cd to the directory to keep it simple...
opendir(DIR, ".");   # opendir is most portable on current dir ¬
(.)
@txtFiles = grep( -T, readdir(DIR));
closedir(DIR);
```

Here the **grep** function applies the **-T** operator to test each file in the list of file-names returned by **readdir** and thus passes on to **@txtFiles** a reduced list containing only the text files in the directory. Binary executables, GIF images, and other directories, for instance, should fail the **-T** test. HTML files and Perl scripts should pass.

**Initializing the @keep Array for Use as a "Silo"**  Once you have a list of files to search, you can open each one and search it for matching lines. As in the previous example, this script uses the file input operator **<FILE>** to read in one line at time, but it temporarily stores each line in an array called **@keep**, which holds exactly **$Context*2 + 1** lines at a time. As it reads through a file, it pushes each new line onto the top of this array and shifts the rest down, eliminating the oldest one to make way for the new. In this way, the array is like a silo: first in, first out. Another way to imagine it is as a window in a moving car or train that lets you view a constant number of fence posts as you pass by.

To optimize the whole algorithm for speed, the script must initialize this holding array before the main loop begins:

```
undef @keep;          # Re-initializing @keep is essential!
for $j (0 .. $Context) {
    $keep[$Context - $j] = '';  # Add blank line before.
    $_ = <FILE>;                 # Get next line from FILE.
    s/$tags//go if $StripHTML;  # Remove whole and partial tags.
    $keep[$Context + $j] = $_ if $_;  # Add next line after.
}
```

Here **$keep[$Context]** is assigned the first line in the file, and the other entries in **@keep** are assigned their values using indices that are computed relative to this center. As explained above, if the "Ignore Tags" option is specified, all tags are removed from the lines as they are input. You might have noticed that **$keep[$Context]** is actually initialized twice. Nevertheless, this is the most compact and probably the most efficient initialization possible.

Once the inner search loop gets underway, however, there will be no more references to the elements of **@keep** using variable indices. Instead, at the end of every iteration, the **shift** operator will be used to shift the oldest line out from the beginning of **@keep**, and the **push** operator will push a new line onto the end of **@keep**, maintaining it at its fixed size of **2*$Context + 1** lines for the main part of the loop. Perl's shift and push are two members of a family of index-free array-manipulating functions that also includes **unshift** and **pop**.

Perl's **shift** function pulls the first value out of an array, decreasing the array's size by 1 and shifting the remaining entries down. The **unshift** function prepends a list of one or more scalar values to the beginning of an array, increasing its size by the number of new elements. The function of **push**, on the other hand, can be thought of as the opposite of either **shift** or **unshift**; it pushes a list of one or more scalar values onto the end of an array, increasing its size. A series of comments in tdsearch.cgi shows an alternative technique for initializing **@keep** that uses **unshift** and **push** instead of explicit indices. If you want to understand thoroughly how tdsearch.cgi works, it will be worth your while to read those comments, as well as the comments annotating the rest of the script. Since **unshift** is the inverse of **shift**, it provides a natural way of initializing the beginning of **@keep**, as if it were loading the silo from the bottom. Once the main loop begins, the **shift** and **push** functions are all that are needed to send every line of text through **@keep** from top to bottom.

**Evaluating the Search Loop Using the eval Function** Although Perl is not truly a compiled language, there are many ways in which Perl interpreters act like compilers. In particular, a Perl interpreter can greatly optimize certain constructs, notably search patterns and array references, if it can determine their values and/or logic at start-up. Search patterns that are already known at compile time can be "hardwired" into the compiled executable, saving the expense of re-evaluating them every time they are used. In a program such as tdsearch.cgi, however, the search pattern is never known at start-up, because it has to be entered by a user. That's where Perl's **eval** function comes in.

The **eval** function parses and executes an expression as if this expression were a mini-program within a program. In effect, **eval** invokes a new Perl interpreter to execute an expression whose values and logical syntax have been fully determined by the surrounding program and are now ready for optimization.

In the case of tdsearch.cgi, the entire search loop is evaluated only once for each input file, and even then it is evaluated as a single expression in which most of the variables are "frozen" in value. When the loop is actually evaluated, only the variables whose names were escaped using the backslash character are still subject to change. The rest are interpolated as parts of **eval**'s argument just as they would be inside a quoted string used as an argument to the **print** operator. In particular, **$Context**, **$Query**, and **$StripHTML** are all replaced by constant values, and even some of the branching decisions, such as whether to eliminate or escape HTML tags, can be made before the loop even begins. Using **eval** to run the loop in this way can significantly boost the program's performance.

It can also make the program harder to debug, however. Inside an **eval**, mistakes that would normally cause Perl to abort execution of the entire script will only cause it to terminate the **eval**, and Perl will not automatically output any error or warning messages. Even basic syntax errors may go undetected if you don't look for them. To find such problems, you should always check the special variable **$@** after any complex **eval** operation. If any errors are encountered during an **eval**, Perl puts the error messages in **$@**. Thus it is quite common to see a statement like

```
    die("$0: $@") if $@;              # $@ catches errors from eval.
```

immediately following a call to **eval**. The combination of **eval** and **$@** provides Perl with a basic error catching mechanism.

**Inside the Search Loop** The algorithm of the main search loop is to search for **$Query** (possibly as modified by options) in every new line of text, precisely when that line of text is in the middle of the **@keep** array. If the line contains a match, a link to that line's file is printed. If this is the first match for that particular file, the file's size and last modification date are also printed, as obtained from the **stat** and **ctime** functions. Either way, the line numbers are printed, followed by the entire contents of **@keep**. Whether the current line matches or not, the next line from the file is read in using the **<FILE>** operator, and if **$StripHTML** is true, this new line is stripped of any tags. Finally, the oldest line in **@keep** is shifted out to make way for the new, the new line is pushed onto the end, and everything is ready for the loop's next iteration.

## Example 8C: Recursively Searching a Directory and All Its Subdirectories

This final example shows one way to search every text file in a directory and all its subdirectories for a set of keywords. Like the script in the previous example, it obtains a list of filenames and then searches each file individually. The main differences are that it uses the **index** function instead of regular expressions to search for matching strings and that, instead of obtaining its list of files all at once, it pipes in the output from the Unix **find** command to get the filenames one at a time. The main loop begins with the **FILE:** label, and if any of the files whose names are returned by the **find** command cannot be opened, the program jumps back to this label to get the next file. Listing 8.3 shows the complete script, and Figure 8.3 shows the page that it generates.

---

**LISTING 8.3** **nph-find.cgi, a script that searches all the files in a directory and all of its subdirectories**

```perl
#!/usr/local/bin/perl
# nph-find.pl - an example of searching a directory and all of its
# subdirectories. Copyright (C) 1996 Stephen Lines <spraxlo@ai.mit.edu>.
require "FormData.pl";
$findProg = '/usr/bin/find';  # standard location in Unix
$txtdir   = '../web/me';       # relative path of directory to search

if ($ENV{'SCRIPT_NAME'})  {
  &getFormData(*Form);
  $| = 1;
  print "$ENV{'SERVER_PROTOCOL'} 200 OK\n";
  print "Server: $ENV{'SERVER_SOFTWARE'}\n";
  print "MIME-version: 1.0\n";
```

**LISTING 8.3**    nph-find.cgi, a script that searches all the files in a directory and all of its subdirectories (Continued)

```perl
  print "Content-type: text/html\n\n";
  $Query  =  $Form{'Query'};
  @ARGV   =  split(/\s/, $Query);
  print <<EOF;
<HTML><HEAD><TITLE>
Keyword Search in a Directory and all its Subdirectories
</TITLE></HEAD><BODY BGCOLOR=#AAFFDD><DIV ALIGN=CENTER><H2>
Keyword Search in a Directory and all its Subdirectories
</H2></DIV><FORM>
Keywords to search for under $txtdir:<BR>
<INPUT TYPE=TEXT SIZE=60 MAXLENGTH=255 NAME=Query VALUE="$Query">
<INPUT TYPE=SUBMIT  VALUE=Submit>
<INPUT TYPE=RESET   VALUE=Reset><BR>
Words are separated on spaces and matched exactly (no regular expressions).
</FORM><HR><PRE>
EOF
}


$Query = join(', ', @ARGV);   # This script also works in a shell.


if ($Query) {
  open(FIND, "$findProg $txtdir -print |") || die "Can't run find: $!\n";
  print "Searching all text files under $txtdir for: $Query\n\n";
  $foundLines = $foundFiles = 0;
  FILE:
  while ($filename = <FIND>) {
    chop $filename;
    next FILE unless -T $filename;
    if (!open(TEXTFILE, $filename)) {
      warn "Error opening $filename ($!) — continuing...\n";
      next FILE;
    }
    $files++;
    $found = 0;
    while (<TEXTFILE>) {
```

**LISTING 8.3    nph-find.cgi, a script that searches all the files in a directory and all of its subdirectories (Continued)**

```perl
      foreach $word (@ARGV) {
        if (($i = index($_, $word)) >= 0) {
          s/</&lt;/go;
          s/>/&gt;/go;
          print "$filename\n" unless $found++;
          printf("%7d %4d: %s", $., $i, $_);
        }
      }
    }
    if ($found) {
      # $filename =~ s|^.*/||; # Uncomment to keep only name, not path
      print "Found $found matches in $filename\n\n";
      $foundLines += $found;
      $foundFiles++;
    }
  }
  print "Totals: $foundLines matches in $foundFiles file"
  , ($foundFiles != 1 ? 's' : ''), ", out of $files files searched.\n";
}
print "</PRE></BODY></HTML>\n" if $ENV{'SCRIPT_NAME'};
```

Perl's **index** function searches a string for a substring and returns the position of its first occurrence; if the substring is not found, it returns **-1**. Its typical usage is:

```perl
$position = index($string, $substring, $start_pos);
```

The third argument is optional and specifies only where to start looking, not the origin from which to reckon **$position**. Typical uses of the **index** function do not often overlap with those of regular expression matching, but in some situations it provides an alternative.

## Index-Based Search Facilities

If your site is large or will be searched quite often, you should consider basing your search facility on a precompiled index. An indexing program can search your entire site for a list of keywords and compile the results into an index file. The list of keywords may be specified in advance or generated from the contents of the searched documents themselves at run time, and the indexer only needs to run periodically instead of every time a user initiates a search. Instead of searching the files themselves, the CGI interface can then search only the index file, which contains all the necessary data for constructing links, file descriptions, match counts, or whatever other information you want to present to the user. This scheme reduces the CGI program's task from searching an entire site to searching a single file.

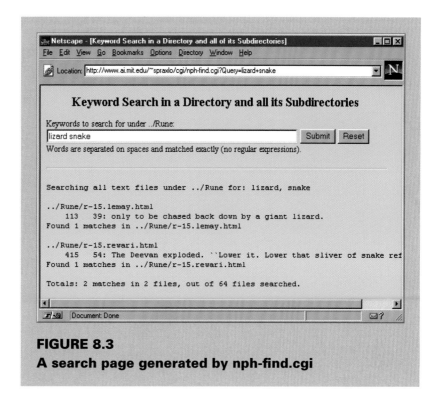

**FIGURE 8.3**
**A search page generated by nph-find.cgi**

Designing and implementing an indexer is not necessarily any more difficult that creating an ordinary search program like the ones presented in this chapter. What an indexer should look for and how it should organize the resulting index, however, may vary greatly, depending on your site's size, contents, and the end purposes of your search facility.

A variety of commercial and noncommercial indexing systems have been offered for personal and/or business consumption, and even some of the systems freely available as source code kits are fairly flexible. Almost all of them, however, are written in C, and are not exactly easy to install. One such indexing system that is implemented in Perl is ICE, by Christian Neuss, available from http://www. informatik.th-darmstadt.de/~neuss/ice/ice.html and http://ice.cornell-iowa.edu/. It consists of two Perl scripts, which are quite easy to install and customize. The indexer, ice-idx.pl, creates an index as a plain text file that the CGI script ice-form.pl can then search. Figure 8.4 shows a customized front end for a search facility based on ICE.

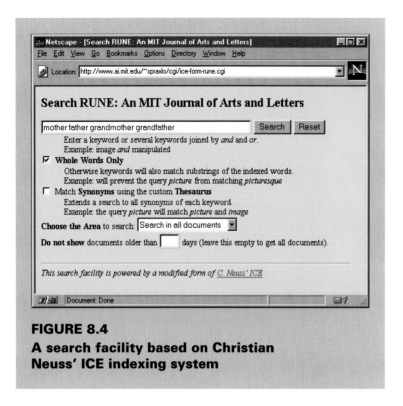

**FIGURE 8.4**
**A search facility based on Christian Neuss' ICE indexing system**

# When to Disallow Searching and/or Indexing

You may have some documents or CGI programs on your site that you don't want users to be able to search, or that you don't want to be indexed or accessed by automated programs outside of your site. In the last few sections of this chapter, I'll discuss some typical situations in which you might want to disallow searching and/or indexing. I'll also present some techniques for curtailing your own search engines, as well as an (almost) standard method for excluding external robots from indexing specified parts of your Web site.

## When and How to Limit Your Own Search Engines

The example scripts in this chapter illustrate powerful techniques for searching entire files, directories, and directory trees. The only things those scripts exclude from their searches are non-text files or, optionally, in the case of tdsearch.cgi, the interiors of HTML tags. Before installing such a script on your Web site, you might want to make it exclude CGI scripts and text-like data files as well.

If you can, it's generally a good idea to keep all of your CGI programs in one directory, from which searching is always excluded, and all of the data files that you wouldn't want to be served as-is in directories entirely outside of your public Web server's document tree. Some ISPs, however, won't automatically give you your own private disk space outside the server's document tree unless you pay for shell access. (If you find yourself in this situation, ask for the extra space or demand something better!) Otherwise, your search program may waste time processing files such as a count.txt file meant to be used only by an access counter, or worse, it may be plied into serving up private information. Remember that your CGI programs generally run as if they were part of the Web server itself, and yet are not automatically restricted to outputting documents in the server's document tree. Depending on how you implement your CGI application as a whole, these same properties can be used to increase the security and reliability of your Web site, or to compromise the security of an entire server installation.

If you do decide to keep data and program files in the same directories as your serve-able HTML documents, there are many tricks for keeping them invisible and/or unretrievable. One trick for hiding files is to use a index.html or index.cgi file to place a cover over the contents of a directory (or if you control the Web server, to disable directory listings entirely). For better or worse, however, such "hidden" files are still accessible by their full URLs. Some servers do not support these particular options, but provide other methods for hiding and/or disabling access to files. Many servers, for instance, can be configured to ignore files with certain extensions. (Official, documented methods are usually better than hacks like naming a data file data.cgi and denying it execute permissions.) To keep your own search programs out of these same files, however, you'll have to program that functionality into them yourself. To prevent tdsearch.cgi from searching any file whose extension is .cgi or .tmp, for instance, you could change it's directory-scanning statement to the following:

```
@txtFiles = grep( -T && !/\.(cgi|tmp)$/, readdir(DIR));
```

A different approach would be to allow your search engine to search only the files in a predefined list of files or directories. Both tdsearch.cgi and nph-find.cgi are hardwired to search under a preconfigured directory, but it would be exceedingly easy to change that into a user-selectable choice of directories.

## How Robots Crawl the Web

Robots, in the context of the Internet, are simply programs that automate tasks such as acknowledging all incoming e-mail with a form letter. Spiders are robots that crawl the Web by automatically selecting links and jumping from page to page. Other metaphors for these programs include scooters, Web walkers, wanderers, agents, and even worms; but like any other Web client, they in fact never leave home. Instead, the Web comes to them, as it would to a browser running on autopilot. Spiders are typically set loose on the Web in order to gather statistics about the Web itself, check for invalid links, or add pages' URLs to some form of database. AltaVista, Lycos, OpenText, WebCrawler, Yahoo!, and many other large-scale search sites use spiders to download the texts of millions of pages for indexing. Because of their great speed, spiders are invaluable for these purposes, but they also increase Internet traffic and can put a heavy strain on the servers they visit, impeding the access of ordinary users or even causing the servers to fail.

The visitations of spiders may have other side effects, too; they can increase hit counters, vote, or repeatedly invoke computation-intensive CGI programs.

In this book, for instance, the script www-cart (Example 7B) is capable of dynamically generating "new" pages with "new" links back to itself every time it is invoked. Although the basic URL of every page and in every link ends with www-cart.cgi, each URL is "new" because it also contains a query string with a new cookie and/or a different value for the next page. This application was designed in such a way that the client must submit a form before the script will output any pages that contain such links, but submitting a form is not beyond the capabilities of spiders. A "smart" spider might record only the basic URL and move on, but a poorly written one might actually get caught in its own web, so to speak, and also tie up resources on your Web server.

A rule of thumb for regulating robots might be to bar robots from accessing any URL that points to the cgi-bin directory, but HTTP requests issued by robots are not necessarily distinguishable from those issued by an ordinary browser, nor do all sites require CGI programs to reside in cgi-bin. And what about textual information that appears on the same page as a form? Should that be unavailable to the spider-fed search sites?

Spiders also raise certain issues of privacy. Now that spiders are capable of finding every recent message you've posted to Usenet, and their associated search sites can then make this information available to anyone on the Internet, the old protection of privacy through obscurity no longer applies. Some Web domains require passwords (or credit card payments); this may effectively prevent or dissuade spiders from entering, but many proprietors of special interest sites would prefer not to require users to log in.

Spiders tend to operate with a very limited understanding about what they are perusing. Unless such information is encoded in the text of the pages themselves, a spider generally cannot determine whether a page it has accessed will soon expire, is still under construction, was intended to be accessed only through a special link, or should not be indexed for some other reason. On the other side of the client/server connection, some tags, such as <META>, <NAME>, and <TITLE>, can be used to aid robots or other indexers in classifying the contents of a page.

## How to Exclude Robots from Your Site

An unofficial standard known as the Standard for Robot Exclusion (SRE) was developed in 1994 to give site administrators a way of keeping spiders out of designated areas of their Web sites. Servers do not actually enforce this standard, but most robots, at least those that belong to the major search sites, do comply with it.

To exclude an SRE-compliant robot from all or part of a Web site, place an HTTP-accessible text file named robots.txt in the server's document root directory so that it will have the URL http://your.site/robots.txt. In this file, entries of the form

```
User-agent: robot-name
Disallow: /directory-name/
```

tell the named robot to keep out of the named directory and all of its subdirectories. The wildcard entry

```
User-agent: *
Disallow: /
```

tells all robots to skip your site entirely, whereas the following combination excludes all robots from the tmp and staff directories except for a robot named linkchex, which is granted carte blanche:

```
# Sample robots.txt file
User-agent: *
Disallow: /tmp/
Disallow: /staff/
User-agent: link-chex
Disallow:
```

Note that comments preceded by the pound sign are ignored by SRE-compliant robots but might not be by the rest of the world, which can access this file through any common browser. For more information on spiders, see the World Wide Web Robots, Wanderers, and Spiders page at http://info.webcrawler.com/mak/projects /robots/robots.html. For a copy of the Standard for Robot Exclusion, see http://info.webcrawler.com/mak/projects/ robots/norobots.html.

# Chapter 9
# Designing and Implementing Interactive CGI Applications

Designing a small CGI program is usually easy—the input/output is practically taken care of by the server, and the work the program must accomplish between the input and output phases is often task-specific and very narrowly defined. Yet some of the same characteristics of CGI that make it easy to create small programs can make it difficult to design and implement large, interactive applications. CGI's inherent lack of state and its default practice of treating users as anonymous entities are usually at the top of this list. Add to these difficulties the facts that CGI provides no immediate, ongoing feedback from the back end and that it necessarily shares resources, and you'll see that building a larger CGI application can be quite a challenge.

In this chapter, I discuss the design of CGI applications in somewhat more general terms than in the previous chapters. Instead of explaining fully implemented example programs, I'll illustrate various CGI and Perl programming techniques with functions and code fragments that you may or may not want to integrate into your own applications. When I really need a concrete instance of an application, I'll return to the examples from earlier chapters, but only to suggest how they might be modified, not to actually build all the changes into a new working application. You can learn a lot by studying the code of a completed program, but the more polished it is, the less insight it's likely to give about the process of its own creation. To build your own applications, you also need to know how to construct the initial scaffolding and fix the inevitable mistakes in your original plans or first pass at the actual coding.

## CGI Applications Are Based on Transaction Processing

CGI programs run by request only. A browser sends a request to a Web server, and the Web server invokes the CGI program and passes to it the input from the browser. The CGI program might call upon a database management system or some other server-side resources to help it process this input, or it might not. But it is generally the CGI program itself that processes the request as a whole, and one thing that a CGI program always does is return a new document, which is in effect what the browser requested in the first place. The role of the Web server is essentially just to pass the request along to the CGI program. It is the CGI program that is responsible for turning the request around, and this is the center of the whole transaction between the browser and the Web server/CGI program. When the CGI program has sent back the new document, it dies. Thus you could say that CGI programs live only to process transactions.

This is fairly typical of programs that are invoked by servers in a network environment, but it is quite different from what happens when users invoke interactive applications on their own local computers. Local applications typically run as interactive sessions of indefinite duration, and they are best understood not as programs that occasionally process transactions but as programs that handle many small events in series. Before you start designing your own larger CGI applications, it's worth your while to compare the two cases in terms of basic software design.

# Differences between Local and CGI-Based Applications

A local application normally persists throughout the span of an interactive session as a single process, whereas a CGI program has to be contacted through a network and restarted to process every new transaction. Therefore, as you might expect, local applications tend to be event-driven. A local application can offer almost instantaneous response to small, discrete user input events (such as mouse clicks in one of the application's windows). CGI programs must rely on a transaction model of processing. They are driven by requests that represent the results of multiple local events (such as keystrokes in one of the browser's windows). Table 9.1 summarizes the main differences between local and CGI-based applications.

In terms of how the programs work internally, a local application can perform many tasks just once, at the beginning or end of a single interactive session, but a CGI program will have to perform the same tasks repeatedly to handle each and every transaction. Although CGI applications can save state information between their short-lived instances, this information is usually quite minimal when compared to the complete internal state of a running application, and at any rate it is no substitute for having continuous access to local input devices. Since the state of

**TABLE 9.1    DIFFERENCES BETWEEN LOCAL AND CGI-BASED APPLICATIONS**

| A Local Application... | A CGI-Based Application... |
| --- | --- |
| Consists of one session of indefinite duration | Is processed in multiple short-lived instances |
| Is characterized by modes | Is characterized by states |
| Is event-driven | Is driven by requests for transactions |
| Is implemented by a single user | Can be implemented by multiple users |
| Uses resources that all belong to the local owner by default | Uses resources that are shared by remote, anonymous users |
| Is processed locally, on a single machine | Is processed between local and remote machines |

a local application changes literally with every keystroke, such applications are often characterized in terms of their *modes*. An application's current mode often determines how it handles input events; for example, some text editors distinguish between insert and overlay modes.

The following outline shows a control sequence that is typical of a session-based, local, interactive application:

▶ **Begin session**   Read in any state and configuration information saved from the last session. (An example would be opening a document that contains a set of style templates or preferences.)

▶ **Perform main event loop**   Wait for an event from any of the input devices; on any event, call the appropriate event handler, which may produce output, and then return to the beginning of the loop. In other words:

   ▶ Wait for the next event (input).

   ▶ Process the event.

   ▶ Output the response, if any.

▶ **End session**   Save the current state and configuration information for the next session.

The control sequence for a CGI program nearly turns this scheme inside out—it's as if the main event loop were outside the program, surrounding it. The input starts at the user's browser, before the CGI program even starts, and the output phase is not finished until the browser has loaded at the remote site, most likely after the CGI process on the server has exited.

The following outline shows a control sequence that is typical of a transaction-based, interactive CGI application:

▶ **Begin instance**   Get the CGI input and environment from the Web server.

▶ **Perform main transaction procedure**   Identify the user and request; retrieve any appropriate state and local information; process the new and old information together. In other words:

  ▶ Use part of the input to identify the user/browser, if possible.

  ▶ Retrieve any needed local information and/or the state saved from the user's last transaction.

  ▶ Process the rest of the input along with the state information. This determines the output for this instance and sets the application's new state.

▶ **Output document**   Send the new document to the user/browser.

▶ **End instance**   Save the appropriate state information for the user's next transaction and/or for offline processing (actually filling an order, for instance).

Whereas the local application's input and output take place inside the session's inner loop, the CGI application's input and output begin and end outside the actual program instance, at the browser. And the only "event loop," so to speak, is the loop that connects the browser to the server via HTTP and the Internet. This "inverted" control sequence accounts for much of the difficulty you'll face when building complex, multiple-page CGI applications. Keeping a clear view of the differences, however, can help you both in designing and in implementing your own CGI-based applications.

## The Basic Elements of Interactive CGI Applications

The basic ingredients that go into nearly any interactive CGI application can be read off from the outline above. They include functions or techniques that get the CGI input, identify the remote user/browser, store and retrieve state information (either locally or remotely), and generate new documents as well as send old ones. You already have a number of functions for doing these kinds of things, and some of them are quite general—for instance, **getFormData**, **newCookie**, **openDBM**,

**sendFile**, **sendParsedFile**, and **mailForm**. Perl provides many library functions of its own and makes many other tasks so simple that they don't need their own programmer-defined subroutines. In this chapter, I will present a few more functions of intermediate complexity.

In addition to managing the kinds of tasks that can be performed by subroutines or a few oft-repeated lines of code, you must also decide how to design your application's larger framework, which corresponds to the above outline as a whole. Many of the example programs in earlier chapters shared the same basic strategy for handling requests, but only a few called attention to this common framework. The following section makes this structure explicit and generalizes it further.

## A Generic Framework for Interactive CGI Applications

The first and last steps in the outline above are fairly straightforward. If the application uses forms, as most interactive CGI programs do, its input phase will most likely begin and end with a call to a function such as **getFormData**. And although the state or other information saved in the final, shutdown step will vary greatly depending on the particular application, the techniques for saving it vary little; basically the information will be saved to some type of file.

The action that happens between the initial input and final wrapup stages is less settled, but it can be reduced to a few basic steps that are almost as simple as the main event loop at the center of most local applications:

1 Determine the origin of the request, in terms both of the user/browser and of the page. This is equivalent to obtaining the next event.

2 Handle any special cases in the information found in step 1; this includes retrieving locally saved state information. This is equivalent to calling an event handler to process the specific event.

3 Process all the information from steps 1 and 2, which should determine the output. Actually outputting the new document is equivalent to re-entering the event loop at the top, because it sends the ball back into the user/browser's court.

## Control Structures for Single-Page CGI Applications

A CGI application that generates a single Web page as its user interface can come in any shape or size, and in principle such applications can be as varied as the Web pages they output. From this diversity it is not so easy to abstract a common or "correct" program structure. As a general rule of thumb, it's best to put the input in the beginning and group your output together at the end—unless it's more convenient to do it some other way.

Quite often you'll begin a script by calling a function such as **getFormData** and, based on the input it finds, start outputting a return document almost immediately. Because the order of information in a document that you send back to your users is all-important, the document's structure will often determine the structure of your program. If the output document is to be plain text or HTML, you might even consider writing an example or template of its output first and then incorporate that text into your script.

## "Turning the Page" in Multiple-Page Applications

In CGI applications that generate and/or handle the input from multiple pages, it is often helpful to name the pages explicitly and then base the main control procedure on those page names. The steps above can then be restated in terms of turning the page: find out what page the request came from, treat any special cases, and/or select and output the next page. The following code fragment shows one way to do this:

```
&getFormData(*Form);
$FromPage = &FromPage(*Form);
if ($FromPage eq $SpecialPage) { &specialTreatment(*Form); exit; }
$NextPage = &NextPage(*Form);  # Didn't exit, so output the next page
&sendNextPage( $NextPage, *Form );
```

Listing 9.1 shows a similar but more elaborate code fragment, along with possible implementations of the functions **FromFile** and **NextFile** . The bulk of the code for "turning the page" is quite generic, although you'll recognize the filenames and some of the implied functionality of **mySendParsedFile** (not defined here) from the shopping cart examples of Chapter 7.

> **LISTING 9.1    A code fragment for "turning the page" in a generic CGI application**

```
# pageTurn.txt - this is only a code fragment, not a script; it is
# meant to suggest a framework for building a multi-page Web application.
# Copyright (C) 1996 Stephen Lines <spraxlo@ai.mit.edu>, distributed
# under Artistic License (as defined in the Perl 5 distribution).
require 'FormData.pl';


$RelPath    = "../v/"; # Path to files relative to this script
```

**LISTING 9.1    A code fragment for "turning the page" in a generic CGI application (Continued)**

```
$BasePath    = "cgi/v/"; # Used with both HTTP_REFERER and PATH_INFO
%Title2File = ( "The Apartment"  => "vApartment.html"
              , "Apartment Zero" => "vApartmentZero.html"
              , "The Landlord"   => "vLandlord.html"
              , "The Tenant"     => "vTenant.html" );
@ValidFiles = sort(values(%Title2File));
# NB: The path/filenames in @ValidFiles must be underneath $BasePath.

### Strategy: Think of files as objects, and the app as an object server:
### Get name of submitting file as part of the event context;
### act any special cases, i.e., handle the particular event internally,
### then respond by serving the appropriate next file.

if (&getFormData(*Form)) {

    # What file did this apparent form submission come from?
    $FromFile = &FromFile(*Form);

    # Handle any special cases of $FromFile and/or Form values here:
    if    ($FromFile eq $CheckOut) { &CheckOut(*Form); }
    elsif ($FromFile eq $SearchIt) { &SearchIt(*Form); }

    if    ($Form{'Save'} eq 'Yes') { &Save(*Form); }
    elsif ($Form{'Quit'} eq 'Yes') { &Quit(*Form); }

    # Determine the next file to send:
    $NextFile = &NextFile(*Form, $FromFile);
}
else {
    $NextFile = $ValidFiles[0];      # default to first file
}


# Send $RelPath.$NextFile, where $RelPath is the path to the
# files relative to this script. In other words, the absolute
# path $ENV{'SCRIPT_FILENAME'}.$RelPath names the same actual
```

**LISTING 9.1    A code fragment for "turning the page" in a generic CGI application (Continued)**

```
# directory as represented by $BasePath.

&mySendParsedFile( *Form, $NextFile, $FromFile, $RelPath);
exit;

############### Local Subroutines: ##############################

sub FromFile {
    local(*Form)    = @_;
    if(($FromFile) = split('/\0/', $Form{'FromFile'})) {
        $FromFile  = $Title2File{$FromFile} if ($FromFile !~ /\.html$/i);
    } elsif($FromFile = $ENV{'HTTP_REFERER'}) {
        if ($FromFile eq "http://$ENV{'SERVER_NAME'}$ENV{'SCRIPT_NAME'}") {
            warn("$0 apparently served a file with no FromFile field.\n");
        } else {
            $FromFile =~ s/^.*$BasePath//;
        }
    } else {
        $FromFile = $ValidFiles[0]; # Assign default $FromFile here
    }
    $Form{'FromFile'} = $FromFile;  # Return new entry in %Form
}


sub NextFile {
    local ($FromFile, *Form) = @_;

    if(($NextFile)= split(/\0/, $Form{'NextFile'})) {
        $NextFile = $Title2File{$NextFile} if ($NextFile !~ /\.html$/i);
    } elsif ($NextFile = $ENV{'PATH_INFO'}) {
        $NextFile =~ s/^.*$BasePath//;
    }
    if ($NextFile) {  # Check whether $NextFile is in @ValidFiles:
        for ($FileNum = $#ValidFiles; $FileNum >= 0; $FileNum--) {
            last if ($NextFile eq $ValidFiles[$FileNum]);
        } # If there's no match, this loop ends with $FileNum == -1
```

---

**LISTING 9.1 A code fragment for "turning the page" in a generic CGI application (Continued)**

```perl
        if ($FileNum == -1) {   # Who is trying to get invalid files?
            warn("$0 called by $ENV{'REMOTE_ADDR'} w/ NextFile=$NextFile\n");
            $NextFile = $ValidFiles[0];
        } else {
            $NextFile = $ValidFiles[$FileNum];
        }
    } elsif ($FromFile) {
        for ($FileNum = $#ValidFiles; $FileNum >= 0; $FileNum--) {
            last if ($FromFile eq $ValidFiles[$FileNum]);
        } # If there's no match, this loop ends with $FileNum == -1
        $NextFile = $ValidFiles[($FileNum + 1) % @ValidFiles];
    } else {
        $NextFile = $ValidFiles[0]; # Assign default $NextFile here
    }
    $Form{'NextFile'} = $NextFile;  # Return new entry in %Form
}
```

---

The basic page-turning algorithm described above should be apparent from the comments and in the structure of the code itself. By hiding the implementation details, the functions **FromFile** and **NextFile** streamline the main program, making it easier to read, as well as easier to generalize or customize for re-use in different applications.

**FromFile: Where Did this Submission Come From?** The **FromFile** function first checks for a value in **$Form{'FromFile'}**:

```perl
    if(($FromFile) = split('/\0/', $Form{'FromFile'})) {
```

This form value could come from a self-identifying input element such as

```
    <INPUT TYPE=HIDDEN NAME=FromFile VALUE=thisFile.html>
```

where *thisFile*.html is the actual filename of the form's source document. This hidden field is inserted automatically into files parsed and sent by the implementation of **mySendParsedFile** shown in the same listing (Listing 9.1). A different technique would be to place such a self-referential hidden field into all the original, static files that **mySendParsedFile** will be used to send. It is generally good practice to be consistent, but **FromFile** does not depend on consistency; instead, it is designed to support either technique, or even a mixture of both.

The point of calling the **split** function is to handle cases in which a form contains more than one input element whose NAME attribute is set to **FromFile**. If the submitted form data were to contain more than one *name=value* pair for **FromFile**, **getFormData** would put all the values into one null-separated list. Ideally, this redundancy shouldn't occur, but once you start automatically parsing files and inserting hidden fields, such redundancies are much more likely. In this case, the call to **split** makes **FromFile** more robust by removing the potential redundancy. The assignment to the single-element list (**$FromFile**) retains only the first item returned by **split** and ensures that no more than one filename or page title is assigned to **$FromFile**.

If **$Form{'FromFile'}** is set but its value does not end in **.html**, the **FromFile** function assumes that this value is a page title instead of a filename and attempts to convert it into a filename, using **%Title2File** as a translation table:

```
$FromFile = $Title2File{$FromFile} unless ($FromFile =~ ¬
/\.html$/i);
```

Otherwise, the function tries the value of the environment variable HTTP_REFERER:

```
} elsif($FromFile = $ENV{'HTTP_REFERER'}) {
    if ($FromFile eq "http://$ENV{'SERVER_NAME'}$ENV¬
{'SCRIPT_NAME'}") {
        warn("$0 apparently served a file with no FromFile ¬
field.\n");
    } else {
        $FromFile =~ s/^.*$BasePath//;
    }
}
```

This **elsif** clause would yield the correct value if the user had arrived at the script from one of the static page .html files in **@ValidFiles** rather than from one of the pages that was parsed and served up by **mySendParsedFile** in a previous execution of the script.

Finally, if all other designs and heuristics fail, the first valid file in the list is assigned to **$FromFile** by fiat:

```
$FromFile = $ValidFiles[0]; # Assign default $FromFile here
```

To ensure consistency, the final value of **$FromFile** is also (re)entered into **%Form** at the same time that it is returned:

```
$Form{'FromFile'} = $FromFile;  # Return new entry in %Form
```

Depending on how **%Form** is subsequently used, this step may not be necessary, but it results in one less wrinkle to have to worry about. Some other part of your script may tacitly assume that the value of **$Form{'FromFile'}** is always set by the most recent form submission; this statement at the end of **FromFile** doesn't exactly justify such an assumption, but it does validate it.

**NextFile: Determining Which Page to Sent Next**   The **NextFile** function is similar to **FromFile**. It checks the value of **$Form{'NextFile'}** first, but if that is not set, it tries PATH_INFO instead of HTTP_REFERER as a candidate for **$NextFile**. It also performs strict checking to ensure that the returned value of **$NextFile** is actually an element in **@ValidFiles**. This is crucial, because **$NextFile** is then passed on to **mySendParsedFile**, which is capable of sending any file on the system, as long as the Web server can read it. If the checking were not so strict, this script would pose a serious security risk. A knowledgeable user would be able trick it into sending any file to which the Web server had access—for example, the Unix password file /etc/passwd. If you don't care to log apparent attempts to retrieve unsanctioned files, you can simply set the loop to terminate when **$FileNum** reaches **0** instead of **-1**:

```
if ($NextFile) {  # Check whether $NextFile is in @ValidFiles:
    for ($FileNum = $#ValidFiles; $FileNum > 0; $FileNum—) {
        last if ($NextFile eq $ValidFiles[$FileNum]);
    } # If there's no match, this loop ends with $FileNum == 0
    $NextFile = $ValidFiles[$FileNum];
```

If neither the form data nor the extra path information specifies a value for **$NextFile**, the **NextFile** function attempts to obtain the **$FileNum** associated with **$FromFile**. If it succeeds, it assigns to **$NextFile** the next filename in the list of valid files. In any event, the last step is always an assignment of the form

```
$NextFile = $ValidFiles[number];
```

which ensures that **$NextFile** is a valid file more or less by definition.

# Filtering Information and Parsing Files with CGI

The code in Listing 9.1 represents only a fragment of a multiple-page application. The rest of the application could be whatever you imagine it to be. This section returns to an earlier discussion of one of CGI's most common tasks, filtering (begun in Chapter 7), and then the remainder of the chapter is given over to a set of programming tips that I hope will be useful to you as you create your own CGI applications.

The need to reformat, reduce, augment, or otherwise transform stored information before serving it over a network was a major impetus behind the invention of the Common Gateway Interface, and such filtering is still one of CGI programming's most common and well-defined tasks. As the breadth and depth of the information accessible via the Web continues to increase, the need for filtering will grow with it. Some other common tasks, such as user authentication and context maintenance, have also been emerging, and in some cases, CGI will have to change to keep pace. Right now, however, the capacity of CGI for filtering information between servers and clients is paramount.

In this book, most of the examples from Chapter 6 onward implement one form of information filtering or another. The pie chart example (Listing 6.4) converts a set of names and numbers into a graphical analog. The shopping cart examples of Chapter 7 reformat plain text into HTML (www-mart.cgi) and parse static files, replacing preset patterns with dynamic data (www-cart.cgi). Chapter 8 is all about reducing large amounts of text to a few lines that match a search pattern, and reformatting these matching lines for display inside a Web page. The next two sections review several techniques that make use of regular expression matching to filter static files and to reformat dynamically generated text.

## Using Regular Expressions to Filter Files

Applying filters to turn template files into dynamic Web pages is very common in multiple-page CGI applications, and that is the purpose of the **mySendParsedFile** function, which was called but not defined in the code fragment of Listing 9.1. The functions in filters.pl, shown in Listing 9.2, fill in this gap. Each of them is a variation on the theme began by the **sendParsedFile** function of www-cart.cgi (Example 7C), and each one implements its own strategy for parsing a file. Some of them replace entire lines in the parsed file, for instance, while others replace matching strings within lines. These functions are not meant to be used exactly as-is, but to be modified according to the needs of particular applications and incorporated into them as local subroutines. All of the pattern and string variables, such as **$Pattern1** or **$StringA**, are meant to be replaced by literal strings or defined outside the function. If you want to turn any of these functions into a library routine, you should modify it to accept these pattern or string variables as parameters (but read on for further caveats).

**LISTING 9.2    Some examples of functions that filter files**

```
# filters.pl - example subroutines that illustrate several
# variations on filtering/parsing/serving files.
# (c) 1996 Stephen Lines <spraxlo@ai.mit.edu>


# This one replaces the whole line when it finds a match.
sub  sendParsedFileReplaceLines {
  local ( *Form, $File ) = @_;
  my     ( $line );
  open(File, $File) || die("$0: sPFRL died on $File ($!)\n");
  while ($line = <File>) {
    if ( ($_) = ($line =~ /^<!—#insert\s+(\w+)\s*->/i)) {
      if (/($pattern1|$pattern2|$pattern3)/io) {
        &myFunc1(*Form, $File, $1);
      }
      elsif (/^$PatternA$/i) {
        &myFuncA(*Form, $File);
      }
    # else { print $line; } # Don't output any insert directives.
    }
    else { print $line; }    # Do output all other lines unchanged.
  }
  close (File);              # Return 1 on success.
}


# This one replaces tags within lines.
sub  sendParsedFileReplaceTags {
  local( *Form, $File ) = @_;
  my    ( $line );
  open(File, $File) || die("$0: sPFRT died on $File ($!)\n");
```

**LISTING 9.2    Some examples of functions that filter files (Continued)**

```perl
  while ($line = <File>) {
    while (  ($_) = ($line =~ /<!-#insert\s+(\w+)\s*->/i)) { # No /g!
      print   $`;          # Print beginning of $line up to match.
      $line = $';          # Reset $line to remainder after match.
      if (/^($pattern1|$pattern2|$pattern3)$/io) {
        &myFunc1(*Form, $File, $1);  # Functions called from within
      }                              # this loop are free to change $_.
      elsif ($_ eq $StringA) {
        &myFuncA(*Form, $File);
      }
      else {               # Remove entire <!- ... -> directive:
        s///;              # s/// searches $_ for the last matched
      }                    # string and replaces it with nothing.
    }
    print $line;           # Always output (remainder of) line.
  }
  close (File);            # Return 1 on success.
}

# This one calls a function on two found arguments.
sub  sendParsedFileReplaceTagsByFunc {
  local ( *Form, $File ) = @_;
  open(File, $File) || die("$0: sPFRTBF died on $File ($!)\n");
  while (<File>) {
    while (/<!-#insert\s+(\w+)\s+(\w+)\s*->/gi) { # /g iterates.
      print $`;            # Print beginning of $line up to match.
      $_  = $';            # Reset $_ to remainder of line after match.
      &Func($1, $2);       # Beware of functions that change $_, however.
    }
    print;
  }
  close (File);            # Return 1 on success.
}
```

**LISTING 9.2    Some examples of functions that filter files (Continued)**

```perl
# This one replaces tags *in place*; it's efficient but fragile.
sub  sendParsedFileReplaceTagsInStrings {
  local( *Form, $File ) = @_;
  open(File, $File) || die("$0: sPFRTIS died on $File ($!)\n");
  while (<File>) {
    # The /g option on the pattern below makes the pattern matching
    # operator start where it last left off, instead of
    # starting over at the beginning of the line on each iteration.
    # The parsing still proceeds recursively, but more efficiently.
    while ( ($arg) = (/<!-#insert\s+(\w+)\s*->/ig)) {
      if    ($arg eq $StringA) {
        s//$ReplacementA/;
      }
      elsif ($arg =~ /$StringB/) { # The new search replace
        s//$FromFile/;             # $StringB *within* the directive.
      }
      if ($_ eq $StringB) {
        my $s = $_;                      # Functions called from within
        $ReplacementB = &myFuncB($_); # this loop definitely shouldn't
        $_    = $s;                      # change $_, unless you save and
        s//$ReplacementB/;             # restore $_ locally.
      }
      elsif ($_ eq $StringC) {
        s//&myFuncC($_)/e;  # This is almost guaranteed to fail except
      }                     # in Perl 5 under Unix (realloc errors).
      else {                # Remove the entire <!- ... -> directive:
        s///;               # s/// searches $_ for the last matched
      }                     # string and replaces it with nothing.
    }
    print;                  # Output $_, including all substitutions.
  }
  close (File);             # Return 1 on success.
}
```

Each one of the functions defined in filters.pl reads a static file and searches it line by line for matches to a variation of the following regular expression matching operator:

```
/<!-#insert\s+(\w+)\s*->/i
```

This operator matches patterns of the form

```
<!-#insert ARGUMENT->
```

where *ARGUMENT* matches the parenthesized subexpression **(\w+)**. Thus *ARGUMENT* can be any word composed entirely of alphanumeric characters (including the underscore character). As in the discussion of www-cart.cgi in Chapter 7, let us call such a pattern an Insert directive. You can make up your own directive types, of course, and search for them in place of, or in addition to, Insert directives, but you will probably want to avoid using the same identifiers that Web servers use to identify SSI directives.

### Breaking the Search Down into Multiple Levels

When an insert directive is found, the parentheses in the regular expression cause Perl to place the argument in the special variable **$1**. Some of the functions in filters.pl immediately copy the Insert directive's argument into **$_** as well, so that it becomes the default argument for subsequent pattern matching operators and **print** statements and **$1** can be reassigned. In the following code fragment, for instance, each line read from a file is searched for the above regular expression, and if it matches, the found argument is in turn searched for any of the patterns specified by **$pattern1** or **$pattern2**:

```
while ($line = <File>) {
  if ( ($_) = ($line =~ /<!-#insert\s+(\w+)\s*->/i)) {
    if (/($pattern1|$pattern2)/io) {
      &myFunc1(*Form, $File, $1);
    }
```

If either pattern is found, the substring that actually matches it (as opposed to the pattern itself) is automatically placed in **$1**, which is then sent to **myFunc** as a parameter.

The main reason for breaking the search up into two levels this way is to make it more efficient. At the top level in the loop, each file input line is searched only once, for one general container pattern. Only substrings that match the general container pattern are searched further for the particular directives they may contain.

If you define other types of directives besides Insert directives (or decide to search for more than one argument), then it would be most efficient to break the search down into *three* levels, as in:

```
while ($line = <File>) {
  if ( ($cmd, $arg) = ($line =~ /<!—#\s+(\w+)\s+(\w+)\s*->/i)) {
    if ($cmd =~ /^insert$/i) {
      if ($arg =~ /($pattern1|$pattern2)/io) {
      &myFunc1(*Form, $File, $1);
      } elsif ($1 =~ /^myDirectiveTypeName$/i) {
        . . . my sub-search code . . .
      }
```

Here the words matching the first and second instances of **(\w+)** are assigned to **$cmd** and **$arg**, respectively, just to head off any confusion that might result from the reuse of the "memory" variables **$1** and **$2**. These memory variables are reset every time a pattern matching operator is applied, but since they are always local to the innermost block in which they are set, you could in fact safely use **$1** and **$2** for **$cmd** and **$arg** and still use **$1** in **&myFunc1(*Form, $File, $1)**. The question is how easy will it be to understand your code when you (or somebody else) looks at it again six months later?

## Replacing Entire Lines, One Directive per Line

The loop fragments above are good for when you want to substitute dynamically generated data for entire lines in the parsed file. When a line containing a directive is found, just output the new data, and don't output that line. To implement this approach, either of the loops above may end as follows:

```
# else { print $line; } # Don't output any insert directives.
}
else { print $line; }    # Do output all other lines unchanged.
}                         # End of outer-most loop
```

If you replace entire lines in the parsed file, naturally you need to be careful to put each one on its own line. Any other text in the same line, even if it is another directive, will be lost. On the other hand, you could choose to view this limitation as a feature, and use it to your advantage, as was done in www-cart.cgi (Example 7C). Either way, since browsers generally ignore line breaks in a Web page's HTML source, the stipulation of one directive per source line is a small price to pay for the simplicity and speed of this parsing scheme.

## Replacing Substrings within Lines As You Go, or ASAP Parsing

For some purposes, however, you may want to replace a pattern within a single line, or even to modify one directive inside another. For instance, you may want to replace an attribute or field inside an HTML tag, and keep the tag all on one line. To replace a matching substring within a line, you can use a pair of nested loops that begin as follows:

```
while ($line = <File>) {
    while (  ($_) = ($line =~ /<!—#insert\s+(\w+)\s*->)/i)) { # No /g!
        print    $`;        # Print beginning of $line up to match.
        $line = $';         # Reset $line to remainder after match.
```

Whenever a pattern matching operator succeeds, Perl locally resets the pair of special variables **$`** and **$'**; **$`** is assigned whatever part of the search string precedes the successfully matching substring, and **$'** is assigned any remaining part of the search string that follows the match. Thus if either **$`** or **$'** is non-null after a successful pattern match, what matched must have been a proper substring rather than the string as a whole. In the code fragment above, the first part of any matching line is printed immediately, before the found directive is processed, and the **$line** variable is reassigned the value of **$'** so that it will be searched for additional directives upon the loop's next iteration. If there are multiple directives in the same line, only the first one is matched and processed on each loop iteration. (Beware: this means that the **/g** modifier should *not* be specified on the main search pattern. If there are two directives in a line and the global search option is specified, **$_** would be assigned the argument from the first directive, but only the second directive would be replaced in the output stream, and it would be replaced with the results of processing **$_** — the first argument!) The inner loop terminates after all the directives in a line have been processed in the order of their occurrence, and only then is the remainder of a matching line printed, in the same place where any line that contains no directives is printed. This strategy for parsing a file can thus be characterized as "print ASAP."

## Replacing Substrings within Lines Recursively, or JIT Parsing

A different approach is to output each line only after it has been fully processed, just before reading the next line from the file. This strategy can be characterized as outputting the parsed line just-in-time, or as "print JIT." For maximum efficiency, you might implement a JIT file filter with a pair of nested **while** loops that begin as follows:

```
while (<File>) {
  while (/<!-#insert\s+(\w+)\s*->/ig) { # /g iterates through $_
    if ($1 eq $StringA) {
      s//$ReplacementA/;
    }
  /<!-#insert\s+(\w+)\s*->/i
```

The special default variable **$_** is used here with a vengeance. The **s/PATTERN/REPLACEMENT/** operator actually references two default variables: since it is not bound to a search string by a **=~** operator, it searches **$_**, and since there is no **PATTERN** string, what it searches for is the last matched string, which in this case can only be **$StringA**. If the Insert directive's argument is in fact **$StringA**, the entire directive is replaced in **$_** by the current value of **$ReplacementA**. If the argument is not **$StringA**, the inner loop may go on to compare it against other pre-defined values, as in:

```
elsif ($1 eq $StringB) {
  s//$ReplacementB/;
}
```

If the directive's argument fails to match any of the known values, **s///** should be applied without any **PATTERN** or **REPLACEMENT** strings in order to delete the entire directive from **$_**. This step is necessary for ensuring that the loop terminates, because the next iteration of the inner loop will search the same line again. The **while** loops should end as follows:

```
    else {          # Remove the entire <!- ... -> directive:
      s///;         # this searches $_ for the last matched
    }               # string and replaces it with nothing.
  }                 # End of inner while loop.
  print;            # Output $_, including all substitutions.
}                   # End of outer while loop.
```

There is only one **print** statement in the whole subroutine, and it outputs each line only after it has been completely processed and any substitutions have been made in place.

In this scheme, the inner loop's top-level search expression *should* include the **/g** modifier:

```
/<!-#insert\s+(\w+)\s*->/ig
```

This option makes the pattern matching operator remember its place in the search string and start the next search of the same string wherever it broke off the previous search. This is more efficient than the default of starting the search over from the beginning of the line. After a match, however, the remembered place will be at the *beginning* of the matching substring, not at the end.

This means that with or without **/g**, every directive in a line must be replaced by a non-directive before the inner **while** loop can terminate. It also means that this file parsing scheme is recursive: directives can be replaced within directives, and one directive can be replaced by a string containing another directive, which in turn may be replaced on the next iteration.

In many cases, such a "print JIT" strategy for parsing files is more efficient than "print ASAP," but it is much less robust. It is highly optimized for replacing patterns with precomputed strings, and easily breaks if you try to use it for more generalized filtering purposes. For instance, if you want to call a function from within the inner loop, you must take care lest the function unintentionally alter the global value of **$_**. You could save the value of **$_** to a local variable before the function call and then restore it afterwards, but if you try to optimize that, you'll soon arrive back at the "print ASAP" strategy. Thus you might want to take the just-in-time approach only when efficiency is important and you can easily obtain all the necessary replacement strings before entering the inner loop.

# CGI Programming Tips and Techniques

At this point, you are no doubt way beyond ready to write your own interactive CGI applications. The fundamentals of CGI and most of the basics of programming in Perl were covered in the first five chapters, and from there I went on to introduce several advanced topics. I tried to illustrate each topic with examples that not only demonstrated the essential programming techniques but that also showed how the techniques might be integrated into real-world applications. When writing those chapters, I felt that it was even more important to explain each technique in terms that were so general that you could immediately start using it in your own scripts, knowing why you were using it as well as how it worked. The examples were only a means to this end. If you can conceive your nascent application's functionality and algorithms apart from the particulars of its implementation, you are already ahead of the game, but true programming freedom comes from knowing your tools so well that they never tell you what to do.

Rather than furnish any more example scripts or detailed explanations of Perl's semantics, then, I'll devote the remainder of this chapter to CGI and Perl programming tips and a few observations on general practices in software development. These notes are organized under two main headings: common programming tasks, and testing and debugging. Under both headings you will find tips, tricks, small-scale techniques, and out-and-out advice.

## Common Tasks in CGI/Perl Programming

The material that might fill this section has been the main focus of this book, and most of it I've already covered. Nevertheless, some of it bears repeating, and there are a few things here that didn't seem to belong in any particular chapter.

### Define Subroutines and Store Them in Your Own Libraries

My first two pieces of advice are very easy to give:

▶ Define subroutines for performing oft-repeated tasks

▶ Create your own library files in which to save and maintain subroutines

Many a beginner seems to abhor the vacuum that his or her program might turn into if he or she were to replace large jumbles of code with a few compact function calls. Or perhaps people are put off by the extra time it would take to isolate one piece of code from the rest and make its capabilities just a little more general than its immediate context calls for. Whatever it is, don't be loath to define functions. In Perl there is almost nothing to it, and even ad hoc subroutines can make your code much more readable and easy to modify. The extra attention such an approach focuses on a piece of code is often just enough to allow you to spot potential problems and fix them.

Likewise, some programmers seem to feel that creating a library of subroutines is a job for software professionals. But maintaining your own personal library of subroutines can save you a great deal of time and is an excellent way to deepen your understanding of Perl as a language. Making the acquaintance of many different scripts and coding styles will give you breadth, but mastery starts with becoming very familiar with a relatively fixed body of code. Creating a Perl library is actually a cinch. You might start by gathering some or all of the library functions defined in this book into one file. To turn it into a Perl library, all you really have to do is add the statement **1;** at the bottom of the file, so that the **require** operator will be satisfied when you use it to include this file inside a script. You do not need to mark the file executable, start it off with a pound-bang command line, or name it with any particular extension (although .pl is customary). To create your own functions, follow the example of any library function defined in this book. If you are converting a subroutine that was originally defined only for use in one script, the most important thing is to replace any references it makes to global variables with localized variables that are passed to it as parameters.

### When to Abstract, Ad-lib, or Add Libraries

Go forth and multiply your subroutine libraries. That's easy to say, but knowing where and how to abstract the pieces of code that you might end up re-using in different contexts is a skill that grows from years of experience. Unless you have a personal guru you can consult, the best way to avoid learning everything the hard way is to study the code of accomplished programmers and make their techniques work for you. If you have paid attention to the examples in this book, you've gotten a sense of how at least one programmer orders his abstractions and organizes his function naming and calling conventions. I'm not aware of following any very rigid set of rules, but I feel that I know the makings of a subroutine when I see them. Beyond the example subroutines in this book, I have only a few comments to offer.

When you are developing a new application and need a function to play a role similar to that of **NextFile** or **mySendParsedFile** (in Listing 9.1), or **displayCart** (in Example 7C), all of which heavily depend on the global variables in their surroundings, it will probably work out to your best advantage to copy your last-modified version into the new script and retailor it to fit its new surroundings. It would not be easy, or in the end worthwhile, to convert the version of **sendParsedFile** in Example 7C into a general purpose library routine. The main obstacle is the hardwiring of the Insert directive names. The same directive names must also appear in the HTML files that **sendParsedFile** parses, and modifying them there is not simply a matter of changing a function parameter. Another obstacle is that it refers to script-specific global variables. These might be turned into proper function parameters, but this function also calls other local subroutines, such as **displayCart**, which are even more dependent on their surroundings and specialized to the script in which they are defined. Passing a function both a set of search patterns and a set of corresponding actions as parameters would be a little baroque for most CGI applications. Therefore it's better to let **sendParsedFile** remain a local subroutine, and to cut and paste modified versions of it into new scripts as needed.

For very general tasks such as parsing form submissions or updating an access counter, on the other hand, it would probably not be an effective use of your time to reinvent **getFormData** or **countf**. You are better off banking such functions in a library for safekeeping and using calls to them as the building blocks for other functions, even when these other functions do less, not more.

For example, you may want to write a script that accepts only POST requests and rejects all others with an error message. One approach would be to go into a copy of **getFormData,** yank out the code for handling GET requests, and then rewrite its error message to reflect this. Having one less contingency to handle, your modified function *might* run a microsecond or so faster than the original **getFormData**. Or you might accidentally leave out a semicolon, in which case the new version would run infinitely slower. Worse, you could inadvertently break the function in some less obvious way and then have to do some real debugging.

An easier approach would be to test for the POST method outside of **getFormData**, as in:

```
if ($ENV{'REQUEST_METHOD'} ne 'POST') {
    &bitterlyComplainAndDie("Request method must be POST!");
} elsif (&getFormData(*Form)) {
    &breakOutTheEggNog(*Form);
}
```

True, checking the request method both inside and outside of **getFormData** is redundant, but it's far less redundant than maintaining several nearly identical copies of what should really be one library routine.

## Use Well-Written Scripts as Examples or Templates for Your Own Projects

Using well-designed programs and subroutines as templates for your own scripts will not only save you time in the short run but may also accelerate your learning curve. On the other hand, basing your programs on bad examples can set you back. If you're not sure about the overall quality of a script, judge it on the parts that you best understand. If you do end up using a significant amount of somebody else's code, acknowledge them by name at the top of your script, in a README file or any other documentation that accompanies your script, and in any output from the script that includes your own name as author. (What's good for the programming community is good for you.)

## Try to Understand Every Bit of Code that You Use

Whether you base your code on good examples, bad examples, or no examples at all, you won't get very far if you don't understand the code you are using. Ideally, you should understand every single statement, whether it comes from a professional software engineer or a self-taught dabbler. Blindly copying somebody else's code rarely works for long, especially in Perl; there are just too many small things that can go wrong. If you are not sure what one of Perl's functions does, or what one of its special variables means, look it up in your online (or Web-accessible) documentation. (Unlike the number of bugs, the number of functions and variables is finite.) And if you don't understand what a certain piece of code is doing, don't assume that the lack of understanding is yours alone—there are many free CGI scripts on the Web that aren't worth the asking price.

## Optimistic vs. Pessimistic Assumptions and Coding Styles

The best way to ensure that your script will work is to assume that it won't—unless you understand every statement in it and make it work. Such pessimism can also be good for your coding style. There are three basic attitudes you can take toward error handling:

- ▶ Nothing will ever go wrong (the Pollyanna approach).

- ▶ Everything will work as expected, except when it doesn't (the optimistic approach).

- ▶ Everything that can go wrong will go wrong, except when it doesn't (the pessimistic approach).

Code written in the Pollyanna programming style wishfully neglects error handling altogether, whereas an optimistically written code fragment might look like a V-shaped flock of if-else clauses heading East:

```
if (open(SRC, "<$SRC")) {
    if (($rbytes = read(SRC, $record, $bytes, $off)) == $bytes) {
        if (open(DST, ">$DST")) {
            if (seek(DST, $off, 0)) {
                if (print DST $record) {
                    print "Copied $bytes bytes from $SRC to $DST\n";
                } else { die("Couldn't print $bytes in $DST"); }
            } else { die("Couldn't seek to offset $off in $DST"); }
        } else { die("Couldn't open destination file $DST"); }
    } else { die("Couldn't read $bytes from $SRC, got $rbytes"); }
} else { die("Couldn't open source file $SRC for reading"); }
```

A more pessimistic style would bring this code back toward the left-hand side of the page and put the error messages right next to the function calls, making it easier to understand the code's functional content:

```
if (open(SRC, "<$SRC")) {
open( SRC, "<$SRC") || die("Couldn't open source file $SRC");
$rbytes = read(SRC, $record, $bytes, $off);
```

```
$rbytes == $bytes    || die("Couldn't read $bytes from $SRC, got ¬
$rbytes");
open( DST, ">$DST") || die("Couldn't open destination file $DST");
seek( DST, $off, 0) || die("Couldn't seek to offset $off in $DST");
print DST $record    || die("Couldn't print $bytes in $DST");
print STDOUT "Copied $bytes bytes from $SRC to $DST\n";
```

It's also easier to write and maintain pessimistic code, because if you deal with problems as they occur and where they occur, you can worry about them one at a time. In the larger picture, this gives you flexibility. If you find the optimistic code's V shape pretty, answer me quickly: Where would be the most sensible place in it to add a **close(SRC)** statement? And now picture that with 20 or so lines of code added to the positive branch of each **if-else** clause.

## Testing and Debugging Your Scripts

It may seem much more difficult to test and debug CGI programs than ordinary single-user, single-console programs, but it doesn't always have to be. CGI calling and response procedures are inherently distributed but not hidden. With a few windows open at the right places, you can often contrive to monitor the whole process from start to finish.

### Set Up an Isolated Test Environment

One of the very first things you should do is set up your own isolated test environment. There are several ways to do this, from managing your own Web server(s) to simply setting a few environment variables inside a command shell or test script.

**Running Your Own Web Server**    The most isolated environment you could set up would be your own Web server on a computer isolated from the network. The downside of this approach is that if you disconnect a computer from a local area network, you are likely to lose services, such as remotely mounted disks and the Domain Name Server (DNS) service. But even without DNS, you can usually connect to a Web server that runs on the same computer as your Web browser by specifying **localhost** as the server name. If that doesn't work, try using the IP address **127.0.0.1** in place of the server name. Any machine capable of connecting to the Internet should have **localhost** aliased to this "loop-back" address, which is necessary for some network connectivity tests and self-connections. If you disable DNS look-ups on a Windows 95 or Windows NT machine (using the Network

Control Panel), you might have to create a hosts file (c:\windows\hosts) yourself. The file should have the following contents:

```
# Stand-alone hosts file defining the loop-back address and ¬
  (optionally) the machine's own IP addresses and aliases
127.0.0.1       localhost

128.52.38.148   bzrq www bzrq.ai.mit.edu
```

If you are on a PC or Macintosh and connect to the Internet via modem, starting the server may automatically initiate the dial-up process, and the server may even refuse to finish starting up until you are "logged onto the network." That's fine. Let it start up, and then close the modem connection manually, turning off the modem to prevent further redials if necessary. With all the software I have tried, the Web server has continued to serve pages and CGI output to the local host, even after its connection to the outside world was gone.

**Hiding Your Scripts from View on a Public Server** If it isn't practical to develop and test your scripts on your own server, you might be able to hide them from public view on a publicly accessible Web server. There are several different ways in which you might be able to isolate a whole directory or shield most of its contents from public access, depending on the type of Web server you're using and its current configuration.

Most Unix and Windows Web servers are configured to look for index.html as the default document to serve from a directory when the pathname in a requesting URL ends on a directory name instead of a filename. Some also support index.cgi as a default file, usually lower in precedence than index.html. Some other servers look for default.html; this should be a configurable feature. (See your server documentation or site administrator for details.) In a directory that serves index.html (or the equivalent) as a default, you can place other documents to which there are no links. These documents will be accessible only to those who know their full URLs. Alternatively, most Unix servers allow you to turn off directory views entirely. Either way, if you are the only person who knows that a script is there, nobody else is likely to request it. Spiders (automatic Web indexing robots) generally have no more access than human users do, which means that they end up following links rather than recursively scanning whole directory trees. If your test scripts have no links, and if they are in a shielded directory, they shouldn't end up in the indexes compiled on HotBot or AltaVista.

On the Macintosh platform, the popular server MacHTTP and its commercial successor WebStar never presented directory listings in the first place. (CGI programs can be run from any subdirectory.) Hiding a script on a Macintosh is thus only a matter of choosing an obscure pathname.

**Testing Your Scripts without Using a Server** One of the questions most frequently asked by new CGI programmers is, "Do I need a Web server to run my scripts?" Invariably, the answer is "Yes." It's true that you need to install your script on a Web server to make it run *as* a CGI program, but for testing purposes, you can run it as an ordinary command-line program and simulate the conditions of the Web server. The most important thing is to have a local copy of Perl that is identical or as close as possible to the version running on the Web server machine on which your script would normally be installed. Beyond that, it's usually only a matter of setting environment variables, either in the command shell itself or inside the script. You can even automate such testing by calling your CGI script from another Perl script that has set up the right environment variables and input stream. Another variation of this kind of testing is to write a script that calls communications library routines or a program like **telnet** to send simulated browser requests directly to a Web server.

Several example scripts in this book already include provisions for standalone testing outside of a Web server. The tdsearch.cgi script (Example 8B) contains the following conditional:

```
unless (defined($ENV{'SCRIPT_NAME'})) {   # this is only a test...
  $ENV{'SCRIPT_NAME'}    = $0;
  $ENV{'REQUEST_METHOD'} = 'GET';
  $ENV{'QUERY_STRING'}   = 'Query=Cologne&StripHTML=CHECKED';
  $ENV{'CONTENT_LENGTH'} = length($ENV{'QUERY_STRING'});
}
```

If the script is invoked as a CGI program, the Web server will have placed the script's own partial URL in the environment variable SCRIPT_NAME, and the statement inside the conditional will not be executed. If **$ENV{'SCRIPT_NAME'}** is not defined, the script infers that it is being tested, and these statements set up a few of the most salient parts of a running CGI program's environment. Adding such a conditional to a script allows you to test it as a simulated CGI program in a Unix shell, in a MacPerl console window, or at a DOS command line. To simulate a posted form submission, you can save the URL-encoded form data that you want to test in a plain text file named stdin.txt, say, and change the above conditional to something like the following:

```
unless (defined($ENV{'SCRIPT_NAME'})) {    # this is only a test...
  $ENV{'SCRIPT_NAME'}    = $0;
  $ENV{'REQUEST_METHOD'} = 'POST';
  my  $STDIN             = 'stdin.txt';
  $ENV{'CONTENT_LENGTH'} = (-s $STDIN);
  open(STDIN, $STDIN) || die("Couldn't open $STDIN ($!)");
}
```

Here the **open** statement will close the default standard input and replace it with an open filehandle to stdin.txt. Any function that does the work of **getFormData** will then read that file's contents as the posted message body. If you want to control the data file's contents from inside your script, you can replace the last two statements above with the following:

```
my  $query_string      = "name1=value1&name2=value2";
$ENV{'CONTENT_LENGTH'} = length($query_string);
open( STDIN, ">+$STDIN") || die("Can't write/read $STDIN ($!)");
print STDIN $query_string;
seek( STDIN, 0, 0)          || die("Can't rewind $STDIN ($!)";
```

These statements write the value of **$query_string** to a new file and then reposition the filehandle so that Perl's **read** function or diamond operator (**<>**) will then input the contents of the file specified by **$STDIN**.

## Debug during Development, or Test as You Go

You should test all your scripts as your develop them, obviously. What may not be so obvious is that you should periodically stop development work and retest a script from the beginning and then test it all over again when your are done. It's all too common for a programmer to pay attention only to the part of the program that he or she is currently working on and see only the output that he or she expects from it. Yet bugs seem to have ways of propagating themselves and hiding in just the places where you aren't looking for them. In the context of debugging as you go, Murphy's law might be stated as "If it can go *right*, it will—until you stop testing it."

**Be Objective (Never Trust the Programmer)**     This is part of the larger rule that states that you are the worst person to test your own scripts. If you test your script with the same assumptions you had in mind while you were developing it, you shouldn't be surprised if you find nothing wrong. In particular, the input you use for testing is very likely to be influenced by your knowledge of how the program is supposed to work. It may conform exactly to the program's expectations, or it may blatantly violate them. A problem might only appear, however, when the input is only a little off kilter, perhaps in some unforeseen way. If you can get others to test your scripts for you, do so. If you must do all the testing yourself, do it methodically. "Shotgun" testing, in which you barrage your program with more-or-less random input, is rarely effective.

A case in point is the tdsearch.cgi script of Example 8B. Almost the last change I made to this program was adding the option to "Ignore Tags," and when I got it to "work," I thought that I was practically finished. As I systematically tested all the other options to make sure that they still worked, I felt I was being very objective. In fact, I completely blundered. Here is what I did to test my own program. In the program's form interface, I turned the "Ignore Tags" option on, and reran the program with every possible combination of its three other checkboxes on and off.

First I ran the program with all the other checkboxes off, and then I tested these other options one at a time, making sure that each one did what it claimed to do. Next I tried all three combinations of two out of three checkboxes on. It wasn't enough that the program merely ran and found *something* in the files it searched; it had to find and output the *right* thing, and not be fooled even in special cases where the options might interfere with each other. I frequently edited one of the files in the directory it was searching, trying to devise strings that would throw my program for a loop. (Would the Match Whole Words option still work as expected when the search string was **\bThe\b** and the option to match regular expressions was also on? Yes, because in any regular expression, two **\b**'s match the same word boundary as one **\b**. That's obvious, right? Well, I was pretty sure of it, and I was even surer that my program would do the right thing, but I tested it anyway.) Finally I verified that nothing broke when the three of the other options were all on together. Everything seemed fine, so I packed up the script and sent it off to the tech editor, imagining that he would test it in the same methodical way and certify it to be bug-free. "*Of course* it passes every test," said the programmer's voice in my head, "did you really expect your new feature to *lose*?"

The trouble was, I hadn't tested the script with the new feature *off*. Since all of its checkbox options are off by default, that's the way the tech editor first tried it, and for him, the script couldn't find anything. My testing had been methodical, but not methodical enough. I had systematically tested all 8 combinations of 3 options, when I should have tested the 16 possible combinations of all 4 options. In fact, *none* of the 8 combinations I did not test would have worked. My expectations as the programmer blinded me to a bug that others couldn't miss.

(If you read between the lines in the corrected script's comments, you can guess where the bug was. When Ignore Tags was off, the value of the corresponding variable **$StripHTML** was null (''), so that inside the **eval**, every occurrence of **$StripHTML** was replaced by nothing at all. The **eval** was not only telling Perl to interpret the conditionals **unless ()** and **if ()**, which are syntax errors, but was also catching the resulting error messages. Thus Perl never aborted the program as a whole, but only the **eval** itself.)

The moral of this story is that there is no substitute for methodical testing. Spot checking is not enough, nor is testing only the new features as they are added. A pessimistic programming style can make it much easier to diagnose errors after the fact, but it does not prevent them from occurring in the first place. Everything that can go wrong, will go wrong, but the point of testing is to make sure that it does so before you release your program to the public.

**Add Debugging Flags and Conditional Output Statements to Your Scripts** When you know you have a bug in your script but can't easily figure out *what* went wrong, the next best thing is to figure out *where* it went wrong. A quick-and-dirty way to accomplish this is to add **print** or **warn** statements that output your data or control variables at strategic "before" and "after" points in your program. (Recall that the main difference between these is that **print** sends its output to STDOUT, whereas **warn** sends its output to STDERR.) Start with a wide field of inquiry, and then narrow the search down on each successive re-execution until you've found the precise location of the error. Once you can see *where* the error occurs, the diagnosis and remedy are quite often immediately recognizable. If not, at least you'll find out what you have to study up on to correct the problem.

When you are trying to trap a bug between output statements, it's a good idea to separate or at least distinguish your debugging output from the program's normal output.

If you are doing your testing on a Unix system (or any other system that distinguishes between STDOUT and STDERR), send your debugging output to STDERR if you possibly can, even if it ends up in the same terminal window as the normal output. If you are testing your script as a CGI program on a Unix Web server, your script's STDERR will normally be redirected to the server's error log file. If you have shell access to this server, you can monitor its error logging almost as it happens by using the **tail** command with the **-f** option, as in:

```
Unix% tail -f /usr/etc/httpd/logs/error_log
```

The **tail** command normally prints out the last 24 lines or so of a file or input stream, but when the **-f** option is specified, **tail** will keep checking the file to see if any new data has been appended, and print out the new lines if there are any.

If you do not have shell access, you can use **open(STDERR,">STDOUT")** to redirect your script's standard error output to its standard output filehandle, and thus send your debugging output to your browser. This technique was explained in Chapter 5, in the section called "Redirecting Diagnostic Output from STDERR to STDOUT or to a File." Make sure that your script will still output all its HTTP headers before it sends any debugging information. If they are not there already, you may have to (temporarily) move the Content-type and other headers to the very beginning of your script.

If you cannot separate your debugging output from the script's normal output, you can at least mark it as different by including your own special symbols in a conspicuous manner.

One way to distinguish your debugging output from the script's ordinary output, and at the same time to distinguish your debugging statements from the rest of the code inside your script, is to insert your own initials or some funky symbol such as **DBG** in all the output strings, as in:

```
warn("DBG: after the fall, \$theTree is $theTree");
```

When you are finished debugging, you can search for this token and destroy or comment out all occurrences.

I prefer to define my debugging symbol as a file-global or package-global variable at the beginning of my script and to make all my debugging output pass through one or two simple subroutines that test this variable, as in

```
local $DBG = 1; # bitmask debugging flag; 0 turns off all output

sub dbg {        # Usage: &dbg(flag, message1, message2 ...);
    my $flag = shift @_; # get flag as the first parameter
    warn("DBG $flag: @_") if ($flag & $DBG);
}
```

This scheme has the advantage of allowing you to turn all the debugging output on or off by setting the value of one variable, **$DBG**. In simple cases, you can always call **dbg** with a flag value of **1**, as in

```
&dbg(1, "the data before crunching:", $data, $dada, $doodah);
    . . . your errant data-crunching code here . . .
&dbg(1, "same data after crunching:", $data, $dada, $doodah);
```

If **$DBG** is **1** (or, in fact, any odd number), **($flag & $DBG)** will evaluate to **1** inside **dbg**, and the debugging statements will be printed. Otherwise, they won't.

In more complicated or recalcitrant cases, you can use **$DBG** as a bitmask for selectively turning debugging statements on and off. For example, suppose you were debugging a complex script that performs three kinds of computations: binding, winding, and grinding. To avoid having to remember numbers, you might define your debugging flags as follows:

```
$DBG_OTHER =  1;
$DBG_BIND  =  2;
$DBG_WIND  =  4;
$DBG_GRIND =  8;
$DBG       =  $DBG_OTHER | $DBG_BIND | $DBG_WIND;
```

Here **$DBG** is assigned the value **7** as a bitwise *OR* of the defined symbols. This defines which debugging flags are on and off, and as a result, the subroutine call

```
&dbg($DBG_BIND, "Can't bind", $dada, "to", $doodah);
```

will print all of its arguments (separated by single spaces), whereas

```
&dbg($DBG_GRIND, "Can't grind", $dada, "for", $doodah);
```

will not print anything at all. As individual bits in a bitmask, the debugging flags can be turned on and off independently of each other.

For formatted output, you can define a subroutine that calls **printf** instead of **print**. Here is one such definition:

```
sub dbgf {          # usage: &dbgf(mask, format, arg1, arg2 ...);
    my $flag   = shift @_;  # Inside a subrouting, @_ is,
    my $format = shift @_;  # actually shift's default argument.
    printf(STDERR "DBG $flag: $format", @_) if ($flag & $DBG);
}
```

The fact that the string "dbg" does not normally occur in English (or Perl) makes it easy to search for and remove all the **dbg** and **dbgf** statements when you are finished debugging. If you have redirected STDERR into STDOUT or a file, that is also very easy to undo. In general, your debugging statements should be conspicuous, and once you have finished constructing or repairing your application, it should be easy to take down the scaffolding.

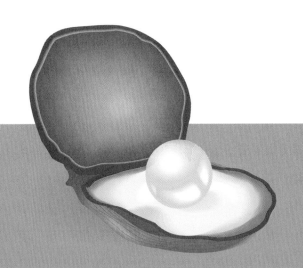

Building a
Gateway: From
Information
Servers to
Application
Servers

The Advantages and
Disadvantages of
Using CGI Today

Proposed Enhancements
and Alternatives

What, Then,
Is the Future of CGI?

# Chapter 10
# The Future of CGI

What is the future of the Common Gateway Interface? Before I attempt to answer this, let me pose two related questions: What is the general problem that CGI should be concerned with solving, and what would a solution that improves upon or goes beyond the current version of CGI be like?

## Building a Gateway: From Information Servers to Application Servers

The original intentions behind the Common Gateway Interface were fairly modest: It was built to provide a means for Web users to query databases or other information resources on remote servers. The term "gateway" commonly refers to any application or system that provides this kind of service, in which the emphasis is on information retrieval rather than on full-fledged interaction. Wide Area Information Server (WAIS) gateways, for instance, predate the Web by several years. (WAIS is an Internet publishing and textual database system that allows clients to use a standard protocol to interrogate database servers.) The Common Gateway Interface was thus invented as a standard query-and-response mechanism to be shared by browsers, Web servers, and gateway programs.

CGI's humble origins are still apparent in its language of "request methods" and "query strings," but from there it has grown to fulfill a more general purpose. CGI has become a mechanism that allows more-or-less anyone and everyone to send input to a specified program at a remote Web site and get back the program's output. CGI programs can input and output anything that can be transported over the Internet (using the very flexible HTTP protocol, that is), from live audio segments to electronic money, executable code, compressed video clips, or even a personalized horoscope. And in between input and output, these programs can perform any kind of computation imaginable. In practice, creating a Web-accessible gateway to a database can be a nontrivial task, but it is certainly less of a chore than building, say, a networked multiuser 3-D flight simulator, which is one of the directions in which CGI may be headed. CGI has become a mechanism for running a wide variety of server-based applications over the Web, and its future will thus be affected by the general impetus to make these applications ever more powerful and complex. In short, what began as a set of interface conventions designed to be shared by gateways to information servers has become a de facto standard gateway interface and input/output mechanism shared by a great many networked applications.

## CGI as a Solution to a Set of Technical Problems

Any application gateway mechanism must take into account such issues as user identification, user-application interfaces and context maintenance, system and data security, and overall system performance. Some of the problems are as obvious as they are potentially devastating, yet their solutions are far from certain. For instance, any user identification scheme must weigh issues of privacy and liability against those of efficiency, the desire to offer user-sensitive services, and the benefits of standardization. Likewise, there will always be trade-offs between maximizing the richness of responses and minimizing overall response times.

Nevertheless, if the general problem were *only* (!) the technical one of providing a gateway mechanism for network applications, the future of CGI might lie in the development of better technical solutions to each of these particular sub-problems. However, CGI is more than a mechanism. It is also a programming practice and a widely implemented standard interface.

## CGI Programming as an Ongoing Practice

As a programming practice, CGI competes against other, overlapping practices. Two kinds of competing practices are those that make use of server-specific APIs (application programming interfaces) and those that take a more client-centered approach, such as Java and JavaScript programming. API-based applications are capable of completely replacing the functionality of CGI programs, whereas Java and JavaScript applets are capable (at least in principle) of usurping some of the roles currently played by server-resident CGI programs. CGI programming has enjoyed a large head start over the others, and there are still many more programmers competent at CGI programming in Perl and C than there are programmers who know Java or JavaScript. (As for the future of CGI programmers, their skills should adapt well to programming with CGI enhancements or replacements.)

## CGI as a Widely Implemented Standard

As a widely implemented standard interface, CGI is very unlikely to disappear overnight. CGI is perfectly adequate for performing many tasks on a great many servers, and it is often much easier to clone and modify existing CGI programs than to create new API-based or client-centered programs from scratch. CGI is currently the only alternative that is supported by virtually all browsers and servers. In addition to the inertia of the installed base, there is the promise of backward compatibility in the future. Other solutions hoping to gain precedence over CGI would face not only the difficulty of gaining recognition but also the task of implementation in a global setting.

## CGI's Problematic Dependence on HTTP

The fact that CGI is piggybacked on HTTP accounts for some of its major weaknesses as a remote application interface. For instance, it is actually HTTP 1.0 that is stateless, not CGI itself. Using some of the techniques illustrated in this book, especially in Chapter 7, you can make your CGI applications maintain a persistent context with a user, but because CGI lives in the stateless environment of HTTP, this is a matter of programming rather than a matter of course.

Not only do CGI programs extend the capabilities of HTTP as a protocol, they also routinely violate the current HTTP specification. According to the specification for HTTP 1.0 and the draft for HTTP 1.1, for example, the GET request method should be both "safe" and "idempotent." The *safe* stipulation means that the request method "should never have the significance of taking an action other than retrieval." And the *idempotent* stipulation, when applied to the request method, means that "(aside from error or expiration issues) the side-effects of [performing] $N > 0$ identical requests [are] the same as for a single request" (from the Internet draft of the Internet Engineering Task Force memo "Hypertext Transfer Protocol — HTTP/1.1" <URL:ftp://ietf.org/internet-drafts/draft-ietf-http-v11-spec-07>, page 46>). In particular, sending more than one GET request with the same URL should always retrieve the same document and have no other side effects. Because extra path information and query strings are technically part of a URL, many CGI programs actually are HTTP-compliant in this regard. (This is why it "works" to save their URLs as bookmarks.) But any CGI program that answers identical GET requests by sending different page contents, or maintains state using the equivalent of a cookie in a query string, does so in clear violation of the current and proposed next update of the HTTP specification.

If HTTP compliance were actually enforced, it could thus seriously undermine much of the current practice of CGI programming. Likewise, if HTTP were to change significantly—for instance, if it should switch to a scheme of maintaining state information at the transport layer—CGI might either have to adapt or face obsolescence. A more likely scenario is that HTTP and CGI will change together to better accommodate current practice and the future needs of Web programmers.

## Taking All the Factors into Account

When trying to predict the future of CGI, one should take into account the practical implementation and human factors as well as the purely technical problems of inventing a better mechanism for remote operability and a better communications protocol for transporting data across an open network.

Any application gateway interface must confront the same challenges, but the combination of CGI 1.1 and HTTP 1.0 is particularly amenable to improvement. Most of the proposed enhancements or alternatives to CGI have been formulated in terms that address one or more of the following goals:

▶ Increase application performance by decreasing system overhead

▶ Increase the sensitivity and responsiveness of the user interface by placing a greater portion of the application itself on the user's local computer

▶ Take greater advantage of existing technologies for networked application environments, such as dynamically linked object libraries

▶ (Better) ensure the security (integrity and privacy) of transmitted data

▶ Provide a standard mechanism for maintaining a persistent context throughout a user session

▶ Provide a standard mechanism for identifying users and maintaining account status across multiple sessions

The first three of these design goals are concerned with the drawbacks of CGI as a currently implemented standard. The second three are more concerned with the drawbacks of HTTP 1.0 as a communications protocol and general network application environment. Overall, the issues of server performance and transmitted data security have received the most attention, and in the near future, changes in these areas are likely to have the greatest impact on CGI programming as we know it.

# The Advantages and Disadvantages of Using CGI Today

There are many advantages to using the Common Gateway Interface as currently specified and implemented. Some of the main benefits are

- ▶ **Portability**    CGI is the de facto open standard for developing Web-based applications. Practically every Web server implements some form of CGI.

- ▶ **Simplicity**    CGI is simple to implement and configure in a Web server (at least on a Unix platform) and easy to learn to program—in Perl, of course! Installing a CGI script is as easy as installing an HTML page.

- ▶ **Process isolation**    CGI programs run as separate processes and thus cannot crash the Web server or access each other's internal states. This also makes them easier to debug.

- ▶ **Language and architecture independence**    Because CGI programs run as separate processes, they can be written in any programming language and are not constrained to match the server's own internal architecture (for instance, in terms of multithreading, dynamically linked objects, and so on). Binary executables need only match the machine architecture (basically, the CPU and the operating system).

The main disadvantages to using CGI come from some of the same basic properties:

- ▶ **Performance**    The overhead involved in starting a new process for each request or execution slows the server down for everybody. Interpreted programs such as Perl scripts can be particularly inefficient, because the entire interpreter must be loaded and run to execute even a single line of code. On a Unix machine, a Perl 5 process typically starts out with half a megabyte of memory and allocates more to itself as needed.

- ▶ **Restricted (and short-lived) functionality**    The role of a CGI program is only to respond to a request and exit. Because the Web server waits for the program to die before it closes the connection to the client browser, the CGI process really can't go on living to perform another day. This makes maintaining state between requests troublesome and costly. It also creates a barrier against linking CGI programs into other roles, such as user authentication or tracking.

▶ **Lack of server-side supervision**    Paradoxically, a CGI process's actions might not be monitored closely enough. Although CGI programs are initiated by Web servers, they are not supervised and generally run with all the permissions of the Web server itself. They can gobble up arbitrary amounts of memory and other resources and use their nearly direct connection to the network to do things with blatant disregard for the HTTP specification (especially if they are non-parsed-header scripts). A CGI program can even survive its own death.

Server vendors and various third parties have cited each of these disadvantages as an impetus to create alternatives to CGI, placing the greatest emphasis on CGI's performance problems.

## Proposed Enhancements and Alternatives

At present, there are two competing Web application technologies whose functionalities greatly overlap that of CGI:

▶ Application programming interfaces (APIs) that support the servers produced by Netscape, Microsoft, Apache, and other server vendors

▶ Open Market's FastCGI

Web server APIs provide a means for dynamically linking application code into the server application itself. FastCGI can be used as a partial or complete replacement for CGI and retains much of the same interface to the Web server that standard CGI does. In this respect, the face that FastCGI presents to programmers is one of enhancements to, rather than an outright replacement of, standard CGI programming techniques. Server APIs and FastCGI offer the most direct competition to CGI.

In addition to these, Microsoft's ActiveX controls, as interfaced with its Information Server API (ISAPI), have been touted as an integrated solution that replaces major aspects of CGI's functionality. Sunsoft's various Java programming models, notably applets and servlets, have staked out claims to much of the same territory. The Java and ActiveX programming technologies are better known for their client-side capabilities, but either of them could have an impact on server-side applications. If these technologies can live up to their advance marketing hype, they will come to play increasingly important roles in the field that is now dominated by CGI. At this point, however, it is too early to say whether either or both of these technologies will replace much of the installed base or current development of CGI programs.

## Server-Specific Application Programming Interfaces (APIs)

Apache, Microsoft, Netscape, Process Software, O'Reilly, and other developers of Web server software have all created APIs for use with their servers. Applications based on these Web server APIs are typically written in C/C++, following the guidelines and including the header files provided by the vendor. Microsoft's ISAPI is wrapped up in an OLE/ActiveX package, which allows ISAPI applications to be written in Visual Basic, Java, Delphi, or any other OLE-enabled programming language. The resulting application is not a standalone program but a shared object or dynamically linked library. In most schemes, the application is linked into the Web server at startup time, as specified by the server's configuration files.

API-based applications enjoy the following advantages over CGI programs:

▶ **Efficiency and lower overhead** Because the API-based application is linked into the server process, its initiation doesn't incur the cost of starting a new process, nor is there the overhead of starting up an interpreter or loader just to execute one small program.

▶ **Speed** Lower overhead means greater speed. In addition to solving CGI's startup problem, the API solution also requires no interprocess communication of synchronization. The server doesn't wait for the API application to die, and if the server is multithreaded, it may not even have to wait for the program to begin.

▶ **Increased functionality** Depending on the server's configuration, the API-based application might have full access to the server's data and internal state information. It might also be integrated into any part of the server's response to a request, such as user authentication and tracking (logging).

▶ **Supervision (security)** Again depending on the server's configuration, the actions of an API-based application may be limited or monitored by the Web server into which it is linked. In present implementations, this property is more of a side effect than an explicitly designed feature.

A list of the disadvantages of the API approach to building server-side applications reads like a line-by-line veto of CGI's advantages:

▶ **Proprietary guidelines**  An application developed for a particular server vendor's API will not be easily portable to another Web server.

▶ **Complexity**  APIs are complicated and might require programmers to climb a steep learning curve just to get started. In addition to that, implementation might be time-consuming and might require maintenance work every time the server is updated.

▶ **Lack of process isolation**  Because applications share the same process identification and address space as the server, a buggy or malicious one can corrupt, crash, or compromise the security of the others or of the server itself. Conversely, bugs in the server can affect applications. All of these problems can be very difficult to debug.

▶ **Language dependence**  Applications must be written in a language supported by the API (usually ANSI C or C++). Perl is not supported by any existing API, not is it likely to be supported in the future.

▶ **Architecture dependence**  If the server is multithreaded, the application must be thread-safe. Conversely, if the server is single-threaded, a multi-threaded application won't enjoy any advantage in performance. Obviously, the application must also be ported and recompiled to run on different platform architectures.

## Open Market's FastCGI

FastCGI is a nonproprietary CGI-like server/program interface that is capable of partially, incrementally, or fully replacing standard CGI. Its developer, Open Market, Inc., claims that it is "fast, open, and secure," and "combines the best aspects of CGI and vendor APIs." Web servers that support FastCGI still run CGI programs as separate processes, but they manage these processes in a different way.

The main difference is that an ordinary Web server starts a new process to respond to each new CGI request and then waits for it to die, whereas a FastCGI-compliant Web server starts the process only once and leaves it running to handle subsequent requests. Between requests, the FastCGI process can simply sleep, waiting for new connections or requests from the Web server. Instead of communicating with the FastCGI process through filehandles linked together as dedicated input/output pipes and environment variables (which can be created only at startup), the Web server can multiplex the environment information and standard input/output/error channels over a single full-duplex connection. This allows FastCGI programs to run either on the same machine as the Web server or on remote machines, using TCP connections. If the program is local and single-threaded, the server would normally run the program as a pool of nearly identical processes. Each running copy would handle one request at a time; this is the same trick that single-threaded Web servers use to handle overlapping client requests simultaneously. If the FastCGI program is multithreaded, a single running copy will be able to handle multiple requests simultaneously, or if each request is mediated by a TCP connection to a remote machine, the server can wait for the next available process. In a very literal sense, then, each FastCGI program becomes a secondary, highly specialized server in its own right, and the Web server itself is the FastCGI program's client.

The basic calling and response sequence is as follows:

1 The Web server creates FastCGI application processes either at startup or the first time they are requested by a Web client/browser.

2 Each particular FastCGI program initializes itself as a running process and waits for new connections from the Web server.

3 When a client request comes in, the Web server opens a connection to the FastCGI process. The Web server sends the CGI environment variable information and standard input over the connection.

4 The FastCGI process sends the standard output and error information back to the server over the same connection.

5 When the FastCGI process closes the connection, the request is complete. The FastCGI process then waits for another connection from the Web server.

Because of the basic similarities between FastCGI and standard CGI as interfaces, FastCGI applications enjoy the same advantages over API-based applications. FastCGI also solves the main CGI performance problem by avoiding the creation of new processes, and it provides ground-level support for distributed computing. The cost of these advantages lies in the persistence of FastCGI processes between requests. Each multithreaded application or process pool is kept in a ready state, waiting to respond to a request as soon as the Web server can open the connection and send the request information through it. Although a waiting process uses practically no CPU time, it can still tie up memory (or at least virtual memory). The major trade-off is thus memory for speed, but this is hardly unique to FastCGI, and it's a trade-off with which many administrators of busy Web servers can be comfortable.

# What, Then, Is the Future of CGI?

For the most part, the relative advantages of using CGI-based, FastCGI-based, and API-based server-side applications speak for themselves. In the near future, each of these alternatives will vie for market share, but as a simple, standard technology, CGI itself will continue to be used for a great many basic tasks. The biggest threat to its continued use may come not from APIs or persistent, multiplexed processing schemes such as that of FastCGI, but from changes to the transport layer underlying HTTP itself. Nevertheless, the best way to keep up in an area of rapidly changing technology is usually to master the established tools first, before going on to pursue the latest-breaking developments. If you thoroughly understand how CGI is used as an interface for network applications, and if you master the skills needed to create real-world CGI programs in Perl, you will be well prepared for the future of Web programming.

# Appendix
# Regular Expressions in Perl

Perl's regular expression handling is one of its most powerful features and is one of the main reasons that Perl is a nearly ideal language for CGI programming. Text manipulation is central to many CGI applications, and the proficiency with which regular expressions search and replace text is without parallel. To beginners, however, the terse notation, the many options, and the alternative ways of forming a pattern can be somewhat daunting. If you are new to regular expressions, don't expect to master all the rules on your first pass through the summary below. As is the case with most other features in Perl, you don't need to know everything there is to know about regular expressions in order to begin using them effectively. If, on the other hand, you are already familiar with regular expression matching, you will still find this appendix helpful for its description of the usage of regular expressions in Perl 5 as opposed to earlier implementations (such as Henry Spencer's original design, used by the Unix **egrep** command).

## The Rules of Regular Expression Matching

A regular expression consists of zero or more alternative *patterns*, which are strings of *elements*. Patterns are separated by the vertical bar character (I), and the whole expression is usually delimited by forward slashes (/), followed by zero or more of the option characters **g**, **i**, **m**, **o**, **s**, or **x**. Regular expressions almost always appear within delimiters, and these delimiters are spoken of as if they were a part of the regular expression itself, even though they do not participate in the matching. An element is either an *atom*, quantified or unquantified, or an *assertion*. An unquantified atom always matches a single character, whereas a quantified atom can match zero or more characters. An *assertion* matches a contextual condition, such as the beginning or end of a string, and does not absorb any of the matched string's characters. A regular expression matches a string if any one of its patterns matches some part of that string, element-for-element. Testing always proceeds from left to right and stops at the first complete match. The individual elements match as described in the following sections.

## Unquantified Atoms

As an unquantified atom, each character matches itself, unless it is one of the special characters **+, ?, ., *, ^, $, (, ), [, ], {, }**, |, or \ (not including the commas, which are used here only for readability). The actual meanings of these special characters will become apparent below. To match one of them as a literal character, you can precede it with a backslash to "escape" its special meaning. For example, the special character **.** (period) is a wildcard that matches any single character, but **\.** matches only a period. In general, a preceding **\** escapes the special meaning of any non-alphanumeric character, but it converts most alphanumeric characters *into* special atoms or assertions. Thus you can also use **\** on itself, or on **/**, which is a special character only when it is being used as the delimiter; for instance, the **/**-delimited regular expression **/\/\\/** matches **/\** inside any string. (For an explanation of using other non-alphanumeric characters as delimiters, see the sections on Perl's **m//** and **s///** operators, later in this appendix). All of the special atoms are enumerated below, and match as follows:

**.** (period)   Matches any character except a newline. Will match a newline if option **s** (single-line match) is specified.

**\w**   Matches any alphanumeric character, including _.

**\W**   Matches any non-alphanumeric character, excluding _.

**\s**   Matches one whitespace character; that is, a tab, newline, vertical tab, form feed, carriage return, or space (ASCII 9 through 13 and 32), which individually match **\t**, **\n**, **\v**, **\f**, **\r**, and **\040**, respectively.

**\S**   Matches one non-whitespace character.

**\d**   Matches a digit, 0 through 9.

**\D**   Matches any non-numerical character.

**\NNN**   Matches the character specified by the 2- or 3-digit octal number **NNN**, unless it would be interpreted as a back-reference (see the definition of **/N** below). For example, **\177** matches the DEL character (ASCII 127).

**\xXX**   Matches the character represented by hexadecimal value **XX**; for example, **\xA9** matches the copyright character © (ISO Latin-1 169).

**\cC**   Matches the control character Ctrl-**C**, where **C** is any single character; for example, **\cH** matches a backspace (ASCII 8). This atom is the same as **\NNN**, where **NNN** is the octal value of **ord(C) + 64**.

**[*S*]**     Matches any character in the class *S*, where *S* is specified as a string of literal characters (as in **[abc$%^&]**), a range of characters in ASCII order (as in **[a-z]**), or any combination thereof (as in **[a-c$-&^]**). Most of the special characters lose their special meanings inside the square brackets, but the hyphen must be escaped as **\-**, the **\b** character matches a backspace (**\010**), and most other backslashed characters retain their special meanings as atoms or assertions.

**(*E*)**     Matches any regular expression *E* and stores the substring matching the $N^{th}$ parenthesized expression in the special read-only memory variable **$*N*** (that is, in **$1**, **$2**, etc.). The parentheses serve both to group a string of elements or patterns into one atom and to mark that atom for future reference.

**\\*N***     Matches whatever the $N^{th}$ parenthesized atom actually matched, where *N* = 1, 2, 3....up to the total number of preceding parenthesized atoms. Such an atom is called a *back-reference* to a subexpression.

**(?:*E*)**   Matches the regular expression *E* but does not store the match in any **$*N*** variable for back-referencing.

## Quantifiers and Quantified Atoms

The regular expression *quantifiers* are the special characters **+**, **\***, **?**, and the expressions **{*N*}**, **{*N*,}**, and **{*N*,*M*}**. A quantified atom is an atom that is followed by a quantifier. If *A* is any atom, *A*+ matches *A* one or more times; that is, it matches one or more adjacent substrings that each match *A* individually. Similarly, *A*\* matches *A* zero or more times, and *A*? matches zero or one occurrence of *A*. Furthermore, *A*{*N*} matches *A* exactly *N* times, *A*{*N*,} matches *A* *N* or more times, and *A*{*N*,*M*} matches a minimum of *N* and a maximum of *M* occurrences of *A*. A quantified atom matches as many characters as possible, unless a **?** is appended to the quantifier, in which case the atom matches the smallest substring allowed by the context. Thus **/(ab+)([bc])/** and **/(ab+?)([bc])/** both match **abbc**, but the first expression sets **$1** and **$2** to **abb** and **c**, respectively, whereas the second expression sets **$1** and **$2** to **ab** and **b** (for the meanings of **$1** and **$2**, see the parenthesis rule above, in the table entry for (*E*)).

## Assertions

An *assertion* is different from an atom in that it doesn't match any characters but rather matches a *contextual condition*, such as a difference between two adjacent characters. Because assertions cannot add any characters to a matched substring, they are said to have zero width. Assertions match as follows:

| | |
|---|---|
| **\A** | Matches the beginning of a string. |
| **\Z** | Matches the end of a string. |
| **^ and $** | These are like **\A** and **\Z** except that in multiline mode (option **m**), **^** and **$** match the beginning and end of every line (that is, after and before every newline character), respectively. |
| **\b** | Matches a word boundary. |
| **\B** | Matches a non-boundary. |
| **\G** | Matches the point at which the previous global search (option **g**) left off. |
| **(?=E)** | Matches the beginning of the regular expression **E**, without including **E** as part of the matched substring. In other words, **E** must be present for **(?=E)** to match, but the match has no effect on subsequent matching or processing. This is called a zero-width positive look-ahead assertion. |
| **(?!E)** | Matches the absence of the regular expression **E**. This is called a zero-width negative look-ahead assertion. |
| **(?#T)** | Matches anything and nothing; **T** is only an embedded comment. That is, **/(?#T)/** always returns **1**, no matter what string is searched, but the matched substring is always null. |
| **(?M)** | Matches anything, like **(?#T)**, except that **M** is an embedded pattern-match modifier, namely one or more of the options **i**, **m**, **s**, or **x**. (For a description of these options, see the discussion of **m//** below.) The specified options(s) affect the entire search, the same as if they are appended to the ending delimiter as modifiers. |

# Examples of Regular Expressions

The following list of examples and the descriptions of what they match covers the essentials of regular expression matching in Perl 5.

| **Regular Expression** | **What It Matches in Perl 5** |
|---|---|
| **/abc/** | **abc** anywhere in the search string. |
| **/^abc/** | **abc** at the beginning of the string. |
| **/abc$/** | **abc** at the end of the string. |

| **/(abc)/** | **abc** anywhere in the string; the matched expression is stored in **$1**. |
|---|---|
| **/ab\|cd/** | **ab** or **cd**, whichever comes first. |
| **/a(b\|c)d/** | **a** followed by **b** or **c**, then **d** (**abd** or **acd**, not **abcd**). |
| **/ab{3}c/** | **a** followed by exactly 3 **b**'s, then by **c**. This is the same as /abbbc/. |
| **/ab{1,3}c/** | **a** followed by 1, 2, or 3 **b**'s; then by **c**. This is the same as **/abb?b?c/**. |
| **/ab?c/** | **a** followed by **c** with an optional **b** in between (**ac** or **abc**). This is the same as **/ab{0,1}c/**. |
| **/ab*c/** | **a** followed by zero or more **b**'s, then **c** (**ac**, **abc**, **abbc**, etc.). This is the same as **/ab{0,}c/**. |
| **/ab+c/** | **a** followed by one or more **b**'s, then **c** (**abc**, **abbc**, etc.). This is the same as **/ab{1,}c/**. |
| **/[abc]/** | Any single character in the bracketed class, namely, **a** or **b** or **c**. This is the same as **/[a-c]/** and **/a\|b\|c/**. |
| **/[abc]+/** | Any string of one or more characters from the bracketed class (**a**, **b**, **c**, **aa**, **ab**, **ac**, **ba**, **bb**, **bc**, etc.). |
| **/[^abc]/** | Any single character not in the class inside the brackets. (Note that the **^** character has a different special meaning at the beginning of a character class than at the beginning of a pattern. In the interior of a character class, or as an element in the interior of a pattern and not preceded by **\n**, **^** matches itself. |
| **/\w+/** | Any string of alphanumeric characters, including _. This is the same as **/[0-9A-Z_a-z]+/**. |
| **/\W+/** | Any string of non-alphanumeric characters. This is the same as **/[^\w]+/**. |
| **/abe\b/** | **abe** followed by a word boundary (the zero-width space between alphanumeric and non-alphanumeric characters, that is, between characters matched by **\w** and **\W**); this expression will not match the **abe** in **abecedarian**. |
| **/./** | Any single character except a newline (**\n**). |

| | |
|---|---|
| **/((.\n)+)/** | Any string of one or more characters, including **\n**; **$1** will contain the whole string, and **$2** will contain only the last character matched. |
| **/name=([^&]*)&ident=\1(&\|$)/** | A string of the form **name=val&ident=val**, followed either by **&** or the end of the string; **val** can be made up of any characters besides **&** and **\n** and will be placed in the special read-only memory variable **$1** (see the parenthesis rule in the section on "Unquantified Atoms," above). |
| **/(ab+)([bc])/** | **a** followed by one or more **b**'s (as many as possible), then either a **b** or a **c** (**abb**, **abc**, **abbb**, **abbc**, etc.). If the last character matched is **c**, all of the **b**'s will be placed in **$1**, following the initial **a**, and **$2** will be assigned the value **c**. Otherwise, the matched string must contain at least two **b**'s, and **$2** will be assigned the last matched **b**. |
| **/(ab+?)([bc])/** | **a** followed by one or more **b**'s (as few as possible, because of the **?**), then either a **b** or a **c**. In other words, this expression can match only the substrings **abb** or **abc**. After a match, the only possible value for **$1** is **ab**, whereas **$2** will be either **b** or **c**. |
| **/<[^>]*?(>\|$)\|(^\nG)[^<>]*?>/** | Any full tag delimited by angle brackets, or any partial tag broken by a line ending. That is, any substring that begins with **<** and ends with either **>** or the end of the string as a whole, or any substring that starts at the beginning of the string and ends with **>**. |
| **/<[^>]*?>/m** | Any angle-bracket-delimited tag, even one that spans many line endings within the search string. |

# Operators That Use Regular Expressions in Perl

Perl has three operators that search strings for regular expression matches: **m/pattern/**, **?pattern?**, and **s/pattern/replacement/** (also known simply as **//**, **??**, and **s** or **s///**). The first of these is usually written without the optional **m**; indeed, **/pattern/** is practically synonymous with regular expression matching in Perl and other programming languages.

The **?*pattern*?** operator is just like **/*pattern*/**, except that it matches only once between calls to the **reset** operator. This can be useful when you want to see only the first match in a file, for instance, but there are better ways to accomplish this, and the **??** operator may be removed from future versions of Perl.

The usage of the search-and-replace operator, **s/*pattern*/*replacement*/**, also closely follows that of **m//**, except that with **s///** any part of the search string that matches the regular expression *pattern* is replaced by *replacement* (which is not a regular expression). This extra step makes the **s///** operator so powerful that entire programs can be written using almost nothing else.

The following sections go into more detail about how to use the **m//** and **s///** operators. For further examples (and a great deal of other valuable reference information), see Perl's online documentation, especially perlop.html and perlre.html. In the NTPerl distribution, these files can be found in the docs subdirectory under the main Perl directory, and in MacPerl, they can be found in the pod subfolder. In Unix installations, these files are usually kept in a directory such as /usr/local/lib/perl5/pod and may have to be converted to HTML format with the **pod2html** utility program, which should reside in the same directory as the Perl interpreter itself. (Try /usr/local/bin/pod2html.)

## Perl's Regular Expression Matching Operator: m//

Perl's pattern matching operator **m//** is used as follows:

```
$match = (string =~ m/pattern/options);
```

This construct searches a string for a regular expression and assigns the return value true (**1**) or false (**''**) to **$match**. If *string* contains the regular expression *pattern*, as modified by the *options*, the value of **$match** will be **1**; otherwise it will be **''**. The **=~** is called the *pattern binding operator*. Despite its appearance (and its association with the search-and-replace operator, **s///**), **=~** is not some kind of fancy assignment operator but is a logical operator like **==** or **eq** (which denote numerical and string equality, respectively). Its opposite is **!~**, which causes the expression **(*string* ~! /*pattern*/)** to evaluate to true if and only if *string* does *not* match *pattern*.

The value of the whole expression **(*string* =~ m/*pattern*/)** depends on both of the operands *string* and **m/*pattern*/**, and neither is changed as a result of the operation. If you omit the search string, Perl will search the special variable **$_**. You can also leave out the **m**, as long as you are using slashes to delimit the regular expression. Thus **/*pattern*/** all by itself is equivalent to **($_ =~ m/*pattern*/)**. If you keep the **m**, you can use almost any character as the pattern delimiter, as long as it doesn't explicitly appear within the pattern. The **#** character is often used to delimit patterns that contain **/**'s, as in

```
print "local\n" if ($path =~ m#/usr/local/bin/#);
```

On the other hand, the slashes are not a problem in

```
$pattern = "/usr/local/bin";
print "$pattern\n" if ($path =~ m/$pattern/);
```

You can also use the *bracketing character* pairs **[]**, **()**, **{}**, and **<>** as the opening and closing delimiters. Otherwise, the same character must be used to mark both the beginning and the end of the regular expression.

The options tell Perl how to optimize and perform the matching: **g** will cause the search to match as many times as possible (in other words, to perform a "global" search); **i** will cause the search to be case-insensitive; **o** will interpolate any variables in the pattern only once; **m** will cause the string to be searched as multiple lines (slower); **s** will cause the string to be searched as a single line only (faster; this is the default); and **x** enables Perl's extensions to regular expressions. The only such extension documented in Perl 5 is to ignore any white space in a search pattern. This can make the pattern much easier to read, but it also means that a literal white space character in the pattern string will not match itself in the search string. (The very last to example in this appendix illustrates an effective use of the **/x** modifier along with embedded comments.)

## Perl's Search-and-Replace Operator: s///

Perl's search-and-replace operator, **s///**, is used as follows:

```
$matches = (string =~ s/pattern/replacement/options);
```

This construct searches **string** for the regular expression **pattern**, replaces one or all of any matching substrings with **replacement**, and returns the number of substitutions made. If there were no matches, the **s** operator returns false (**''**). If no string is specified via the **=~** or **!~** operator, the special variable **$_** is searched and modified. If specified, **string** must be an lvalue—that is, either a variable that evaluates as a scalar value or an assignment to such a variable.

As with the **m//** operator, the pattern delimiter can be nearly any non-alphanumeric character instead of **/**, and a few such delimiters have special meanings. (You can think of the **??** operator in this way.) If the delimiter chosen is the single quote character, no variable interpolation is done on either the **pattern** or the **replacement**. Otherwise, if **pattern** contains a **$** followed by an alphanumeric character (so that it looks like a variable rather than an end-of-string test), the variable will be interpolated into *pattern* at runtime. Variables in *replacement* will also be interpolated. (The **/e** modifier forces this behavior even if the delimiter is the single quote character.) If backquotes are used as delimiters, the replacement string will be executed as a shell command and its output will be used as the actual replacement text. If *pattern* is delimited by a pair of bracketing characters, *replacement* must have its own pair of delimiters, which need not be the same. Two examples of this approach are **s(foo)[bar]** and **s <foos>/ball/**.

The options are the same as for **m//**, except that the **/g** modifier causes the pattern matching operation to replace all occurrences of the pattern (in other words, to perform a global replacement), and to return the total number of replacements. There is also one additional option: the **/e modifier** causes the operation to evaluate the replacement string as a full-fledged Perl expression (possibly using the equivalent of an **eval**), as in:

```
$escapes = ($name =~ s/%([0-9A-Za-z][0-9A-Za-z])/pack("C", ¬
hex($1))/eg);
```

Here the value of the special "memory" variable **$1** will be whatever has just matched the parenthesized sub-expression **([0-9A-Za-z][0-9A-Za-z])**, namely, a 2-character string representing a hexidecimal number. The **hex** function returns the decimal equivalent of this hexidecimal number, and the **pack** function with the parameter **"C"** returns the ASCII character corresponding to this number. Thus the overall effect of this expression is to replace a URL-escaped character with the equivalent literal character. (Note that **%** is not a special character; it matches only itself.) Further examples of **/e**'s usage are given below, as well as a caveat.

## Examples of s///'s Usage

Many of the following examples are identical or similar to those on Perl's manual page (as converted to perlre.html), but here they are accompanied by explanations:

The following statement replaces all occurrences of **green** as a whole word in the current contents of **$_**:

```
s/\bgreen\b/mauve/g;          # don't change wintergreen
```

This statement replaces uses **I** instead of **/** as the delimiter, and replaces the first occurrence of **/usr/bin** with **/usr/local/bin** in **$path**:

```
$path =~ s|/usr/bin|/usr/local/bin|;
```

This one substitutes the current values of **$foo** and **$bar** in the search pattern and the replacement string, respectively, before performing the search and replacement operation:

```
s/Login: $foo/Login: $bar/;        # pattern computed at runtime
```

If **$foo** or **$bar** is not defined, it is replaced by nothing. Note that when **$** appears in the interior of a search string, it loses its special meaning as an assertion that matches the end of a line or string. To match **$** as a literal character, however, you have to use **\$**.

The following statement assigns the value of **$bar** to **$foo** and then replaces the first occurrence of this with that in **$foo** but not in **$bar**:

```
($foo = $bar) =~ s/this/that/;
```

This one uses memory variables to reverse the first two space-separated substrings in **$_**:

```
s/([^ ]*) *([^ ]*)/$2 $1/;   # reverse the first two fields
```

In the next example, the replacement string is actually a Perl expression, so you have to use the **/e** modifier:

```
s/(\d+) elf/($1 != 1 ? "$1 elves" : $&)/ge;
```

This statement replaces all substrings in **$_** that consist of a number followed by the word **elf** with the same number followed by the word **elves**, unless the number is **1**, in which case a matching substring is replaced by itself. The special variable **$&** always contains the string matched by the last (successful) pattern match.

With the **/e** modifier, you can also call your own subroutines (as opposed to Perl's built-in functions) within a replacement expression:

```
s/^=(\w+)/&myFunc($1)/ge;        # use function call
```

In my experience, however, this only works well in Perl 5 on a Unix platform. Both NTPerl and MacPerl NTPerl are prone to abort execution with diagnostic messages such as "Out of memory" or "panic: realloc," so beware.

You can even nest the **/e** modifiers; the following statement will expand simple embedded variables in **$_**:

```
s/(\$\w+)/$1/eeg;
```

The following statement finds all the relative hyperlinks in the text stored in **$html** and replaces them with forms:

```
$html =~ s[<A\s+HREF\s*=\s*"?/(.*)"?\s*>\s*(.+?)\s*</A>]
{
<FORM ACTION=/cgi-bin/myParser.cgi/$1>
<INPUT TYPE=SUBMIT NAME=SubmitFromLink VALUE="$2">
</FORM>
}ig;
```

The hyperlink reference field from the HREF attribute is turned into extra path information at the end of the FORM tag's ACTION attribute, and the link's anchor text becomes the VALUE field in the INPUT element that defines a SUBMIT button. The line breaks between the bracketing delimiters **{}** are included in the replacement string.

This last example removes all SSI-style directives from the text stored in **$html**:

```
$html =~ s {
    <!--#    (?# Match the opening delimiter)
    .*?      (?# Match a minimal number of characters)
    -->      (?# Match the closing delimiter)
} []gsx;
```

Here the **/s** modifier causes the search string to be treated as a single line, and the **/x** modifier causes any white space in the search pattern to be ignored. (Note that this is not the same things as ignoring white space in the search string; for that, use **\s***, as in the previous example.) The expressions delimited by **(?#** and **)** don't match anything; they are merely comments embedded in the search expression. The replacement string, delimited by **[]**, is nothing.

# Index